EROTICISM AND CONTAINMENT

GENDERS 20

EROTICISM AND CONTAINMENT
Notes from the Flood Plain

Edited by Carol Siegel
and Ann Kibbey

NEW YORK UNIVERSITY PRESS
NEW YORK AND LONDON

NEW YORK UNIVERSITY PRESS
New York and London

ISBN 0–8147–7998–0 — ISBN 0–8147–7999–9 (pbk)

New York University Press books are printed on acid-free paper, and
their binding materials are chosen for strength and durability.

Manufactured in the United States of America

10   9   8   7   6   5   4   3   2   1

Contents

v

PART ONE

Identity and Its Discontents

ONE

Coming to the Table: The Differential Politics of *This Bridge Called My Back*

Kayann Short

As a text, *This Bridge Called My Back* has many beginnings. The second edition has not one but three forewords, two title pages, an acknowledgment in Spanish and English, a preface, and an introduction. Yet for me, *Bridge* really begins with its own history as recounted in two brief paragraphs that lie facing the collection's first foreword. These words stand as testimony to the struggle behind and beyond the book's existence as mere paper and ink:

When Persephone Press, Inc., a white women's press of Watertown, Massachusetts and the original publishers of *Bridge*, ceased operation in the Spring of 1983, this book had already gone out of print. After many months of negotiations, the co-editors were finally able to retrieve control of their book, whereupon Kitchen Table: Women of Color Press of New York agreed to re-publish it.

The following, then, is the second edition of *This Bridge Called My Back*, conceived of and produced entirely by women of color.[1]

It is no mistake that *Bridge* opens with this deceptively simple statement, its inherent challenge to hegemonic feminism so intentionally understated that allusions such as "a white women's press," "months of negotiations," and "retrieve control" cannot help but leap off the page. There is a story here and, like all tales of struggle, it speaks of power, pain, and loss. Yet there is also pride in the words "conceived of and produced entirely by women of color," and a final sense of restitution, celebration, and homecoming.

Intriguing in their brevity, these three sentences serve as my entry into

3

Bridge, the circumstances of its publication(s), and its radical position vis-à-vis a feminist movement dominated by white, educated, economically privileged women. Until its first publication in 1981, nothing like *Bridge* had ever existed.[2] Its appearance marked a vital shift in feminist publishing by introducing feminist theory by women of color. In this chapter, I will trace the publishing trajectory of *This Bridge Called My Back* from its conception to its current status as the premiere multicultural text within academic and grass-roots feminism. However, my methodology is neither precisely historical nor objectively journalistic: I do not have all the "facts." Rather, I am interested in locating *Bridge* within the theoretical and material conditions of second-wave feminist publishing and politics in the United States.[3] To this end, I will conclude with a discussion of *Bridge* as exemplary of U.S. Third World feminist politics, an ideology and practice that Chicana theorist Chela Sandoval has labeled "differential consciousness."[4]

A WHITE WOMEN'S PRESS

This Bridge Called My Back was conceived in February 1979 by Gloria Anzaldúa at a women's retreat outside of San Francisco for which she had received a $150 scholarship to attend as the only woman of color. Made to feel like "a non-entity" who "wasn't worth listening to" because of her skin color and last name, Anzaldúa confronted the pain of that experience by deciding to create a book examining the racism of the U.S. women's movement.[5] When the national feminist writers organization to which she and Cherríe Moraga belonged as the only two Chicanas refused to address its racist and elitist practices, they quit the group and began work on the anthology. According to the original letter circulated in April 1979 to solicit contributions from Third World women in the United States, *Bridge* was intended to confront the very circumstances out of which it originated: "We want to express to all women — especially to white middle-class women — the experiences which divide us as feminists; we want to examine incidents of intolerance, prejudice and denial of differences within the feminist movement. . . . We want to create a definition that expands what 'feminist' means to us."[6]

In July of 1980, Moraga traveled to Massachusetts to find a publisher. While in Boston, she and Barbara Smith attended a New England Women's Studies Association organizational meeting. According to Moraga, it was one more meeting at which the issue of racism "lay like a thick immovable paste above all our shoulders, white and colored, alike."[7] Yet from this meeting the title of the anthology, originally something like "Smashing the Myth," was born:

And there it was again; you had to explain everything like from step one. You were meeting a mass of ignorant women, white women, and there were some Third world women there who were very patiently, again, trying to explain. So, I came out of there feeling so totally exhausted, like somebody had walked over me. And Barbara said to me, "It's so hard to be a bridge: that's the thing, a bridge gets walked over."[8]

Returning to San Francisco, Moraga suggested to Anzaldúa that they call the book *This Bridge Called My Back*, using the idea of political and cultural bridging but making it physical by adding "my back" because "it acknowledges the fact that Third world women *do* lay their bodies down to make a connection."[9] At the same time, the self-declaration "I am a bridge" empowers a woman of color to be not only the bridge from "the white feminists to the Black church folks the Black church folks / To the ex-hippies the ex-hippies to the Black separatists," etc., but to be "the bridge to nowhere / But [her] own true self."[10]

South End Press in Boston, Persephone Press in Watertown, Massachusetts, and another press were all interested in the anthology. As Moraga writes in the preface, a collection like *Bridge* was "in high demands" both by the Left, who hoped to counter "its shaky and shabby record of commitment to women," and by feminists, who hoped to ease "the boredom setting in among [its] white sector."[11] Ultimately the feminist publisher Persephone Press was selected and the book was published in June of 1981, in time for the National Women's Studies Association annual conference. In the space of two short years, Anzaldúa and Moraga had created a book that "was already long overdue," that "should already have been in our hands," a book that could serve as a "catalyst" and a "revolutionary tool," a book intended "to reflect an uncompromised definition of feminism by women of color in the U.S."[12] To celebrate its publication (and, of course, to promote sales), Persephone sponsored a catered "Evening of Readings, Music, Art, and Food by Radical Women of Color" at the Arlington Street Church in Boston on June 5. Readers included Aurora Levins Morales, Barbara Cameron, Barbara Smith, Beverly Smith, hattie gossett, Kate Rushin, Nellie Wong, Rosario Morales, editors Moraga and Anzaldúa, and illustrator Johnetta Tinker. Five hundred people attended and Persephone later received many appreciative letters from women whose lives had been affirmed by the event.[13]

This Bridge was Persephone's eighth book and, according to one press release, was marketed as "the classic consciousness-raising/organizing tool for both women of color and non-colored women committed to eradicating racism within the feminist movement and society in general."[14] While it was the first anthology collectively devoted to writings by Black, Asian American, Latina, and Native American women published by any press, it was not the first anthology, nor the first book written by a woman of color, to be published by Persephone. More than previous books, however, *This Bridge* fully met the press's stated intention of "confronting and challenging heterosexism, racism, and conglomerate control/seizure of publishing."[15]

Persephone Press was founded in April 1976 as a branch of the collective Pomegranate Productions, organizers of women's cultural events in the Boston area. Involved in women's studies research, Pomegranate had discovered many examples of radical writing by nineteenth-century feminists that had been suppressed and were now virtually unknown and inaccessible. This discovery led to a realization of the vital connection between feminist publishing and feminist activism. Like predecessors such as Daughters, Inc., Diana Press, and the Women's Press Collective, Persephone's goal was "to build an autonomous lesbian-feminist publishing network to encourage and ensure global communication among women, without patriarchal censorship."[16] "We are using publishing as a strategy for the building of a women's revolution," declared co-owners Gloria Greenfield and Pat McGloin in 1980. "We publish the innovative and the provocative. . . . We see gaps and want to bring books to the public on those subjects."[17]

According to Persephone's sales figures for January 1981, the public — or at least its feminist/lesbian segment — was ready and waiting for some of those gaps to be filled. Their first book, *A Feminist Tarot*, by Sally Miller Gearhart and Susan Rennie, had sold eleven thousand copies by the beginning of 1981, while Gearhart's powerful and imaginative lesbian utopian novel, *The Wanderground*, had sold seventeen thousand copies since its release in February 1979. Julia Penelope Stanley and Susan J. Wolfe's *The Coming Out Stories*, the groundbreaking anthology on lesbian life in the United States, sold ten thousand copies in its first ten months, Nancy Toder's novel *Choices*, released in fall 1980, sold thirty-nine hundred copies in its first six weeks, while West Indian writer Michelle Cliff's autobiographical essays on racism and heterosexism, *Claiming an Identity They Taught Me to Despise*, sold sixteen hundred copies in its first two weeks.[18]

Unfortunately, this success was in large part responsible for the press's demise in the spring of 1983. Backlist books were selling more rapidly than Persephone could reprint them, while stores and distributors could not pay for the books as quickly as the reprint capital was needed. (Generally, production costs must be paid for up front, yet products are paid for only after they sell. Because bookstores and distributors are often slow in paying their bills, a book that sells out in six months may not bring in any income until months after it is out of print.) Because Persephone's vision was expansive — best-selling books, lavish promotional receptions, and higher-than-industry royalties — they were continually involved in raising capital by acquiring large bank loans, soliciting readers for contributions and loans, organizing promotional fundraisers, and even forming their own book club. To raise the money to publish *This Bridge*, *Lesbian Poetry*, and *Lifetime Guarantee*, for example, the press sent out a promotional packet that included budget estimates for these books' production costs. Breakdowns for *This Bridge* alone projected costs of $9,651.45 for a run of five thousand copies and $11,429.85 for seventy-five hundred. These figures were only for production (typesetting, printing, binding, and illustrations); promotion and distribution costs were not even included. Persephone asked supporters for loans of at least one thousand dollars for a minimum of one year and hoped to raise $40,433 to print the three new books and reprint two others.[19] Ironically, their success required expansion, which in turn required capital, which in turn forced Persephone constantly to confront its lack of funding.

From the beginning, however, Persephone had been creative in its fundraising strategies. In fact, Persephone had gotten its start when Gearhart and Rennie gave Pomegranate Productions the manuscript for *A Feminist Tarot* to help defray the cost of a National Women's Spirituality conference in Boston. The first three hundred pamphlets sold out in one day, followed by another one thousand in six months. The first printed edition of five thousand sold out rapidly and enabled the publication of *The Fourteenth Witch*, a book of poetry by Shelley Blue and photographs by Deborah Snow, and Gearhart's *The Wanderground*, whose second edition comprised a run of fifteen thousand. Originally working other jobs while investing their salaries and free time in Persephone, McGloin and Greenfield quit their jobs in September 1979 to run the press full time and immediately experienced an increase in productivity and sales.[20]

With the editors devoting all their energies to the press, Persephone was able to publish some of the movement's most influential books of the early 1980s, including the 1981 anthologies *Lesbian Poetry*, edited by Elly Bulkin and Joan Larkin, *Lesbian Fiction*, edited by Bulkin, and *This Bridge Called My Back*, followed in 1982 by *Nice Jewish Girls*, a collection on Jewish lesbians edited by Evelyn Torton Beck, and *Zami*, Audre Lorde's unprecedented biomythography. Plans for 1983 included the publication of the novels *Abeng* by Michele Cliff and *Law of Return* by Alice Bloch, as well as the anthology *Home Girls*, edited by Barbara Smith, a book that in fact was almost completed when Persephone went out of business in May of that year.

Like the closing of Diana Press and Daughters, Inc., Persephone's closing came as a shock to its community. Carol Seajay wrote in *Feminist Bookstore News*, "Part of the loss is the loss of what Persephone might have brought into publication in the future and now won't. What they did publish will continue to affect and influence our community for years to come."[21] At the time they closed, the press had lost twenty-two thousand dollars each of the last two years of operation and Persephone's owners estimated that they would need investments of at least one hundred thousand dollars to stay in business.[22] In debt for back taxes, lacking capital to print their new list, and unable to find another publisher to buy them out, McGloin and Greenfield sold off what office equipment they could, distributed the remaining books between other publishers, and declared bankruptcy. *Nice Jewish Girls*, *Zami*, and *Abeng* went to Crossing Press, *A Feminist Tarot*, *The Wanderground*, *Choices*, *Lifetime Guarantee*, and *Law of Return* went to Alyson, and the newly established Kitchen Table: Women of Color Press agreed to publish *Home Girls* and *This Bridge*, which by the time of Persephone's closing was already out of print.

RETRIEVING CONTROL

In 1977, feminist lesbian activist Barbara Smith, one of the first literary critics to write about Black women's studies, published an essay entitled

"Toward a Black Feminist Criticism."[23] In it she spoke of the need for a book that could change her life and the lives of the women around her:

I finally want to express how much easier both my waking and my sleeping hours would be if there were one book in existence that would tell me something specific about my life. One book based in Black feminist and Black lesbian experience, fiction or nonfiction. Just one work to reflect the reality that I and the Black women I love are trying to create. When such a book exists then each of us will not only know better how to live, but how to dream.[24]

A few years later, Smith would have the opportunity to fulfill this quest in an even more expansive vision as a cofounder and then chief publisher of Kitchen Table: Women of Color Press.

Kitchen Table Press was established in 1981 as the first press publishing works exclusively by women of color. Because the Kitchen Table Collective was composed of women who were already published, including Audre Lorde, Cherríe Moraga, and Barbara Smith, they never intended to publish the works of its own members. However, according to Smith, Kitchen Table's current publisher and only remaining collective member, Persephone's closing "left a number of Third World Women without publishers for their books. So [we came] to realize that even those of us who've published before don't always have access to being published in the future."[25]

It was from this realization that women of color had no options for getting published "except at the mercy or whim of others" that Kitchen Table evolved.[26] In October 1980, Audre Lorde called Barbara Smith to say, "We really need to do something about publishing."[27] Despite Lorde's success as a published poet, she painfully recognized the difficulties women of color, and particularly lesbians of color, encountered within a publishing industry that afforded them little autonomy from mainstream control over acceptable subject matter and writing style. An organizational meeting was held a month later in Boston and the press was officially founded in October 1981 at the second Women in Print conference held in Washington, D.C.[28] Like *This Bridge*, then, Kitchen Table Press was formed to fill a need felt by women of color for resources with which to confront the "geometric" oppression of their daily lives.[29] The press's name was chosen to emphasize that it is a grass-roots operation, supported by women who do not have class privilege or access to corporate amenities. The name also honors traditional women's work as a source of empowerment because "the kitchen is the center of the home, the place where women in particular work and communicate with each other."[30]

Kitchen Table's first published book, *Cuentos: Stories by Latinas*, appeared in 1983 and was edited by Alma Gómez, Cherríe Moraga, and Mariana Romo-Carmona. However, Kitchen Table initially began by exclusively distributing Cheryl Clarke's self-published poetry collection, *Narratives: Poems in the Tradition of Black Women*, which the press agreed to reprint after the first edition sold out. They also distributed books from other alternative presses, including the Persephone edition of *This Bridge*. However, when Persephone closed in the summer of 1983, leaving *This Bridge* and *Home Girls* without a publisher, Kitchen Table suddenly found itself with a doubled booklist. Although the "extreme trauma" of having *Home Girls* dropped by Persephone just weeks before its publication date was "incredibly wrenching," according to Smith, the move of both books to Kitchen Table was fortuitous for the authors, editors, and publisher.[31] *Home Girls* and *This Bridge* remain Kitchen Table's two top sellers, with twenty-seven thousand copies and eighty-six thousand copies in print, respectively, as of fall 1993.

This success is no coincidence, however. The concurrence between these anthologies and their press is evident from the original statement of Kitchen Table's mission: "Kitchen Table: Women of Color Press is the only publisher in North America committed to publishing and distributing the writing of Third World women of all racial/cultural heritages, sexualities, and classes." According to Smith, a work published by Kitchen Table is "not simply [written] by a woman of color" but also "consciously examines, from a positive and original perspective, the specific situations and issues that women of color face."[32] However, although Kitchen Table was founded as a press to publish the writings of *women* of color, and well-educated women of color are their biggest customers, the press views their primary audience as *people* of color. According to Smith, "Other women's presses can more logically define women as their priority constituency, since white, Christian, middle-class women do not share an oppressed identity and status with their white male counterparts."[33]

However, because women of color both share oppressions with men of color and experience sexism and heterosexism in relation to men of their own cultures, as well as in relation to white men, Kitchen Table books are intended to "shake up the total communities that [women of color] live in."[34] Therefore, marketing is never viewed simply as a matter of sales strategies but is redefined as the ability to reach as many people of color as possible. Ensuring that their target audience has access to books has always been an important part of Kitchen Table's work. Since its inception, the press has placed priority on bringing its books physically to conferences, book fairs, concerts, and readings held by people of color, such as the Asian/Pacific American Heritage Festival and the Latin American Book Fair. Kitchen Table's attendance at events such as these is designed "not simply to sell books, but to spread the word about our work among individuals who do not necessarily get their information through the women's movement."[35]

Such participation is also consistent with Kitchen Table's view of its publishing work as inherently political. Smith admits that as a lifelong activist she initially was hesitant "to view the cultural work of the press as identical to the grueling work of directly taking on the power structure around such issues as economics, housing, education, jobs, racial violence, violence against women, and reproductive rights." Yet after the press was established, she began "to experience the difference it makes for women of color to control a significant means of communication, a way to shape ideology into a foundation for practical social and political change."[36] She now emphatically asserts that "by our publishing choices, we're acknowledging that our political situation is indeed crucial."[37] In fact, in 1984 Kitchen Table added the following to its original statement of purpose: "Our work is both cultural and political, connected to the struggles for freedom of all of our people. We hope to serve as a communication network for women of color in the U.S. and around the world."[38]

One of Kitchen Table's "publishing choices" grew directly out of the press's commitment to reaching people of color outside of the United States. The Freedom Organizing Pamphlet series includes articles that address women of color's political resistance to oppressions encountered in their daily lives. The series includes Audre Lorde's essays "Need: A Chorale for Black Woman Voices," "I Am Your Sister: Black Women Organizing across Sexualities," and "Apartheid U.S.A.," the latter co-published with Merle Woo's "Our Common Enemy, Our Common Cause: Freedom Organizing in the Eighties"; Barbara Omolade's "It's a Family Affair: The Real Lives of Black Single Mothers"; Angela Davis's "Violence against Women and the Ongoing Challenge to Racism"; and the classic articulation of Black feminist theory, "The Combahee River

Collective Statement."³⁹ The series was conceptualized by Barbara Smith in response to a need to share information about Black feminism with participants at a conference in the summer of 1984.⁴⁰ She realized that the Combahee River Collective statement was ideal for the situation so she wrote an introduction and distributed five hundred copies from *Home Girls*. Later, it was printed as a pamphlet independent of the anthology and was soon joined by other essays. Each is packaged with a button such as "Fight Racism, Fight Rape" and contains a list of organizing resources. Quick and inexpensive to produce, these pamphlets follow the tradition of grass-roots publishing and are ideal organizing and teaching tools for both movement and classroom use.

In a similar grass-roots response, Kitchen Table printed a poster in protest against the U.S. Senate's disregard for Anita Hill's testimony at the Clarence Thomas Supreme Court confirmation hearings in October 1991. The poster commemorates an advertisement placed by African American Women in Defense of Ourselves in the *New York Times* and six Black newspapers that protested the hearing with the words "no one will speak for us but ourselves" and reproduced the signatures of 1603 supporters inside a woman's silhouette.

Kitchen Table's dedication to political outreach is also practiced through its distribution of books published by other presses, its service as a resource on Third World feminism, including a huge and often overwhelming volume of correspondence, and its filling of requests for free books to people in prisons and psychiatric institutions (both disproportionately women of color) and to people with AIDS.

Yet Kitchen Table's political work is also performed in less obvious ways, and it is perhaps in the quiet performances of these publishing choices that Kitchen Table's truly radical vision can be found. For example, unlike many other feminist presses, Kitchen Table does not publish such generally lucrative genre fiction as mysteries, romances, or sci-fi. Neither does it publish erotic writing, sex manuals, or love poetry. While Smith acknowledges the market for such writing and hopes that someday there will be other women-of-color presses able to publish it, she strongly believes that Kitchen Table must publish books that "will help us," books that challenge institutionalized oppression: "I really feel that literature, if it's going to do its work, should be about changing the world and changing consciousness on an incredibly profound level. It's not enough just to have a lot of writing available."⁴¹ Smith would like to publish more "explicitly political writing" that addresses current issues, books like Kitchen Table's *A Comrade Is as Precious as a Rice Seedling*, written by Mila Aguilar, a Filipina dissident who was imprisoned during the Marcos dictatorship and was released by Corazon Aquino in 1986 after her book drew attention to her plight. Books such as *Comrade* are more than "writing that is literary in style with good politics," for they also raise international awareness of political events.[42]

The anthology format of many of Kitchen Table's books is another political publishing choice in that it consciously attempts to promote the writings of as many women of color as possible. At the same time, the combination of multiple genres within a collection exhibits the complexity of these writers' styles, as well as the many ways in which they creatively employ language to reflect a diversity of lived experiences. For these reasons, anthologies are popular within movement politics, and they are also practical for classroom use. Kitchen Table stresses the pedagogical value of all its books, and *This Bridge* and *Home Girls* in particular continue to be widely used as textbooks in women's studies and ethnic studies courses more than ten years after their initial publications.[43]

Text and cover design is an integral element of every Kitchen Table book. (Hisaye Yamamoto's *Seventeen Syllables and Other Stories* and Aguilar's *A Comrade Is as Precious as a Rice Seedling* have even been redesigned.) In order for its books to visually represent the writing they contain, the press often uses traditional graphics from indigenous cultures in both the production and promotion of a work. Kitchen Table's logo represents a clay pot or woven basket decorated with concentric circles, both handmade items of practical use and simple beauty. Additionally, each book's cover makes explicit reference to the fact that it is written by a woman of color and that it critically reflects a race-, sex-, and class-conscious perspective.[44] For example, the subtitle of *Home Girls* is "A Black Feminist Anthology." According to Smith, "There aren't many books that say 'Black Feminism' on the cover, unless the word 'debate' or something is after it — or 'Black and White Women and Feminism' — or what have you. It's important that we finally have something that says that Black feminism is a reality."[45]

Kitchen Table's most radical undertaking, however, is its commitment to publishing works by all women of color — not just African American women, not just Native American women, not just Asian American women, and not just Latinas. Neither does it publish exclusively lesbian or heterosexual writers. This union of women from many different cultures, races, ethnicities, and sexualities presents a unique opportunity to practice the kind of coalition politics found at the heart of the press's mission. Cherríe Moraga, who was Kitchen Table's first non-Black member, identified the challenges posed by such a collaboration: "It's difficult for anyone to admit ignorance of another person's racial or ethnic group, yet those were the kinds of risks we all took — and are still taking. . . . The fact that we even attempt to work together is something we're proud of."[46]

Kitchen Table's latest anthology, entitled *The Third Wave: Feminist Perspectives on Racism*, is an impressive example of how women of color, joined in their struggles by white women, can organize around the issue of racism. Coedited by three women of color and two white women, the book is the first published by Kitchen Table to include work written by white women since "you need to have white people address [racism] — because it is, after all, their baby."[47] Smith initiated the project herself in 1987 after talking to other feminist publishers and white women about the timely need to compile such an anthology, but found no one willing or able to edit it. Rather than wait for someone else to do it, Smith took on the work herself. Smith believes that the feminist movement, particularly in a lesbian context, "is one of the few places in this society that people of different racial and nationality backgrounds actually do interact with some commitment above and beyond window-dressing or superficial things," and she wanted to document the collaborative efforts of women and lesbians of all races, cultures, and nationalities working to end oppression.[48] It took her six years to make this book, whose strength lies in its explicitly political focus on antiracist organizing. Featuring the writing of over fifty authors, the anthology embraces an international perspective and includes articles on economic neocolonialism and resistance struggles in Third World countries, as well as in the ghettos, barrios, reservations, and ethnic "towns" of the United States.

Following the model set by *This Bridge Called My Back* eleven years earlier, *The Third Wave* fits Smith's definition of feminist publishing as political activism and places Kitchen Table within the tradition of early feminist presses such as the Women's Press Collective, Diana Press, and Daughters, Inc. For Smith, their books worked to change women's lives:

I remember those books: those books were like lifelines for us because you couldn't go into B. Daltons and find anything that reflected our reality. Now you have feminist publishing at both ends of the spectrum, and it's very, very different. In those days, the women's presses really performed a function that no one else was doing. See, I see Kitchen Table in that tradition. We're like the old school, the old-fashioned kind of women's presses.[49]

However, Smith believes that "that original political vision, that was very radical and encompassing . . . has gone by the by, and what we have now is people who are trying to make money." This emphasis on the commercial rather than political nature of feminist publishing has alienated Smith from other feminist presses: "I don't see the women's presses, by and large, as being allies for Kitchen Table because I don't think they publish books to really complement what it is we're doing."[50] Instead, she aligns the press with other leftist presses such as South End Press in Boston, and at the American Booksellers Association (ABA) conference exhibits the press in the independent political publishers aisle, a group of ten publishers and distributors "committed to progressive, radical, and revolutionary change."[51]

After the 1993 annual meeting of feminist publishers at the ABA convention, women representing three presses — Barbara Smith, Lillien Waller, and Mattie Richardson from Kitchen Table; Jamie Lee Evans of Aunt Lute Books in San Francisco; and Martha Ayim and Deborah Barretto of the Women's Press in Toronto — discussed the meeting's racism with *Sojourner* magazine.[52] Smith expressed her disappointment and anger at the changes she has seen in many parts of the feminist publishing movement: "I think women come to these meetings now primarily as professional publishers, not as feminist activists who see publishing as a means to inspire other women and strengthen the movement."[53] Jamie Lee Evans of Aunt Lute, a press that is committed to employing women of color as well as to publishing more books by women of color, such as Gloria Anzaldúa's second anthology, *Making Face, Making Soul/Haciendo Caras*, commented on how this emphasis on money over message contributed to the racist marginalization and silencing of the women of color at the ABA meeting: "A white woman stood up, again with no self-consciousness, and said, 'Well my consultant said to me, "Edit books, don't pack cartons." ' And I just thought, How many of us have the luxury of making a statement like that? And how can this woman not see the obvious classism, racism, and elitism in her comment?"[54] All three presses remarked on the lack of discussion of audience — the people who buy and read feminist books — at the meeting and how this is symp-

tomatic of the way some feminist publishers, like their mainstream counterparts, are primarily concerned with money rather than political and
social change. Publishing works by women of color, for example, is often
viewed as only part of a "multicultural trend," and now that the trend is
supposedly over, "what they gonna do with all these books they can't
sell?"[55]

Clearly, Kitchen Table is not concerned with being part of any "multicultural trend," for its commitment to publishing women of color is
ongoing. For Kitchen Table, publishing is "a revolutionary tool because
it is one means of empowering society's most dispossessed people, who
also have the greatest potential for making change."[56] Likewise, unlike
some other feminist publishers, Barbara Smith does not worry about the
trade publishers competing with Kitchen Table for "their" authors: "I'm
not worried about Random House taking my authors. Why should I
worry? I don't have to worry. And if they do take them, I'll find some
more. [She laughs.] I just can't see someone beating down the door of
Kitchen Table to get a lesbian feminist of color who's a radical. They're
never going to publish that stuff."[57]

SUBJECT TO CHANGE

As *This Bridge Called My Back* is not written in stone, neither is our political vision.
It is subject to change.
— Cherríe Moraga, foreword to second edition

In 1981, at the same National Women's Studies Association conference at
which *This Bridge* was introduced, Chicana cultural critic Chela Sandoval
presented her work on the oppositional consciousness of U.S. women of
color. Published ten years later in the interdisciplinary journal *Genders*,
Sandoval's essay circulated in five additional versions throughout the
decade and has been highly influential in naming and theorizing the
political and intellectual work of women of color, which she labels "U.S.
Third World feminism."[58] Having just provided information about the
two publishers of *This Bridge*, I want to introduce the work of Sandoval
and other women of color as a theoretical framework within which to
read *This Bridge Called My Back*. In examining these theories, I am interested
not only in providing a critical context for the anthology's essays and
poems but also in conceptualizing how *This Bridge* circulates within and

without the shifting parameters of the print apparatus of feminist production.[59]

Sandoval's article, "U.S. Third World Feminism: The Theory and Method of Oppositional Consciousness in the Postmodern World," traces the practice of U.S. Third World feminism across a four-part typology constructed from histories of hegemonic feminist consciousness – "the official stories by which the white women's movement understands itself" – including Elaine Showalter's "Towards a Feminist Poetics," Hester Eisenstein and Alice Jardine's *The Future of Difference*, and Allison Jaggar's *Feminist Politics and Human Nature*.[60] Drawing upon a synthesis of these representative works, Sandoval schematizes a typology of the phases of hegemonic feminism in the following manner:

1. Liberal feminism: Women are the same as men.
2. Marxist feminism: Women are different from men.
3. Radical/cultural feminism: Women are superior to men.
4. Socialist feminism: Women are a racially divided class.

It is Sandoval's contention that the reification of this typology "sets limits on how the history of feminist activity can be conceptualized" while simultaneously assimilating or making invisible a Third World feminism that exists "just outside the rationality" of this four-part structure (9–10).

In an attempt both to describe the limitations of this typology and to create a theoretical space for an alternative history of feminist consciousness, Sandoval proposes an alternate *topography* – comprising, but not exclusive to, feminism – in which "individuals and groups seeking to transform oppressive powers constitute themselves as resistant and oppositional subjects" (11). Unlike the previous typology of hegemonic feminism, this topography is not historically organized, does not privilege one form of consciousness over another, does not insist that categories remain mutually exclusive, and recognizes the potential effectiveness of all methods of resistance. Furthermore, it reflects methods of oppositional consciousness that have been in operation in the United States throughout this century:

1. Equal rights: difference only exists in appearances; common humanity affirmed.
2. Revolutionary: difference necessitates social transformation.
3. Supremacism: difference provides moral and ethical superiority.

4. Separatism/utopianism: difference is protected and nurtured through complete separation from the dominant order.

Yet beyond its description of modern liberation movements, Sandoval's topography goes a step further by adding a fifth mode — differential consciousness — which has a "mobile, retroactive, and transformative effect" on the other four (12). Additionally, Sandoval's revised five-part schematic includes the categories of hegemonic feminism as conceptualized by white feminists but provides a space for the Third World feminism that has always functioned within dominant feminism — "but only as the unimaginable" (1). The theorization of this mode is necessitated by the geometric oppressions faced by women of color: "What U.S. third world feminism demands is a new subjectivity, a political revision that denies any one ideology as the final answer, while instead positing a *tactical subjectivity* with the capacity to recenter depending upon the kinds of oppression to be confronted" (14).

However, this fifth mode represents not simply an additional ideological practice but a movement "between and among" the others (14). The difficulty of describing this "mobility of identity" is apparent from the metaphorical language Sandoval employs to illustrate this theory (1). Differential consciousness, she writes, is "cinematographic," "a kinetic motion that maneuvers, poetically transfigures, and orchestrates" (3); like the clutch of a car, it "permits the driver to select, engage, and disengage gears in a system for the transmission of power" (14). Yet the concrete nature of such analogies is instructive, for differential consciousness is, above all, a subjectivity born of practice, a "tactic," not a "strategy" or, to borrow from *This Bridge*, a "theory in the flesh."[61] Differential consciousness "depends upon the ability to read the current situation of power and of self-consciously choosing and adopting the ideological form best suited to push against its configurations, a survival skill well known to oppressed peoples" (15). It is not surprising, then, that Sandoval's theory is drawn in part from the writing of women of color — writing like *This Bridge Called My Back*, which describes "a lived experience of difference" — as well as from the political activism of women of color, including Sandoval herself.[62] Sandoval's essay stands in answer to both white feminist and mainstream academic theorists who claim that women of color have no theory, that their work is descriptive rather than analytical, or that it exists at the level of narrative rather than abstraction. Such a claim — or accusation —

is inherently racist and sexist both because it ignores the social, educational, and economic oppression faced by women of color, which limits their access to intellectual or academic environments, and because it discounts the actual accomplishments made by women of color despite such limitations.

Barbara Christian's frequently cited essay, "The Race for Theory," describes the negative effect an emphasis on "theory" has on the survival of writings by people, and particularly women, of color, as well as on those academics committed to reading, teaching, and promoting such literature.[63] Yet it is not theory per se that Christian protests, but rather the current privileging as a commodity within the academy of a particular kind of theory — "with its linguistic jargon; its emphasis on quoting its prophets; its tendency toward 'biblical' exegesis; its refusal even to mention specific works of creative writers, far less contemporary ones; its preoccupations with mechanical analyses of language, graphs, algebraic equations; its gross generalizations about culture."[64] This emphasis denigrates and ignores the way in which people of color have always theorized through narrative forms, hieroglyphs, riddles, proverbs, and other types of language play. Such theorizing, of course, is not readily accessible to those scholars ignorant of nonhegemonic discourses and their cultural contexts.

For Christian, the purpose of reading, teaching, and interpreting the emerging literatures of women and men of color is to understand how "[their] theorizing, of necessity, is based on [their] multiplicity of experiences," as well as to ensure that future generations will have access to a literary tradition that "has always been in danger of extinction or co-optation, not because [people of color] do not theorize but because what we can even imagine ... is constantly limited by societal structures."[65] Like Sandoval, Christian rejects fixed categories of analysis and instead proposes a theoretical method in which "every work suggests a new approach."[66] Rather than subsume all differences under one monolithic theory, such approaches necessitate attention to the specific historical, social, and political contexts in which any work is created and circulated. Sandoval's "differential consciousness" is exactly the kind of theory Christian advocates. "Rooted in practice," it both describes and provides the "necessary nourishment" by which people can "come to understand their lives better."[67]

Black feminist theorist Patricia Hill Collins also examines the way theories of knowledge that challenge hegemonic interests are discredited and suppressed within the academy. She furthermore suggests that because any epistemology "reflects the interests and standpoints of its creators," any attempt to validate alternative knowledge claims within the terms of the dominant paradigm can be counterproductive or even harmful to the political concerns of an oppressed group. According to Collins, "The goal [of Black feminist scholarship] is not one of integrating Black female 'folk culture' into the substantiated body of academic knowledge, for that substantiated knowledge is, in many ways, antithetical to the best interests of Black women. Rather, the process is one of rearticulating a preexisting Black women's standpoint and recentering the language of existing academic discourse to accommodate these knowledge claims."[68]

Like Christian and Sandoval, Collins is concerned with creating theories based on "strategies of everyday resistance."[69] Collins's work articulates a shared standpoint among Black women regarding the nature of their oppression and the possibiliities for individual and collective resistance to it. This standpoint is characterized by Black women's unique experiences of material reality and their interpretation of that reality counter to the dominant society's. In other words, a Black feminist standpoint draws a connection between "what one does and how one thinks."[70] For example, the domestic worker who cooks the meal views it differently than the person who is served it. This connection is a common theme in literature by women of color. In "Poem for the Young White Man Who Asked Me How I, an Intelligent, Well-Read Person Could Believe in the War between Races," Chicana poet Lorna Dee Cervantes writes,

> I believe in revolution
> because everywhere the crosses are burning,
> sharp-shooting goose-steppers round every corner,
> there are snipers in the schools . . .
> (I know you don't believe this.
> You think this is nothing
> but a faddish exaggeration. But they
> are not shooting at you.)[71]

However, the articulation of any alternative standpoint is always difficult. In the same poem, Cervantes writes of her "stumbling mind," her "'excuse me' tongue," and "this nagging preoccupation / with the feeling of not being good enough."[72] Alternative standpoints are systematically suppressed by the dominating culture precisely because they encourage resistance to domination. Thinking about one's oppression differently allows for the development of different tactics to resist that oppression. Here we see how the connection between thinking and doing moves in both directions: what one thinks determines what one does.

The importance of articulating a standpoint for women of color lies in the way it "calls into question the content of what currently passes as truth and simultaneously challenges the process of arriving at that truth."[73] A good example of this challenge was offered by the June 1989 airing of a Donahue talk show that featured five Black feminists for the first time in the program's history.[74] The panelists — Barbara Smith of Kitchen Table, Byllye Avery of the National Black Women's Health Project, Loretta Ross from Women of Color for NOW, scholar Paula Giddings, and entrepreneur Dorothy Hughes — articulated how Black women's invisibility within both the women's and Black rights movements, as well as in the dominant society, threatens their ability to cope with intersecting oppressions by denying the legitimacy of their problems and their right to political agency. Rather than being understood as a function of a racist and sexist society, this invisibility is blamed on Black women themselves. Ironically, despite the talk show's promise to provide space for the expression of Black feminism, in various ways Donahue himself systematically recreated the same oppressive dynamics he purportedly opposes.

First, Donahue's initial question ignored the viability of Black feminism by asking why Black women have hesitated to join the "white women's movement." The panelists dually responded that there *are* Black women in mainstream women's groups such as NOW *and* that a Black feminist movement has always existed as an integral part of the women's movement as a whole. Furthermore, the panelists' insistence on the need for an autonomous Black feminist movement reinterpreted a misperceived absence or separatism as potential coalition.

Second, because one purpose of the Donahue format is to reduce all experience to sociological trend, the individual differences between the panelists were continually elided. For example, Donahue's questions were never directed to any particular panelist, and in this way he overlooked the diverse organizations represented on the panel. The panelists, however, insisted on reiterating their different identities and political strategies.

Finally, Donahue's attempt to place himself outside a privileged position with statements such as "if I were a Black man" merely served the phallic privilege of misarticulating the voices of those for whom he thinks he speaks. Joined by women of color in the audience, the panelists consistently refused his posturing by reminding him that he *is* a white man and, further, that the white male definition of what people will do "only predicts what other white men will do."

The panelists constantly reinterpreted the patriarchal, Eurocentric knowledge presented by Donahue and white audience members by offering new Black feminist paradigms for understanding experience that both confronted hegemonic definitions of Black women's lives and presented alternative epistemologies. In one of the most angry exchanges of the entire program, the panelists and Black audience members responded to a white man's inquiry as to why there were "no high-profile" Black women by listing names such as Shirley Chisholm, Whoopi Goldberg, and Alice Walker; by explaining how the media is a function of white men who "want you to know what they want you to know"; and by questioning what is meant by a "high-profile" Black woman.

This multiple response illustrates the kind of differential consciousness Sandoval theorizes. While the first and second answers refute the question on its own terms — "you want some high-profile women, we'll give you some high-profile women" and "there *are* high-profile Black women; you're just not allowed to see them" — the third answer challenges the terms of the question itself. Rather than contradict each other, the answers are, in fact, one answer, designed to expose the intersecting biases experienced by Black women within both the media and the society at large. There is no need for — indeed, there is no benefit in — insisting on the viability of one type of answer over another, for they are all correct. Instead, what is absolutely necessary is a flexible political consciousness open enough to recognize and resist what Audre Lorde calls "the many varied tools of patriarchy."[75]

Although articulated from differing methodological bases, the works of Christian, Collins, Sandoval, and other women of color are allied in their emphasis on the material basis of a political consciousness that operates "among and between" the interstices of hegemonic culture. This "survival mode" discounts the stability of any singular political affiliation as a luxury and liability that few can afford. Furthermore, it recognizes that when adopted by political movements, ideologies often preclude the kind of "street tactics" adaptable to situations encountered in daily life. As Barbara Smith states so acutely, "I don't live in the women's movement; I live on the streets of North America."[76] As with Lorde and her "many varied tools of patriarchy," Smith and other women of color recognize that "the identity of the oppressors we face in our day-to-day lives is fluid and constantly changes."[77] Clearly, given oppression's invidious ability to mutate in cancerous proportions, any feminism not "subject to change" is wholly inadequate as an oppositional practice.

However, in its most inclusive impulse, feminism as defined by Smith and others can provide an alliance for women who have "no ground for unity as *women* except in the context of feminism in the United States."[78] This desire for unity has always been feminism's most hopeful gesture, although one unfortunately distorted by disagreement over what constitutes women's oppression. While movement unity has often been "misnamed as . . . homogeneity," women of color and lesbians have insisted that "'one becomes a woman' in ways that are much more complex than in a simple opposition to men."[79] As Sandoval's essay on differential consciousness so lucidly illustrates, this insistence has provided a significant critique of identity politics within hegemonic feminism by exposing how "one's race, culture, or class often denies comfortable or easy access to either category, [and how] the interactions between social categories produce other genders within the social hierarchy" (4).

Identity politics — that is, basing one's political consciousness and practice upon an aspect or aspects of one's self-identification, even if that identification has originally been externally imposed — has had a long history within U.S. Third World feminism. The Combahee River Collective statement, for example, claims identity politics as the most cogent factor motivating social change: "We believe that the most profound and potentially most radical politics come directly out of our own identity, as opposed to working to end somebody else's oppression."[80] However, while recognizing the benefit of identity politics for Third World feminism, Barbara Smith warns of its limited use when it is divorced from political activism:

The concept of identity politics . . . has undoubtedly been most clarifying and catalytic when individuals do in fact have a combination of non-mainstream identities as a result of their race, class, ethnicity, sex, and sexuality; when these identities make them direct targets of oppression; and when they use their experiences of oppression as a spur for activist political work. Identity politics has been much less effective when primary emphasis has been placed upon exploring and celebrating a suppressed identity within a women's movement context, rather than upon developing practical political solutions for confronting oppression in the society itself.[81]

Like the connection between thinking and doing / doing and thinking in Collins's Black feminist standpoint theory, Smith's caveat proposes a reciprocal relationship between the statement "I am a . . . " and the actions that enable and enlarge the "being" of that identity. In other words, the phrase "identity politics" itself indicates how the concepts are coterminous: neither "identity" nor "politics" can assume a stable position prior to the other; instead, the two concepts are mutually informing.

Within Third World feminism, identity politics has been most success-ful when aligned with the practice of coalition politics. The fundamental conjunction between the two is implicit, for example, in Smith's declara-tion: "As a Black feminist I believe in our need for autonomy in determin-ing where we stand on every issue. I also believe in the necessity for short and long term coalitions when it is viable for various groups to get together to achieve specific goals."[82] In fact, identity politics and coalition politics enable each other by allowing people from particular identity groups to "come together to be validated by each other." As Byllye Avery explained during the Donahue program, "Once that validation happens and they start to break down the conspiracy of silence and the barriers that have kept them from talking, they then develop a prospective [sic] as to who we are which makes us go to the table in a different way. We are not coming to the table to sit at the foot of the table — of anybody's table. We are coming to the table to sit as peers."[83]

The most frequently cited essay on coalition politics in the context of Third World feminism is undoubtedly "Coalition Politics: Turning the Century," by Bernice Johnson Reagon, founder of the women's a capella musical group Sweet Honey in the Rock and curator of the Community Life division at the Smithsonian's National Museum of American His-tory.[84] Based on a talk given at the 1981 West Coast Women's Music Festival held in California's Yosemite National Forest, the essay was published in *Home Girls* in 1981.[85] As the writer of the last essay in the book, Reagon gets to have the final word on a theory of coalition politics that, according to editor Barbara Smith, pervades the entire collection: "Everybody's basically talking about [coalition politics] in the book. Clearly those politics are going to make a real difference in how we decide to move and whether we have any hope, too."[86]

COMING TO THE TABLE 25

Reagon's essay, however, is characterized less by a sense of hope than by a sense of expediency. According to Reagon, coalition politics offers our last chance to change the kind of society we live in, and the sooner we face that fact, the better: "We've pretty much come to the end of a time when you can have a space that is 'yours only' — just for the people you want to be there. Even when we have our 'women-only' festivals, there is no such thing. . . . There is no hiding place. There is nowhere you can go and only be with people who are like you. It's over. Give it up."[87]

Throughout the speech/essay, Reagon sets up an opposition between the metaphors of "home" and "the streets," between "a space that is 'yours only' " and coalition. Yet Reagon's essay subverts any nostalgic sense of security associated with either home or political movement: neither of these locations is safe. If coalition is the place where "you feel threatened to the core," you are no less vulnerable at home in your "barred room" because "the door of the room will just be painted red and when those who call the shots get ready to clean house, they have easy access to you."[88] Reagon further aligns the metaphor of home with cultural nationalism, lesbian separatism, and other exclusionary practices. One cannot have a home without excluding others, yet Reagon points out the limitations of such actions. If women's music festivals exclude men, what about male children? Must heterosexual women check their relationships at the gate? Can racism be checked too? What about homophobia? At the same time, home is absolutely necessary as a place of comfort and nurturance, "someplace for you to go to so that you will not become a martyr to the coalition."[89] Coalition politics, then, involves a movement between home and the street, between comfort and danger. Such movement creates an "our" that "must include everybody you have to include in order for you to survive," even "somebody who could possibly kill you."[90]

Although never explicitly delineated within the terms of Sandoval's theory of differential consciousness, coalition politics — between women of color from different racial or ethnic backgrounds, as well as between men of color and women of color, women of color and white women, lesbian and heterosexual women, lesbians and gay men, among other configurations — circulates within the essay as an ideal imperative that is not utopian but is functioning within feminism at this precise historical moment.[91] For example, Sandoval writes, "U.S. third world feminism represents the political alliance made during the 1960s and 1970s between a generation of U.S. feminists of color who were separated by culture, race, class, or gender identifications but united through similar responses to the experience of race oppression" (17). As Sandoval illustrates, this political alliance has always interacted within the white women's feminist movement, "but rarely for long, and rarely adopting the kind of fervid belief systems and identity politics that tend to accompany their construction under hegemonic understanding" (13). Misinterpreted as "disloyalty, betrayal, absence, or lack" (13), women of color's affiliative mobility advanced from the recognition that "there is no way that one oppressed group is going to topple a system by itself," while single-issue feminism, a political ideology constructed only in opposition to male gender privilege, stalled on its refusal to acknowledge the legitimacy of coalition politics.[92] Differential politics, then, departs from hegemonic feminism as a politics of both opposition *and* coalition.

That Sandoval's theory of differential consciousness evokes coalition politics is not surprising given her location in U.S. Third World feminism's development during the 1980s. Indeed, traces of her theory are evident in her published account of the 1981 NWSA conference in Connecticut, where the political alliance of women of color in which Sandoval participated exemplified the practice of coalition politics.[93] In a report that she wrote as secretary to the National Third World Women's Alliance, Sandoval asserted that, despite the conference's theme and title, "Women Respond to Racism," the conference's structure divided participants into the oppositional categories "Third World" and "white." All participants were expected to attend morning consciousness-raising (CR) groups, but while the white women were offered a variety of choices such as "white/immigrant," "white/working-class," "experienced in CR groups," and so on, all the three hundred women of color were placed in a single CR group. Additionally, the conference's "shopping mall" approach in scheduling an overabundance of workshops and panels made it difficult to identify or attend those presentations focused most effectively on racism. Finally, no time was allotted within the conference as a whole for women of color and white women to meet collectively in an effort to address the issue of racism within the women's movement in general or women's studies in particular. By the conference's end, many white women felt that they had "put in their time" dealing with racism, while women of color were frustrated at the lack of flexibility and commitment evidenced by the conference organizers and participants.

However, although the women of color were initially suspicious of being represented within a supposedly homogenous category, the Third World CR group ultimately constituted a "conference within a conference" through its exploration of a united Third World women's standpoint. Working together to confront their own internalized racism, the women in this group began to consider their differences "not as idiosyncratic and personal, but as a rich source of tactical and strategic responses to power."[94] This examination of difference led to the formulation of a theory that Sandoval would later conceptualize as "differential consciousness." This theory is clearly recognizable in rudimentary form throughout Sandoval's report in passages such as the following: "What U.S. third world feminists are calling for is a new subjectivity, a political revision that denies any one perspective as the only answer, but instead posits a shifting tactical and strategic subjectivity that has the capacity to re-center depending upon the forms of oppression to be confronted."[95]

Gloria Anzaldúa has written that writings by women of color "are not only *about* survival strategies, they *are* survival strategies — maps, blueprints, guidebooks that we need to exchange in order to feel sane, in order to make sense of our lives."[96] This characterization is certainly fitting of Sandoval's work, for her writing goes beyond description (and by this I also mean it goes beyond theory). Indebted in the most collective sense to a concept of coalition as practiced by women of color within and without the women's liberation movement, Sandoval's work is truly oppositional in that it both describes *and* exemplifies a method of differential politics.

I have been concerned in this section with tracing the genesis of this theory and connecting it to work by other women of color in order to provide an expansive framework within which to examine *This Bridge Called My Back* as both a product and a process of differential consciousness. As with Sandoval's essay, the writing and reading of *This Bridge* cannot be separated from the conditions of its publication. From those first two remarkable paragraphs, it is a text that can never forget the moment of its own making. In the following final section, I will use *This Bridge* to consider textual production as a liberatory tactic within the differential practice of U.S. Third World feminism.

CONCEIVED OF AND PRODUCED ENTIRELY BY WOMEN OF COLOR

¿Cara a cara con el enemigo de qué valen mis palabras?
(Face to face with the enemy, what good are my words?)
— Cherríe Moraga, foreword to the second edition

Face to face with *This Bridge Called My Back*, I am haunted by Moraga's words, for they ask the question that informs this entire chapter. If words are worthless, what difference does the publication of *This Bridge* make to women's lives? Yet, holding it in my hands, looking at the pictures, and reading the words, I am struck by its complexity and passion. Like Michelle Cliff, I find that "so much is here in this book, for myself, for other readers, that it is difficult to begin — or at least, to know where."[97] In an effort to find that beginning, I return to the design and structure of the book as a physical object.

This Bridge Called My Back is 261 pages long, with an additional seven unnumbered pages at the beginning of the second edition. It features twenty-eight writers in forty-five essays, speeches, letters, and poems organized into six sections; biographical notes; and a bibliography of works by and about Third World women in the United States, including the addresses of periodicals and presses cited there. Each of the six sections is preceded by an illustration and introduced by either Anzaldúa or Moraga. Only six of the forty-five pieces are reprinted from previous sources.

The book's cover features a sketched outline of a faceless, naked woman on her hands and knees. Resting on her shoulders and back are the words "This Bridge Called My Back." However, this bridge formed by the woman's body is not stationary, for her arms and legs are not closed together. Rather, one arm and one leg are ahead of their mates, in stride, in motion, *going somewhere*. Such movement is described by Anzaldúa in her foreword to the second edition: "Caminante, no hay puentes, se hace puentes al andar" (Voyager, there are no bridges, one builds them as one walks).[98] This notion of creating a temporary bridge across culturally and historically specific divides could also be used to conceptualize differential consciousness. What better figure to represent differential consciousness than a mobile female body, a bridge that moves from crossing to crossing?

Embodied in this image, however, is the conflict faced by women of color between being a bridge that "gets walked over" and a bridge "to nowhere / But [one's] own true self." Women of color are always being asked to bear the weight of white women's racism, of men of color's sexism, of the world's injustice. They are expected to be the bridge, the liaison, the connection between groups of people too lazy or ignorant or scared to meet each other halfway. Yet this bridging can also be a source of empowerment as it creates new frameworks, perspectives, and possibilities for coalition.

The structure of *This Bridge* manifests this tension between danger and reward. As discussed earlier, Anzaldúa initiated the book as a reaction against racism within the women's movement. However, Moraga envisioned the book as "erasing the walls between women of color, as well as between women of color and white women."[99] What emerged as the book evolved was the realization that complex differences existed among Third World women themselves. This realization led to attempts to "construct a politic out of those complexities."[100] In the process, the critique of white feminism became only one section of the book, "And When You Leave, Take Your Pictures with You." As Toni Cade Bambara notes in her foreword (vi), by coming together to critique the "would-be alliance" with white feminists, women of color discovered "new tasks,"

and a new connection:	US
a new set of recognitions:	US
a new site of accountability:	US
a new source of power:	US

The emergence of this "US" marked a new kind of coalition between women of different races, ethnicities, and cultures. Third World feminists were wary of reproducing the same structures of invisibility enforced by a homogenization of "sisterhood" within the the women's liberation movement that ignored "the divisions forged between women of color from varying backgrounds and heritages." Instead, women of color struggled to "respect the history of these divisions while at the same time they moved to mend them."[101]

As women of color articulated their specific issues and understanding of power, they also began to "come to the table" with white women who were starting to confront their own internalized racism and naive assumptions of privilege. This kind of political alliance created a space where differences could be both respected and mended. It is not surprising that in the following description of this type of political work, Anzaldúa alludes to a method of differential consciousness:

The process you go through is you get very specific about differences. But when it comes right down to it, you don't choose your friends or your allies by virtue of class, color, etc. You don't build a movement that defines people by purely their class and their color. People are *pissed* at the white women, but I think that, in the long run, nobody will ever say that a white woman can never be an ally. So, it's basically both those things: naming specific differences, but feeling like the real political movement has to do with being able to cross over those differences.[102]

This differential movement between "naming specific differences" (identity politics) and "crossing over" (coalition politics) forms the structure of *This Bridge Called My Back*. While the first two chapters articulate the connection between lived experience and political consciousness — "the roots of radicalism" and "theory in the flesh" — the middle two chapters focus on alliance struggles between feminists of color and white feminists, as well as among women of color themselves, and the final two chapters address writing and spirituality as processes of political transformation. This structure is not meant to enforce a politically linear teleology, however, for all the sections overlap thematically and can be read in any order. The essays engage in a dialogue with each other across their various sections in an attempt to "reflect an uncompromised definition of feminism by women of color in the U.S." (xxiii). This is a feminism conceived not merely in opposition to male privilege and power, but feminism as a *political alliance* that offers "solutions to the numerous paradoxes and contradictions that riddle the fabric of [all women's] lives."[103]

It is out of the paradoxes and contradictions faced by women of color that the differential consciousness of *This Bridge* arises. Moraga specifically addresses this mode of consciousness in the preface to both editions: "Our strategy is how we cope — how we measure and weigh what is to be said and when, what is to be done and how, and to whom and to whom and to whom, daily deciding/risking who it is we can call an ally, call a friend (whatever that person's skin, sex, or sexuality). *We are women without a line. We are women who contradict each other*" (xviii-xix, my emphasis).

Again and again throughout the book, women from diverse cultural, racial, and sexual backgrounds and perspectives refuse an "easy explana-

tion" of multiple oppressions and offer instead a "theory in the flesh."
Like the theory advocated by cultural critics such as Christian, Collins,
and Sandoval, it is never abstract, but evolves from a space "where the
physical realities of our lives – our skin color, the land or concrete we
grew up on, our sexual longing – all fuse to create a politic of necessity"
(23). Titles such as "For the Color of My Mother," "I Am What I
Am," "Dreams of Violence," "La Güera" (The Light-skinned Woman),
"Invisibility Is an Unnatural Disaster," and "It's in My Blood, My Face –
My Mother's Voice, the Way I Sweat" reflect the connection among
identity, experience, and political consciousness and activism. Mitsuye
Yamada, for example, writes of how her invisibility as an Asian American
woman was conditioned by racism and sexism. When after eleven years
she filed a grievance against the college for which she taught, the administration was shocked that she would feel discriminated against. Their
reaction surprised her, for she had always believed herself to be perceived
differently from the stereotypical "submissive, subservient, ready-to-
please, easy-to-get-along-with Asian woman" (37). Her sense of identity
became politicized as she placed her life within the historical context of
U.S. racism, Japanese American internment, and cross-cultural sexism:
"Because I was permitted to go to college, permitted to take a stab at a
career or two along the way, given 'free choice' to marry and have a
family, given a 'choice' to eventually do both, I had assumed I was more
or less free, not realizing that those who are free make and take choices;
they do not choose from options proffered by 'those out there'" (37).[104]

Essays like Yamada's are valuable in that they articulate the specific
historical conditions that have led to the oppression of women of color.
Once articulated, this knowledge can be used to confront misconceptions
or lack of information about Third World women's lives. In "An Open
Letter to Mary Daly," Audre Lorde offers a productive and compassionate model for such confrontation. Writing in response to Daly's *Gyn/
Ecology*, Lorde questions why all the "goddess-images" in this book on
female myth and ritual are "only white, western-european, [and] judeo-
christian," why all the non-European women are portrayed as "victims
and preyers-upon each other," why non-European archetypal experience
is "distorted and trivialized," and why Lorde's own words were used to
"testify against [herself] as a woman of color?" (94–95). Lorde asks Daly
to connect her own racism with violence against women of color in her
own city, Boston, where twelve Black women were murdered in the

spring of 1979, and reminds her that "the oppression of women knows no ethnic nor racial boundaries, true, but that does not mean it is identical within those boundaries" (97). Finally, Lorde thanks Daly for what she has learned from her and offers her letter in repayment for that knowledge.

Lorde's letter exemplifies on a literal level the "naming" and "crossing over" dynamic of differential consciousness practiced throughout the book. It provides a missing historical and cultural context while challenging the inaccurate assumptions based on that lack. It criticizes a narrow and biased perspective while acknowledging the value of the impulse behind that perspective. It also attempts to communicate across pain and silence toward mutual recognition and understanding.

Like all of the essays in *This Bridge*, Lorde's letter reiterates the need for coalition within feminism, for the formation of a community without "a shedding of differences, nor the pathetic pretense that these differences do not exist" (99). In "Letter to Ma," for example, Merle Woo writes, "The outlines for us are time and blood, but today there is breadth possible through making connections with others involved in community struggle" (147). In "I Paid Very Hard for My Immigrant Ignorance," Martha Quintanales declares, "It is pure folly to think that a small group of Latina or Black or Chinese American lesbians can, on its own, create a feminist revolution. It is pure folly to think that middle-class wasp feminists can do so" (154). Similarly, in "Lesbianism: An Act of Resistance," Cheryl Clarke asserts, "So all of us would do well to stop fighting each other for our space at the bottom, because there ain't no more room. We have spent so much time hating ourselves. Time to love ourselves. And that, for all lesbians, as lovers, as comrades, as freedom fighters, is the final resistance" (137).

Yet as Moraga cautions in the unpaginated introduction to the second edition, coalition provides no "easy political framework," for it must be "buil[t] from the inside out." Women of color form no "'natural' affinity group" but instead "have come together out of political necessity." Three years after the initial publication of *This Bridge*, she writes that the "*idea* of Third World feminism has proved to be much easier between the covers of a book than between real live women." At first glance, this statement appears to set up an opposition between writing and living, which then privileges lived experience as the most appropriate arena for political activism. However, such a reading would misleadingly refute

Moraga's own political work, as well as *Bridge*'s emphasis on writing as an effective form of political activism.

In *This Bridge*, writing is not opposed to living, but is itself a lived activity. In "Speaking in Tongues: A Letter to 3rd World Women Writers," Anzaldúa describes writing as a physical, material action: "As I grope for words and a voice to speak of writing, I stare at my brown hand clenching the pen and think of you thousands of miles away clutching your pen. . . . I can see Cherríe going about in her terry cloth wrap, barefoot, washing the dishes, shaking out the tablecloth, vacuuming. . . . Watching her perform those simple tasks, I am thinking *they lied, there is no separation between life and writing*" (169–70). Furthermore, writing expresses lived experiences from which theoretical models can be developed. Just as Smith asked for "one book . . . that would tell me something about my life," Moraga expresses the need to read "something that put what I don't have a name for in some kind of context and gave me room to live." [105]

It is exactly *because* the idea of Third World feminism is easier between the pages of a book that writing becomes so necessary. The publication and distribution of written language can transmit ideas to a wide-ranging audience that can then implement those ideas toward personal and social transformation. The importance of *This Bridge* in this regard is obvious from the testimonials it received from its readers and reviewers. Moraga begins her foreword to the second edition by stating, "I have heard from people that the book has helped change some minds (and hopefully some hearts as well)," and she quotes a young Puerto Rican reader, Alma Ayala, who wrote that the book "seemed to be speaking to me . . . telling me I had a right to feel as I did." Reviewer Deborah Aslan Jamieson writes, "This anthology's existence is important for us to start to unravel the lies that have been told on each ethnic group. We must find our way to each other, strengthen each other and form a unified front so that we can accomplish what is important to *us*." [106] While Ayala exclaims, "It is remarkable to me that one book could have such an impact," Michelle Cliff states simply, "I want this book in the world." [107]

Technologies of print culture provide a material space where writing and publishing as lived activities can take place. Because access to such space has been severely limited for most women of color in the United States, writing for them is an "act of defiance" (163). Anzaldúa writes because "the world I create in the writing compensates for what the real world does not give me" (169). One of the primary purposes of *This Bridge*, then, was to enlarge this space for U.S. Third World women. By publishing *This Bridge*, Moraga and Anzaldúa hoped that "the fact that our voices are in print [would be] a tool to encourage other third world women writers to take up the pen so that it's not something exclusive to a certain class and race of people." Their ideal was "not to make the thirty women in *Bridge* recognizable as third-world women writers, but for the *Bridge* to be a catalyst for more third-world women recognizing themselves as writers." [108]

For *Bridge*'s editors, the most difficult problem encountered in compiling the anthology came not in providing a material space for the voices of women of color, but in "the fact that Third World women are so new to believing that we have a right to be writers, period." [109] In the "reprinted" introduction to her then unpublished volume of poetry, hattie gossett poignantly expresses how internalized oppression creates a crisis of confidence for Third World women writers:

who the fuck do you think you are to be writing a book? i mean who do you think you are? and who cares what you think about anything enough to pay money for it during these days of inflation and cutbacks and firings and unemployment and books costing at least $15 in hardcover and $5 in paperback? plus theres a national literacy crisis and a major portion of your audience not only cant read but seems to think readin is a waste of time? plus books like this arent sold in the ghetto bookshops or even in airports? on top of that you aint nothing but a black woman! who told you anybody wanted to hear from you? (175)

Gosset's passage exposes the connection between writing as an individual intellectual/spiritual/psychological act and the material conditions necessary for its reception. People must have the money to buy the book, the literacy skills to read it, and access to it in the first place. But even the fulfillment of these criteria is not enough to provide an audience for writing by women of color. As Anzaldúa argues in her introduction to the *Bridge* section devoted specifically to writing as a radical act, women writers of color "must also actively engage in establishing the criteria and the standards by which our work can be viewed" (163). With its lack of capital letters, for example, Gossett's introduction obviously departs from standard writing practices. Similarly, Rosario Morales's long poem, "I Am What I Am," consists of descriptive phrases unpunctuated except for an occasional exclamation mark and a period at the end ("Take it or leave me alone.") (15).

In addition to such stylistic deviations, the writings in *This Bridge* refuse generic categories; rather than being poems, essays, and stories, they are "cables, esoesses, conjurations and fusile missles [sic]" (vi). This refusal of traditional genres and styles was part of the original selection process, for Moraga and Anzaldúa rejected academic prose in favor of writing "that's intellectual, but at the same time, heart-felt and experiential."[110] Many of the entries selected came from women who wrote that they couldn't write, and "why they couldn't write an article ended up being the article."[111] This selection method defined previously unrecognized literary forms of writing for women of color and extended to language as well. When Anzaldúa writes of "speaking in tongues," she refers not only to writing that is bilingual but also to writing that challenges the assumption that there is only one way to write. In reviewing *This Bridge*, West Indian writer Michelle Cliff reminds us that "one of the consequences of being colonized is that you are told, in both overt and subtle ways, that you must speak in the language of your oppressor, or else your speech is not real — it is dialect, patois, pidgin English. Just as you are trained in the language, so are you trained in his ideas: a package deal."[112] From its bilingual dedication on, *This Bridge* insists on the power of writers "reclaiming their tongue" to manifest social change.

Still, as Moraga's disappointment three years after *Bridge*'s initial publication proves, "change don't come easy." Moraga's discouragement is echoed by Chicana theorist Norma Alarcón in her 1990 essay in *Making Face, Making Soul*, "The Theoretical Subject(s) of *This Bridge Called My Back* and Anglo-American Feminism."[113] This essay provides a densely provocative analysis of hegemonic feminism's resistance to the work of *This Bridge Called My Back*. Alarcón's critique is based on Anglo-American feminism's substitution of "woman" for "man" as subject of knowledge, without a reconfiguration of consciousness as woman's "relational position to a multiple of others, not just white men."[114] By pursuing a "common denominator" approach to the constitution of a female subject, Anglo-American feminism overlooks the way female subjectivity is also "constructed in a crisis of meaning situation which includes racial and cultural divisions and conflict."[115] Part of this exclusion stems from a lack of awareness of how language is "reflective of material existence" that is apparent in the assumption of "a speaking subject who is an autonomous, self-conscious individual woman," thus denying *Bridge*'s theoretical construction of consciousness as "the site of multiple voicings."[116]

I agree with Alarcón's analysis of hegemonic feminism's commitment to an educationally and economically privileged subject of knowledge that, although gendered or, more accurately, because gendered, fails to account for both relations of domination *between* women and relations of multiple (Smith's "geometric") oppression. I also agree that white feminist theorists have often ignored or appropriated theory by women of color for their own politically correct ends. Yet I am not so pessimistic about either *Bridge*'s influence upon mainstream feminism or the political viability of alliances within feminism as a coalitional movement. For Alarcón, the fact that *This Bridge* has "problematized many a version of Anglo-American feminism" and "helped open the way for alternate feminist discourse and theories" is not enough.[117] In fact, she ends her essay by arguing that "to privilege the subject, even if multiple-voiced, is not enough."[118] What I believe Alarcón is critiquing here is the privileging of "the subject" as an abstraction rather than as a flesh-and-blood person who struggles to survive within a complex network of historically specific power relations. Alarcón faults Anglo-American feminism for theorizing abstract notions of *subjectivity* rather than concrete relations of *subjugation* to the detriment of those who are "disenabled not only from grasping an 'identity,' but also from reclaiming it."[119]

What Alarcón seems to be calling for is an oppositional theory of the subject that can account for a "struggle of multiple antagonisms, almost always in relation to culturally different groups and not just genders." I suggest that Sandoval's theory of differential consciousness can serve Alarcón's purposes in that it resists privileging any one subject of knowledge in favor of enabling movement between standpoints (which are not themselves subjects, but are created by subjects) and the concurrent practice of those standpoints (thinking and doing). I also believe that *Bridge*'s problematizing of hegemonic feminism and its creation of alternate political practices should not be underestimated. In fact, these tactics are exemplary of the differential politics from which *Bridge* was produced. That *This Bridge Called My Back* continues to be in demand thirteen years after its initial publication is testimony to the breadth of its vision and its unique position within feminist print culture. Even within the currently favorable university and trade press market for feminist writing, *This Bridge* is still only one of a handful of books "conceived of and produced entirely by women of color." In conclusion, I would like to suggest how

This Bridge employs differential politics to circulate within an apparatus of feminist production.

This Bridge Called My Back was originally published by "a white women's press" because no women-of-color press existed prior to 1981. However, the same forces that made possible Persephone Press's publication of *This Bridge* also enabled the establishment of Kitchen Table Press. That is, the simultaneous empowerment ("sisterhood") and marginalization (racism/classism) of women of color within the feminist movement constructed a political and material basis from which a publication network for and by U.S. Third World women could emerge. By the time Persephone ceased operation, the future of Kitchen Table was secure enough to allow republication of *This Bridge* and first-time publication of *Home Girls*. In turn, these books helped solidify Kitchen Table's reputation and financial foundation. As the only press devoted exclusively to writing by women of color, Kitchen Table was the obvious choice for publishing *This Bridge*, but it was not the only choice. Given only the book's topic ("Writing by Radical Women of Color"), the Feminist Press, Crossing Press, and South End Press, among others, could reasonably have opted to republish it.

By locating *This Bridge* within the larger historical and political contexts of its publication narrative, however, we can conceptualize it not only as a *book* — a material object produced by feminist print culture — but also as a *function* of feminist ideology and movement. Published by Persephone, *This Bridge* problematized "sisterhood's" erasure of difference; published by Kitchen Table, it also enables a material space for the articulation of alternate feminist discourses. As a function of U.S. Third World feminism, it seeks to impact the process by which feminism constitutes itself as an idea and a practice, to "create a definition that expands what 'feminist' means" (xxiii).

In fact, *This Bridge* was never regarded as only a "book." From the beginning, it was conceived of as a "resource," a "catalyst," a "revolutionary tool," a "consciousness-raiser," an "educator and agitator" (xxvi). This personification of *Bridge* as an active agent is not accidental, for its editors, contributors, and publishers have always self-consciously presented it as autonomous of anyone's individual agency. Instead, the promotion of *This Bridge* as a coalitional effort with the ability to move among and between even adverse material spaces reveals an awareness of the book's transformative power. Over a decade after the initial publication of *This Bridge Called My Back*, feminists of color like Barbara Smith no longer have to ask for one book that would tell them how to live and how to dream. That book exists in *Bridge*.

However, *Bridge*'s power is not manifested solely in its discursive agency. While as a textual object *This Bridge* privileges writing, as a function it demands the recognition that the written word alone is not enough. Like a song by Sweet Honey in the Rock, "not enough" becomes a refrain in the lives of women of color. Just as Smith argues that "it's not enough just to have a lot of writing available," and Nellie Wong writes that "poems and stories will do some of the work . . . but poems and stories alone aren't enough" (180), we must admit that, viewed only as a singular object or event, the publication of *This Bridge* is not enough to change the world. Placed within a framework of differential politics, however, publication as a kind of "textual activism" becomes not just one tactic among many, but one tactic that exists only in relation to many. Coalition politics, reclaiming language, theory in the flesh, the politicization of writing, audience outreach, literacy, access to print technologies, even multiple beginnings are all differential tactics that *This Bridge* deploys "to make revolution irresistible" (viii). As Toni Cade Bambara writes in her introduction, "Quite frankly, *This Bridge* needs no Foreword. It is the Afterward that'll count" (viii).

NOTES

1. Cherríe Moraga and Gloria Anzaldúa, eds., *This Bridge Called My Back: Writings by Radical Women of Color*. The first edition was published by Persephone Press of Watertown, Massachusetts, in 1981; the current edition has been published since 1983 by Kitchen Table: Women of Color Press, P.O. Box 908, Latham, New York 12110.
2. However, an anthology written entirely by Black women had previously been published as the periodical *Conditions 5: The Black Women's Issue* in November 1979 and was later reprinted in part in *Home Girls*, edited by Barbara Smith and published by Kitchen Table in 1983. *Conditions 5* sold three thousand copies in three weeks from an initial printing of five thousand and was followed by a second printing of another five thousand in December. *Home Girls* was to have been published by Persephone Press in 1983 but the press went out of business just weeks before its publication date. Only after hiring

a lawyer and threatening to sue Persephone for the time she had invested in the book was Smith able to retrieve her already-typeset manuscript. *Home Girls* continues to be one of Kitchen Table's bestsellers. For more information on publishing by Black women, see Smith's introduction.

3. The term "second wave" refers to the current women's liberation and feminist movements, which had their roots in the civil rights, antiwar, and student movements of the 1960s. Some feminists of color use the term "the third wave" to identify a new feminism that is led by and has grown out of the challenge to white feminism posited by women of color. Kitchen Table recently published an anthology entitled *The Third Wave: Feminist Perspectives on Racism*, which examines this challenge.

4. Chela Sandoval, "U.S. Third World Feminism: The Theory and Method of Oppositional Consciousness in the Postmodern World," *Genders* 10 (1991): 1–24.

5. Gaye Williams, "Anzaldúa and Moraga: Building Bridges," *Sojourner* 7 (October 1981): 14.

6. Introduction to *This Bridge*, xxiii.

7. Preface to *This Bridge*, xv.

8. Williams, 14.

9. Ibid., 14. Earlier works by people of color that used the bridge metaphor in their titles were *Sturdy Black Bridges: Visions of Black Women in Literature*, ed. Roseann Bell, Bettye Parker, and Beverly Sheftall (New York: Doubleday, 1978) and the journal *Bridges: An Asian American Perspective*, which included two special issues on Asian American women (Winter 1978–1979 and Spring 1979).

10. Donna Kate Rushin, "The Bridge Poem," in *This Bridge*, xxi-xxii.

11. Preface to *This Bridge*, xiii.

12. Introduction to *This Bridge*, xxv, xxiii.

13. Mary Fiorenza, "Persephone: Revolution in Process," *Sojourner* 6 (August 1981): 15, 26. In this interview, however, Greenfield and McGloin reported that one thousand people attended the reading for *Lesbian Poetry* and attributed the difference in audience size to racism. Flyers for the event were circulated in both English and Spanish. For more information on the reading, see *Gay Community News*, June 27, 1981, 7–9.

14. From a January 7, 1981, promotional fundraising packet sent to the Lesbian Herstory Archives in New York. My deepest appreciation to the archives for their help in collecting and researching materials on feminist publications. For more information, write to them at LHEF, Inc., P.O. Box 1258, New York, N.Y., 10116 or call them at 718-768-DYKE.

15. Ibid., no page numbers.

16. Ibid.

17. Marilyn Weller, "Women's Own Media," *Equal Times*, October 13–26, 1980, 1.

18. Promotional packet; see note 13 above.

19. Ibid.
20. Cynthia Rich, interview with Persephone Press, *Sinister Wisdom* 13 (Spring 1980): 81–85.
21. Carol Seajay, "Persephone Press Closes," *Feminist Bookstore News*, September 1983, 11.
22. *Gay Community News*, August 6, 1983, 1. For more on Persephone's closing see Seajay, "Persephone Press Closes," 10–13, and "Persephone: Profile of a Feminist Publisher," in *Words in Our Pockets*, ed. Celeste West (Paradise, Calif.: Dustbooks, 1985), 104–12.
23. The essay was originally published in *Conditions* 2 (October 1977) and then printed as a pamphlet by Out and Out Books and distributed by Crossing Press. It has since been reprinted many times, including in Smith's Black women's studies anthology, *All the Women Are White, All the Blacks Are Men, but Some of Us Are Brave*, coedited with Gloria T. Hull and Patricia Bell Scott (New York: Feminist Press, 1982), 157–75.
24. Ibid., in *But Some of Us Are Brave*, 173.
25. Michelle Parkerson, "Some Place That's Our Own: An Interview with Barbara Smith," *off our backs* 14, no. 4 (April 1984): 11.
26. Barbara Smith, "A Press of Our Own: Kitchen Table: Women of Color Press," *Frontiers* 10 (1989): 11.
27. Ibid., 11.
28. For more information on the conference itself, see *off our backs* 11 (December 1981): 2–3, 10–11, 27.
29. I borrow the idea of "geometric" oppression from Barbara Smith's analysis of class, racial, and sexual oppression as "not merely arithmetic — one plus one plus one — but geometric." See "Notes for Yet Another Paper on Black Feminism, or Will the Real Enemy Please Stand Up?" *Conditions* 5 (1979): 123.
30. Smith, "A Press of Our Own," 12.
31. Parkerson, 12.
32. Smith, "A Press of Our Own," 12.
33. Ibid., 12.
34. Parkerson, 10.
35. Smith, "A Press of Our Own," 12.
36. Ibid., 13.
37. Terri L. Jewell, "Barbara Smith and Kitchen Table: Women of Color Press," *Hot Wire* 6 (May 1990): 21. This interview is also published in the *Bloomsbury Review* (May-June 1990).
38. Smith, "A Press of Our Own," 12.
39. For more information on ordering these pamphlets or other Kitchen Table publications, write to the press at the address in note 1.
40. Jewell, 22.
41. From my interview with Barbara Smith in Albany, New York, August 14, 1991, and from a January 13, 1991, interview by Kate Brandt published in her

Happy Endings: Lesbian Writers Talk about Their Lives and Work (Tallahassee, Fla.: Naiad, 1993), 114.

42. Parkerson, 11.
43. Stella Dong, "Kitchen Table: Publishing for Third World Women," *Small Press* 2 (January-February 1985): 27.
44. Smith, "A Press of Our Own," 12.
45. Parkerson, 12.
46. Dong, 29.
47. Jewell, 21. *The Third Wave: Feminist Perspectives on Racism* is edited by Lisa Albrecht, M. Jacqui Alexander, Sharon Day, and Mab Segrest, with Norma Alarcón (Latham, N.Y.: Kitchen Table: Women of Color Press, 1994).
48. Ibid., 20.
49. From my interview with Barbara Smith.
50. Ibid.
51. From the 1993 catalogue.
52. "Packing Boxes and Editing Manuscripts: Women of Color in Feminist Publishing," *Sojourner* 9 (August 1993): 10–11B.
53. Ibid., 10.
54. Ibid., 10. Aunt Lute is currently composed of eight women of color, one Jewish woman, and one white woman, its founder, Joan Pinkvoss, and is consciously structuring its operations to promote power sharing and diverse publishing.
55. Ibid., 11. The comment was Mattie Richardson's paraphrase of some feminist presses' concerns.
56. Smith, "A Press of One's Own," 13.
57. From my interview with Barbara Smith.
58. For Sandoval's response to the racism of the 1981 NWSA conference, see her "Feminism and Racism: A Report on the 1981 National Women's Studies Conference," in *Making Face, Making Soul/Haciendo Caras*, ed. Gloria Anzaldúa (San Francisco: Aunt Lute Foundation, 1990), 55–71. For an elliptical discussion of how Sandoval's work has both influenced and been appropriated by white feminists, see Katie King's "Producing Sex, Theory, and Culture: Gay/Straight Remappings in Contemporary Feminism," in *Conflicts in Feminism*, ed. Marianne Hirsch and Evelyn Fox Keller (New York: Routledge, 1990), 91. The identification of Sandoval as a cultural critic comes from her contributor's note in *Genders*. I was fortunate to have worked at *Genders* during the publishing of Sandoval's important essay and am deeply indebted to her insights.
59. I am borrowing here from Katie King's concept of a "feminist apparatus of literary production." See her essay, "Producing Sex, Theory, and Culture," where she defines cultural feminism as "the apparatus for the production of feminism 'culture'" (92). See also her essay "Bibliography and a Feminism Apparatus of Literary Production," in *Text: Transactions of the Society for Textual Scholarship* 55 (1991): 91–103, and her dissertation, "Canons without

Innocence: Academic Practices and Feminist Practices Making the Poem in the Work of Emily Dickinson and Audre Lorde" (University of California-Santa Cruz, 1987).

60. Sandoval, 5. Further references will be cited parenthetically in the text.

61. Sandoval writes that "within the realm of differential consciousness, oppositional ideological positions, unlike their incarnations under hegemonic feminist comprehension, are tactics – not strategies" (15). "Theory in the Flesh" is one of the subheadings from *This Bridge*.

62. Ibid., 4. See Sandoval, 4–5, for a list of the authors whose work portrays such lived experience.

63. Barbara Christian, "The Race for Theory," *Feminist Studies* 14 (Spring 1988): 67–79. This version is reprinted with changes from *Cultural Critique* 6 (Spring 1987): 51–63. It is also reprinted in *Making Face, Making Soul*, 335–45.

64. Ibid., 69.

65. Ibid., 76, 78.

66. Ibid., 78.

67. Ibid., 69.

68. Patricia Hill Collins, "The Social Construction of Black Feminist Thought," *Signs* 14 (1989): 751, 772.

69. Ibid., 745.

70. Ibid., 748.

71. Lorna Dee Cervantes, "Poem for the Young White Man Who Asked Me How I, an Intelligent, Well-Read Person Could Believe in the War between Races," in *Emplumada* (Pittsburgh: University of Pittsburgh Press, 1981), 35. This poem is reprinted in *Making Face, Making Soul*, 4–5. Reprinted here by permission of University of Pittsburg Press.

72. Ibid., 36.

73. Collins, 773.

74. "Black Women and the Feminist Movement," show #60989, aired on June 2, 1989. Quotations are from the transcipts of the program.

75. Audre Lorde, "An Open Letter to Mary Daly," in Lorde's *Sister Outsider* (Ithaca, N.Y.: Crossing Press, 1984), 67.

76. Barbara Smith, "Between a Rock and a Hard Place: Relationships between Black and Jewish Women," in *Yours in Struggle: Three Feminist Perspectives on Anti-Semitism and Racism* (Brooklyn, N.Y: Long Haul Press, 1984; repr. Ithaca, N.Y: Firebrand, 1988), 84.

77. Smith, "Notes for Yet Another Paper on Black Feminism," 126.

78. King, "Canons," 55.

79. Norma Alarcón, "The Theoretical Subject(s) of *This Bridge Called My Back* and Anglo-American Feminism," in *Making Face, Making Soul*, 360. The phrase "misnamed as . . . homogeneity" comes from Audre Lorde's "Age, Race, Class, and Sex" in her collection *Sister Outsider*, 119.

80. The statement first appeared in *Capitalist Patriarchy and the Case for Socialist Feminism*, ed. Zillah Eisenstein (Monthly Review Press, 1978), and has been

reprinted in *But Some of Us Are Brave*, 13–22; *Home Girls*, 272–82; and *Ms.*, July-August 1991, 40–44. The above quotation is from page 275 of *Home Girls*.
81. Smith, "Between a Rock and a Hard Place," 84.
82. Ibid., 83.
83. Byllye Avery, "Black Women and the Feminist Movement," Donahue show #60989, aired on June 2, 1989.
84. For more information on Sweet Honey in the Rock, see "Sweet Honey: A Cappella Activists," by Audreen Buffalo in *Ms.*, March-April 1993, 24–29.
85. Bernice Johnson Reagon, "Coalition Politics: Turning the Century," in *Home Girls: A Black Feminist Anthology*, 356–68.
86. Parkerson interview, 12.
87. Reagon, 357.
88. Ibid., 358.
89. Ibid., 361.
90. Ibid., 365, 357.
91. Although I have used their work to different ends here, I am indebted to King's juxtaposition of Reagon and Sandoval in her "Canons," 34–37.
92. Barbara Smith and Beverly Smith, "Across the Kitchen Table: A Sister-to-Sister Dialogue," in *This Bridge Called My Back*, 126.
93. Sandoval, "Feminism and Racism."
94. Ibid., 67.
95. Ibid., 67.
96. Gloria Anzaldúa, "Haciendo caras, una entrada," in *Making Face, Making Soul*, xviii.
97. Michelle Cliff, "Making Soul, Creating Alchemy," *Sinister Wisdom* 19 (1982): 26.
98. Gloria Anzaldúa, Foreword to the second edition of *This Bridge*, no page number. Further references to this edition will appear parenthetically in the text.
99. Jil Clark, "A Book about Difference . . . *This Bridge Called My Back*," *Gay Community News*, June 27, 1981, 6.
100. Ibid., 6.
101. Cliff, 28.
102. Williams, 14.
103. Deborah Aslan Jamieson, "Review of *This Bridge Called My Back*," *off our backs* 12, no. 4 (April 1982): 6.
104. Sonia Saldivar-Hull has written of Chicanas, "Autobiography for the new mestiza is the history of the colonization of indigenous southwestern peoples by Anglo-American imperialists intent on their manifest destiny." I believe this juncture of autobiography and repression is applicable in various ways to the understanding of all marginalized groups in the United States. See her essay "Feminism on the Border: From Gender Politics to Geopolitics," in *Tradition and the Talents of Women*, ed. Florence Howe (Champaign: University of Illinois Press, 1991), 297.

105. Williams, 14.
106. Jamieson, 6.
107. Cliff, 31.
108. Lorraine Sorrel, "Interview: *This Bridge* Moves Feminists," *off our backs* 12, no. 4 (April 1982): 4.
109. Williams, 14.
110. Sorrel, 4.
111. Ibid., 4.
112. Cliff, 28.
113. Norma Alarcón, "The Theoretical Subject(s) of *This Bridge Called My Back* and Anglo-American Feminism," in *Making Face, Making Soul*, 356–69.
114. Ibid., 359.
115. Ibid., 359.
116. Ibid., 363.
117. Ibid., 357.
118. Ibid., 366.
119. Ibid., 364. I am indebted to Lorna Dee Cervantes for suggesting this distinction between subjectivity and subjugation.

Talking about Sex: Sexology, Sexual Difference, and Confessional Talk Shows

Deborah Lupton

Let's talk about sex, baby, let's talk about you and me, let's talk about all the good things and the bad things that can be, let's talk about sex
— Salt 'n Pepa, 1992

In late-capitalist societies, the popular media have become important forums for the uncovering of sexual secrets and the production and circulation of a proliferation of knowledges and experiences relating to sexuality. Many of these come under the rubric of "sexology," a "science of sexuality" developed to document, prescribe, and provide advice about the sexual government of the body. Sexology has a complex cultural history and is underpinned by powerful ideologies that shape its formulation and its reception.[1] Foucault argues that the change to sexuality as medicalized, monitored, recorded, and categorized in great detail has resulted in sex becoming "an object of great suspicion . . . the fragment of darkness that we each carry within us."[2] He asserts that such an intense focus upon sexuality has rendered it ever more amenable to the deployment of power; the discourses of sexology produce sexuality, inscribe the sexual body, and mark out its boundaries of acceptable behavior.

The contemporary urge toward the discussion of sexuality is supported by the accepted liberal humanist position that it is important to be "open" about sexuality, for people to know as much about the varieties and vagaries of human sexual behavior as possible, so that their own sexual

45

activities are not hindered by the development of inappropriate psychoses and feelings of guilt.[3] Sexual identity has become conflated as one's true identity: *"You are* your sexual nature or problem or whatever. . . . Sexology is the new identification, the roll-call of that 'sexuality' that defines our lives, us, you and me, who we are."[4] Sex manuals, selling in the millions, have extolled the virtues of an accomplished sex life to the extent that genital gratification and the "sexualization of the self" have been elevated as the principal sphere of adult pleasure.[5] In the 1970s, such manuals espoused a change in morality, advocating less focus on the sexual act and more concern with the communicative context. It was argued that people could engage in any sexual activity they enjoyed as long as it was ensured that their partners were willing to participate and that any problems were discussed openly and at length.[6] Lifestyle and fashion magazines have also constituted important arenas for the obsessive and incessant dissection and discussion of sexuality. The sexual advice offered by women's magazines such as *Cosmopolitan* places an emphasis on "finding yourself through sex," achieving satisfaction through communication by telling one's partner what one wants in bed, as well as instructing women on how to turn themselves into the ultimate sexual commodity for their partners' pleasure.[7] This position constantly valorizes the notion of "talking over" one's problems, encouraging both men and women to articulate their fantasies and desires as well as their dissatisfactions to their sexual partners and others deemed appropriate, such as counselors. To keep such thoughts to oneself is viewed as potentially damaging, either to an individual's psyche or to that person's relationship with his or her sexual partner/s.

However, since the early 1980s, the discourses of self-expression and the achievement of happiness through sexuality have been problematized by the advent of AIDS. Sexuality and its dangers have become the subjects of intense public debate and private anxiety. Indeed, some commentators have identified a *fin de millennium* discourse prevailing in the public culture of the West in the late twentieth century, in which anxieties about viral invasion, control of body boundaries, death, and sexual expression are interlinked.[8] Much public discussion of sexuality has been narrowed to "a discourse of disease."[9] Sexual partners are now urged to learn about each other's sexual history before any contact is made, presumably with the intention of abstaining from sex or insisting upon condom use if a partner were to reveal a past that included "unsafe" sexual contact. Negotiation and "talking about sex" are privileged as strategies, for heterosexual women in particular, for avoiding HIV infection by persuading their partners to use condoms. Sex manuals in the late 1980s and early 1990s, including those for gay men, now routinely privilege monogamous and long-lasting sexual relationships, portraying casual sex as dangerous and pathological.[10]

The emergence of sexology, the compulsive discussion of sexuality in the popular media, and the pathologizing of both homosexual and heterosexual sexual activities in the age of AIDS have given the confession a new, secular importance. In its original religious context, the confession had formed part of a broader apparatus of moral control, used since medieval times to draw distinctions between acceptable and nonacceptable behaviors, not only those that are sinfully sexual.[11] Foucault views the confession as the integral mechanism by which Western societies have traditionally "talked about sex" in the form of a religious ritual that centers on the production of "truth." He suggests that in contemporary times,

We have since become a singularly confessing society. The confession has spread its effects far and wide. It plays a part in justice, medicine, education, family relationships, and love relations, in the most ordinary affairs of everyday life, and in the most solemn rites; one confesses one's crimes, one's sins, one's thoughts and desires, one's illnesses and troubles; one goes about telling, with the greatest precision, whatever is most difficult to tell.[12]

In the contemporary secularized and post-Freudian episteme, confessions are nearly always of a sexual nature, and they no longer merely relate the details of the act but go well beyond that, "reconstructing, in and around the act, the thoughts that recapitulated it, the obsessions that accompanied it, the images, desires, modulations, and quality of the pleasure that animated it."[13] The confession is deemed to be a difficult but rewarding process. The "truth" that emerges from the confession is corroborated by the difficulties and obstacles that have been surmounted in order for it to be formulated. Whether in church or in a counseling session, whether disclosing oneself to a friend or a sexual partner, the confessor is rendered purified through the process. Simply bringing the "truth" out in the open becomes almost an end in itself, a cathartic experience that is believed to lead to greater self-awareness and the release of negative feelings. The burden of shame, anxiety, and guilt that surrounds the keeping of a secret is believed to be alleviated by its telling, for "if we believe that the truth about sex is repressed and hidden, sexual secrets become by definition sexual truths."[14]

The confession hence is positioned in popular, religious, and medico-scientific discourses as ultimately therapeutic. Despite possible negative consequences for the person with the secret and those whose feelings may have been spared by its keeping, it is considered better if the secret is revealed, not just because doing so unburdens the confessor but also because it allows that party to "discover" his or her "true identity": "Sexology gives itself as its object and proclaims itself as the very basis of human being, of who we really are. It is our *duty* to open up and be a sexual story, to confess and overcome (the path of the 'fundamental questioning'), showing our true humanity and entering thereby the sexological kingdom of heaven, the happy family of confirmed individuals."[15] However, as Foucault insists, the power of the secularized confession generally resides not in the confessor but in the individual hearing the confession. That individual is usually an authority who requires the confession and passes judgment, prescribes punishment, or consoles: priest, judge, interrogator, physician, psychoanalyst, teacher, parent, counselor . . . and high-rating talk-show host.

The American television talk show has become a central media site for the discursive construction of "normal" and "abnormal" sexualities. The discourses that are produced and reproduced in popular cultural artifacts such as television talk shows construct both speaking and reading positions, attempting to persuade audiences to accept certain "ways of seeing" over others, to resolve contradictions and suppress alternative viewpoints. The talk-show genre frequently uses the confession as a commodity, selling to audiences the prurient pleasure of hearing about other people's intimate sex lives and feelings. Unlike most confessions, the confession that takes place on such talk shows is highly public. The confessors' identities are known, and their names (if only their first names) and their faces are broadcast to millions of viewers worldwide. As a result, this type of confession may be viewed as more like the Protestant activity of testifying to one's sins before a group, signifying a transition from private to social citizen.[16] The lure of the confessional talk show is not celebrity guests but ordinary people just like the audience's friends, family, and neighbors, who have a dark secret they are willing to share. This secret is often of a sexual nature. The majority of guests appear, upon first viewing, as consummately "normal," ordinary, and all-American. Most are white, young adults or middle-aged, married with children, reasonably articulate and personable, neat and conservatively dressed, sometimes overweight. Few guests conform physically to stereotyped notions of sexual "deviance." Indeed, much of the fascination of the show is the schism between the apparent normality and banality of the guests' external personae and their wicked, lust-filled sexual lives. The audience is attracted to participating voyeuristically in the inquisition of the guests, to find out why they have chosen deviance and how they reconcile their dark secrets with their everyday, workaday lives.

While several cultural theorists have written about confessional talk shows, few have analyzed in detail the discursive structure of this genre. As Masciarotte has commented, "There are very few articles that pay close attention to the structure of the talk on these shows: Who gets to talk? About what can/do they talk? How do they talk? Why?"[17] To address these issues, the remainder of this essay discusses in detail the discursive processes by which an extremely "deviant" topic was negotiated in an episode of the popular *Donahue* talk show. The episode used as a case study for the purposes of the present discussion screened on Australian television in early 1992. This particular episode was chosen for analysis as a typical example of the type of confessional talk-show program that centers around discussing the private sexual lives of "ordinary" people.[18] Its topic was marriages between men and women in which one partner actively engages in sexual activities with members of the same gender, while the other remains exclusively heterosexual. Three couples participated as guests in front of the usual mainly female and white studio audience. The analysis centers around a number of exchanges that took place among Donahue, the guests, members of the studio audience, and people who participated in the discussion by calling in.

Donahue is taped in the United States but is syndicated all over the world, including Australia, where the episodes are screened a matter of days following their live taping. In Australia, *Donahue* screens each weekday during the daytime television period. The show tackles a combination of serious and trivial topics, although the latter seem to be taking preeminence over the former.[19] *Donahue* is the longest-running program of the confessional talk-show genre (the twenty-fifth anniversary of the show was recently celebrated).[20] The format of the *Donahue* show (and others of the genre such as *Oprah Winfrey* and *Sally Jessy Raphael*) is simple: it involves verbal interaction between the guests (sometimes there is only one guest if he or she is a celebrity, but more commonly the show features several noncelebrity guests), who sit on chairs mounted on the low stage and are questioned first by the male host of the show, Phil Donahue, and later by members of the studio audience. Members of the television audience viewing the show live are also invited to participate by telephoning the show, and their comments are relayed to the guests and studio audience by use of a telephone microphone. Donahue himself is rarely seated on the stage; instead, he roams around the studio, interspersing his own comments and questions with those of chosen audience members to whom he offers his microphone, often turning his back on the guests to do so.

It is within the discourse of achieving greater therapeutic openness about sexuality that *Donahue* is positioned. The program, like other confessional talk shows, privileges knowledge, truth, unburdening oneself, not keeping secrets, and emphasizes the cleansing, cathartic process of the confession, the belief that as long as problems can openly and honestly be discussed, all will be resolved. This ideology justifies the imposition upon the guests' private lives that is required of them. The show uses the perceived need to unburden oneself as the prime motive for the guests to appear. Donahue plays the role of the father confessor: middle aged, dressed in a tie and suit, white haired, liberal but also conservative, fatherly, concerned. He often refers to his Irish-Catholic ancestry on the show, emphasizing his link with Catholicism, the priesthood, and the tradition of the confession. Another role played by Donahue that is appropriate to the confession format is that of the judge, with the studio audience as jury. As judge, Donahue interrogates the "guilty" confessors, guiding the audience into asking the "right" questions and making the right judgments, and occasionally stopping to provide his pronouncements on the issues as the "expert." Although there is often a bona fide "expert" invited on the show to provide the "expert opinion" (usually a psychologist or therapist who has written a pop psychology book on the issues involved or who has published research in the area), that person rarely is allowed much time to give his or her interpretations of the guests' behavior. Instead, the show's format positions Donahue himself as the undisputed authority who has the power to devote as much time as he likes to his own theories and to restrict the time allowed for others' interpretations. To extend the therapy metaphor, the audience members also act as lay therapists, questioning the guests, providing their opinions on how they should behave, seeking to guide them into appropriate behavior to "improve" (normalize) their lives.

From the moment the guests' visages appear upon the screen, they must work to establish their normality. Simply by having a show devoted to them, the guests are positioned as unusual, worthy of special interest, the "other." At their first introduction, the guests are presented under labels that condense their individuality to a single title related to their sexuality — for example, "Lee and Joanne Dubin. Married couple. Husband sleeps with men" — and introduced in a way that explicitly describes the "shocking" details of their sexual lives. One example is this excerpt, in which Donahue first introduces Cindy and Alan:

> DONAHUE: Cindy and Alan. They've been dating for four years and they are in love. Yes, both profess to each other. She wants to get married even though he admits that he sleeps with men. He used to meet men in gay bookstores and have sex with them. He actually has brought a date over to their house for dinner . . . uh . . . they do live together. She cooked, he and the date went out to a concert, and the date came home with him for sex while you were upstairs, is that right, Cindy?

In short, sharp sentences, Donahue constructs a thumbnail sketch of the couple's relationship, centering on their feelings for each other, their living arrangements, and most importantly, the "unusual" sexual behavior of the male partner and his de facto wife's equally unusual acceptance of the behavior. This introduction notably contravenes the rules of the standard introduction in social life, in which the first details to be elicited about strangers usually relate to their occupation or place of residence, and certainly never to their sexual proclivities (except in the special case of such social events as swingers' parties or gay bars or "beats," where all those present share the assumption that meetings between strangers are performed on the basis of the promise of mutual sexual pleasure rather than purely social intercourse). The scene for the ensuing discussion is thus set from the first introduction of the guests as sexual "deviants." We hear about their family life in the context of "deviant" sexuality, or their personal happiness or fulfillment in response to the unusual behavior, or the impact upon children of sexual expression that flouts the rules. The audience has little opportunity to learn much else about the guests.

This standard introduction also sets the scene for the incitement of moral indignation on the part of the audience. Beginning with the introduction, and throughout the discussion, Donahue acts as interpreter between guests and audience, explaining each other's statements and reactions as if neither were capable of making sense of the other. He therefore sets up a division between audience and guests, marking the guests out as "strange" and "unusual," forced to justify their choice of lifestyle to an audience positioned as uncomprehending, hostile, confused, viewing the guests' narrative with suspicion as abnormal and inexplicable. For example, Donahue responds to the audience's gasps of shock and disbelief about Cindy and Alan's unconventional arrangement and explains their response to Cindy:

DONAHUE (to audience): Now just hold it [audience mutters]. Is there another audience out there? Well, you know, before you just expire from indignation, let's accept Cindy and Alan's . . . they are entitled to be believed — they love each other [pause] . . . Uh . . . Cindy, you understand the response of the audience . . . I mean, come on, let's get this over with and get outta here . . . to which attitude you would say what, Cindy?

CINDY: I love him and I want to spend the rest of my life with him.

And later in the show:

DONAHUE: Cindy, how . . . share with us your feelings? You love Alan, and you are . . . are you engaged?

CINDY: No.

DONAHUE: You cohabit. You *are* interested in marriage, are you not?

CINDY: Yes.

DONAHUE: Tell us, now, what's the deal here? You know that he's had sex with another man at least once while you were upstairs, and, er, you hated it, did you not, when he would meet men in gay bookstores to have sex? Or did you?

CINDY: The only part that bothered me about that was, uh, AIDS, and the quick, anonymous sex, that's the only part that bothered me. As far as him being with another man does not bother me [gasps from the audience, as the camera focuses upon members of the audience looking shocked, and shaking their heads in disbelief and disapproval].

DONAHUE: And you would be willing to accommodate a marriage that includes this kind of open, honest activity as long as, as long as you knew?

CINDY: Correct.

JOANNE (another guest): That's very important. This honesty is . . . the most important aspect.

It is notable that throughout the discussion, as in the excerpt above, all three featured couples emphasize liberal sexual values, *as long* as they are accompanied by honesty and openness. The narcissistic ideology of sexology prevalent in the pre-AIDS epoch, that people should be allowed to express their sexuality in the way they feel is right for them even if it does not conform to the accepted norms of heterosexuality, is reiterated. The argument used is that the individual engaging in homosexual extramarital sex cannot exist as a "whole person" without this contact, for his or her identity is inextricably interlinked with his or her sexuality. As one woman guest, Charlotte, who had decided after over twenty-five years of marriage that she wanted to have sex with women, describes her feelings,

CHARLOTTE: I didn't, um, I don't think the way is in the closet, I don't think the way I was given a life was to hide it. And given a choice I chose to live my total life as a complete person. Each of us have that choice, instead of [scattered audience applause] . . . instead of either/or, I chose and and both. And that's my lifestyle.

And later:

DONAHUE (to Charlotte): Do you not long for a lesbian lover?
CHARLOTTE: Yes, that's real, that's a part of me, that's a part of the person that I am.

It is not only the guests who insist that their happiness depends on their freedom to be "true to themselves" and to be allowed to express their "real" sexual feelings. Donahue himself, in keeping with his presentation of self as a liberal humanist despite his conservative appearance, also frequently emphasizes the importance of sexual liberation. For example, in the episode examined, when an audience member challenges Alan's need to continue with casual male-to-male sexual relationships, Donahue takes it upon himself to speak for Alan, explaining his need to "express himself" fully, without "denying part of who he is":

DONAHUE (to the audience member): Look, I can appreciate the way you feel. I think we have responsibility, though, to understand that apparently, if all the research is correct, and a lot of people are doing work on this, he's going to have these feelings for the rest of his life. And he is, he is saying . . . to her . . . as long as this exists, I'm not going to put myself through a wringer and become, kind of a, you know, screwball, who's denying part of who he is and so our relationship is somehow, going to have to accommodate some opportunities, with your knowledge and without cheating, for me to see another man on occasion . . . aaarh! [mock growl of dissent] [audience laughs and exclaims in response].

In this complex speech, Donahue provides his version of Alan's response. Donahue first presents himself as "understanding the way you [the dissenting audience member] feel," for to respond negatively to these statements of "deviance" is a perfectly natural response. Donahue thus places himself on the side of righteous indignation. However, he goes on to emphasize the importance of understanding the position of those who are "different," a "responsibility" that is supported and made respectable by his reference to "all the research" that "a lot of people are doing work on." According to Donahue, Alan's unusual sexual desire is permanent — "he's going to have these feelings for the rest of his life" — and if he continues to deny them, he will end up psychologically disturbed and incomplete, "a screwball, who's denying part of who he is." Yet, Donahue distances himself from these statements at the end of the speech by way of his mock growl, which encapsulates his expectation of audience members' moral indignation in response to his liberal statements, showing them that he sympathizes and understands their indignation in the same way that his humorous rhetorical question in the excerpt quoted earlier — "Is there another audience out there?" — validates the response of the audience. Given the mocking tone of these remarks and the fact that Donahue also often refers to the extreme liberalism of his New York audiences, such remarks, rather than silencing the indignation of the audience, serve to reinforce the position of audience members as "normal folk" who are understandably surprised and shocked by the revelations they are witnessing.[21]

Toward the end of the show, when a self-identified gay male telephone caller challenges the right of people to marry and continue to have sex with other people, Donahue again speaks for the guests by expressing their need to be "true to themselves" and not to suppress their "real" sexuality, despite the caller's objections that such expression can be hurtful and emotionally damaging for others:

CALLER: I'd like to know why these people got married in the first place, because . . .
DONAHUE (interrupting and raising his voice): Because they were living in a homophobic world and they didn't want to break their parents' heart and they had no opportunity to really look in the mirror and say, "Who am I?"
CALLER: But that's ridiculous, because you're playing with a person's mind and emotions and you lead them on to things that . . .
DONAHUE (interrupting): He thought he could change! He didn't get married with the idea of going to gay bookstores . . . or public parks!
CALLER: Speaking as a homosexual male, I know, you can't suppress it, it's always with you, you can fight it off as hard as you can but it's always there.

DONAHUE: Yes, but . . .
CALLER: Why get married and involve somebody in this type of situation and put them through this type of hell . . . [*DONAHUE* (interrupting): Right] . . . I mean . . . [audience applauds loudly].
DONAHUE (interrupting): And that's why we gotta get out of this closet! *That's* why we want to get rid of the closet!

As demonstrated in these excerpts, Donahue, therefore, encourages the airing of the need for self-expression on the part of the guests and even espouses it himself as an accepted ideology, but at the same time allows space for, and in fact encourages, members of the audience to emphasize the deleterious effects of such self-indulgence upon others if it is accepted that sex and love should not and cannot be separated. The tension between the dominant ideologies of the importance of truth and honesty, liberal narcissism centered around being true to one's sexual identity and conservative moral indignation, is never really resolved for the confessors on the show, who are forced to choose between the negative choices of either denying their "true" identity or expressing themselves and in the process hurting others.

These discourses are paradoxical: as long as openness and honesty are valorized as desirable, then any sexual infidelity in the search of identity must be confessed, with the risk of destroying relationships. For example, the moral indignation inspired by the couples' stories on the part of the studio audience is largely incited by the apparent acceptance, by both partners in each couple, that a marital relationship can accommodate extramarital infidelity on a regular basis. The couples draw upon the notion of the separation of spiritual love from physical sexual attraction as a strategy for emotionally dealing with and rationalizing their situations. They each try to explain that the extramarital sex is based not on "love" but on physical attraction. The audience, however, is not persuaded by the couples' protestations that they can deal emotionally with the drawing of a distinction between sex and love, and contests their definitions with hostility:

CINDY: I love [Alan] and I want to spend the rest of my life with him.
AUDIENCE MEMBER (young female): Does he want to spend it with you?
ALAN: Yes, absolutely.
SAME AUDIENCE MEMBER (to Alan): Why not give up the guy then, if you love her that much?
ALAN: Because I can't.

SAME AUDIENCE MEMBER: Excuse me, but I'm 21 years old and I'm in love with
my boyfriend. Can you explain to me what love is if you love her and you love
another man, what is love to you?
ALAN: I *don't* love another man.
SAME AUDIENCE MEMBER: But you have sex, what is sex to you?
ALAN: With them it's just sex.
SAME AUDIENCE MEMBER: Is it like a chore, like doing the dishes? [audience
laughs] This is a woman who *loves* you, don't you know she loves you?
DONAHUE: And cut it out.
SAME AUDIENCE MEMBER: Then reciprocate the feelings.

When another audience member asks if Cindy is allowed to engage
in extramarital sexual activities, Donahue reframes her question. Before
allowing Cindy to answer, he jokes again about the lack of tolerance
of members of the studio audience (thus again inflaming their moral
indignation) and interprets their response to the couple by explaining that
the audience cannot accept that the couple could accommodate such an
unconventional arrangement and live happily:

DONAHUE: How about Cindy sleep . . . having a lesbian relationship they want
to know, Alan, or with a man? Can she go cheat on you? [audience applauds
and cheers] . . . [Donahue pauses, then laughs] Oh, this audience, they just
came from the Giants . . . grrrr [mock growl] [audience laughs]. . . . I understand, though I don't mean to say that . . . uh . . . we have to, I mean they just
can't just get the, they think that, uh, you look like real nice people to them,
so they want you to both go your married ways and be happy and stop this.
CINDY: We're happy *this* way [audience gasps]. And yes, I *can* date, I *can* see other
men if I choose to, yes I can [audience mutters].
DONAHUE: Why get married, they want to know? Why get married, they're
saying . . . do you . . . you want to get married, don't you Cindy?
CINDY: Yes.
DONAHUE: And Alan, can you, is this possible, I'm asking you, you've given more
thought to this than we have, I mean really, can this be?

Thus Donahue constantly reinforces the "otherness" of the guests' relationships and reinforces the position of the audience as "normal," even
while the guests themselves protest that they are able to accommodate
the "deviance," that they are perfectly happy, that after much discussion
they have come to a mutually acceptable and stable arrangement between
themselves. Donahue again speaks for the audience — "you look like real
nice people to them, so they want you to both go your married ways and
be happy and stop this" — emphasizing the homogeneity of the audience's
view that "niceness," "normality," happiness, and marriage are all incom-

patible with marital infidelity. The voice of the "majority" is held up as opposing the deviant minority views and lifestyles of the guests. Despite the guests' protestations, they are time and time again forced to justify themselves, as in the above excerpt when Donahue presses Cindy to explain why she would want to get married to such a man, and asks Alan, "Is this possible . . . can this be?"

In their analysis of the discussion of "delicate" issues in AIDS counseling, which includes sexual matters and "dreaded issues" such as death, Silverman and Perakyla noted the use of perturbations, or speech disturbances such as pauses, hesitations, "ers," or "ums" that mark items that members of the discourse perceived to be delicate. They point out that these do not indicate difficulties in communication; on the contrary, such disturbances represent "elegant interactional work in which both parties subtly attend to the local consequences of the labels they use to describe people, and by implication, themselves."[22] As the exchange above demonstrates, Donahue is skilled in using such perturbations to display his sensitivity to the issues involved but also to signal his distance from the "deviants" he has invited to speak on his show. His stammering attempts to sum up the situation for both audience and guests are carefully couched so as to suggest his own embarrassment about the sensitive issues but simultaneously his desire to overcome natural modesty for the sake of public enlightenment. Part of the process is his tendency to use bourgeois euphemisms when referring to sexual behavior — "intimacy" for sexual intercourse, "some opportunities . . . to see another man" for extramarital homosexual activity, for example — while at the same time subtly but relentlessly requesting the confessors to reveal their most personal feelings and behaviors.

The following excerpt is demonstrative of Donahue's typical style of asking personal and intrusive questions in an extremely oblique manner. Pete makes a long speech in which he talks about the mutual love that he and his wife have for each other, how they have worked through their problems, how they have sought spiritual guidance from their church. As if he is bored with this account of emotional stability, Donahue interrupts abruptly at the end, pruriently asking Pete about the possibilities of a threesome:

DONAHUE: Right. Is it is possible that she should bring a woman home, that you would consider to be feminine and with whom she had some emotional satisfaction, and that the intimacy would involve all three of you?

Like a doctor or counselor talking with a patient about sexual matters, Donahue presents himself as being slightly discomforted at his impropriety in having to ask direct questions about "private" matters but at the same time aware of the need to do so. The suggestion is that the guests on the show, who are revealing so much to so many but who are not rewarded with similar revelations from their inquisitors, are themselves benefiting, helping to promote liberal social attitudes and, perhaps, greater self-awareness by "getting rid of the closet." It is notable that while Donahue grills the guests to reveal extremely private aspects of their lives, he does not usually reciprocate by providing juicy personal tidbits from his own life, preferring to position himself as an "impartial observer" (again like a counselor, doctor, or judge). While, for example, on her show, Oprah Winfrey frequently talks about her personal experiences as a victim of sexual abuse and weight problems, providing her own confessions to facilitate (and perhaps to reward) the unburdening of her guests, Donahue works to maintain the distinction between his public persona and his private life. (Although he may represent the type of talk-show host who is more conservative than, for example, the black and female Oprah Winfrey, the other male American confessional talk-show host, Geraldo Rivera, tends to state openly his repugnance of some of his guests' behaviors.)²³

In the post-AIDS era, issues dealing with male-to-male sex invariably raise concerns as to the health aspects of such behavior. Inevitably, the specter of AIDS is raised twice during the show, once when Cindy remarks that the only thing that bothers her is the risk of Alan contracting AIDS through "quick, anonymous sex" (quoted in an earlier excerpt) and again when a caller talks about her own situation, which involves adapting to a husband who engages in male-to-male sex:

DONAHUE: Right. Now do you . . . do you allow him then, or is there an agreement whereby, similar to what we discussed here?
CALLER: There was, but right now he's quite ill.
DONAHUE: He's ill?
CALLER: Yeah — he doesn't have AIDS, he had a heart attack [*Donahue* (interrupting): Uh huh] and so, I don't worry about it right now, but we did, we had an agreement, he had his time off, it was like one of the women said, I don't remember her name, I didn't want to know where he was going, I just knew that he came back to me, and he loved me and he loved my children.
DONAHUE: Right. Have you been tested?

CALLER: Yes, very often, my children too, I had them tested.
DONAHUE: And your husband?
CALLER: My husband gets tested all the time. And we're all negative, thank God.

The euphemistic use of the phrase "being tested" alludes delicately to the threat of HIV infection. The context of the discussion — homosexuality — and the woman's need to clarify that her husband's illness is *not* AIDS and that he is "tested" regularly make it clear that "the test" referred to is for HIV, not the more "innocent" diagnostic tests such as those for blood cholesterol level or diabetes. This example demonstrates how, in the age of AIDS, there is a reemergence of a moralism overtly based on public health concerns but covertly harkening back to ideals of morality based upon marital monogamy and fidelity.[24] The "test," as well as the need to take it regularly, has become a marker of difference, of unjustified risk taking that places others in danger, a discourse that again conflicts with the ideology of liberal sexual self-expression that is rapidly losing its credibility in the *fin-de-millenium* era of panic bodies and panic sex.

In most episodes of *Donahue*, the final word belongs to Donahue and the audience. Audience members are given the opportunity to express their views or give advice to the confessors, to which the guests have little chance of replying. In the particular episode here examined, the majority of conclusions made by audience members criticized the choice of the couples to accommodate infidelity and refused to accept their reasons for staying together, as in the following example:

AUDIENCE MEMBER (young woman): Um, I think that life is too short to go through, to go through your life with an ache in your heart, and I think it's a pity, you're a beautiful woman, you're an attractive woman, you're a nice, handsome man, and those, the good years of your life are just going to be sitting with an ache in your heart [*Cindy* (interrupting): I don't have an ache in my heart] . . . and regrets [*Cindy* (interrupting): I don't] . . . you will though, you'll be an older woman some day, and you're gonna say that all those great years of your life are just spent hurting.

The episode ends, then, with audience members giving their judgment of the narratives they have heard, deciding that despite their protestations of love, the couples, and Cindy and Alan in particular, will never be able to reconcile one partner's search for sexual satisfaction outside the marriage.

The tensions and contradictions inherent in the *Donahue* episode here examined point to the existence of competing and paradoxical representa-

tions of sexuality in contemporary popular culture. There are two potential ways that audiences may respond to the publicized revelations of
sexual deviance uncovered in the confessional talk-show genre. First,
there is the potential for such representations to encourage plurality of
sexual expression. Confessional talk shows satisfy people's need in an
increasingly alienated society to connect, to know about the intimate
details of other people's lives (and particularly their sex lives), to be
involved in their problems and to give supportive advice. Such support
may well be forthcoming for those guests who are acceptably controversial. Just as the readers of sexology books may be reassured by the answers
provided to the question "am I normal?" so it may be argued that members of the audience who do engage in sexual activities commonly categorized as perverse or deviant, or who have a partner or close relative who
does so, may feel reassured in knowing that there are others, "normal" in
every other respect, who are like them in their sexual proclivities.[25] People who may be experiencing difficulties reconciling their own or their
partner's seemingly perverse sexual desires may derive comfort from the
discussion of sexuality on talk shows that dissects the reasons for these
desires, providing some explanation and overt acceptance. Sometimes the
secret is revealed, debated, and ultimately accepted as part of the rich
tapestry of human variance and quirks. Sympathy may be proffered and
similar secrets from the audience revealed to demonstrate that the guest
is not alone in harboring such a secret. This is essentially the argument of
some cultural commentators, who see confessional talk shows as allowing
deviant "others" to speak for themselves rather than being spoken about,
"defusing shame, guilt, and fear along the way."[26] In this perspective,
confessional talk shows are sites for the constitution of the new public
sphere, democratically allowing members of the public to express their
views and providing the space for alternative discourses to give voice.
For example, Mellencamp views such shows as privileging reception and
listening and using personal experience rather than professional advice as
the final arbiter:

Walking or running around the *mise-en-scène* . . . the host can align him- or herself
with any and every position — embodied as "persons" who are half-object, half-
subject, both spoken about and speaking. Significantly, the hosts, unlike many of
the interrupting guests, are superb listeners, letting others be heard and allowing
new information to sway them. The hosts take the new politics of pluralism and

deregulation to shocking limits, sanctifying scandal and blanding the aberrant Others.[27]

However, other critics have noted how alternative positions are often effectively silenced by the discursive structure of confessional talk shows, which tends to limit debate and confrontation around restrictive binaries and, "having limited the terms of the debate to the acceptability of lifestyles and sexual practices, pit[s] mostly female audiences, guests, and callers against one another, in a no-win situation that ultimately militates against both gender and class interests."[28] If the secret is "deviant" enough, the discussion is structured so that the audience responds with disapproval and overwhelmingly rejects the confessors' assurances that the situation is not as destructive or strange as it may seem. It may therefore be argued that the potential for confessional talk shows to provide space for spirited discussion and even confrontation is limited to the topic; the more controversial and "deviant" the topic, the less likely it is that positions alternative to hegemonic views will get an airing. Some topics resist closure, and the discussion of such topics on the talk show presents so many scattered and pluralistic viewpoints that no agreement can be resolved, and the show ends with the participants continuing to argue vigorously. Others invite closure, either by their close conformity to accepted values or their too controversial flouting of norms dear to American mythologies. Prostitution, as McLaughlin points out, is one of the topics that is simply too deviant to maintain a harmonious plurality of opinion. She observes that "it is much more common for audience members of 'callers' (those who telephone the *Donahue* show while it is taping) to express their disapproval of prostitution, unloading a barrage of epithets on prostitutes, and questioning their maternal abilities . . . than to speak out on the decriminalization or even the regulation of prostitution."[29]

Other such topics include incest, child abuse, and marital infidelity, especially if it involves homosexual extramarital sex, as the analysis here demonstrates. Those guests who fall into these categories are routinely punished by their public confession, in which they subject their secrets to an audience of millions, some of whom they will have to face on an everyday basis (their relatives, close friends, workmates). Thus such shows can be regarded as the modern equivalent of the stocks as well as a secularized version of the confessional, in which offenders are held up to public ridicule and chastised for their sins, accepting their punishment in return for experiencing a cathartic release of guilt. Indeed, the outward normality of the guests serves to incite a greater level of moral outrage and anxiety, simply because their normality is an effective screen for their deviance. If sexual deviance can flourish within the context of a middle-American family, which on the outside seems wholly to be conforming to accepted norms, then the corollary is that sinfulness and perversion may be flourishing everywhere, invisibly, invading the typical American home and leaving no outward signs. One's own friends, neighbors, relatives, one's own spouse, or even oneself may be capable of sexual perversions. This suggestion is frightening, for it implies that deviance is almost impossible to detect and control. Hence the seductiveness, fascination, and terror of confessional talk shows such as *Donahue*.

In striving for openness, frank discussion, and the chance for the "other" to speak, then, the *Donahue* show produces archetypes of deviance, allowing them to have a voice only within strictly defined limits and in the context of a manufactured moral outrage that serves to disempower and punish the more extreme representatives of sexual plurality. The guests who willingly participate, the studio audience, the television audience, the show's producers and researchers, and Donahue himself are all voluntary participants in the exertion of disciplinary power in the panoptic sense by means of exposing sexual difference to the full glare of publicity and dissecting it. Just as sex manuals have been criticized for privileging phallocentric heterosexuality while giving only brief attention to other forms of sexual expression, and *Cosmopolitan* magazine includes features on understanding lesbianism but does not ask "what makes a woman heterosexual?" so, too, *Donahue* and other talk shows routinely feature guests who deviate from the norm but rarely question the norm itself.[30] "Talking about sex" in such popular cultural artifacts as *Donahue* therefore renders sexuality more amenable to discipline and surveillance and the deployment of power. The ideologies of popular sexology and the confession together encourage us to maintain close attention to our sexual feelings and activities, deemed as they are to be so important to our subjectivity, and also to exercise surveillance over those of our partners and friends. In doing so, they encourage us to become obsessive about sexuality; sexuality is rendered overly important, constantly dominating private and public discourses. Remaining in the closet, keeping one's perversions or fantasies to oneself, refusing to share one's "dark secret" has become unacceptable, but perhaps there needs to be a turn away from disclosure and toward repression if pluralities of desires, pleasures, and sexualities are to be able to flourish, which requires avoiding the constraints of binary dualisms such as normal/abnormal, masculine/feminine, and Self/Other that so frequently are invoked in debates over sexuality in popular culture.[31]

NOTES

1. Michel Foucault, *The History of Sexuality*, vol. 1 (London: Penguin, 1978), 88. See also Janice M. Irvine, *Disorders of Desire: Sex and Gender in Modern American Sexology* (Philadelphia: Temple University Press, 1990); Steven Seidman, "Constructing Sex as a Domain of Pleasure and Self-Expression: Sexual Ideology in the Sixties," *Theory, Culture & Society* (1989): 293–315; L. Birken, *Consuming Desire: Sexual Science and the Emergence of a Culture of Abundance, 1871–1914* (Ithaca, N.Y.: Cornell University Press, 1988).
2. Foucault, *History of Sexuality*, 69.
3. Steven Seidman, *Embattled Eros: Sexual Politics and Ethics in Contemporary America* (New York: Routledge, 1992).
4. Stephen Heath, *The Sexual Fix* (Basingstoke: Macmillan, 1982), 27, emphasis in the original.
5. Seidman, "Constructing Sex."
6. Ibid., 295.
7. Janice Winship, *Inside Women's Magazines* (London: Pandora, 1989); Kathryn McMahon, "The *Cosmopolitan* Ideology and the Management of Desire," *Journal of Sex Research* (1990): 381–96.
8. Arthur Kroker, "Sacrificial Sex," in *Fluid Exchanges: Artists and Critics in the AIDS Crisis*, ed. James Miller (Toronto: University of Toronto Press, 1992); Arthur Kroker and Mari-Louise Kroker, "Panic Sex in America," in *Body Invaders: Sexuality and the Postmodern Condition*, ed. Arthur Kroker and Mari-Louise Kroker (Toronto: Macmillan Education, 1988); Deborah Lupton, *Moral Threats and Dangerous Desires: AIDS in the News Media* (London: Taylor and Francis, 1994); Elaine Showalter, *Sexual Anarchy: Gender and Culture at the Fin de Siècle* (New York: Viking, 1990); Linda Singer, *Erotic Welfare: Sexual Theory and Politics in the Age of Epidemic* (New York: Routledge, 1993).
9. Irvine, *Disorders of Desire*, 284.
10. Steven Seidman, *Romantic Longings: Love in America, 1830–1980* (New York: Routledge, 1991), 197; Ralph Bolton, "AIDS and Promiscuity: Muddles in the Models of HIV Prevention," *Medical Anthropology* (1992): 182.
11. Mike Hepworth and Bryan S. Turner, *Confession: Studies in Deviance and Religion* (London: Routledge & Kegan Paul, 1982).
12. Foucault, *The History of Sexuality*, 59.

13. Ibid., 62.
14. M. Altman, "Everything They Always Wanted You to Know: The Ideology of Popular Sex Literature," in *Pleasure and Danger: Exploring Female Sexuality,* ed. Carol Vance (New York: Routledge & Kegan Paul, 1984), 116.
15. Heath, *The Sexual Fix,* 77–78.
16. Gloria-Jean Masciarotte, "C'mon Girl: Oprah Winfrey and the Discourse of Feminine Talk," *Genders* (1991): 85.
17. Ibid., 82.
18. On the basis of the author's intermittent viewing of *Donahue* and monitoring of program topics (which are printed in the television guide) over a period of some four years, the episode was judged to be typical of those dealing with sexual "deviance." The program format has generally remained the same throughout this time, as has the manner in which Phil Donahue structures the discussion and the response of audience members to confessions of "deviance." The program can therefore be regarded as formulaic, with one particular episode dealing with sexual difference being very similar to others on a similar topic.
19. For example, in one week in late 1992, the episode titles of *Donahue* included the following: "My Mother Has 53 Personalities and My Lawyer Has 100," "What Happens to Strippers When They Get Old? – They Keep on Stripping," "An Eyewitness Report on the New Democratic Russia," "Safe Sex Orgies," and "Studs or Pigs: Men Who Say They Are God's Gift to Women."
20. Two other American talk shows employing the "confessional" format are screened in Australia: *Sally Jessy Raphael* and the *Oprah Winfrey Show.* They are shown during the daytime period between Monday and Friday, along with *Donahue,* all on the same television channel. These talk shows also devote much time to the discussion of sexuality: on one notable day in October 1992, the topics of the three shows included "I Have a Secret Sexual Fetish" (the *Sally Jessy Raphael* show), followed by "How to Have Satisfying Sex Every Time You Try" (*Donahue*), capped off by "How to Tell Your Lover You Need More Sex" (*Oprah Winfrey Show*).
21. Lisa McLaughlin, "Chastity Criminals in the Age of Electronic Reproduction: Re-viewing Talk Television and the Public Sphere," *Journal of Communication Inquiry* (1993): 51.
22. David Silverman and Anssi Perakyla, "AIDS Counselling: the Interactional Organisation of Talk about 'Delicate' Issues," *Sociology of Health and Illness* (1990): 293–318, 307.
23. Patricia Mellencamp, *High Anxiety: Catastrophe, Scandal, Age, and Comedy* (Bloomington: Indiana University Press, 1992), 215.
24. Cf. Simon Watney, *Policing Desire: Pornography, AIDS, and the Media* (London: Comedia, 1987); Richard Davenport-Hines, *Sex, Death, and Punishment: Attitudes to Sex and Sexuality in Britain since the Renaissance* (London: Collins, 1990); Singer, *Erotic Welfare*; Lupton, *Moral Threats and Dangerous Desires.*
25. Altman, "Everything They Always Wanted You to Know," 116.
26. Mellencamp, *High Anxiety,* 218.

27. Ibid., 214.
28. McLaughlin, "Chastity Criminals," 52.
29. Ibid., 50.
30. Seidman, "Constructing Sex"; Winship, *Inside Women's Magazines*, 117–18.
31. There is, of course, an irony here; in critiquing the compulsive interest in discussing and dissecting sexual behavior evident in the confessional talk-show genre, and the potential for public discussion to render sexuality more amenable to the deployment of power, scholars themselves are simultaneously contributing to this very proliferation of discourses. This begs the question, to what extent should scholars relinquish their own obsession with endlessly defining and redefining sexuality?

Henry James's Thwarted Love

Wendy Graham

Much has been written of late concerning "the feeling between men." A perusal of texts on homosexuality, perversion, and gender, from Eve Sedgwick's *Epistemology of the Closet* to Jonathan Dollimore's *Sexual Dissidence* to Kaja Silverman's *Male Subjectivity at the Margins*, suggests that the debate has moved well beyond the question, "Did he or didn't he have boyfriends?" Without losing sight of the contributions of recent theorists of sex and gender (specifically, a greater awareness of multiple, nonexclusive affective investments and subjectivities), I want to call attention to the uses of literary biography for gay culture studies. Operating under the premise that sexual identity is temporally contingent, one can dismantle as well as construct past and present identity categories; one can foreground their inherent contradictions. In this regard, Henry James's complex relationship with his brother William is instructive. Although William James characterized intimate contact with persons of one's own sex as "repulsive" and defined homosexuality as a "pathological aberration," he nevertheless encouraged Henry's near-obsessive attachment to himself well into middle age.[1] Indeed, William's sexual panic informed Henry's struggle to come to grips with his own sexual identity, as William not only served Henry as a virile ideal but also played the part of an authority on medical and psychiatric concerns.

William's counsels regarding Henry's physical complaints and susceptibility to depression and overwork were partly responsible for Henry's monastic existence, as this was considered the prudent course for a neuropath to adopt. It is quite important that, prior to the theoretical elaboration of homosexuality at the end of the nineteenth century, a typology

66

already existed to account for gender and sexual variants: that of hereditary degeneration. While Henry James was adversely affected by the
emerging medical discourse on homosexuality, he appears to have been
comfortable, up to a point, with the notion of gender inversion. What I'm
after in this essay is a better understanding of Henry James's participation
in the construction of homosexuality at the fin de siècle, particularly
the way in which James's effeminacy anticipated the majority of late-
nineteenth-century medical, psychiatric, and legal representations of male
homosexuals as psychical hermaphrodites.[2] James's life is exemplary of
nineteenth-century sexuality in that it mirrors the turmoil produced and
the introspection encouraged by the new scrutiny of marginal identities,
albeit among a rarefied group of intellectuals whose constructions of
homosexuality have proven highly influential. Moreover, at a time when
gays are rejecting the historic association of male homosexuality with
effeminacy as retrograde, it is well worth considering the meaning and
allure of this identity sign. Jonathan Dollimore remarks that "the perception of the homosexual as feminized remains strangely disturbing — the
supreme symbol, in the eyes of those like Norman Mailer, of a range of
deep failures including the demise of masculinity, the abdication of masculine power, the desire for self-destruction, and, beyond that, the loss of
difference."[3] Richard Dellamora and Kaja Silverman have acknowledged
this difficulty in their own work, which focuses on rehabilitating the
domain of the feminine so that the rhetorical wish or fantasy of becoming
a woman may be read as an empowering (subversive) move.[4] This strategy
is constructive in that it addresses present concerns about negative cultural stereotypes but counterproductive in that it submits historical am-
bivalences and anxieties to erasure. I highlight Dellamora's and Silverman's discussion of the place of femininity in male homosexuality
because the charge of effeminacy has bedeviled James enthusiasts,
whether or not they have been willing to acknowledge his homosexuality.
As early as 1902, a critic insisted that no comprehensive account of
James's work could fail to take account of his effeminacy.[5]

As Jonathan Freedman points out, homosexuality is the "unspoken
subject that clearly underlies the language of effeteness and effeminacy
that anti-Jacobites persistently used to describe James's putative aestheticism, and for which the term 'aesthete' has long served as a virtual
synonym."[6] For as long as critics have been proclaiming, hinting at,
ignoring, or denying the homoerotic elements in James's life and works,

they have participated in a critic's compact, a set of rules and guidelines for representing and, more to the point, for concealing sexuality. In 1979, Richard Hall, lay scholar and editor of *The Advocate*, chided James specialists for ignoring the question of homosexuality in James's life and works. Singling out Leon Edel, who "by avoiding a frank discussion of James' homosexual leanings . . . had failed to present a full and complex picture of the man," Hall threw down the gauntlet before a generation of academics who accepted Edel's theory that James had sublimated eros in the service of art.[7] Following Edel's lead, most critics have been content to see James, in Richard Hall's words, as "the golden capon of world literature."[8]

We might forget that this was the state of James criticism until very recently, with no less an authority than Eve Sedgwick reminding us of "biographically inobliterable" evidence of James's homosexual desire.[9] Sedgwick herself has characterized James as one whose passional impulses were expressed indirectly through "homosexual panic" or homophobia. In her fine reading of "The Beast in the Jungle," Sedgwick notes, "To judge from the biographies of Barrie and James, each author seems to have made erotic choices that were complicated enough, shifting enough in the gender of their objects, and, at least for long periods, kept distant enough from *éclarcissement* or physical expression, to make each an emboldening figure for a literary discussion of male homosexual panic."[10] While Sedgwick's work has been widely influential, it has received some intelligent criticism. For example, Dellamora complains that Sedgwick virtually ignores self-aware male homosexuals in *Between Men* and focuses on homophobic, rather than homoerotic, tendencies in writers in her later work.[11] Sedgwick's reinvention of James as a self-deceiving or sexually dormant homosexual, while a step forward, is not entirely satisfying, for, in spite of herself, she seems to equate genital activity (end-pleasure) with sexual identity. Without attempting to categorize James, I would argue that his sexual escapades probably emphasized fore-pleasure and belonged to the regions of the mind where fantasies evolve. Ross Posnock has suggested that James's love letters to male friends were "themselves pleasurable forms of sexual activity and not simply substitutes."[12]

James's biographers and critics have made much of his passionlessness. In 1902, F. M. Colby acidly described James's erotic universe as "a land where the vices have no bodies and the passions no blood, where nobody sins because nobody has anything to sin with."[13] In 1925, Dr. Joseph

Collins, a fashionable New York neurologist who had treated James for depression and heart disease over a two-month period in 1911, shared his impressions of James's personality with the public in a book called *The Doctor Looks at Biography*. Describing James as an amalgam of feminine and infantile personality traits, Collins concluded, "The great defect in the makeup of Henry James was in the amatory side of his nature."[14] Apparently, James confided in Collins, avowing that he had remained celibate throughout his life.[15] The autobiographical *Notes of a Son and Brother* (1913) contains a much-discussed revelation of a "horrid even if an obscure hurt" James sustained while turning a water crank in an attempt to extinguish a fire, an injury that deprived eighteen-year-old Henry of his virility and health, or so James implied.[16] This chronic debility has been variously interpreted as castration, impotence, or an incapacitating spinal disorder.[17] It has been argued that Henry unconsciously chose disability as a way out of the trials of masculinity gathering around him in 1861 (courtship and the Civil War). He describes the injury as a token badge of honor: "This was at least a negative of combat, an organised, not a loose and empty one, something definitely and firmly parallel to action in the tented field."[18] However, James's reminiscences suggest that he saw himself as a spiritless poltroon throughout his childhood, particularly in relation to his bullying, supercompetent older brother, William; Henry favors the word "impotent" in *A Small Boy and Others* to such an extent that he seems to be proclaiming his psychic emasculation well before he reveals his alleged castration in the flesh in *Notes of a Son and Brother*.

Saul Rosenzweig suggested that the "obscure hurt" be read as an act of "filial submission" to a "gifted sibling rival," a suspension of masculine identification occasioned by guilt and inferiority complexes.[19] But what kind of ego need was served by James's representation of himself as a clueless, hapless youth castrated on the brink of manhood? Donald Moss has recently stressed the coexistence of "aim-limited homoeroticisms" and "fiercely articulated interdictions against *serious* same-sex erotics," which remind the individual that "the only permissible way to love the forbidden object is via (dis)identification with it."[20] The established paradigms of biological sex, gender, and desire also produce reflex models of deviance; as Judith Butler puts it, "Spectres of discontinuity and incoherence [are] themselves thinkable only in relation to existing norms."[21] In other words, James's effemination was an unconscious response to his incestuous longing for his brother, a heterosexualization of same-sex desire. Moreover, as if reading from some master script of monolithic sexuality, Henry can be said to have reinvented his neurasthenic brother as a manly man. While documenting his own foundering attempts to succeed at anything in his *Autobiography*, Henry marveled at his older brother's talents: "One of these, and probably the promptest in order, was that of my brother's occupying a place in the world to which I couldn't at all aspire — to any approach to which in truth I seem to myself ever conscious of having forfeited a title."[22] Henry's memory is remarkably selective. Henry doesn't dwell on William James's nervous troubles in the period 1861–1874, capped off by a full-blown nervous breakdown in 1870. He doesn't mention the fact that this paragon used his nervous illnesses to avoid self-reliance and Civil War service. William couldn't be described as self-supporting before 1874, when he turned thirty-two. And he lived at home, mostly, prior to his marriage at the ripe age of thirty-six.

Georges-Michel Sarotte suggested that William James was implicated in "the atrophy of masculine feelings from which Henry James appeared to have suffered all his life."[23] Setting aside Sarotte's morbid characterization of this relationship, any reader of Henry's autobiography must concur that William contributed to Henry's effemination. During childhood, William exacerbated Henry's inferiority complex by abandoning his milksop baby brother, a mere fifteen months his junior, in search of sport and masculine companionship in other quarters: "I play with boys who curse and swear."[24] William also feminized Henry throughout their lives, designating Henry by the moniker "Angel" while referring to himself as the "Demon" in his letters home.[25] In their correspondence, one gets a sense of two male siblings playing house well beyond their infant years. The roles of mother and father are surprisingly well defined. In 1873, William wrote his family from Italy, "At present Harry is my spouse. I have been here with him boarding in a hotel for two and a half weeks."[26] At another time, flushed with a renewed sense of health and vitality, Henry wrote William, "I am as broad as I am long, as fat as a butter-tub and as red as a British *materfamilias*."[27] When William married in July 1878, Henry wrote to convey his congratulations as well as his sense of desolation: "I have just heard from mother that you had decided to be married on the 10th ult: and as I was divorced from you by an untimely fate on this unique occasion, let me at least repair the injury by giving you, in the

most earnest words my clumsy pen can shape, a tender bridal bene-
diction."[28]

Richard Hall wondered whether Henry James, in "writing about Daisy
Miller and Isabel Archer and Catherine Sloper . . . is maintaining the core
of female identity which William created for him and whose marriage
now denied it? That the unconscious demands of his life required such an
identity, which now moved from life to art?"[29] Leon Edel was the first to
claim that Henry identified increasingly with his female protagonists after
William's marriage in 1878.[30] Indeed, it was this observation that inspired
Hall to conceptualize the relation between James's sexual inactivity and
his homosexuality as a repressed incestuous passion for his brother. The
psychoanalyst Howard Feinstein enlarged on this theme in his biography
of William James: "Henry James's early stories can be read as the creation
of a young artist who had become painfully aware of himself as a female
consciousness masquerading in the body of a man. It is not surprising that
the brothers' 'singular life' blurred sexual distinctions between them. And
it should not come as a shock that in Henry's fictive world there is a
strong homosexual strand linking him to his brother William."[31]
Feinstein's observation that Henry "had become painfully aware of himself as a female consciousness masquerading in the body of a man" reveals
the antiquated outlook built into his psychoanalytic perspective. It rules
out diversity in masculine, as well as homosexual, identifications and it
denies any pleasure in the fantasy of "being a woman."

Moreover, by attributing a feminine "psychological core" to Henry
James, Feinstein, Edel, and Hall accord ontological status to a drag
performance; they confuse James's incorporation or mimicry of the feminine with an essential self. What we have here is an example of "fantasmatic femininity," where the male ego disports itself with the fantasy of
alterity.[32] According to Judith Butler, the notion of a "psychological core"
veils "the political constitution of the gendered subject and its fabricated
notions about the ineffable interiority of its sex or of its identity."[33] The
internal core is a generally accepted truth enabling a false stabilization of
gender roles in the interests of heterosexual dominance and the regulation
of reproduction.[34] Although the norm stifles certain impulses, it is com-
plied with because it satisfies the individual's longing for coherence. In
this regard, James's obscure hurt may represent an unconscious attempt
to bring gender identity, sexual preference, and anatomy into pseudoco-

herence by effecting an imaginary sex change. Krafft-Ebing's accounts of
male homosexuals who experienced menstrual cramps, birth pangs, and a
longing for "authenticity" so strong they contemplated emasculation ("I
should not have shrunk from the castration-knife, could I have thus
attained my desire"; "If I had been single, I should long ago have taken
leave of testes, scrotum, and penis") suggest that gender identity, whether
inverted or conformist, is a "personal/cultural history of received meanings subject to a set of imitative practices," as Butler contends.[35] Krafft-
Ebing's would-be transsexuals challenge the notion that anatomical sex is
the ground zero of gender identity, and they subvert patriarchy through
their willingness to sacrifice the penis-phallus.

In "From the History of an Infantile Neurosis," Sigmund Freud indicates the contrary impulses influencing the patient's tentative resolution
of castration anxiety: "In the end there were to be found in him two
contrary currents side by side, of which one abominated the idea of
castration, while the other was prepared to accept it and console itself
with femininity as a compensation."[36] In context, Freud argues that the
Wolf-man's identification with his mother was confined to the fantasy of
assuming her place in relation to his father in the primal scene, where his
own anus would function as a womb. In no respect is the patient effemi-
nated or seen as a case of interior androgyny. As Henry Abelove has
demonstrated, Freud explicitly rejected Ulrichs's notion of "anima mu-
liebris in corpore virili inclusa" (appropriated by Krafft-Ebing as "psychical hermaphroditism") as well as Hirschfeld's proposition that homosexuals constituted a "third sex."[37] In Three Essays on the Theory of Sexuality,
Freud remarked, "The theory of bisexuality has been expressed in its
crudest form by a spokesman of the male inverts: 'a feminine brain in a
masculine body.' But we are ignorant of what characterizes a feminine
brain. There is neither need nor justification for replacing the psychological problem by the anatomical one."[38] Freud's successors are chiefly
responsible for characterizing homosexuality as a pathological form of
gender inversion, and they waited until Freud's death in 1939 before
doing so publicly.[39] In taking this position, Freud's disciples were actually
invoking a late-nineteenth-century theory, shared by homosexual advocates and sexologists alike: "Here the soul which is doomed to love a man,
and is nevertheless imprisoned in a male body, strives to convert that
body to feminine uses so entirely that the marks of sex, except in the
determined organs of sex, shall be obliterated."[40]

As it happens, Freud was an early defender of homosexual rights, both as a contributor to Hirschfeld's festschrift and as a signatory of a public appeal for the decriminalization of homosexuality in Austria and Germany.[41] Nevertheless, it is wise to remain circumspect about the metamessages of his concepts, as they have lent themselves to certain prejudicial misconstructions. In "Deconstructing Freud (2): Perversion against the Oedipus Complex," Dollimore criticizes the normative aspects of psychoanalysis, its privileging of the heterosexual path of psychosexual development.[42] In his "Leonardo, Medusa, and the Wish to Be a Woman," Dellamora attributes to Freud heterosexist and homophobic anxieties that prevent him from conceptualizing the erotic possibilities of the male fantasy of becoming a woman.[43] Freud should probably not be faulted for steering clear of Ulrich's, Krafft-Ebing's, and Hirschfeld's variations on the theme of homosexual difference when his aim was to affirm the humanity of homosexuals; he insisted that "psycho-analytic research is most decidedly opposed to any attempt at separating off homosexuals from the rest of mankind as a group of a special character."[44] However, Dollimore and Dellamora are right to harp on the interrelated concepts of identification, introjection, and object choice.

The real problem is not Freud's homophobia but his male chauvinism. While acknowledging Freud's stated denial of any attempt to disparage the feminine psyche, Kenneth Lewes believes early psychoanalysis clearly revealed a masculine orientation and ethos that saw women and effeminate men alike as inferior.[45] Moreover, as Frank Sulloway has richly illustrated in *Freud: Biologist of the Mind*, Freud often struck a compromise between essentialist and nominalist positions.[46] Sometimes Freud overstated the case for biological determinism, as in "The Passing of the Oedipus-Complex" (1924) and "Some Psychological Consequences of the Anatomical Distinction between the Sexes" (1925), where he cannot seem to shake the supposition that "anatomy is destiny."[47] Yet, if I have correctly characterized James's obscure hurt, it would appear that Henry James overcame his narcissistic interest in his penis, accepted castration, and retained the homogenital parent (his surrogate) as a love object. It would appear that "the little possessor of the penis" ignored his anatomical destiny and followed a "feminine" path to the resolution of the Oedipus complex, right down to the wish to bear a child.[48] The one persistent feature of James's incorporation of a feminine identity is the extent to which he identified artistic creativity with pregnancy. In an 1891 letter to

William James, Henry conflated the production of his new play with the birth of the William and Alice James's third son: "The anecdote of Margaret Mary and her babe [is] most delightful. It seems trivial at such a time to trouble you with my deliveries, but by the time this reaches you, you and Alice will have got a little used to yours. However, you are to receive news of the coming into the world of my dramatic first born" (*HJL* 3:317). Henry's sense of being married to William, of collaborating in the production of infants, is evident in an 1884 letter in which Henry recommends that William name his second son after a character in *Roderick Hudson*. Henry writes, "If I had a child I would call him (very probably) Roland! 'Roland James' is very good" (*HJL* 3:40). Following William's death in 1910, Henry wrote of his undying attachment to his ideal elder brother: "My life, thank God, is impregnated with him" (*HJL* 4:562).

What I am arguing against is reading James's gender confusion apart from its historical context, as some kind of eternal truth about unhappy and unfortunate males predisposed to homosexuality. James's self-portraits (fictional, epistolary, and autobiographical) are consistent with sexologists' constructions of homosexuality during his lifetime. J. L. Casper published in the 1850s and 1860s. Karl Ulrichs and Carl Westphal published in the 1860s. By the 1880s, a mass of information on homosexuality had accumulated, and much of it was remarkably uniform in outlook, stamping homosexuality as gender inversion pure and simple. By the 1880s, inversion had become a mainstream concept, familiar not only to European specialists on sexual disorders but also to American asylum superintendents: "The hair on the face is sometimes thin, the voice almost always soft. The 'Urnings' have a mincing gait, and sometimes the hips are broad like those of women";[49] "A dandified man is always ridiculous, but when he adds to his foppery, effemination, he then becomes contemptible";[50] "These are the conditions which have been prolific in producing the antisocial 'new woman' and the disgusting effeminate male, both typical examples of the physiological degenerate."[51] Homosexuals also became topics of discussion in the lay press. The 1871 trial of the transvestites Ernest Boulton and Frederick William Park, known as Stella and Fanny to their intimate friends, arrested and charged with "conspiring and inciting persons to commit an unnatural offense," caused a stir on both sides of the Atlantic.[52]

While effeminacy in men was increasingly associated with sexual inversion in the late Victorian period, it was not rigidly codified. Sexual inversion was primarily associated with sex acts rather than sexual persona at this time.[53] While "excessive" or "unnatural" effeminacy in a man would certainly have excited suspicion, James probably felt he could cultivate the feminine side of his personality without incurring the opprobrium attached to overt homosexuality. The point is that James had a lot more latitude in which to indulge his femininity and homoeroticism than has been supposed. Leon Edel assumed that James was "greatly shocked to find his old Parisian friend [Joukowsky] in a veritable nest of homosexuals" (*HJL* 2:289). Richard Ellmann has suggested that James was only tolerant of closeted gays: "Pater's homosexuality was covert, Wilde's was patent. Pater could be summed up as 'faint, pale, embarrassed, exquisite,' but for Wilde James found other epithets embracing his mind, manners, and probable sexual proclivities ('unclean beast')."[54] Critics have unduly emphasized James's disdain for Wilde as somehow emblematic of his attitude toward homosexuals. This move is reductive in more than one sense, for it implies that James had no other motive for loathing Wilde (such as jealousy over his dramatic success, contempt for his self-promotion) than his dandified dress and manner. Fred Kaplan falls into this trap when he observes that, for James, Wilde was "abhorrent insofar as he dramatized a flamboyant caricature of unmanly effeminacy."[55] If this were the case, James should have despised Howard "the Babe" Sturgis, a nurturing and tender man whose hobbies included knitting and embroidering as well as novel writing.[56] While Kaplan has contributed to our knowledge of James's romantic friendships with gays and bisexuals, among them Paul Joukowsky, Hugh Walpole, Jocelyn Persse, Jonathan Sturges, Morton Fullerton, and Hendrik Anderson, I think Kaplan underestimates the erotic possibilities of James's passionate correspondence, a nineteenth-century equivalent of "party lines" and "phone sex." Along the same lines, Edel, Ellmann, and Kaplan have naively interpreted James's insistence that immorality and perversity disgusted him. Feelings of disgust and shame, as well as claims of moral and aesthetic ideals, may be reaction-formations against too keen an interest in unsanctioned sources of erotic gratification.[57] They may also signify plain dissimulation.

The decadent literature James devoured, from Gautier to D'Annunzio to Huysmans, not only served James as mild homoerotic pornography but also enabled him to devise a sexual persona for himself consistent with his determination to abstain from physical love. In "The Image of the Androgyne in the Nineteenth Century," A. J. L. Busst explains, "It must not be thought, however, that because it is the product of the mind, it is removed from sexuality or from lasciviousness. On the contrary. For the lechery which is associated with the pessimistic symbol of the androgyne is above all cerebral; indeed, cerebral lechery is the *vice suprême* which best characterizes the attitude of disillusionment and withdrawal from practical life which conditions the symbol."[58] Busst continues, "This particular perversion, cerebral lechery, is by no means incompatible with total sexual abstinence."[59] James's choice of the name "Hyacinth" for the sexually ambiguous hero of *The Princess Casamassima* aligns him with the decadent writers who used this name to blur the gender boundaries between heroines and heroes from 1798 (Novalis's *Marchen*) to 1891 (Huysmans's *Là-Bas*) and 1893 (Pater's "Apollo in Picardy").[60] Of James scholars, Posnock has the keenest appreciation for the sexual dimensions of his friendships, fantasies, and fictions. Describing James as an example of the "rarest and most perfect" sublimation, in which curiosity takes the place of sexual activity, Posnock stresses "the near hallucinatory force of James's power of sublimation to express desire."[61]

For if James genuinely found Aubrey Beardsley's illustrations sickening and "extraordinarily base," why did he bother to read *The Last Letters of Aubrey Beardsley* or to acknowledge the receipt of the book with a warm note to André Raffalovich, the book's editor and the one-time author of a tract on "urningism"? (*HJL* 4:691–92). James was clearly aware of Raffalovich's past indiscretions and promiscuity, for he makes light of the latter's conversion to Catholicism in a letter. James beseeched his sexually active friends Hugh Walpole and Morton Fullerton to give him fuller accounts of their private lives. He tells Walpole, "I could have done even with more detail — as when you say 'Such parties!' I want so to hear exactly what parties they are. When you refer to their 'immorality on stone floors,' and with prayerbooks in their hands so long as the exigencies of the situation permit of the manual retention of the sacred volumes, I do so want the picture developed and the proceedings authenticated" (*HJL* 4:695). And James was himself capable of titillating gossip with a homoerotic undertone, as when he provided Edmund Gosse with the rough outline of a "fantastic tale" of Guy Maupassant's concerning a ménage à trois between "two Englishmen, each other, and their monkey!" (*HJL* 4:630).

James's curiosity about sexual matters was insatiable. James didn't turn a hair while reading Byron's account of his incestuous passion for his half-sister, Augusta Leigh, though his colleague, John Buchan, reported that he himself was positively sickened by it: "His only words for some special vileness were 'singular' — 'most curious' — 'nauseating, perhaps, but how quite inexpressibly significant'" (*HJL* 4:536). James's scopophilia is prominent in all these illustrations; he would rather watch than participate in sexual activity; however, Freud's theory of component instincts permits us to recognize the exhibitionistic counterpart to James's voyeurism.[62] In writing these letters, in traversing safe borders of gender identity (in a letter to Fullerton, James complained that a snapshot made him "resemble her late Britannic majesty" and protested "je suis mieux que ça"), James was courting some kind of exposure (*HJL* 4:215). James's sensationalism of his own prudery is yet another kind of drag performance, for he cloaks his lusts behind a spinster's irreproachable petticoats.

Scholars read "The Author of Beltraffio" as an attack on the aesthetic movement and, implicitly, on the homosexuals who were its figureheads. In *Professions of Taste*, Jonathan Freedman calls the story "a tale of Gothic horror in which a mother lets her child die rather than grow up with a homosexual father."[63] Freedman also highlights the notions of contagion and tainted inheritance implicit in the story: "The novelist's highly moralistic wife allows their child to die of diphtheria, convinced by proofs of his latest book that Ambient's immoralism would inevitably infect their son. In this story, then, aestheticism is (as it was, paradoxically, for both the advocates and the detractors of 'decadence') linked with corruption and disease, and leads inevitably to moral tragedy."[64] These aspects of the story are compatible with extraliterary representations of both homosexuals and aesthetes in late Victorian culture. In 1889, the former chief of the police department for morals in Paris, where homosexual activity was protected under the Napoleonic Code, expressed his conviction of "the contagiousness of antiphysical passion."[65]

Mrs. Ambient's suspicions were also echoed in the work of the American alienist William Lee Howard, who claimed, "The invert and the pervert is to be found among the aesthetic class. . . . Ninety per cent of these abnormal individuals are engaged in artistic pursuits."[66] Lucien Arreat described the unmanning "nervous erethism" and "infeverishing passions" of creative individuals in an 1893 essay, "Pathology of Artists"; he concluded, "Artists are the most feminine of men."[67] Mrs. Ambient's self-righteous conduct speaks volumes about the general hostility to homosexuals at this time and goes some distance toward explaining why it was difficult for James to come to Wilde's defense or to identify himself publicly with the burgeoning homosexual rights movement. In his *Notebooks*, James expresses no liking for, no sympathy with, Mrs. Ambient. He styles her a "narrow, cold, Calvinistic wife, a rigid moralist."[68] James favors Mark Ambient, whose "godless ideas" are said to belong to the literary career and not to enter into his "perfectly decent" life.[69]

This contrast between works of imagination and actions is extremely important. James's avoidance of full genital sexuality made his passion for other men possible. James's celibacy and his equivocations on sexual matters, in particular his animosity toward certain gay men, have been taken at face value by scholars. But the amount of drapery necessary for decency in the Victorian context was ample. Literary scholars should consider what it cost someone of James's class, background, not to mention personality, to emerge from the closet. John Addington Symonds may serve as a foil for James. Conscious of his predilections early on, Symonds nevertheless held himself aloof from the debauches of Harrow and sought to transcend "crude sensuality through aesthetic idealization of the erotic instincts."[70] Homophobia, self-loathing, and prudery were in equal measure responsible for Symonds's ability to master his passion: "While I was at school, I remained free in fact and act from this contamination. During the first half year the 'beasts,' as they were playfully called, tried to seduce me. But it was soon decided that I was 'not game.' "[71] In 1859, Symonds exposed the love affair between a school fellow and Harrow's headmaster, a man called Vaughan. Apparently, Symonds's conscience was pricked by the reflection that he felt "a deeply rooted sympathy" with the man he brought down, but his greater allegiance, at the time, was to the conventional pieties.[72] This tension between moral training and romantic inclination, resulting in a sexual stalemate — celibacy — was fairly common in the nineteenth century. In 1883, J. C. Shaw and G. N. Ferris published "Perverted Sexual Instinct," one of the first articles to translate and summarize European case studies of sexual inversion for an American audience. Several case histories, those of respectable and talented men, addressed the patients' profound shame at their inability to suppress homosexual inclinations and their proportionate misery at being unable to indulge them. One individual "had often longed to have intercourse with young men, which, however, he never had had. On account of this affection for men, he considered himself a complete reprobate" and "damned for all eternity." Another was "a well-educated young man, twenty-four years of age, of excellent character, [who] during an acute attack of melancholia confessed his perverted desires toward his own sex to his physician. When seen a few days later by Westphal, all traces of his melancholy had disappeared. Recognized his sexual desire as perverted, and wished to be cured of it." A third "felt attracted by young, handsome, strong men; desired to please them, and show them the many little attentions usually shown to a young lady; had never given way to these desires, but still could not control his imagination."[73]

Beyond the physicians' characterization of homosexuals as self-loathing deviants, the forums in which such articles appeared are significant: *The Journal of Nervous and Mental Disease*, *The American Journal of Insanity*, *Alienist and Neurologist*, and the like. The association of homosexuality with insanity, neurasthenia, hysteria, and melancholy is extremely important. Nineteenth-century physicians, sexologists, and psychiatrists divided homosexuals into two camps: the congenital invert, who had inherited his or her inclinations from a forebear, and the debauchee, who merely indulged his or her salacious whims. Congenital inversion was associated with two bugbears of the nineteenth century: moral insanity (Henry Maudsley's term for amoral behavior) and degeneration (atavism, devolution) In "Perverted Sexual Instinct" (1884), George Shrady observed, "In the reported cases of congenital perversion, the abnormal instinct begins oftenest as early as the eighth or ninth year, but shows itself at first, perhaps, only in an inclination to adopt the manners and practices of girls and women. The victims show the somatic basis of their trouble in various ways. There is often an hereditary psychopathic or neuropathic taint."[74] Frank Lydston, physician and criminal-anthropologist, warned that acquired perversion could be transmitted to the next generation: "Men and women who seek, from mere satiety, variations of the normal method of sexual gratification, stamp their nervous systems with a malign influence which in the next generation may present itself as true sexual perversion."[75] In "Viraginity and Effemination" (1893), James Weir argued that these conditions are "due directly to the influence of that strange law laid down by Darwin — the law of reversion to ancestral types. It is an effort of nature to return man to the old hermaphroditic form from which he was evolved."[76] Even Symonds believed the laws of evolution and devolution were inescapable: "We cannot evade the conditions of atavism and heredity. Every family runs the risk of producing a boy or a girl whose life will be embittered by inverted sexuality."[77]

Sexual aberrations figured prominently within the more extensive framework of degeneracy theory, which covered functional and organic diseases, insanity, alcoholism, criminal propensities, nervous exhaustion, and alopecia. The James family was well acquainted with this doctrine. Mrs. James's letters to her children regarding their work habits and potential for nervous exhaustion read like crib notes from S. Weir Mitchell's *Wear and Tear: Hints for the Overworked* (1871). William apparently got the message. In his correspondence, he mentioned the "increasing wear and tear" of his life in Berlin and dedicated himself to "economizing [his] feeble energies" (*LWJ* 1:134, 75). Henry also showed facility with the concept of overwork: "I am delighted to hear [William] was reassured on the subject of poor B[ob]'s balance of intellect and rejoice in the latter's having got rid of his unhappy newspaper. I hope he won't (whatever he does) embark in an *irritating* profession" (*HJL* 2:231). Howard Feinstein's major contribution to our understanding of the Jameses was his insight into the role nineteenth-century concepts of heredity played in the family's psychic economy. As Feinstein pointed out, three of the eleven children of William of Albany who reached maturity, Henry, William, and Jannett, had breakdowns. Their youngest brother, Howard, was an alcoholic. Feinstein concluded that "the incidence of affective disorder, alcoholism, and other forms of psychopathology in the first three generations of this family [was] high."[78] In *A Small Boy and Others*, Henry joked about "tipsy" Albany uncles and family members who "without exception had at last taken a turn as far as possible from edifying."[79] This notion was echoed, more grimly, in *The Princess Casamassima*, where a character reflects, "The family, as a family, had gone downhill to the very bottom."[80] In Henry James's immediate family, Henry Senior had a nervous breakdown in 1844; Alice in 1868; William in 1870; Robertson in 1881; Henry Junior in 1910. Robertson was also an alcoholic, who had himself committed to an asylum. Alice spent her adult life in bed suffering from psychosomatic complaints. In 1884, Garth Wilkinson, the only James sibling to have escaped nervous illness, died a physical wreck at age thirty-nine. Henry Junior had lifelong attacks of gastritis, constipation, sick headaches, and back pain, in addition to episodes of severe depression.

The fear of passing along a tainted heredity is evident in the family correspondence. When Robertson contemplated marrying his cousin in 1869, William wrote to discourage him: "After all, what results from every marriage is a part of the next generation and feeling as strongly as I do that the greater part of the whole evil of this wicked world is the result of infirm health, I account it a true crime against humanity for anyone to run the probable risk of generating unhealthy offspring. . . . I want to feel on my death bed when I look back that whatever evil I was born with I kept to myself, and did so much toward extinguishing it from the world."[81] People like Henry and William James, who recognized any of the somatic or characterological warning signs of hereditary degeneration in themselves or family members, believed that their minds and bodies would slowly, surely betray them. Feinstein explains that "the scion of such 'tainted' stock was at best condemned to a lifelong program of wilful resistance to his defective nature."[82] Though William had moved well beyond nineteenth-century notions of degeneracy by the time he published *Varieties of Religious Experience* in 1902, the most famous portions of that work, devoted to "The Sick Soul," reveal a palpable terror of an insane diathesis. Thirty years had passed between James's encounter with an epileptic idiot at a local asylum and his report of that incident in 1902, which he attributed to a depressed French correspondent. The account seems to have lost none of the poignancy of the original experience:

Simultaneously there arose in my mind the image of an epileptic patient whom I had seen in the asylum, a black-haired youth with greenish skin, entirely idiotic, who used to sit all day on one of the benches, or rather shelves, against the wall, with his knees drawn up to his chin, and the coarse gray undershirt, which was his only garment, drawn over them, enclosing his entire figure. He sat there like a sort of sculptured Egyptian Cat or Peruvian mummy, moving nothing but his black eyes and looking absolutely non-human. This image and my fear entered into a species of combination with each other. *That shape am I*, I felt, potentially. Nothing that I possess can defend me against that fate, if the hour for it should strike for me as it struck for him. There was such a horror of him, and such a perception of my own merely momentary discrepancy from him, that it was as if something hitherto solid within my breast gave way entirely, and I became a mass of quivering fear.[83]

In *Disease and Representation*, Sander Gilman contends that William's "Sick Soul" resembles a case of masturbatory insanity. Gilman likens William's depiction of the alleged epileptic to a plate in Esquirol's famous 1838 work on mental illness, which contained full-length portraits.[84] Certainly, William's figure, clothed in a coarse grey undershirt and seated on a shelf with his knees drawn up against his chin, assumed an identical posture. Moreover, the greenish cast of the idiot's skin links William's figure to nineteenth-century representations of masturbators: the skin "acquires a yellowish, leaden hue."[85] Finally, epileptic insanity was frequently described as the most serious consequence of self-abuse.[86] As "The Sick Soul" was originally conceived as one segment of a longer presentation on religious despondency delivered under the auspices of the Gifford Lectures on Religion at the University of Edinburgh, 1901–1902, James undoubtedly wished to avoid an "overtly autobiographical" presentation, as Gilman suggests.[87]

Throughout the 1860s, William struggled with his melancholy and hypochondria; he was incapacitated, in turns, by visual disturbances, digestive disorders, back pain, and general malaise. One may infer from his letters that William contemplated suicide in 1867 (*LWJ* 1:95). At the same time, William prayed fervently for an ennobling practical calling that might rouse him from his lucubrations and raise him from his sickbed. The subtext of these aspirations is even more interesting than William's self-exhortations to a kind of deliberate sublimation: "Through a knowledge of the fact that that enjoyment on the whole depends on what individuals accomplish, lead a life so active, and so sustained by a clean conscience as not to need to fret much"; "but I really don't think it so *all*-important what our occupation is, so long as we do respectably and keep a clean bosom" (*LWJ* 1:130, 128). William's reflections on moral hygiene should be read in light of nineteenth-century descriptions of sexual neurasthenia and masturbatory insanity. Samuel Tissot's 1758 text on onanism inaugurated a booming market for publications of this kind. William Acton's *The Functions and Disorders of the Reproductive Organs* was widely available after its appearance in 1857 and his ideas were rapidly disseminated by boarding-school administrators, parents, and doctors. In "The Spermatic Economy and Proto-Sublimation," G. J. Barker-Benfield summarizes the content of Victorian advice books, such as *The Student's Manual*, which warned against the enervating effects of masturbation through loss of vital fluids and recommended tonics, stimulants, exercise, and cold showers as a means of controlling the base impulse to self-abuse.[88] In William's case, the appeal for self-control and clean living appears internally generated, but it stemmed from terrifying medical and popular reports of the consequences of masturbation: impotence, immorality, madness, and failure in professional and business pursuits.

William's malaise, inanition, indigestion, and lack of concentration were symptomatic of sexual neurasthenia. As an invalid given to solitary contemplation and bedrest, he was a prime candidate for this "vice." William's lamentations regarding his listlessness and want of purpose are highly instructive: "But my habits of mind have been so bad that I feel as if the greater part of the last ten years had been worse than wasted, and now have so little surplus of physical vigor as to shrink from trying to retrieve them. Too late! too late!" (*LWJ* 1:119). What hope did science hold out to this young medical student who had enfeebled himself by recklessly expending his vital store of nervous energy (seminal fluid)? Self-discipline was the obvious remedy and, failing that, mechanical measures such as rings with sharp teeth for preventing erections, masturbation drawers, manacles, and potions: "Man is distinguished from the brute by his self-control. Let him bear this fact in mind and raise himself above the animals by a determined effort of the will. Pure thoughts, and chaste associations, vigorous physical exercise and a resolute effort to act a manly part will always be successful."[89] By 1873, William had recovered from his depression and declared himself "restored to sanity" (*LWJ* 1:169). Henry Senior wrote to Henry Junior, transcribing William's account of the reasons for his improved outlook. The two most significant were the acceptance of Renouvier's doctrine of the freedom of the will and the rejection of the notion that all mental disorder is produced by physical catalysts. In addition, William's 1874 reading of Henry Maudsley's *Responsibility in Mental Disease* strengthened his one real hope, that through self-control and will power he could halt his decline into madness: "But an opposite course of regeneration of the family by happy marriages, wise education, and a prudent conduct of life is possible; the downward tendency may be thus checked, even effaced in time."[90]

Henry Junior was in America from April 1870 through May of 1873 and observed William's breakdown first-hand. In October of 1873, William visited Henry in Rome. At this time, William very likely expounded his views on the means to health and sanity to his brother, whom he was in the habit of advising on such matters. In 1869, William, the budding physician, counseled Henry on his constipation. And in May of 1873, Henry's gastrointestinal problems had resurfaced. William evidently thought that Henry was a hypochondriac, like himself. In 1869, William diagnosed Henry's back ailment as "dorsal insanity."[91] William would not have been the only source of the doctrine of will power and abstinence. In "The Lessons of the Father: Henry James, Sr., on Sexual Difference," Alfred Habegger has provided a somewhat distorted picture of the paterfamilias: "Evidently Henry James, Sr., had a dream of what used to be called free love." [92] It is true he once wrote a letter to the editor of *The Nation* condemning marriage as presently administered in society as a "hotbed of fraud, adultery, and cruelty, . . . the parent consequently of our existing lasciviousness and prostitution." [93] But his hyperbole served different ends than those Habegger (and Henry Senior's contemporaries) attributed to him; Henry Senior's emphasis was on the hypocrisy and iniquity of socially sanctioned relations between the sexes. Although Henry Senior had the reputation of a nonconformist and sexual libertine, he certainly exposed his boys to the gospels of chastity and self-control, very likely because he regretted his own youthful indiscretions: inebriety, gambling, licentiousness. In a letter to his son Robertson during the Civil War, Henry Senior advised, "Avoid all impure intercourse with the other sex; I mean all intercourse with impure people. And in your intercourse with pure women study to do nothing and say nothing and feel nothing but what would elevate them in their own self respect." [94] Of all the James boys, Bob showed the greatest inclination toward the vices of Henry Senior's youth. In the 1870s, Henry Senior sensed that Robertson, though superficially stable — married and pious — was sorely tempted by drink and extramarital affairs: "It would kill me if one of my boys, especially you, turned out an unkind husband, or a base man." [95] Whether Henry himself had such advice directly from his father and brother or indirectly from advice books and advertisements, he was surely exposed to it.

Although the fear of tainted heredity may explain why Henry James remained single, while many homosexuals he knew (Gosse, Symonds, Wilde, Sargent) married and fathered children, it is not yet clear how this apprehension influenced James's decision to remain celibate. Feinstein characterized Henry's and William's early relationship as a "psychological twinship." [96] In spite of their strongly individual natures, their divergent career paths, their increasing alienation from one another over the years, they remained closely identified. In 1901, William spent the better part of five months at his brother's home, Lamb House, working on a draft of *Varieties of Religious Experience*, in which his account of "The Sick Soul" appeared for the first time. According to John Auchard, "In conversation, in draft, in composition, and in final published form, *Varieties of Religious Experience* was perhaps the work of his brother which Henry James knew on most intimate terms." [97] William's remarkable anecdote had tremendous resonance for Henry. In 1908, it provided the donnée for one of his greatest stories, "The Jolly Corner," in which Spencer Brydon returns to his childhood home and stalks the spirit of what might have been, which is none other than the repressed *"alter-ego* deep down somewhere within [him], as the full-blown flower is in the small tight bud."[98] Brydon expects to discover in his alternate self merely a capacity for business and worldly concerns. He considers himself the dissolute twin: "I've not been edifying — I believe I'm thought in a hundred quarters to have been barely decent. I've followed strange paths and worshipped strange gods."[99] Spencer Brydon is the second coming of Mark Ambient. Brydon is an aesthete who has remained "perfectly decent in life" in spite of his "surrender to sensations"; he is homosocial rather than homosexual.[100] Significantly, Brydon is horrified to discover that he is the pair's better half, and so he denies fraternity with the figure that confronts him at tale's end: "Such an identity fitted his at *no* point, made its alternative monstrous."[101] It is precisely because the alter ego represents exactly what Brydon should have come to had he lived a fuller life that it is disowned:

The stranger, whoever he might be, evil, odious, blatant, vulgar, had advanced as for aggression, and he knew himself to give ground. Then harder pressed still, sick with the force of his shock, and falling back as under the hot breath and the roused passion of a life larger than his own, a rage of personality before which his own collapsed, he felt the whole vision turn to darkness and his very feet give way. His head went round; he was going; he had gone.[102]

To some degree, James's response to Wilde ("unclean beast") may be read as a protest against the perception of "the merely momentary discrepancy" between them. For, significantly, the distinction between the homosexual and homosocial in "The Jolly Corner" hinges on the notion of synchronic existence. It is not the person but the time and place that determine the advent of the beast: "I just transferred him to the climate, that blighted him for once and for ever."[103] As we have seen, the suppression of sexual impulses was the only means of keeping this beastly self at bay. "The Jolly Corner," like "The Beast in the Jungle," is replete with Bengal tigers, great bears, and monstrous stealthy cats waiting to spring upon the unwary, just as Brydon's double pounces on him with "the hot breath and the roused passion of a life larger than his own." This trope, which links anomalous or hyper-sexuality with degeneracy, had currency in James's day. In *La Bête Humaine* of 1890, Zola described the atavistic bloodlust of Jacques Lantier as a "wild beast inside him."[104] In

Vandover and the Brute, written in 1895 but unpublished until 1914, Frank Norris reprised Spencer Brydon's vision of his monstrous alter ego: "For now at last it was huge, strong, insatiable, swollen and distorted out of all size, grown to be a monster, glutted yet still ravenous, some fearful bestial satyr, grovelling, perverse, horrible beyond words."[105] Symonds described his thwarted lust in these same terms in his memoirs: "Oftentimes the beast within roars angrily for that its hunger was not satiated."[106]

For most of his life, Henry James went out of his way to avoid this fate, sealing himself off from physical intimacy, consoling himself with pen-and-ink fantasies. After twenty-five years of friendship, James still came across as "a fountain sealed" to his close friend Edmund Gosse, who suspected that "life stirred his intellect while leaving his senses untouched."[107] It is noteworthy that Gosse himself employed the figure of the "wild beast" when he wrote of his secret passion for other men in 1890: "I have reached a quieter time — some beginnings of that Sophoclean period when the wild beast dies. He is not dead, but tamer; I understand him and the trick of his claws. . . . And the curious thing is that it is precisely to this volcanic force, ever on the verge of destructive ebullition, that one owes the most beautiful episodes of existence, exquisite in all respects."[108] In "The Beast in the Jungle" (1903), James expressed his tragic sense of what he, like John Marcher, had "insanely missed" by failing to discover that the beast was a figure of love and beauty as well as destructive ebullition:

The sight that had just met his eyes named to him, as in letters of quick flame, something he had utterly, insanely missed, and what he had missed made these things a train of fire, made them mark themselves in an anguish of inward throbs. He had seen *outside* of his life, not learned it within. . . . It hadn't come to him, the knowledge, on the wings of experience; it had brushed him, jostled him, upset him, with the disrespect of chance, the insolence of accident. Now that the illumination had begun, however, it blazed to the zenith, and what he presently stood there gazing at was the sounded void of his life.[109]

In 1899, James fell in love with the sculptor Hendrik Anderson, a man thirty years his junior, who hoped the infatuated novelist would champion his work or, at the very least, introduce him to a rich American patron of the arts. James's letters to Anderson are a gold mine for someone of my critical bent, for they provide "inobliterable evidence" of James's homoerotic inclinations. Flirting with Anderson, James even played the part of the big bad wolf: "What an arch-Brute you must, for a long time past, have thought me! But I am not really half the monster I appear"; "What a cold-blooded Brute my interminable silence must have made you think me!" (*HJL* 4:187, 268). James couldn't sustain this pose for any length of time, primarily because Anderson remained out of reach emotionally and physically: "Don't 'chuck' me this year, dearest boy, if you can possibly help it."[110] Of all James's young men (Joukowsky, Persse, Walpole, Sturges, Fullerton), Anderson appeared the most capable of surmounting the barriers James had erected to physical intimacy, had the sculptor been so inclined. Georges-Michel Sarotte has appropriated the truly momentous passage in their correspondence for the title of his book, *Like a Brother, like a Lover*. Following the death of Hendrik's brother, Andreas, James wrote to console him: "I return to Rye April 1rst, and sooner or later to *have* you there and do for you, to put my arm round you and *make* you lean on me as on a brother and a lover, and keep you on and on, slowly comforted or at least relieved of the first bitterness of pain — this I try to imagine and as thinkable, attainable, not wholly out of the question" (*HJL* 4:226).

During the early years of their acquaintance, while James presumably considered whether sexual intercourse was "thinkable, attainable, not wholly out of the question" for himself, James began to complain of gastrointestinal distress, a problem that had not plagued him this persistently for thirty years. In *Three Essays on the Theory of Sexuality*, Freud argued that many neurotic symptoms, which have their basis in sexual conflicts, surface in nonsexual somatic dysfunctions: "The retention of the faecal mass, which is thus carried out intentionally by the child to begin with, in order to serve, as it were, as a masturbatory stimulus upon the anal zone . . . is also one of the roots of the constipation which is so common in neuropaths."[111] While I am uneasy about the ramifications of diagnosing James's constipation as suppressed anal erotism, I do see the relevance of Freud's articulation of symptom formation. The language of hypochondria (both somatic and literary) figures prominently in Henry James's correspondence with his brother. Throughout the fall of 1869, Henry regaled William with the most intimate details of his illness, describing a proctological examination, bowel movements, piles, enemas, and the like to his keen auditor. Heralding the end of Henry's "moving intestinal drama," William's letters also reached a pitch of urgency and euphoria difficult to write off as the "enthusiasm of a neophyte physician and the compassion of a fellow sufferer."[112] Extolling the "wonderful effect" of electricity, William might have been singing the praises of "masochistic jouissance" when he urged Henry to insert one pole of an electrical battery into his rectum and apply a "strong galvanic current."[113] Henry James's costiveness and diarrhea may or may not represent the conversion of homosexual fantasies focusing on the anus as an erogenous zone into somatic symptoms, but the word play connected with these symptoms is certainly suggestive: "So I've pulled through — and am out — and surprisingly soon — of a very deep dark hole. *In* my deep hole, how I thought yearningly, helplessly, dearest Boy, of *you* as your last letter gives you to me and as I take you, to my heart" (*HJL* 4:227). Wooing Anderson, James pictures himself at the base of his own bowel, yearning for his absent friend — a clear, if unintentional, conflation of disease and desire. Nor is this a unique instance. Critiquing a pair of coolly disposed lovers, a recent addition to Anderson's "great nude army," James advised, "So keep at *that* — at the flesh and the devil and the rest of it; make the creatures palpitate, and their flesh tingle and flush, and their internal economy proceed, and their bellies ache and their bladders fill — all in the mystery of your art" (*HJL* 4:394). In this scheme, indigestion would seem to be commensurate with sexual ecstasy.

In 1904, James had adopted the practice of chewing his food to a pulp in the interests of reducing his corpulent physique and conquering his gastritis and constipation. Later, he blamed this "Fletcherizing" for half-starving him to death and for lowering him into the emotional depths of despond. Early in 1910, Henry James suffered a nervous breakdown, complete with all the trimmings, which, for him, included a "marked increase of a strange and most persistent and depressing stomachic crisis" (*HJL* 4:547). William and his wife arrived in April 1910 and helped Henry through the darkest stages of his depression. Henry's terror of solitude was such that Mrs. William James, at her husband's urging, stayed on with Henry at Lamb House while William traveled to Paris in search of relief for his angina. By August 1910, William was on his death bed and Henry was well on his way to recovery.[114] Many precipitating factors have been urged by scholars who attribute James's depression to wounded vanity (the New York edition had not sold well), loneliness (isolation at Rye), and the loss of loved ones. To my mind, James's unrequited love for Hendrik Anderson was the principal cause. Long convinced that aesthetic sublimation compensated him for the sacrifice of sexual intimacy, James broke down when the sustaining myths of his life were swept aside like dry autumn leaves by the hot gust of passion he felt for Anderson. For what lurking beast of congenital degeneration and sex perversion had emerged to settle him at the end? Like John Marcher and Spencer Brydon, he had grown old without ever having really lived. If the late stories may be taken into evidence, in his late sixties James faced the "sounded void of his life" and prepared to jump at any chance of love. But it was too late; he was too old; he wasn't wanted. And he couldn't bear to drain this bitter cup to the lees, to acknowledge the futility of his passional sacrifice as a means of enabling art and deferring the nervous crisis that had afflicted his family members. In a sense, James's nervous breakdown saved him from the unbearable self-knowledge John Marcher acquired, for it confirmed James's whole cautious plan of existence. The beast had jumped after all.

During the fall of 1910 and the winter of 1911, Henry James had four therapeutic conversations with the distinguished American neurologist James Jackson Putnam, one of William James's closest friends as well as an early convert to psychoanalysis. Though Henry James was out of the darkest patch of his depression by this time, Putnam may have helped him find the courage to carry on. In his correspondence with William James, Putnam conceded that Freud's "terribly searching psycho-genetic explanations correspond only to one pole of human life, and that there is another pole in which he takes no interest," the moral sphere.[115] In a series of letters spanning the period 1909–1911, Putnam encouraged Freud to expand the charter of the analyst: "Our psychopathic patients need, I think, something more than simply to learn to know themselves. If there are reasons why they should adopt higher views of their obligations as based on the belief that this is a morally conceived universe, and that 'free-will' has a real meaning, then these reasons ought to be made known to them."[116] Putnam's determination to wrest the concept of sublimation from Freud's grasp and appropriate the term for his own elevated purposes amused Freud, who never tired of tweaking the American moralist: "What would you have us do when a woman complains about her thwarted life, when, with youth gone she notices that she has been deprived of the joy of loving for merely conventional reasons? She is quite right, and we stand helpless before her, for we cannot make her young again. But the recognition of our therapeutic limitations reinforces our determination to change other social factors so that men and women shall no longer be forced into hopeless situations."[117]

In this excerpt, Freud unwittingly described Henry James's predicament to a nicety. Yet, Putnam's philosophical idealism, his quest for a higher moral synthesis, may have served Henry James better than the talking cure. In praising free will and duty, Putnam echoed the precepts of the late William James, serving as an amanuensis for the philosopher, who had once written, "So that it seems to me that a sympathy with men as such, and a desire to contribute to the weal of a species, which, whatever may be said of it, contains All that we acknowledge as good, may very well form an external interest sufficient to keep one's moral pot boiling in a very lively manner to a good old age" (*LWJ* 1:132). Putnam's morally uplifting message fell on prepared and fertile ground, reminding Henry that he might count on his brother William's wisdom to the last: "He had an inexhaustible authority for me, and I feel abandoned and afraid, even as a lost child. But he is a possession, of real magnitude, and I shall find myself still living upon him to the end" (*HJL* 4:562). Shortly after his sessions with Putnam, Henry James recovered his ability to work, which he described as "an unspeakable aid and support and blessing" (*HJL* 4:596). Surely, the strangest passage in James's history owes something to Putnam's ethic. Following the outbreak of World War I, Henry threw himself into the Allied effort with an energy and conviction that surprised his friends and acquaintances. He visited hospitals and refugee camps, supported the American Volunteer Ambulance Corps, and even wrote articles for war charities.[118] In short, this formerly exclusive and reticent aesthete contributed to the "weal of the species" in a highly practical and public manner. James's formal adoption of British nationality, conceived as a rebuke to the American government's isolationist policy, was also altruistic. Striking a pose worthy of Wilde, though lacking the saving salt of humor, James compared his defection to that of "Martin Luther at Wittenburg" (*HJL* 4:770).

James's tribulations support the conclusions of contemporary theorists, such as Carole-Anne Tyler, who question the subversive potential of drag.[119] James never really escaped the circuit of compulsory (dis)identification with the object of desire. Mimicry may be disorienting, but it is not anarchic, a rejection of paradigms altogether. James allowed the culture he inhabited to interpret his effeminacy *for* him as one of the stigmata of degeneracy. Yet, James willingly sacrificed the penis/phallus. What boon accrued to James from this gesture? Perhaps he overthrew the regime of genital supremacy by this means and freed himself to lead a polymorphously perverse imaginative existence. Tragically, James aborted his personal struggle with flesh and the devil just as it was getting underway, but his autobiography, correspondence, and fiction preserve a record of passion in "letters of quick flame."

NOTES

1. William James, *The Principles of Psychology* (Cambridge: Harvard University Press, 1981), 2:1054.
2. See Richard von Krafft-Ebing, *Psychopathia Sexualis: With Especial Reference to the Antipathetic Sexual Instinct*, trans. Franklin Klaf (New York: Stein and Day, 1978), 231.
3. Jonathan Dollimore, *Sexual Dissidence: Augustine to Wilde, Freud to Foucault* (Oxford: Clarendon, 1991), 263.
4. Richard Dellamora, *Masculine Desire: The Sexual Politics of Victorian Aestheticism* (Chapel Hill: University of North Carolina Press, 1990), 130–46; Kaja Silverman, *Male Subjectivity at the Margins* (London: Routledge, 1992), 339–88.
5. J. P. Mowbray quoted in *Henry James and the Critical Heritage*, ed. Roger Gard (London: Routledge and Kegan Paul, 1968), 331.
6. Jonathan Freedman, *Professions of Taste: Henry James, British Aestheticism, and Commodity Culture* (Stanford, Calif.: Stanford University Press, 1990), xvi.
7. Richard Hall, "Leon Edel Discusses Richard Hall's Theory of Henry James and the Incest Taboo," *Advocate*, September 20, 1979, 49.
8. Hall, "Leon Edel," 49.
9. Eve Kosofsky Sedgwick, *Epistemology of the Closet* (Berkeley: University of California Press, 1990), 197.
10. Ibid., 195.
11. Dellamora, *Masculine Desire*, 9.
12. Ross Posnock, *The Trial of Curiosity: Henry James, William James, and the Challenge of Modernity* (New York: Oxford University Press, 1991), 297, note 14.
13. Gard, ed., *Critical Heritage*, 337.
14. Joseph Collins, *The Doctor Looks at Biography: Psychological Studies of Life and Letters* (New York: Doran, 1925), 92.
15. Ibid., 95.
16. Henry James, *Autobiography: A Small Boy and Others, Notes of a Son and Brother, The Middle Years* (Princeton, N.J.: Princeton University Press, 1983), 415.

17. See Paul John Eakin, "Henry James's 'Obscure Hurt': Can Autobiography Serve Biography?" *New Literary History* 19 (Spring 1988): 675–92.
18. James, *Notes of a Son and Brother*, 417.
19. Saul Rosenzweig, "The Ghost of Henry James," *Partisan Review* 11 (Fall 1944): 453.
20. Donald Moss, "Introductory Thoughts: Hating in the First Person Plural: The Example of Homophobia," *American Imago* 49 (Fall 1992): 288. See also John Fletcher, "Freud and His Uses: Psychoanalysis and Gay Theory," in *Coming on Strong: Gay Politics and Culture*, ed. Simon Shepherd and Mick Wallis (London: Unwin Hyman, 1989), 101: "The law of the Oedipal polarity in effect states: 'you cannot be what you desire; you cannot desire what you wish to be.' "
21. Judith Butler, *Gender Trouble: Feminism and the Subversion of Identity* (New York: Routledge, 1990), 17.
22. James, *A Small Boy and Others*, 7.
23. Georges-Michel Sarotte, *Like a Brother, like a Lover: Male Homosexuality in the American Novel and Theater from Herman Melville to James Baldwin* (New York: Anchor Doubleday, 1978), 198.
24. James, *A Small Boy and Others*, 147.
25. *The Letters of William James*, ed. Henry James III (Boston: Atlantic Monthly Press, 1920), 1:174. Further references to this work will be included parenthetically in the text.
26. William James quoted in Richard Hall, "An Obscure Hurt: The Sexuality of Henry James, Part 1," *New Republic*, April 28, 1979, 28.
27. Henry James quoted in Leon Edel, *Henry James: The Conquest of London, 1870–1881* (New York: Avon, 1962), 2:343. James's emphasis.
28. *Henry James Letters* (Cambridge: Harvard University Press, 1975), 2:177. Further references to this work will be cited parenthetically in the text.
29. Hall, "Obscure Hurt: Part 1," 30.
30. Edel, *Henry James*, 2:392.
31. Howard Feinstein, *Becoming William James* (Ithaca, N.Y.: Cornell University Press, 1984), 233.
32. Silverman, *Male Subjectivity*, 353.
33. Butler, *Gender Trouble*, 136.
34. Ibid., 135.
35. Krafft-Ebing, *Psychopathia Sexualis*, 208, 205, 202, 209; Butler, *Gender Trouble*, 138.
36. Sigmund Freud, *Three Case Histories*, ed. Philip Rieff (New York: Collier, 1963), 275.
37. Henry Abelove, "Freud, Male Homosexuality, and the Americans" (1985), in *The Lesbian and Gay Studies Reader*, ed. David Halperin, Michele Barale, and Henry Abelove (New York: Routledge, 1993), 381–93.
38. Sigmund Freud, *Three Essays on the Theory of Sexuality* (1909; New York: Basic, 1962), 8.
39. Abelove, "Freud, Male Homosexuality, and the Americans," 390.

40. Krafft-Ebing paraphrased in John Addington Symonds, *A Problem in Modern Ethics: An Inquiry into the Phenomenon of Sexual Inversion* (1891; New York: Blom, 1971), 59.
41. Kenneth Lewes, *The Psychoanalytic Theory of Male Homosexuality* (New York: New American Library, 1988), 31.
42. Dollimore, *Sexual Dissidence*, 196.
43. Dellamora, *Masculine Desire*, 136.
44. Freud, *Three Essays*, 11. Footnote added 1915.
45. Lewes, *Psychoanalytic Theory of Male Homosexuality*, 237.
46. Frank Sulloway, *Freud: Biologist of the Mind: Beyond the Psychoanalytic Legend* (Cambridge: Harvard University Press, 1992), 277–319.
47. Sigmund Freud, *Sexuality and the Psychology of Love* (New York: Collier, 1963), 180.
48. Freud, *Sexuality and the Psychology of Love*, 181.
49. George Shrady, "Perverted Sexual Instinct," *Medical Record*, July 19, 1884, 70.
50. James Weir, "Viraginity and Effemination," *Medical Record*, September 16, 1893, 360.
51. William Lee Howard, "Effeminate Men and Masculine Women," *New York Medical Journal*, May 5, 1900, 687.
52. Ronald Pearsall, *The Worm in the Bud: The World of Victorian Sexuality* (New York: Macmillan, 1969), 461–62.
53. See Ed Cohen, *Talk on the Wilde Side: Toward a Genealogy of a Discourse on Male Sexualities* (London: Routledge, 1993), 136, where Cohen remarks that the effeminacy popularly attributed to the male aesthete in the 1880s emerged from newspaper accounts of the Wilde trials of 1895.
54. Richard Ellmann, "Henry James among the Aesthetes," *Proceedings of the British Academy* 69 (1983): 218.
55. Fred Kaplan, *Henry James: The Imagination of Genius: A Biography* (New York: Morrow, 1992), 300.
56. Posnock, *Trial of Curiosity*, 212.
57. Freud, *Three Essays*, 43.
58. A. J. L. Busst, "The Image of the Androgyne in the Nineteenth Century," in *Romantic Mythologies*, ed. Ian Fletcher (London: Routledge and Kegan Paul, 1967), 42. Busst's emphasis.
59. Ibid., 43.
60. See Dellamora, *Masculine Desire*, 187. For another discussion of this myth and its role in fin-de-siècle erotic literature, see Kevin Kopelson, "Wilde's Love-Deaths," *Yale Journal of Criticism* 5 (Fall 1992): 40–43 especially.
61. Posnock, *Trial of Curiosity*, 47.
62. Freud, *Three Essays*, 32.
63. Freedman, *Professions of Taste*, 172.
64. Ibid., 144.
65. Carlier quoted in Symonds, "A Problem in Modern Ethics," 20.
66. William Lee Howard, "Psychical Hermaphroditism," *Alienist and Neurologist* 18 (April 1879): 113–14.

67. Lucien Arreat, "Pathology of Artists," *Alienist and Neurologist* 14 (1893): 86.
68. *The Complete Notebooks of Henry James*, ed. Leon Edel and Lyall Powers (New York: Oxford University Press, 1987), 25.
69. Ibid., 25.
70. *The Memoirs of John Addington Symonds*, ed. Phyllis Grosskurth (New York: Random House, 1984), 96.
71. Ibid., 95.
72. Ibid., 112.
73. J. C. Shaw and G. N. Ferris, "Perverted Sexual Instinct," *Journal of Nervous and Mental Disease* 10 (April 1883): 190, 193, 201.
74. Shrady, "Perverted Sexual Instinct," 70.
75. Frank Lydston, "Sexual Perversion, Satyriasis, Nymphomania," *Medical and Surgical Reporter* 61 (September 1889): 255.
76. Weir, "Viraginity and Effemination," 359.
77. Symonds, "A Problem in Modern Ethics," 4.
78. Feinstein, *Becoming William James*, 304–5.
79. James, *A Small Boy and Others*, 29.
80. Henry James, *The Princess Casamassima* (New York: Scribner's, 1922), 5:66.
81. Feinstein, *Becoming William James*, 304.
82. Ibid., 311.
83. William James, *The Varieties of Religious Experience: A Study of Human Nature* (New York: Longmans, Green, 1905), 160.
84. Sander Gilman, *Disease and Representation: Images of Illness from Madness to AIDS* (Ithaca, N.Y.: Cornell University Press, 1988), 76.
85. Cohen, *Talk on the Wilde Side*, 47.
86. Charles Dana, "Clinical Lecture: On Certain Sexual Neuroses," *Medical and Surgical Reporter*, August 15, 1891, 243.
87. Gilman, *Disease and Representation*, 76.
88. G. J. Barker-Benfield, *The Horrors of the Half-Known Life: Male Attitudes toward Women and Sexuality in Nineteenth-Century America* (New York: Harper and Row, 1976), 175.
89. Charles Dana, "Clinical Lecture," 245.
90. Henry Maudsley, *Responsibility in Mental Disease* (New York: Appleton, 1900), 300–301.
91. *The Correspondence of William James: William and Henry, 1861–1884*, ed. Ignas Skrupskelis and Elizabeth Berkeley (Charlottesville: University Press of Virginia, 1992), 1:82.
92. Alfred Habegger, *Henry James and the "Woman Business"* (Cambridge: Cambridge University Press, 1989), 31.
93. "Mr. Henry James on Marriage," *Nation*, June 9, 1870, 366.
94. Jane Maher, *Biography of Broken Fortunes: Wilkie and Bob, Brothers of William, Henry, and Alice James* (Hamden, Conn.: Archon, 1986), 74.
95. Ibid., 128.
96. Feinstein, *Becoming William James*, 230.

97. John Auchard, *Silence in Henry James: The Heritage of Symbolism and Decadence* (University Park: Pennsylvania State University Press, 1986), 96–97.
98. Henry James, "The Jolly Corner" (1908), in *The Short Stories of Henry James* (New York: Random House, 1945), 614.
99. Ibid., 615.
100. Ibid., 619.
101. Ibid., 635.
102. Ibid., 635.
103. Ibid., 614.
104. Emile Zola, *La Bête Humaine* (London: Penguin, 1986), 66.
105. Frank Norris, *Novels and Essays: "Vandover and the Brute," "McTeague," "The Octopus," Essays* (New York: Library of America, 1986), 159.
106. *The Memoirs of John Addington Symonds*, 127.
107. Edmund Gosse, "Henry James," *London Mercury* 2 (May 1920): 34.
108. Edmund Gosse quoted in Ann Thwaite, *Edmund Gosse: A Literary Landscape, 1849–1928* (Chicago: University of Chicago Press, 1984), 195.
109. Henry James, "The Beast in the Jungle" (1903), in *The Short Stories of Henry James*, 595–96.
110. Henry James Letters (Cambridge: Harvard University Press, 1975), 4:269.
111. Freud, *Three Essays*, 52–53.
112. *The Correspondence of William James*, 1:127; Feinstein, *Becoming William James*, 229.
113. The phrase "masochistic jouissance" is Leo Bersani's. See "Sexuality and Aesthetics," *October* 28 (Spring 1984): 41; *The Correspondence of William James*, 1:113.
114. Kaplan, *Henry James*, 525–31.
115. *James Jackson Putnam and Psycho-analysis: Letters between Putnam and Sigmund Freud, Ernest Jones, William James, Sandor Ferenczi, and Morton Prince* (Cambridge: Harvard University Press, 1971), 79.
116. Ibid., 95.
117. Ibid., 91.
118. Rosenzweig, "The Ghost of Henry James," 450–52.
119. Carole-Anne Tyler, "Boys Will Be Girls: The Politics of Gay Drag," *Inside/Out: Lesbian Theories, Gay Theories*, ed. Diana Fuss (New York: Routledge, 1991), 51–58.

Gender and the Discourse of Nationalism in Anita Desai's *Clear Light of Day*

Sangeeta Ray

The reading of all third world literature as national allegories, proposed by Jameson in his by now in/famous essay, "Third World Literature in the Era of Multi-National Capitalism," has fueled a highly contested debate not only about the primary terms used in the title — "Third World literature" and "national allegory" — but also about the geopolitical consequences generated by a socioliterary critical paradigm that seeks to be all inclusive. This essay seeks to intervene in the ongoing discussion by focusing on nationalism as a gendered discourse. Nationality and gender are in themselves unstable categories that assume stability through their representation and consolidation in discursive acts. When these two contrapuntal categories are yoked together, as in the Indian nationalistic mantra "Bande Mataram" (Glory to the Motherland), the implications and consequences of the hypnotizing gendered trope on the lives of women during and after independence should not be minimized. Even Benedict Anderson's *Imagined Communities* (a household name among scholars of nationalism today),[1] which does address the manner in which issues of ethnicity, race, and class are imbricated in the evolution of nationalist beliefs, ignores the question of gender. As Mary Louise Pratt has pointed out, Anderson's use of the "language of fraternity and comradeship" to capture the idea of the modern nation as an imagined community "displays the androcentrism of modern national imaginings." The absence of gender in Anderson's speculation of the rise and growth of the modern nation cannot simply be explained by arguing that

96

women "don't fit" the descriptors of the imagined community. Rather, the nation by definition situates or "produces" women in permanent instability with respect to the imagined community, including, in very particular ways, the women of the dominant class. Women inhabitants of nations were neither imagined as nor invited to imagine themselves as part of the horizontal brotherhood.[2]

Jameson's essay, some of the responses to his essay, as well as certain other articles dealing with nationalism and its allegorical representation in third world literature,[3] gloss over the problematic relationship resulting from the invidious symbiosis of gender and nationality.[4] My reading of Anita Desai's *Clear Light of Day* addresses the sociopolitical predicaments confronted by women whose position as independent, equal citizens in the nation is thwarted by the appropriation of "woman" (and its related gendered significations) as a metonymy for "nation."

The initial response to Jameson's essay was Aijaz Ahmad's "Jameson's Rhetoric of Otherness and the 'National Allegory.'"[5] Ahmad primarily focuses on the impossibility of postulating a global theory of third world literature. He attempts to invalidate Jameson's major premise that all "Third World cultural productions" can be read as national allegories because they have something in common, namely, that "the story of the private individual destiny is always an allegory of the embattled situation of the public third world culture and society."[6] The most recent entry in the ongoing debate is Madhava Prasad's "On the Question of a Theory of (Third World) Literature."[7] I would like to examine his position at some length here because it offers us an innovative way to theorize about literature by reintroducing the allegorical dimension at the level of class, thereby denying the inviolate bifurcation of the globe into the first and third worlds. Prasad argues for a perception of certain social formations as "a time-space of subject formations, necessarily determined by imperialism, colonialism, developmentalism, and experimentation with bourgeois democracy and other forms of nation-statehood" rather than as a "geography with its millennia of cultural history";[8] then one could retain the signifier "Third World" as used by Jameson in its strategic relational aspect in order to highlight the inequalities that remain the hallmark of global capitalist economy. Prasad's emphasis on subject formations as primarily constituted by their entry into some form of nation-statehood allows him to draw a trajectory that defines all social formations

as structures of administration by representation on the model of the bourgeois democracies of Europe. The nation-state, with a representative rule approximating in varying degrees to the primary models, is the politically, economically and ideologically privileged unit of participation in the global order.[9]

So it is not that Jameson is incorrect when he reads third world texts as national allegories; his mistake is that he restates the opposition between first world and third world texts as that between Freud and Marx. According to Prasad's hypothesis, all literatures at this point in socioliterary history should be inscribed in their national context in order to underline the hypervisibility of the national framework in third world configurations and its apparent invisibility in the Western context.[10] This would entail a collapse of the distinction between the aesthetic and the political in Western literary theories that, in claiming the invisibility of the national framework in Western literatures, seeks to read the individualist emphasis therein as a result of a private libidinal thrust independent of the individual's participation in a social institution that functions as a unit of exchange in a larger, distinctively capitalist global economy. The repression of the allegorical is necessary to advance the theory of a depoliticized realm of the aesthetic that foregrounds the "individualist" and autonomous status of the Western text.

If the intellectual wishes to move beyond a binary representation of world literature as an opposition between the first world and third world, then Prasad insists on a theory of literature that would begin by "redefining the libidinal/private in its allegorical status (its relation to particular nations but especially to particular classes – a class allegory) and collapsing the distinction which originates in capitalist ideology."[11] In this reconfigured allegorical reading, then, the distinction between first and third world texts can still be read within a theory of modes of production. This time, however, the theory is wrenched from its developmental framework, which posits a center of free space, ensuring the formation and participation of a free citizen who enjoys full representation in a putative liberal pluralist democracy that foregrounds a cultural rather than a national identity based on the notion of "free will." To this center is opposed a magnetically charged involuntary field that necessitates the formation of collective communities who in their secondary or tertiary stage of development advocate a nationalist will at the expense of individual subjecthood. If I read Prasad correctly, his notion of class allegory would reintroduce the notion of privilege into the center of free space. This in turn would highlight the obscured formation of class-based communities that would enable us to distinguish between the bourgeoisie,

who thrive under the notion of nation as "a community of private individuals,"[12] from other classes, who continue to conceive nation-states in
terms of territorially biased imagined communities.

Prasad's emphasis on class as an overdetermined signifier that cannot
and should not be overlooked in any discursive undertaking takes away
with one hand what it bestows with the other. Even as he forces us to
recognize the importance of class boundaries in the literary productions
of the first world, he fails to address how gender intersects with class to
confound and contradict class affiliations. One wonders whether Prasad
foresees a kind of Socialist-feminist coalition with class-based labor forces
along the lines of Christine Delphy. This is difficult to assess because his
discussion is so centered on the interjection of space-time-class subject
formations in what has been the first-third world divide. Prasad does not
merely emphasize class in writing from a loosely Marxist "positionality."
My point, which is not just a matter of splitting hairs, is that the widespread influence and practice of feminist studies in every field today
should suggest to every theorist and critic that feminism is not merely a
choice "among competing perspectives" but rather "a choice which cannot but undergird any attempt at a [critical/theoretical] reconstruction
which undertakes to demonstrate our sociality in the full sense, and is
ready to engage with its own presuppositions of an objective gender-
neutral method of inquiry."[13] The active, politically charged presence of
other classes in the nondiscursive realm, significantly absent in the aesthetic examination of the Western discursive theater, surfaces as well in
the last paragraphs of Ahmad's essay, where he correctly interprets Jameson's text as both raced and gendered – it is above all a theory pro-
pounded by a white male critic. However, his argument that Jameson's
reading could not be duplicated by a woman, or a Black writer, suffers
from a similar globalizing tendency for which he faults Jameson. The
distinction between public and private will not be the same for all U.S.
women or for all Black writers, and, on the contrary, for a number of
citizens in a pluralist society, Jameson's reading would have familiar
echoes, irrespective of gender or race.

The emphasis in all the three essays discussed above is the positing of
the discursive formation of nation as a significantly masculinist, public
discourse independent of the machinations of the domestic/familial. It is
true that most theorists of nationalism have been male, but to conve-
niently disregard the play of sexuality and gender as an integral element

in the separation of the libidinal/private from the public/collective seems to come perilously close to the discourse of nationalists who continue to yoke gender to the articulation of the nation even as they seek forcefully to separate the micropolitical from the macropolitical.[14] The desire to keep the two spheres distinct is mandated by the use of the ubiquitous trope of nation-as-woman in all nationalist discourses. As the editors of *Nationalisms and Sexualities* point out, the efficient functioning of this particular trope depends "for its representational efficacy on a particular image of woman as chaste, dutiful, daughterly or maternal."[15] Kumari Jayawardena has argued very convincingly that the emergence of feminist movements in various parts of the so-called third world is intricately tied to anti-imperialist and nationalist struggles waged by a modernized and "enlightened" indigenous middle class.[16] But this alliance has exacted its toll on women whose claims for recognition as equal citizens in the new independent nation-state have been repeatedly set aside by an indigenous government that has to attend to more "pressing" concerns. The form and content of these nationalist movements and independent nation-states, both secular and religious, are multifarious to say the least, but it is crucial that discourses and practices concerning the role and specificity of gender and its relation to the positions of women be analyzed when we seek to examine the proliferation of nationalisms and nationalist discourses. For example, a collection of essays edited by Deniz Kandiyoti seeks to attend to the postindependent trajectories of modern states in their various deployments of Islam to shore up different nationalisms and state ideologies. The various essays in the volume titled *Women, Islam, and the State* show how these various transformations of Islam are used by both hegemonic and oppositional groups to control the problematic space designated by the phrase "the woman question." The essays seek to underline that the

ways in which women are represented in political discourse, the degree of formal emancipation they are able to achieve, the modalities of their participation in economic life and the nature of the social movements through which they are able to articulate their gendered interests are intimately linked to state-building [or nation-building] processes and are responsive to their transformation.[17]

Even though the territories covered are as distinct as Turkey, Bangladesh, Pakistan, Egypt, Iran, Iraq, Lebanon, and Yemen, every single contributor to this volume is a woman. More such studies by men and women are necessary if, as Radhakrishnan has suggested, feminist historiography understands "gender" as a category that is much more comprehensive [than paying mere lip service to the woman question] in its scope. In this sense, feminist historiography speaks post-representationally, activating the category of "gender" beyond its initial or originary commitment to merely one special or specific constituency. . . . To put it differently, the field of historiography [and I would argue the study of nationalism and "Third World Literature"] as such [*must*] be made to acknowledge the reality of the feminist intervention as both micropolitical and macropolitical. (substitution and emphasis mine)[18]

Dipesh Chakravorty, in a very recent essay discussing the status of "Marxism beyond Marxism" (the allusion is to Antonio Negri's text *Marx beyond Marx*), admits that, though the enterprise of the *Subaltern Studies* collective was motivated by an "explicit spirit of opposition to the elitist and teleological narratives that both marxist and nationalist traditions . . . had promoted in Indian historiography," their engagement with feminism as a significant oppositional theoretical grid came only after Gayatri Spivak's critique of the male orientation of their reconstructive projects.[19] In fact, in her brilliant essay "Can the Subaltern Speak?" Spivak reveals that any theory of representation dealing critically with the domains of ideology, subjectivity, politics, the nation, the state, and the law must attend to the specific discursive uses of the category of gender in order not to engender yet another moment of theoretical epistemic violence. She argues that the peasant "consciousness" evoked in the various subaltern countermovements uncovered and charted by the *Subaltern Studies* collective is always already male since "the 'subject' implied by the texts of insurgency can only serve as a counterpossibility for the narrative sanctions granted to the colonial subject in the dominant groups."[20] Thus even though the methodology of the collective cannot be accused of reifying the notion of the feminine as indeterminate, it, in its originary moments, has failed to trace the "doubly effaced" trace of sexual difference in the "itinerary of the subaltern subject."[21] The archival, interventionist historiography of the collective needs to confront the aporia in its methodology, which progresses on the assumption that all forms of silence can be equally measured, retrieved, and represented via the lost figure of the indigenous, insurgent classed/casted subaltern. Spivak addresses a particular gendered issue — *sati* (widow burning) — not only to complicate the notion of free will but also to suggest that in every act of retrieval and reconstruction by the collective, "the ideological construction of gender keeps the male dominant."[22] Carefully scrutinizing both

Brahmanic codes and texts as well as imperialist discourses surrounding the abolishing of *sati*, Spivak comes to the conclusion that "between patriarchy and imperialism, subject constitution and object-formation, the figure of the woman disappears, not into a pristine nothingness, but into the violent shuttling which is the displaced figuration of the 'third-world woman' caught between tradition and modernization."[23] Jenny Sharpe, in her book *Allegories of Empire*, provides an impassioned reading of Spivak's critique of the methodology of the collective. According to Sharpe, Spivak does not fault the collective for ignoring women's participation in rebellions — the collective is scrupulous in documenting such instances. What remains problematic is the failure on the part of the members of the collective to critically examine the moments in their texts where "the symbolic exchange of women appears at crucial moments . . . for explaining the mobilization of peasants across villages. . . . Spivak notes that the project of writing a history from below repeats the subaltern male's indifference to sexual difference."[24]

Even Homi Bhabha, in his essay "Dissemination: Time, Narrative, and the Margins of the Modern Nation," where he seeks to undermine the notion of nation as a fixed, static, and homogeneous entity, fails to undertake a sustained analysis of how the liminal time-space of the modern nation continues to be inscribed in the name and in the gendered narrative of the motherland. He is absolutely correct in his assessment that the narrative of a historically linear nationhood sustains itself by a forced repression of other narratives that might disrupt its hegemony. The nascent presence of the repressed described by Bhabha in terms of the Freudian "uncanny" resurfaces in oppositional practices of signification that are raced, classed, and gendered. This enables Bhabha to re-present the national time-space as a "double time" in which the dominant national temporal narrative (the "pedagogical," in his words) is contested by the performance of "counternarratives of the nation that continually evoke and erase its totalizing boundaries."[25]

However, the positing of counternarratives as minority "performative" (Bhabha's word for oppositional narratives) supplements that rupture the master narrative, not through dialogical confrontation but by "insinuating [themselves] into the terms of reference of the dominant discourse,"[26] produces a curious elision of the term "nation." In all his examples of counternarratives of nation, Bhabha conflates the term "nation" with "culture," so that African American cultural history, Black British working-class women's cultural politics, and the "uncanny" repression of class in the representation of an eighteenth-century worldview through the "common language" of the ubiquitous "English gentleman" appear to have equal force in the disruption of national linear time in their articulation of other national spatial temporalities.[27] This erasure of the differences between nation and culture and the conflation of the discourses of race, gender, and class and/or the strenuous amalgamation of race/gender, gender/class, class/race, race/gender/class under the rubric of migrant metaphoricity evokes a moment of stasis wherein migrant discourse re-emerges in the last analysis as the hypostatized cultural spatio-temporal Other to a linear historical National Sameness.[28] Bhabha seems to want it both ways — to deny the difference between nation and culture in order to argue for a constant dissident minority cultural presence necessary for the articulation of the "double time" of national representation, and to privilege culture over nation so as to preserve the domain of the other as irretrievable in the arena of the same.

This oscillation between containment and analogy is a peculiar hallmark of a certain brand of poststructuralist theory that is cogently captured in Amanda Anderson's notion of the "double gesture" whereby "an ethical voluntarism or 'strategic essentialism' and a theoretical antihumanism are both affirmed."[29] The construction of a cultural spatio-temporal other in terms of either a quintessential Third World (as in Jameson) or the celebration of hybridity *tout court* (as in Bhabha) on the one hand and the denial of difference in the affirmation of a one-world theory (as in Ahmad), as well as the privileging of class as the only site that provides a delimited entry for an allegorical theoretical framework necessary for global cultural critique (as in Prasad, 80) on the other ironically produce an unmediated space for the formation of a national subject. This space is often curiously unmarked by the intersecting axes of class, race, and gender and at times denies the specificities and contradictory material bases that constitute mobility and social positioning.

Gender must be included in any comprehensive theoretical discussion on nationalism. Terms like "motherlands," "mothercultures," and "mothertongues" continue to flourish in this era that is being compelled to witness a global resurgence of violent nationalist discourses. As Susheela Nasta, distilling Elleke Boehmer's argument, writes, we need to begin with the assumption that nationalism is a gendered ideology and that therefore the notion of motherland may "mean neither 'source' or 'home' to women. In the iconographies of nationalism, images of mothers have conventionally invited symbols suggestive of primal origins — birth, hearth, home, roots, the umbilical cord of being — as encapsulated by terms such as 'mothertongue,' 'mothercountry.'"[30] We need to explore the complexities inherent in a preponderantly masculinist ideology that propagates itself through a heavy reliance on feminine ideals. The essays in the collection *Nationalisms and Sexualities* seek to do this by focusing on the complex and often ambiguous relationships among the idea of nation as imagined community, the emphasis on the "proper" nature of the homosocial bonding that characterizes public discourses of dominant official nationalisms, and the trope of nation-as-woman.[31]

In the discussions of third world literatures as national allegories, however, one finds not only a curious absence of gender as a category of analysis but also an ignorance of the ways in which an analysis of the narratives of third world women and women writers may prove useful in the disruption of a self-deluding complacency that often accompanies readings of overt or covert nationalist (read primarily heterosexual male) narratives — interpretations that tend to establish an allegorical correspondence between the psychic crisis of the male protagonist and the sociopolitical crisis of the modern nation-state. Perhaps if they turn to other texts, by women, gay men, and/or lesbians, they might understand how the crisis of individual identity could, as Rhonda Cobham suggests, be read as "a crisis of gender and sexual identities that parallel and intersect with the socio-political manifestations of disorder."[32] The examinations of the numerous ways in which the discourses of imperialism, colonialism, and nationalism have relied on the trope of the feminization of the "other" have led to innovative studies in the fields of ethnography, history, and literary/cultural studies. However, as Sara Suleri has cautioned, the conflation of gender with "woman" and her stereotypical characteristics can, unless one is very scrupulous in one's critical delineation, produce a curious replication of the desire to shroud the "other" in an impenetrable "female" mystery, thereby perpetuating the binary grid set up in imperialist, colonialist, and nationalist discourses. Even though I am not entirely convinced by Suleri's general claim that the "geography of rape as a dominant trope for the act of imperialism" is no longer "critically liberating,"[33] I do believe that attention to surface configurations of the idiom of gender in many imperialist discourses can erase the sexual ambivalence that often marks them. The trope of rape, and feminization, is often complicated by the homoeroticism that underlines the confrontations between colonizer and colonized. Suleri focuses on imperialist discourses surrounding empire building in India and on Anglo-Indian as well as Indo-English narratives, and in her introduction to her book argues for a continuous attention to the production of our own postcolonial feminist critical discourses, which should not serve "as the landscape upon which the intimacy of homoerotic invitation and rejection can be enacted."[34] Readings of encounters between men and between men and women of different races could

provide a highly productive field of study for the epistemological limitations — and their concomitant terror — imposed by an imperial contemplation of the multifariousness of culture. Such [studies] could furthermore provide cultural criticism with a terrain upon which to complicate and to question more literal inscriptions of gender-bound metaphors[35]

onto the politics of colonialism, imperialism, and nationalism.[36] Perhaps then we can begin critically to decode the myths surrounding gender, sexuality, and nationalism that so many critics of third world texts continue to endorse through their critical dis-recognition.

By redirecting Radhakrishnan's encompassing observation "that the field of historiography in general needs to acknowledge the reality of the feminist intervention as both micropolitical and macropolitical"[37] toward the immediate discourse under examination here, that is, nationalism, I wish to open up a space that would allow us to question the homogenizing tendency inherent in the discursive realm of nationalist politics that sets itself up as representing a nongendered ethnic majority. In order to do this, I would like to turn to the novel by Anita Desai. *Clear Light of Day* is often said to be Desai's best book, one of her few novels that, despite her assertions that she does not find the term "feminist" an appropriate description of her writings, depicts two "Daughters of Independence" (to borrow from the title of Joanna Liddle's and Rama Joshi's book)[38] whose lives seem singularly unchanged despite the rhetoric of independence that gave rise to two putatively decolonized nation-states. This particular reading of the novel is not offered as a symptomatic analysis of the body of Desai's works; nor am I suggesting that all bourgeois women's writings from India *must* be read as *primarily* engendered by the discourse of colonialism and nationalism. But since this particular text does strategically use the rise of nationalist fervor, the discord between Hindus and

Muslims, and the death of Gandhi in the construction of its narrative, the postcolonial critic can provide a nuanced reading of the complex function of gender in the tropology of this particular postcolonial novel. Hopefully, this analysis will suggest to feminist postcolonial critics the importance of dialogical readings of other bourgeois Indo-English texts that can wrest nation "from the context of easy allegorization"[39] and provide more comprehensive examinations of the structural function of gender in the political discourse and performance of colonialism and postcolonialism.

Most critics of the book address the links between individual life and history that weave through the book, reading the often-violent domestic upheavals in the Das family against the historic background of an Indian nation born in the wake of a bloody Partition.[40] Instead of plotting the manner in which certain important domestic episodes are inextricably connected to crucial historical events, thereby suggesting the reflection of the macropolitical in the micropolitical, my analysis investigates how the hegemonic discourse of Indian nationalism presents itself as an equalizing, progressive force wresting authority from colonial government by obfuscating its own complicity in the replication of the paternal signifier in the name of national survival.[41] The occasion for the narrative is the present, or, more specifically, a summer in the 1970s, when Tara, the younger sister, returns to the Old Delhi house on one of her regular visits from Washington, where her husband, Bakul, is a functionary in the Indian diplomatic corps. Though Bimala, the older sister, is a teacher of history at a local women's college, her life seems arrested, still circumscribed by the old boundaries that include the Das house and garden and the home of their next-door neighbors, the Misras. Her companion, other than the members of the Misra family, is the silent, psychologically scarred younger brother, Baba, whose only source of solace and entertainment is the reverberating sounds of 1940s Western songs played on a scratchy gramophone.

If during the independence movement issues concerning the rights of women could be strategically included within the immediate nationalist platform, after independence the difference between the genders was effectively deployed to shore up patriarchal power and to establish the firmness of national purpose. The initial demands of freedom for women did generate certain changes in the status of women at the personal and political front,[42] but the alliance between the discourse of nationalism and that of the "woman question" was fraught with contradictions and ambiguities. Even as Indian women were being granted the right to vote (suffrage helped the nationalist cause) and were struggling much harder (the fight was long and bitter) for the passage of a Hindu Code that would reform the areas of personal law such as marriage, divorce, and inheritance, woman as repository of an untainted, unchanging "Indianness" became the sign of the imaginary feminized nation whose chastity had to be safeguarded by virile nationalists against Western penetration. This difference between woman as sign and women as equal personal and political participants in a nation-state produces an unnegotiable conundrum for women, who are constantly struggling to be one and act the other.

This paradox is highlighted by Desai in the character of Bimala. Bimala is the head of a household without being either wife or mother, and she has an occupation. She is not supplant and can participate as an equal in conversations with men; she claims that she loves her pet animals more than any mother could love her children; and she smokes, a vice that further distances her from conventional women. In some ways she resembles an Indian version of the eccentric English bluestocking, attracting men by being handsome, not beautiful. Tara, on the other hand, had married young, and as she acknowledges, her husband "had trained her and made her into an active, organized woman who looked up her engagement book every morning, made plans and programmes for the day ahead and then walked her way through them to retire to her room at night with the triumphant tiredness of the virtuous and the dutiful."[43] Tara does not desire to exchange her life for Bimala's, but there is an element of self-loathing that refuses to be held at bay when she watches Bimala holding court:

Tara was pricked with the realisation that although it was she who was the pretty sister . . . it was Bim who was attractive. Bim who . . . had arrived at an age when she could be called handsome. All the men seemed to acknowledge this and to respond. . . . Tara did not smoke and no one offered her a light. Or was it just that Tara, having married, had rescinded the right to flirt, while Bim, who had not married, had not rescinded? No, it was not, for Bim could not be said to flirt. . . . Bim never bothered." (36–37)

Bim never bothered to be somebody else, or to please anyone. At least this is what Tara believes is true. However, we are privy to Bim's discontent, to her sense of feeling trapped in Old Delhi, where nothing changes, where history has already happened, living a life that stands still while exciting narratives take place elsewhere — London, New York, Canada, the Middle East, and, closer to home, New Delhi (5). In fact, despite Tara's assertion that she and her family need to come back periodically in order to be in touch with the "eternal India" that will continue long after "Nehru, his daughter, his grandson . . . pass into oblivion," along with other postindependent government malpractices such as bribery, corruption, poverty, and "red-tapism"(35), she is frustrated and frightened by Bim's refusal to distance herself from the past. "Why did Bim allow nothing to change? Surely Baba ought to grow and develop at last, to unfold and reach out and stretch. But whenever she saw them, at intervals of three years, all was exactly as before"(12). However, what Tara perceives as Bim's desire to remain rooted in the past is construed by Bim as the inevitable pitfalls of the role she has been forced to play.

In 1947, when the Indian nationalists were struggling to generate the narrative of a united Indian nation, Bimala's life was dramatically overtaken by incidents beyond her control. With the death of the parents, her brother Raja's tuberculosis, and the widowed aunt, Mira-masi's, gradual retreat into alcoholism, Bim by default had to take over the reigns of the Das household. A defiant youthful challenge against the inevitable marriage plot that determined the lives of women — "I won't marry. . . . I shall never leave Baba and Raja and Mira-masi. . . . I shall work — I shall do things. . . . and be independent" (140) — takes an ominous turn as Raja leaves to become a surrogate son of a Muslim family, and Mira-masi dies the horrific death of a hallucinating alcoholic. The desire to be independent having now been overtaken by the need to nurture Baba and Mira-masi and placate Raja, she is apotheosized by her only suitor, the Bengali doctor, as a self-sacrificing domestic goddess. Bimala's lack of desire for a suitor, rather than being read as an act of assertion in the spirit of Joan of Arc or Florence Nightingale (two of the young Bimala's ideals), is revised as a desire to be the female archetype: "Now I understand why you do not wish to marry. You have dedicated your life to others — to your sick brother and your aged aunt and your little brother who will be dependent on you all his life. You have sacrificed your life for them" (97). Bimala finds this speech "horrendous, . . . so leadenly spoken as if engraved on steel for posterity" (97).

Her repression of the doctor's last visit is intimately connected to her denial of this attributed status. Bimala's primal memory of her final encounter (in reality the penultimate one) with the doctor is associated with the assassination of Gandhi; as she flees the doctor's solicitous advances, she stumbles over a cobbler crouching in the dark, murmuring "Gandhi-ji is dead." In her overwhelming need to break the news to Raja, she abandons any pretense of being an interested, subservient girlfriend, and rushes off home. There, once the initial shock and grief over the news has died down, Raja turns to Bimala and asks, "And your tea-party, Bim? How was it? Has Mrs. Biswas approved of you as her daughter-in-law?" (94). Bimala is appalled and angered at Raja's obvious assumption that she wishes to be somebody's daughter-in-law and that she could possibly be interested in as shallow a person as Dr. Biswas. Her initial anger, however, gives way to laughter as she brushes off Raja's words as a brother's natural desire to torment his sister. It is much more difficult for her to erase Dr. Biswas's words, given their idealization of her as a female "*sati savitri*" (a North Indian colloquialism, derived from the mythological character Savitri, the epitome of a self-sacrificing woman). Hence her need to suppress the last encounter: "There was one more time, one that she never admitted and tried never to remember" (94).

The narrative of bourgeois morality and respectability that bolsters the nationalist discourse constantly seeks to protect its boundaries by domesticating and circumscribing the economy of power operable in the non-normative. Nationalist ideology "absorb[s] and sanction[s] middle-class manners and morals and play[s] a crucial part in spreading respectability to all classes of the population."[44] Thus Bimala's sexuality, an aspect that is highlighted in an incident where Bakul bends to light her cigarette, is denied because it is abnormal and dangerously free because not directed at any one man:

There was that little sensual quiver in the air as they [the men] laughed at what she said, and a kind of quiet triumph in the way in which she drew in her cheeks to make the cigarette catch fire and then threw herself back into the chair, giving her head a toss and holding the cigarette away so that a curl of smoke circled languidly about her hand. (36)

Since Bimala refuses the advances of the doctor, he has no other recourse but to inscribe her disdain for his overtures as a defense against anything that might dissuade her from following her natural call to be the angel of her father's house.

Tara, frightened of any emotional confrontation and unwilling to understand or accept the implications of Raja's obsessions with Hyder Ali's family, Baba's uncanny silence, and Mira-masi's gradual deterioration, gravitates toward the Misra household, through whom she meets Bakul, who dutifully asks Bimala for her sister's hand in marriage and leaves for foreign shores. Bakul signifies the typical "modern" (read liberated) Indian man who believes that the true sign of progress is the right balance of tradition and modernity. He courts Tara at the club but dutifully comes to the house to ask for her hand in marriage. Bimala's response is cutting in its sarcasm: "'I'm head of the family now, am I? You think so, so I must be.' ... I don't think you need to ask anyone — except Tara. Modern times. Modern India. Independent India" (81). Bakul feels his position as a desirable suitor undermined by this abrupt, dismissive gesture, and one realizes that even though a "modern" man of Bakul's ilk might initially be attracted by the likes of Bimala, having her as his wife would prove hazardous to his authoritative presence:

[Bakul] wondered, placing one leg over the other reflectively, as he had sometimes wondered when he had first started coming to this house, as a young man who had just entered foreign service and was in a position to look for a suitable wife, *if Bim were not, for all her plainness and brusqueness, the superior of the two sisters, if she had not those qualities — decision, firmness, resolve —* that he admired and tried to instil in his wife who lacked them so deplorably. If only Bim had not that rather coarse laugh and way of sitting with her legs up ... now Tara would never ... and if her nose were not so large unlike Tara's which was small ... and *Tara was gentler, more tender.* (19; Desai's elisions; emphases added)

Raja can deny the division of India and Pakistan and set himself up as the exemplary Indian in independent India by moving to Hyderabad and marrying Hyder Ali's daughter — *Hindu, Muslim bhai bhai!* (Hindu, Muslim are brothers) — only by abdicating his responsibilities as the eldest son. Raja's interest in Moghul culture and his fascination with Urdu language and literature becomes concentrated on the imposing figure of Hyder Ali, the Muslim landlord. His youthful defense of the Muslims against the rabid fundamentalism of his Hindu friends during the precarious days of the last few months of British rule quickly turns into an obsessive concern for the fate of the Ali family at the expense of his own. Raja's infatuation with the strong masculine figure and presence of Hyder Ali is greatly distinguished from his relationship with his own father, who is presented as aloof and unapproachable. It is not that Raja's father is feminized, but his prolonged absences from the household and his impenetrable self-absorption prevent the consolidation of the paternal signifier as the law of the Father. On the other hand, Hyder Ali becomes for Raja the apotheosis of masculinity in relation to which his Hindu family (including his father) appears emasculated. This specific yoking of two heterogeneous cultures (Hindu and Muslim) undermines the usual binary gendered opposition of colonizer and colonized (English and Indian) as male and female. The alliance between Raja and Hyder Ali assumes a homoerotic cast that is not negated by Raja's marriage to Ali's daughter.

Of course Raja's eventual departure for Hyderabad and his marriage to Benazir is equally motivated by Hyder Ali's immense wealth. Raja discards one cocoonlike existence for another, exchanging the dazzle "of the impressive figure of the old gentleman with silvery hair, dressed in white riding clothes seated upon a white horse" (47) for the vision of his son disguised in grand Moghul robes riding a toy white horse. Raja's love of theatricality, buoyed by the grim reality of a burning Delhi and a chaotic country split into two, allows him to dramatically abandon all domestic duties at the death of his father. He refuses to "worry about a few cheques and files in father's office" as "everyone [in partitioned India] becomes a refugee" (66). However, the Das household has to survive, and as Bimala, "dour as her father, as their house," harshly asserts, "No, that's only for me to worry about. . . . That, and the rent to be paid on the house, and five, six, seven people to be fed every day, and Tara to be married off, and Baba to be taken care of the rest of his life, and you to be got well again — and I don't know what else" (67). As Raja and Tara leave Old Delhi for allegedly greener pastures, Bimala is left to pick up where Mira-masi leaves off.

And that, ultimately, is the question with which this text leaves us: what is the real difference between Mira-masi and Bimala? Does Mira-masi's life in colonial India parallel Bimala's life in independent India? True, Mira-masi was a poor relation widowed at fifteen, who had lived with her husband's family serving time as a drudge until she was brought into the Das household to take care of Baba so that his parents could return to their bridge games at the club. But the repression of her sexuality so that she would not fall prey to the appetites of her brothers-in-law and the constant demands placed on her by others to fulfill surrogate roles of woman as maid and as nurturer ultimately force her to erase her memory and her body by slowly and silently drinking herself to death. The children's vision of her as a tree with strong roots and green sheltering branches is eradicated by Mira-masi's own anguished nightmare of being wrapped in "long swaddlings as if she was a baby or mummy — these long strips that went round and round her, slipping over her eyes, crossing over her nose, making her breath stop so that she had to gasp and clutch and tear — " (77). Her very identity in the Das household, captured in the appellation Mira-masi (Aunt Mira), is the final domino in the chain that leads to her breakdown. Mira has never been allowed to be just Mira, and her nephews and nieces who demanded so much of her are transformed by her deluded mind into licking flames that gradually grow taller, towering over her, forcing her to cower as they "pricked her like pins, drawing out beads of blood" (78). She dies denuded, ultimately reduced to a handful of ashes at the bottom of the river.

Bimala, on the other hand, is educated, financially independent, and unmarried; but the bourgeois moral underpinnings of an Indian national-ist ideology are so mythologized that Bimala is ultimately uncomfortable with the freedom granted women during and after independence. Even as she asserts her independence, she is at times paralyzed by the roles she has to enact on demand by relatives. Even as she manages the household and signs financial documents for their insurance company, she daily urges Baba to try to go to work, to assume the role that she believes a man should desire. Even though Tara believes that Bimala refuses to change things, Bimala constantly tries to coax Baba out of his passivity, to take charge so that she can retire to the background and live her life as the unmarried protected sister who teaches history at her leisure.

At various moments in the text we find Bimala acutely burdened by her role as mother, sister, and ersatz father, encompassing as it were the sign of the essential woman and representing the oxymoronic nonphallic paternal signifier. Oscillating between these two sharply divergent ex-tremes, the one signifying an essential indigeny and the other a nontena-ble position in the unambiguous discourse of nation-state-fatherhood, Bimala often cries out in a kind of schizophrenic anguish, "There is never anybody except me" (61). Will she, unlike Mira-masi, be able to prevent the regression into a second childhood? Can she deny the world outside by enveloping herself in an impenetrable cocoon like Mira-masi? Can she withstand the horror of watching her body degenerate and end up "not soft, or scented, or sensual"? Will she in the end refuse to let those around her choke her, suck her dry of substance, reduce her to a desiccated stick or "an ancient tree to which no one adhered" (111)?

Even as the reader notices differences between the passive Mira-masi and the assertive Bimala, similarities keep emerging. Just as we are reminded by Bakul that Bimala does not have the requisite characteristics necessary for a good wife, we recollect that the children, early on, had felt that Mira-masi did not really have

the qualities required by a mother or wife. . . . Looking at her, they could not blame the husband for going away to England and dying. Aunt Mira would not have made a wife. Why, they felt, a wife is someone like their mother who raised her eyes when the father rose from the table and dropped them when he sat down; who spent long hours at a dressing-table before a mirror, amongst jars and bottles that smelt sweet and into which she dipped questioning fingers and drew out the ingredients of a wife — sweet-smelling but soon rancid; who commanded servants and chastised children and was obeyed like a queen. (110–11)

The only time that Mira-masi's body is adorned in anything but a white saree is at her cremation; and though Bimala is not forced by tradition, like Mira-masi, to wear white (widows wear white in India), the aching poignancy of the similar trajectory of their superficially disparate lives is captured in Bimala's words to Tara as they reminisce about their childhood aspirations. Tara can laugh at her childhood dream because it has come true — she wanted to be a mother. But Bimala, who wanted to be a heroine, cannot.

There was a dark shadow across her face from which her eyes glinted with a kind of anger [that frightened Tara]. . . . Bim raised her chin, looked up at her with . . . a horrible smile. . . . "And how have we ended?" she asked mockingly. "The hero [Raja] and heroine — where are they? Down at the bottom of the well — gone, disappeared" [the well, where a cow had drowned, had eventually become marked as an ominous site]. . . . "I always did feel that — that I shall end up in that well myself one day." (157)

The novel ends on a note of narrative harmony. Bim's reflection, occasioned by a memory of the famous line from T. S. Eliot's *Four Quartets*, "Time the destroyer is time the preserver," suggests that she can ultimately draw strength from her "inner eye . . . [through which] she saw how her own house and its particular history linked and contained her as well as her whole family with all their separate histories and experiences. . . . It was where her deepest self lived and the deepest selves of her sister and brothers and all those who shared that time with her" (187).[45] I would argue, however, that the ending strikes a discordant note even though it is predicated on a peace derived from looking deep into oneself and on an intangible power drawn from a belief in essential familial identity that can synthesize the various conflicting trajectories occasioned by traumatic historical and personal events.

This desire for resolution of domestic upheavals, articulated as it is by Bimala, who throughout the novel has struggled against easy solutions, suggests the difficulties women encounter in trying to break away from "'the image of [the] woman [who] is no differently perceived: by the father, the husband, and in a way more troubling still, by the brother and the son.'"[46] Perhaps Desai's reluctance to be labeled a feminist writer suggests her own precarious negotiation of gender issues that continue to permeate various discourses concerning the consolidation of an Indian nation. The ending of the novel then brackets the plight of Mira-masi and others;[47] we are never shown how Mira-masi's "dead and airless" life is transformed into life-giving sustenance (187). Progressive accounts of both colonial and nationalist historiography similarly produce narratives that chart the superficial progress made by Indian women under the aegis of the Raj, or because of the inclusion of women's issues under the nationalist umbrella. But the similarities between a widow in preindependent India and a single, unmarried woman in independent India affirm the obsession with the replication of the ideal woman in the register of the imaginary, thereby reproducing an ever-recognizable symbolic economy. The contradictory and often violent lives of real women, as captured in the fictional lives of Bimala and Mira-masi, ultimately represent a gap, an aporia in a nationalist discourse that in representing itself as fighting against outside enemies needs to repress something within, with the result that "'woman' becomes the mute but necessary allegorical ground for the transactions of nationalist history."[48] Hence, whether one is talking about a theory of third world literature or the reading of third world literature as nationalist allegories, one needs to account for the repressed gendered subject that allows a masculinist nationalist discourse to flourish.

NOTES

I wish to thank Abouali Farmanfarmaian, Samir Dayal, and an anonymous reader for *Genders* for the their valuable comments and suggestions.

1. Benedict Anderson, *Imagined Communities* (New York, Verso, 1983).
2. See Pratt's essay in Jose David Saldivar's *Dialectics of Our Americas: Genealogy, Genre, Cultural Critique, and Literary History* (Durham, N.C.: Duke University Press, 1991).
3. The term "third world" is still highly contentious and its significations never absolute. The essays I discuss seek to highlight the dubious and unstable nature of the category by putting the term within either quotation marks or parentheses; in the case of Jameson, he often capitalizes the two words, which lends the term much more stability and authority than I find desirable. Even as I recognize the provisionality of the semiotic status of the formulation third world, I choose to make the essay less cumbersome by erasing the quotation marks around this much beleaguered category.
4. Besides Ahmad's and Prasad's essays that I briefly discuss here (see notes 5 and 7 below), see Henry Schwarz's "Provocations toward a Theory of Third World Literature," *Mississippi Review* 49–50 (1989): 177–201. For an elaborate exchange of often-divergent positions regarding the phenomena of nationalism see Etienne Balibar and Immanuel Wallerstein's *Race, Nation, Class: Ambiguous Identities*, trans. Chris Turner (London: Verso, 1991). Except for one essay by Wallerstein titled "The Ideological Tensions of Capitalism: Universalism versus Racism and Sexism," which suffers from a formulaic marxist reductivism, the remaining essays fail to address the simultaneous polarization and congruence of the categories of gender and nation. Gillian Beer's article, "The Island and the Aeroplane: The Case of Virginia Woolf," in *Nation and Narration*, ed. Homi Bhabha (New York: Routledge, 1990), 265–90, on the contrary, brilliantly explores the gendered mapping of political space in the interstices of patriarchy and imperialism. For a provocative though brief essay on the politics of citizenship see Chantal Mouffe's "Citizenship and Political Identity" as well as the "Discussion" that follows the essay in *October* 61 (1992): 28–32. I have deliberately mentioned only some of the very recent contributions because the list is too cumbersome. Any one of the books or articles mentioned provides numerous pages of works cited.
5. Aijaz Ahmad, "Jameson's Rhetoric of Otherness and the 'National Allegory,'" *Social Text* 17 (1987): 3–25.
6. Ibid., 69. See Schwarz, "Provocations," and Prasad (note 7 below) for contradictory critiques of Ahmad's position. Since this essay does not concern itself with the feasibility of terminology such as "first" and "third world" and/or the problems generated by such distinctions, I guide the reader to Ahmad's and Prasad's essays for discussions on the subject. Let me briefly say that Ahmad's assertion that we live in one world and that the idea of "third world" is not empirically grounded (7–9) is not always convincing since his analysis relies largely on his own experiences as an intellectual from Pakistan. Despite his marxist affinities with Jameson, Ahmad distinguishes his subject position from Jameson's in terms that recrudesce the familiar opposition between Western and non-Western worlds.

7. Madhava Prasad, "On the Question of a Theory of (Third World) Literature," *Social Text* 31–32 (1992): 57–83.
8. Prasad, 58.
9. Ibid., 71.
10. Ibid., 73.
11. Ibid., 78.
12. Ibid., 75.
13. Kumkum Sangari and Sudesh Vaid, Introduction to *Recasting Women: Essays on Indian Colonial History*, ed. Sangari and Vaid (New Brunswick, N.J.: Rutgers University Press, 1990), 2–3.
14. This consistent oversight by contemporary critics of nationalism is responsible for much of my ambivalence toward their work, which, as Deborah Gordon says in the context of feminist decolonizing ethnography, produces a kind of subordination that "is not located in marginalization nor does it indicate a conspiracy to silence feminists. Rather it is a management of feminism produced out of a masculinist feminism with specific troubles for feminist ethnographers" (or in this case feminist critics of nationalism). See her essay "Writing Culture, Writing Feminism: The Poetics and Politics of Experimental Ethnography," *Inscriptions* 3–4 (1988): 8.
15. Andrew Parker, et al., Introduction to *Nationalisms and Sexualities*, ed. Andrew Parker, Mary Russo, Dorris Sommer, and Patricia Yaeger (New York: Routledge, 1992), 6.
16. Kumari Jayawardena, *Feminism and Nationalism in the Third World* (London: Zed, 1986).
17. Deniz Kandiyoti, Introduction to *Women, Islam, and the State*, ed. Deniz Kandiyoti (Philadelphia: Temple University Press, 1992), 2.
18. R. Radhakrishnan, "Nationalism, Gender, and the Narrative of Identity," in *Nationalisms and Sexualities*, ed. Andrew Parker, Mary Russo, Dorris Sommer, and Patricia Yaeger (New York: Routledge, 1992), 79–80.
19. Dipesh Chakrabarty, "Marx after Marxism: Subaltern Histories and the Question of Difference," *Polygraph* 6–7 (1993): 10.
20. Gayatri Spivak, "Can the Subaltern Speak?" in *Marxism and the Interpretation of Culture*, ed. Cary Nelson and Lawrence Grossberg (Urbana: University of Illinois Press, 1990), 287.
21. Ibid., 287.
22. Ibid., 387.
23. Ibid., 306.
24. Jenny Sharpe, *Allegories of Empire: The Figure of the Woman in the Colonial Text* (Minneapolis: University of Minnesota Press, 1993), 18. Sharpe goes on to emphasize the tremendous significance of Spivak's critique and her undertaking in "Can the Subaltern Speak?": "She [Spivak] identifies the subaltern woman as one who cannot be simply reduced to her class or caste position. She interrupts the project of making subaltern classes the subject of history with a 'text about the (im)possibility of "making" the subaltern gender the subject of its own story'" (*In Other Worlds* [New York: Methuen, 246], 18).

25. In *Nation and Narration*, ed. Homi Bhabha (New York: Routledge, 1990), 300.
26. Ibid., 306.
27. The definition of culture, as Clifford Geertz has pointed out, is extremely difficult; see *The Interpretation of Culture* (New York: Basic, 1973), 4–5, where he reveals the eleven different ways in which Kluckhohn defines culture. Geertz's own definition of culture is a semiotic one in which "culture" is defined as webs of significance that man himself has spun. His analysis of "thick description" is by now common knowledge. As Frantz Fanon has pointed out, the desire to invent a national culture as a means of resistance against colonial domination often reaches beyond the boundaries of a given nation; thus one does not have so much an Angolan culture as an African culture that is used to combat the insidious power and legacy of Western culture (*The Wretched of the Earth* [New York: Grove, 1963], 206–48). Even though one uses cultural icons as symbols for the nation, a symmetrical alliance of the two produces tensions similar to the kind I have pointed out in Bhabha's essay.
28. In *Nation and Narration* Bhabha stresses the power of "wandering peoples" to rupture the boundaries of the modern nation. The reality of migration, he suggests, as in his reading of *The Satanic Verses*, disrupts older national meaning systems. The previous national signifiers, Bhabha argues, have been displaced and/or superseded by "the imaginative geography of the metropolitan space" (318).
29. Amanda Anderson, "Prostitution's Artful Guise," *Diacritics* 21 (1991). 102–27.
30. Susheela Nasta, Introduction to *Motherlands: Black Women's Writing from Africa, the Caribbean, and South Asia*, ed. Susheela Nasta (New Brunswick, N.J.: Rutgers University Press, 1992), xxi.
31. The anthology *Nationalisms and Sexualities* is a groundbreaking collection that explores the intersections in diverse areas of the discourses of gender, sexuality, and nationality. A few of the essays pertinent to the issue of gender and nationalism in third world cultural productions include Radhakrishnan's "Nationalism, Gender, and the Narrative of Identity"; Spivak's "Women in Difference: Mahashweta Devi's 'Douliti the Bountiful'"; Heng and Devan's "State Fatherhood: The Politics of Nationalism, Sexuality, and Race in Singapore"; Katrak's "Indian Nationalism, Gandhian 'Satyagraha,' and Representations of Female Sexuality"; Layoun's "Telling Spaces: Palestinian Women and the Engendering of National Narratives"; and Moghadam's "Revolution, Islam, and Women: Sexual Politics in Iran and Afghanistan."
32. Rhonda Cobham, "Misgendering the Nation: African Nationalist Fictions and Nuruddin Farah's Maps," in *Nationalisms and Sexualities*, ed. Andrew Parker, Mary Russo, Dorris Sommer, and Patricia Yaeger (New York: Routledge, 1992), 43.
33. Sara Suleri, *The Rhetoric of English India* (Chicago: University of Chicago Press, 1992), 17.
34. Ibid., 17. Frantz Fanon, in *Black Skin White Masks* (New York: Grove, 1967), presents an elaborate psychoanalytic study of the relations between black

men/white women, black women/white men, black men/white men, which uncover the complex ways in which, as Suleri puts it, "discourses of rationality are forced to give figurative articulation to the nightmares that the dreams of colonial rationalism may produce, thus indicating the gender imbrication implicit in the classification of culture as an anxious provenance partitioned between the weakness and strength of men" (Suleri, *Rhetoric of English India*, 17). Fanon's *Wretched of the Earth* (New York: Grove, 1963) also discusses the manifestations of male sexuality in relations between the colonizer and colonized. The chapters titled "Concerning Violence," "On National Culture," and "Colonial War and Mental Disorders" are particularly relevant.

35. Suleri, *Rhetoric of English India*, 16.

36. Malek Alloula's *Colonial Harem*, trans. Myrna Godzich and Wlad Godzich (Minneapolis: University of Minnesota Press, 1986) is one such excellent study that unravels the various modes and nodes of transformation of the colonial scene by collecting, arranging, and annotating picture postcards of Algerian women produced by the French in Algeria during the first thirty years of the twentieth century. As Barbara Harlow writes in her introduction, *The Colonial Harem* does not merely expose the analogical links that connect "the imperializing project of colonizing other lands and peoples with the phantasm of appropriation of the veiled, exotic female. The similarity between penetrating the secret, tantalizing recesses of the harem and making the masquerading pilgrimage to Mecca and the holy Kaaba of Islam, which nineteenth-century travellers . . . did, reveals the many guises under which imperialism penetrated the Arab world" (xvi).

37. Radhakrishnan, "Nationalism, Gender," 80.

38. Joanna Liddle and Rama Joshi, eds., *Daughters of Independence: Gender, Caste, and Class in India* (London: Zed, 1986).

39. Suleri, *Rhetoric of English India*, 14.

40. See Dieter Reimenschneider's "History and the Individual in Anita Desai's *Clear Light of Day* and Salman Rushdie's *Midnight's Children*," *World Literature in English* 23 (1984): 196–207; Graham Huggan's "Philomela's Retold Story: Silence, Music, and the Post-Colonial Text," *Journal of Commonwealth Literature* 25 (1990): 12–23; Alamgir Hashmi's "*Clear Light of Day* between India and Pakistan," in *The New Indian Novel in English: A Study of the 1980s*, ed. Viney Kirpal (New Delhi: Allied Publishers, 1990), 65–72; and Shirley Chew's "Searching Voices: Anita Desai's *Clear Light of Day* and Nayantara Sahgal's *Rich like Us*," in *Motherlands: Black Women's Writing from Africa, the Caribbean, and South Asia*, ed. Susheela Nasta (New Brunswick, N.J.: Rutgers University Press, 1992), 43–63.

41. Certain other texts could also generate interesting readings: Ama Ata Aidoo's *Our Sister Killjoy* (Ghana), Merle Collins's *Angel* (Grenada), Bessie Head's *A Question of Power* (South Africa, Botswana), and Sara Suleri's *Meatless Days* (Pakistan), to name just four.

42. See Joanna Liddle and Rama Joshi's *Daughters of Independence* for a full-scale

discussion of the rise and sporadic development of the feminist movement in India.

43. Anita Desai, *Clear Light of Day* (London: Penguin, 1980), 21. Further references to this work will be included parenthetically in the text.

44. George Mosse, *Nationalism and Sexuality: Middle-Class Morality and Sexual Norms in Modern Europe* (Madison: University of Wisconsin Press, 1980), 9.

45. I wish to thank S. Dayal for drawing my attention to this passage.

46. Assia Djebar's words as quoted by Barbara Harlow in her introduction to Malek Alloula's *Colonial Harem*.

47. The plight of two Misra sisters is similarly shelved and also undercuts the finality of the too easily achieved harmonious ending of the novel. These two married sisters are forced to return to their father's house because they have failed to produce children. They keep house and eke out a living for their family — the brothers squander money either on ridiculous business ventures or in their endless pursuit of the excellence of Indian classical music — by teaching music and dance to young children. We are never quite sure of their marital status because the text never makes clear whether they are actually divorced. Their husbands, one presumes, have married again and are living a comfortable and probably bigamous life.

48. Radhakrishnan, 84.

PART TWO

Bad Medicine: Diagnoses and Domestic Desires

Diagnosing the Domestic Woman in
The Woman in White and *Dora*

Lauren Chattman

Mad-houses are large and only too numerous; yet surely it is strange they are not larger, when we think of how many helpless wretches must beat their brains against this hopeless persistency of the orderly outward world, as compared with the storm and tempest, the riot and confusion within: — when we remember how many minds must tremble upon the narrow boundary between reason and unreason, mad to-day and sane to-morrow, mad yesterday and sane to-day.

— Mary Elizabeth Braddon, 1862

This quotation economically illustrates what Patrick Brantlinger has identified as the "crisis in the history of literary realism" represented by Victorian sensation novels of the 1860s.[1] While sensation novelists like Braddon follow in the tradition of domestic realism by exposing the private lives of their characters to the reading public, their investigations into the private reveal not homely stability but horrors unimagined even in the literature of the fantastic. Reality as it is represented in *Lady Audley's Secret* is as often the private subject's "riot and confusion within" as it is the "orderly outward world." In the end, the insane domestic woman functions as a cover for the open secret of nineteenth-century middle-class culture, namely, that *all* subjectivity is constructed as irrational during the period. Lady Audley's private and domestic madness allows her pursuer, Robert Audley, to define himself as a rational, public, professional man. The plot carefully conceals what erupts in the above passage:

that subjectivity, before it is gendered, is defined by mental disturbance, and that even a middle-class professional man might privately lose his grasp on reality at any moment.

As industrial capitalism develops in England during the nineteenth century, the "authentic" subject is increasingly defined as a private person taking refuge at home from the dehumanizing world of work. Private feeling, rather than impersonal objectivity, comes to characterize the real self.[2] The opposition of the "real" private and the "false" public effaces the fact that the private subject could not have existed prior to or apart from the public sphere to which he or she is opposed. Nineteenth-century realism can be characterized by claims similar to those of subjectivity under capitalism. While domestic realism in all its forms privileges as authentic private life over public, it denies its own status as a social and public phenomenon. In its blindness, it is both an effect and a tool of bourgeois culture.

Gender difference is crucial in finessing the contradictions and biases inherent in nineteenth-century subjectivity and its realisms. The separation of spheres divides public and private along the supposedly natural line between men and women and prevents any questioning of the naturalness of the economic system out of which the public/private division arises. As femininity is privatized, middle-class women take on the attributes of the new subjectivity — interiority, domesticity, and leisure — and display these attributes for all the world to see.[3] According to the logic of separate spheres, men must continue to operate in the outside world in order to protect the privacy of their decorative wives. While the division of labor claims to preserve what really matters — the safe haven of home — it also allows for business as usual in the public arena.

Victorian psychiatry is typically realist in basing its account of interiority on the interpretation of women's visible symptoms. Novels underwrite the reality promoted by industrial capitalism by claiming to reveal the deep feelings of domestic women. This paper will examine the contradictory structures of nineteenth-century subjectivity and realism in psychiatric discourse and in two novelistic texts aligning themselves with realism but exhibiting serious ideological cracks. In psychiatry, the sensation novel, and the case study, the struggle to reconcile the home as refuge with irrational subjectivity is thematized. In each instance, the middle-class domestic woman's reason is sacrificed in order to preserve "the orderly outward world." By delving under the surface of nineteenth-century realism, I hope to reveal the necessary irrationality of *all* subjects as they were defined by nineteenth-century middle-class culture. I also want to suggest the effects that the structures of nineteenth-century subjectivity and realism continue to engender today.

As Foucault has described, during the nineteenth century madness begins to be associated with bodily illness rather than with transcendent religious phenomena and can no longer be separated from the population at large. If the eighteenth century is the age of reason, the nineteenth century is the age of *unreason*; psychiatry's scientific objectivity is an attempt to control the irrationality that is perceived to characterize every nineteenth-century subject.[4] Psychiatry emerges and develops along with the irrational subject it investigates. As recent cultural historians of psychiatry have put it, "By a diabolical dialectic of the cunning of reason, the aspiration, widely entertained in 1800, of curing a relatively small population of lunatics, seemed by 1900 in danger of revealing the fundamental craziness of the human mind itself."[5] In response to the shameful suspicion that every nineteenth-century subject is potentially mad, psychiatry defends itself and England by masculinizing itself. In the absence of other markers, the gendered separation of spheres provides the model for clear distinction. As Elaine Showalter has demonstrated, insanity is increasingly figured as feminine during the course of the century.[6] Women bear the burden of madness so that half the population can appear sane.

Richard Sennett has written that the nineteenth-century obsession with objective observation is a response to the fear that the commodity fetishism of capitalism destroys the possibility of objectivity:

To fantasize that physical objects had psychological dimensions became logical in this new secular order . . . there broke down distinctions between perceiver and perceived, inside and outside, subject and object. The celebration of objectivity and hardheaded commitment to fact so prominent a century ago, all in the name of Science, was in reality an unwitting preparation for the present era of radical subjectivity.[7]

Jonathan Crary has also dated the insecurity of the observer to the early nineteenth century. While enlightenment theories of vision are modeled on the camera obscura's clearly delineated relation between subject and object, the nineteenth century brings "an increasing abstraction of optical experience from a stable referent."[8] When the boundary between subject and object is destroyed as a result of capitalist modernization, the observer is transformed from impartial judge to subject with clouded vision. Yet at the moment of this transformation, new "techniques for imposing visual attentiveness, rationalizing sensation, and managing perception" are invented, "disciplinary techniques that required a notion of visual experience as instrumental, modifiable, and essentially abstract, and that never allowed a real world to acquire solidity or permanence."[9]

Crary cites among these disciplinary techniques such inventions as the kaleidoscope and the stereoscope, which emphasize the illusory and unreliable nature of sight but also organize perceptions into recognizable and familiar patterns. More generally, however, psychiatry might be counted among the new techniques for managing perception, since it establishes a framework within which irrational subjectivity itself can be viewed. Psychiatric observation institutionalizes the hopes and fears of the new individual. Even as he longs for the objectivity he has sacrificed to modern culture, the subject suspects the penetrating gaze of strangers into his private life: "In the high Victorian era people believed their clothes and their speech disclosed their personalities; they feared that these signs were equally beyond their power to mold, but would instead be manifest to others in involuntary tricks of speech, body gesture, or even how they adorned themselves."[10] While the nineteenth-century subject is increasingly figured as private, interior, and irrational, the psychiatrist increasingly claims to know that subject's depths from the visual signs conveyed by the body.

Yet because psychiatry, like other supposedly objective sciences, figures itself through the physiological process of flawed human vision, even its most emphatic assertions of knowledge betray a profound uncertainty about what is being observed.[11] Henry Maudsley, the most prominent of the Victorian psychiatrists, declares in a book entitled *Body and Mind* that insanity can be diagnosed by close visual observation:

What are the bodily and mental marks of the insane temperament? That there are such is most certain; for although the varieties of this temperament cannot yet be described with any precision, no one who accustoms himself to observe closely will fail to be able to say positively, in many instances, whether an insane person, and even a sane person in some instances, comes of an insane family or not.[12]

Maudsley goes on to list the possible signs of insanity. Among them are "unsymmetrical conformation of the head," irregular features, "malformations of the external ear," tics, grimaces, prominent eyes, "half-fearful, half-suspicious, and distrustful looks," uncertain walk and manner, spinal deformity, club foot, cleft palate, harelip, deafness, and eczema. In spite of his confidence that madness is easy to observe, his long list of signs, not to mention his assertion that sane people with a family history of insanity carry hereditary marks of madness, suggest two disturbing possibilities: that sane individuals might mistakenly be taken as insane because of some unfortunate physical defect or, considering that the signs of madness are so common and varied, that all of us might be crazy.

Hugh Diamond, the Victorian psychiatrist and asylum keeper famous for his utilization of photography in the diagnosis and treatment of the mentally ill, evinces such uncertainty when he explains why photography is a useful diagnostic tool:

What words can adequately describe either the peculiar character of the palsy which accompanies sudden terror when without hope, or the face glowing with heat under the excitement of burning anger, or the features shrunk and the skin constricted and ghastly under the influence of pale rage? — Yet the Photographer secures with unerring accuracy the external phenomena of each passion, as the really certain indication of internal derangement, and exhibits to the eye the well known sympathy which exists between the diseased brain and the organs and features of the body.[13]

It is as if the doctor, unable to describe what he sees, presents the photograph in place of a rational explanation. Via photography, madness becomes self-explanatory.

During the century body and mind are insistently separated as objects of scientific study. Yet the division signals not an essential difference between the two domains but another management technique. The separation of mind and body allows for the theory that one controls the other, and more generally that an individual is capable of objectivity and self-control. The hierarchization of mind and body recuperates reason for the male subject. When the mind controls the body, the subject is able to view the world rationally and objectively. Bodily disease prevents him from functioning rationally and as he should.

The result of the hierarchical theory of mental health is a professional focus on the outward signs of madness and a rejection of the investigation of the mind per se. While professional psychiatry flourishes in Britain during the nineteenth century, it does so not as an exploration of the uncharted territories of the mind but as an insistence on the inadvisability of delving too deep. In fact, Victorian psychiatrists take self-reflection itself as a sign of an unsound mind. The healthy person should direct his or her attention outward rather than engage in "morbid introspection." Michael J. Clark lists the characteristics that define health and illness: extroversion, "objective" states of consciousness, healthy physical exercise, hard work, altruism, and sociability are good signs, while introversion, "subjective" states of consciousness, idleness, egoism, "selfish vice," and unsociability signal instability.[14] These oppositions reveal how mental health is defined in social and economic terms. Objectivity and hard work define middle-class professional men in nineteenth-century Britain. Subjectivity and idleness are marks of an effeminate and outmoded aristocracy.

During the second half of the century, the proliferation of these middle-class values is heralded as a sign of evolutionary progress. Darwin himself endorses self-control for the maintenance of mental health. In his analysis, visible expression of the emotions is a sign of mental disturbance: "The insane notoriously give way to all their emotions with little or no restraint."[15] But more than this, dwelling on personal feelings can actually lead to madness:

The free expression by outward signs of an emotion intensifies it. On the other hand, the repression, as far as this is possible, of all outward signs softens our emotions. He who gives way to violent gestures will increase his rage; he who does not control the signs of fear will experience fear in a greater degree; and he who remains passive when overwhelmed with grief loses his best chance of recovering elasticity of mind.[16]

Where there are unmistakable class and national biases in his observations (he writes, "Englishmen are much less demonstrative than the men of most other European nations, and they shrug their shoulders far less frequently and energetically than Frenchmen or Italians do"), there is the related middle-class belief that control of one's self-presentation is an act of self-protection.[17]

Women, imagined to be more physical than intellectual, have difficulty fitting themselves into the mind/body model of rational subjectivity. Charged with propagating the race, they are discouraged from intellectual pursuits that might sap their bodily energy and prevent them from successfully reproducing. By cultural definition, women are in thrall to their bodies, a state defined by the psychiatric profession as unbalanced and irrational. They are also uncomfortably allied with morbid introspection and excessive indulgence in emotional display. Exercising proper behavior, the middle-class wife serves as a model for rational self-containment. Yet insofar as repression marks her character, she is implicitly assumed to be repressing the self-absorption and emotionalism that define her in the first place. Because undomesticated femininity is equated with madness, all women are suspected of an irrational subjectivity that must be continually policed.[18]

Since madness is figured in terms of undomesticated femininity, it is not surprising that as the century progresses its treatment comes to be modeled on middle-class domesticity. By far the most important trend in psychiatric treatment is the movement toward the systems of moral management, pioneered by the Quaker layman William Tuke in the 1790s, and nonrestraint, popularized by John Conolly, the famed psychiatrist and asylum administrator, at midcentury. Advocates of moral management reject the notion that lunatics must be harshly punished and physically subdued. Tuke argues that if the insane are treated as members of the asylum community and continually rewarded for what is deemed civilized behavior, they will come to value that community and learn to practice propriety. Tuke's disciplinary system is modeled on the proper upbringing of children within the family, with asylum keepers as parental authorities and the asylum itself as the middle-class home.[19] The "cure" effected by such treatment is a visual one. When patients can demonstrate conventional outward behavior — when they behave like good children — they are deemed mentally healthy and able to return to their real homes.[20]

Nonrestraint is the heir to moral therapy in its view of the family as the exemplary social structure and in its attempt to encourage in patients the desire to belong. Elaine Showalter invokes Jane Eyre's Bertha Mason in describing Conolly's work:

The image of Bertha Mason haunts Conolly's book *Treatment of the Insane without Mechanical Restraints* (1856), and supports his argument that insane women should be treated in asylums rather than at home. Lady patients at home, Conolly writes, are "quite estranged" from all their relatives; "and the house itself is rendered 'awful by the presence of a deranged creature under the same roof,' "[21]

While Bertha Mason is chained to the furniture and confined to a remote chamber, she insistently calls attention to the madness within the home. According to Conolly, undomesticated women like Bertha should be banished from the home until they can prove that they belong there by behaving nicely. The result of this segregation is not only a domestication of the problem patient outside the home but also a denial that home and irrationality have anything to do with one another. One wonders how the novel's plot would have developed had Rochester solicited advice from a contemporary psychiatrist! In no time at all, Bertha might have been brushing her hair (a sure sign of returning sanity, we are assured by Victorian psychiatrists) and otherwise grooming herself to resume her place as a proper wife.[22] As with Tuke, with Conolly there is a tension between public and private in the outward manifestation of mental health. While proper behavior is a sign of rationality emanating from within, it is also a sign of social norms imposed from without.

While moral management and nonrestraint are certainly forms of social control, they operate not as an arm of the state but through the institution of the family. Even as large public asylums are being built around the country to hold increasing numbers of the indigent insane, the argument that such facilities are used to corral dangerous political agitators and other social undesirables skips several crucial steps.[23] That most committals are initiated by the patient's family suggests not overt state control of the unproductive poor, but the way the family has itself become a disciplinary institution. The asylum is not just a way to make poor and working-class families more efficient. Middle- and upper-class families maintain domestic harmony by utilizing private asylums. Charlotte Mackenzie has shown how the private asylum functioned not as place of punishment but as a repository for an unruly relative that allowed for the normalization of domestic life: "For the middle and upper classes, apart from criminal cases which went through the police and courts, it was rather a question of self-regulation. It was families and friends rather than doctors, who made the initial diagnosis of 'insanity' by referring someone for treatment."[24] The private asylum is an alternate domestic space, allowing families to feel that they are treating their ill members humanely and morally according to the private values of the period.

Interestingly, as psychiatry becomes increasingly professionalized and both public and private asylums proliferate and prosper, the conception of medical psychiatrists as greedy charlatans and know-nothings circulates through middle-class culture.[25] Novels like Charles Reade's *Hard Cash* (1863) play on the anxiety that sane individuals will be seen through the professional eye as insane. In her memoir, *How I Escaped the Mad-Doctors* (1878), Georgina Weldon uses sensation strategies in relating her husband's and several psychiatrists' conspiracy to commit her without justification.[26] Louisa Lowe's *Bastilles of England* (1883), which accuses private asylums of horrendous abuses, attests to the reality of mistaken diagnosis, but also to the fear that this could happen to *anyone*. Yet the fact that family members are often the first to diagnose the insane patient suggests that the suspicion of professional psychiatry is really a displaced suspicion of family life itself. And the fine line between the display of true feeling required of proper middle-class women and improper irrationality leaves women especially vulnerable to the diagnoses of their husbands.

It would seem that nineteenth-century British psychiatry, with its valuing of self-control and repression, is diametrically opposed to the exploration of the unconscious proposed by Freud. Clark describes the opposition:

For the psychotherapist, consciousness, and the bringing into consciousness of repressed ideas and feelings, constitute respectively the supreme values and goals of his healing art. But for the late-Victorian psychological physician, consciousness and its phenomena were at best epiphenomenal, and at worst actively detrimental to healthy and efficient mental action.[27]

But as I hope to demonstrate, Freud represents not so much a turnaround as a mutation of already existing techniques through which irrational subjectivity may be coherently viewed.[28]

Freud shares with the Victorians an insistence on the objectivity of his own vision. Ever sensitive to accusations that psychoanalysis is a false science, he repeatedly stresses the disinterestedness of the discipline. In a letter to Fliess in 1900, he distances himself even from the label "observer," preferring to identify with the entirely outward-directed "conquistador" instead:

I am not a man of science at all, not an observer, not an experimenter, not a thinker. I am nothing but a conquistador by temperament, an adventurer if you want to translate this term, with all the inquisitiveness, daring, and tenacity of such a man.[29]

The imperial image separates Freud's project from associations with home, interiority, and femininity. With this description — a nostalgic reference to an earlier investigative mode — he differentiates himself from the subject he investigates.

Nonetheless, his view of his own writing reveals an anxiety about gender and genre. Writing about "Elizabeth von R.," Freud defensively remarks, "The case histories I write read like novellas . . . they, so to speak, lack the serious stamp of scientific method," adding, "[it must be] the nature of the subject, rather than my predilection, that is evidently to be held responsible for this result."³⁰ Again, Freud disavows personal involvement in the styling of his texts, insisting that the case study styles itself on the interior life of the subject studied. But the comparison of the case study with the novella raises questions about psychoanalytic discourse itself. Conquistador metaphors aside, psychoanalysis is an interrogation of interiority, a novelistic and "realist" treatment of a subject's private life. Its intimate conversations take place at the analyst's home, usually the sphere of middle-class femininity. While Freud stood firm in assertions of his own masculinity, he encouraged many women to become professional analysts, his actions suggesting not simply that he was at heart an egalitarian but also that the domestic nature of the enterprise made it a natural career for middle-class women.

Of course, it is Freud's insistent deconstruction of conventional sexuality that sets him apart from the British psychiatrists. While the Victorians take for granted gender difference and the separation of spheres and in fact build their theories on the naturalness and incontestible rightness of difference, Freud historicizes sexuality and claims that social convention gives rise to the mental turmoil of the nineteenth-century subject. Throughout his career, Freud is consistently ignored or rejected by the psychiatrists in England. A threat to the gendered foundations of British psychiatry, psychoanalysis is denied scientific authority by the medical establishment and often classed with hypnosis and spiritualism as a phony and even immoral parlor game.³¹

It is the catastrophe of World War I and the necessity of rethinking madness along new gender lines that opens the way for psychoanalytic theory in England:

In spite of the fact that asylum psychiatry remained out of the limelight during the war, shellshock nevertheless threatened the very foundations of its approach to mental pathology. The monolithic theory of hereditary degeneration upon which Victorian psychiatry had based its social and scientific vision was significantly dented as young men of respectable and proven character were reduced to mental wrecks after a few months in the trenches.³²

While Freud and the Victorian psychiatrists share an impulse toward self-distance and objectivity, Freud in his method and in his anxious self-questioning cannot abandon his own subjectivity. It is well into the twentieth century before the British are willing to concede their professional and masculine objectivity in hope of a "cure" for their irrational men. It would be premature, however, to celebrate this apparent subversion. Professional men's admission of clouded vision hardly destroys the gender hierarchy upon which middle-class culture's construction of "reality" rests. Indeed, as I will discuss in the conclusion of this essay, Freud and his followers' recognition of their own irrationality is quickly recuperated as "self-knowledge." Just as "objectivity" authorized psychiatrists' judgment of what constituted reality during the nineteenth century, so "self-knowledge" authorizes the judgment of professional men today.

In *The Woman in White*, the devious Count Fosco and his impecunious friend Sir Percival Glyde take advantage of an uncanny resemblance between Glyde's wife, the former Laura Fairlie, and her half-sister, the madwoman Anne Catherick, in order to commit Laura wrongfully and steal her fortune. Walter Hartright, Laura's drawing teacher, becomes the hero of the piece by discovering the plot, rescuing Laura from the asylum and restoring to her her rightful identity. After Glyde's death, Walter and Laura marry, and he becomes master of her estate, Limmeridge House.

D. A. Miller, in his seminal essay on *The Woman in White*, remarks that in the novel the asylum is not represented in realistic detail but by the absent memory of Laura Fairlie: "It would be quite difficult to deduce a sociological understanding of Victorian asylums from Collins's novel, which, voiding a lively contemporary concern with the private madhouse, describes neither its structure nor the (medicinal? psychological?) therapies that may or may not be practiced within it."[33] *The Woman in White* does not claim to be a fact-based, crusading account of the abuses of the psychiatric profession. Instead, it presents as real the chaotic minds and secret lives of its characters. It is precisely because Collins makes no direct attempt to address "real" social problems of the public sphere that his text is a believable account of contemporary subjectivity. Equally important to its realism, however, is the way the novel imposes order on its irrational world via the organizing gaze of its middle-class hero. Walter Hartright, a visual artist, sets as his task the representation of the reality of Laura Fairlie's case. In the preamble, he speaks of himself in the third person, indicating the objective state he has achieved through experience: "Let Walter Hartright, teacher of drawing, aged twenty-eight years, be heard first."[34]

One contemporary reviewer compares Collins's strategies of realist representation with those of Hartright: "Mr. Collins possesses the talent of the drawing-master who is his hero. He paints his scenes with a fullness and an accuracy which produces the effect of a stereography."[35] Stereography, one of Crary's "techniques of the observer," is a peculiarly modern method of organizing difficult-to-interpret visual evidence. It utilizes the stereoscope, an optical instrument that combines two separate images in order to create the illusion of depth. Leaving behind gothic images of the madhouse, Collins plunges into the nineteenth-century world of irrational domesticity. Thus Laura's sensible stepsister Marian Halcombe is mistakenly complacent when she first sees Glyde's modernized Blackwater Park: "It is an inexpressible relief to find that the nineteenth century has invaded this strange future home of mine, and has swept the dirty 'good old times' out of the way of our daily life" (177). And as Henry James observes, "Instead of the terrors of Udolpho, we were treated to the terrors of the cheerful country-house and the busy London lodgings. And there is no doubt that these were infinitely the more terrible. Mrs. Radcliffe's mysteries were romances pure and simple; while those of Mr. Wilkie Collins were stern reality."[36] But Collins, like his hero, does more than illustrate the horrors of Limmeridge House and Blackwater Park. In the end, his descriptions attempt to rationalize and control the private chaos that he has exposed.

Early in the novel, Laura's uncle, the aesthete Frederick Fairlie, assures Walter of his privileged place in the aristocratic home: "You will find your position here, Mr. Hartright, properly recognised. There is none of the horrid English barbarity of feeling about the social position of an artist, in this house" (32). But Walter chafes at the role of useless accessory that Fairlie offers him, preferring to make himself useful. By distinguishing between and diagnosing the half-sisters Anne Catherick and Laura Fairlie, he will move Limmeridge House out of its aristocratic malaise and into the busy if "barbarous" nineteenth century.

Walter initially finds the female inhabitants of Limmeridge House inscrutable. His early judgment of Laura is clouded by a seemingly irrational "impression . . . of something wanting." He looks at her, but cannot understand her:

The impression was always strongest, in the most contradictory manner, when she looked at me; or, in other words, when I was most conscious of the harmony and charm of her face, and yet, at the same time, most troubled by the sense of an incompleteness which it was impossible to discover. Something wanting, something wanting — and where it was, and what it was, I could not say. (41)

Hypothesizing that the mystery of Laura's lack is somehow related to the mystery of the woman in white, he is castigated by Marian: "Mr. Hartright, you surprise me. Whatever women may be, I thought that men, in the nineteenth century, were above superstition" (50).[37] Soon the suspicion becomes a controlling paranoia, and Walter begins to doubt his own sanity:

I began to doubt whether my own faculties were not in danger of losing their balance. It seemed almost like a monomania to be tracing back everything strange that happened, everything unexpected that was said, always to the same hidden source and the same sinister influence. (68)

While a lowly drawing master, he is *not* above the feminine superstition that the more rational, more socially elevated, and more masculine Marian rejects. After carefully watching Laura, however, Walter is able to identify the missing quality: "If ever sorrow and suffering set their profaning marks on the youth and beauty of Miss Fairlie's face, then, and then only, Anne Catherick and she would be the twin-sisters of chance resemblance, the living reflexions of one another" (82). When Walter links Laura with the madwoman, he begins to gain control over his own perceptions.

His mode of analysis is surprisingly similar to the asylum doctor's diagnosis of Laura's/Anne's looks:

Insane people were often, at one time, outwardly as well as inwardly, unlike what they were at another; the change from better to worse, or from worse to better, in the madness, having a necessary tendency to produce alterations of appearance externally.... He could not say, of course, that she was absolutely altered in height or shape or complexion, or in the colour of her hair and eyes, or in the general form of her face: the change was something that he felt, more than something that he saw. In short, the case had been a puzzle from the first. (374–75)

While the doctor is sure that madness is visually manifested, he nonetheless identifies the change in Laura's appearance as "something that he felt, more than something that he saw." Like Henry Maudsley and Hugh

Diamond, the doctor claims professional authority by projecting the incoherence of his perception onto the "insane" patient.[38] Out of his confusion, one thing becomes clear. The diagnosis itself changes the way others view Laura, ordering their confused perceptions as well. So persuaded by the testimony of the doctor are the servants at Limmeridge House that they refuse to recognize their former mistress: "The vile deception which had asserted her death, defied exposure even in the house where she was born, and among the people with whom she had lived" (383).

Before Walter can improve on the doctor's diagnosis and rationalize Laura's resemblance to the madwoman, he must develop his powers of observation and reason by taking part in a scientific exploration of Central America. On returning, he applies his new-found logic to eluding and conquering his persecutors: "I had first learnt to use this stratagem against suspected treachery in the wilds of Central America – and now I was practising it again, with the same purpose and with even greater caution, in the heart of civilised London!" (406). Having redefined himself as rational against the irrationality of the jungle, he is able to seize control of the developing plot. But only when Laura actually bears the signs of madness can Walter come into his own as protector, rescuing her and, after Sir Percival's death, marrying her himself. Significantly, the manifestations of Laura's deeply felt mental disturbance are observed but not erased by her second husband:

My closest observation of her detected but one serious result of the conspiracy which had once threatened her reason and her life. Her memory of Blackwater Park to the period of our meeting in the burial-ground of Limmeridge Church, was lost beyond all hope of recovery. At the slightest reference to that time, she changed and trembled still; her words became confused; her memory wandered and lost itself as helplessly as ever. Here, and here only, the traces of the past lay deep – too deep to be effaced. (499)

Now that they are married, it is Walter's role to diagnose and manage her symptoms. In a typical ploy, he attempts to alleviate Laura's depression through occupational therapy, a tried-and-true technique of the Tukes' influential system of moral management.[39] When she complains that she is a useless member of the household, he tricks her into thinking that she can contribute by selling her sketches: " 'Think how useful you are going to make yourself to both of us, and you will soon be as happy, Laura, as the day is long' " (428). Little does she know that "the poor, faint, valueless sketches, of which I was the only purchaser" (429), are hidden away by Walter as soon as she gives them to him. This sort of treatment helps Laura to be cheerfully domestic but does little to help her regain her reason. The gendered organization of middle-class culture in fact *requires* that women remain economically useless and visibly irrational. As Miller has observed, the extreme positions of reason and insanity willingly taken by husband and wife in the novel "no doubt dramatize the supreme value of a norm for whose incarnation no price . . . is too high to pay."[40]

The fate of Count Fosco, the novel's villain, illustrates the cultural necessity of choosing a decided position and sticking with it. Fosco threatens not just Walter's and Laura's interests but also the hierarchical norms of capitalist culture to which Walter, Laura, and the narrative ultimately conform. Public and private, masculine and feminine, old and young, mental and physical, noble and ignoble, foreign and familiar, he defies definition. Ultimately, the Count is undone because he refuses to choose surveillance over self-display. Fosco is a spy, peeping through keyholes and involved in international espionage. Marian locates his power in his mesmeric gaze: "The marked peculiarity which singles him out from the rank and file of humanity, lies entirely, so far as I can tell at present, in the extraordinary expression and extraordinary power of his eyes" (190). Yet even his gaze, while controlling its object, draws attention to itself.[41] When Walter brings Professor Pesca to the opera, they witness this remarkable scene:

Many a burst of applause from the pit, that night, started from the soft, comfortable patting of the black-gloved hands. The man's voracious vanity devoured this implied tribute to his local and critical supremacy, with an appearance of the highest relish. Smiles rippled continuously over his fat face. He looked about him, at the pauses in the music, serenely satisfied with himself and his fellow-creatures. "Yes! yes! these barbarous English people are learning something from ME." (512)

Not content to remain a part of the audience, the Count blurs the line between spectator and spectacle with his flamboyant applause. Because he is such a visible part of the crowd, he is recognized by his invisible assassin.

In the last pages of the novel, Walter views the dead body of Fosco in the morgue and performs a postmortem:

There he lay, unowned, unknown; exposed to the flippant curiosity of a French mob — there was the dreadful end of that long life of degraded ability and heartless crime! Hushed in the sublime repose of death, the broad, firm, massive face and head fronted us so grandly, that the chattering Frenchwomen about me lifted their hands in admiration, and cried, in shrill chorus, "Ah, what a handsome man!" The wound that had killed him had been struck with a knife or dagger exactly over his heart. No other traces of violence appeared about the body, except on the left arm; and there, exactly in the place where I had seen the brand on Pesca's arm, were two deep cuts in the shape of the letter T, which entirely obliterated the mark of the Brotherhood. (561)

Walter, remaining firmly in the audience, ultimately triumphs over the boundary-crossing Fosco. Like a professional psychiatrist, he claims to hold the interpretive keys to the sight of the Italian's mutilated, patholo-gized body and to the secrets of his mind.

While Fosco is an imaginative genius who sees romance in scenes of domestic strife, Hartright is a visual realist, transforming the fantastically gothic into the everyday. Midway through the novel, when Laura is caught up in the horrors of Blackwater Park, she confides to Marian her fantasy of being Walter's middle-class wife:

"I used to see myself in my neat cheap gown, sitting at home and waiting for him, while he was earning our bread — sitting at home and working for him — seeing him come in tired, and taking off his hat and coat for him — and, Marian, pleasing him with little dishes at dinner that I had learnt to make for his sake." (227–28)

Walter eventually turns this fantasy into reality; the Hartrights become a model middle-class couple. The novel ends when he reinstates Laura as the mistress of Limmeridge House:

Mr. Kyrle rose, when I resumed my seat, and declared, as the legal adviser of the family, that my case was proved by the plainest evidence he had ever heard in his life. As he spoke those words, I put my arm round Laura, and raised her so that she was plainly visible to every one in the room. "Are you all of the same opinion?" I asked, advancing towards them a few steps, and pointing to my wife. (557)

Placing Laura on display, he demands that each onlooker conform to his opinion of her case. Once he settles the question of Laura's identity, he rushes off to Paris to investigate for his sometime employer, an engraver, "a French discovery in the practical application of his Art." Not only does the trip provide the opportunity to dispense with Fosco, but it also consolidates his professional position: "I could have no hesitation in thankfully accepting the offer; for if I acquitted myself of my commission as I hoped I should, the result would be a permanent engagement on the illustrated newspaper, to which I was now only occasionally attached" (559). Not for Walter art for art's sake; just as his rational observation of Laura has strengthened his identity as a middle-class man, so his talent for drawing has led to a respectable middle-class job.

Tamar Heller has also analyzed Walter's professional ascent. In her view, Walter's early links with economically powerless femininity and his final dependence on his wife for his connections with the landed gentry radically undercut his participation in any supposed middle-class hegemony. Heller reads the final pages of the novel, in which the triumphant Hartright returns from Paris after Frederick Fairlie's death and is unable to recognize his child as "the Heir of Limmeridge," as subversively unreal: "Hartright's momentary inability to name his son mirrors the reader's incredulity at the fairy-tale ending."[42] I see Walter's progress and his mixed gender and class affiliations more "realistically." The contradictions of Walter's supposedly consolidated identity do not release him from his role; rather, these very contradictions define him as a masculine, middle-class subject. The repression and denial of the male subject's feminine irrationality and aristocratic self-absorption actually give the novel its realist edge. As do nineteenth-century psychiatrists, the deserving professional man in *The Woman in White* escapes culture's threat of irrationality by analyzing the body of the symptomatic woman. In the process he brings middle-class order to an upper-class home and ascends to the social and economic heights appropriate to his moral and intellectual superiority. *The Woman in White* shares with psychiatric discourse the desire to rationalize confused subjectivity and disorderly private life via the analysis of women's symptoms. And yet both the novel and psychiatric writings inevitably contain traces of the *masculine* irrationality they would exorcise from middle-class narratives and from middle-class culture.

In *Dora*, Freud follows both Victorian psychiatrists and analytical heroes like Walter Hartright, defining himself as objective by diagnosing a middle-class woman.[43] Dora's father first brings his intelligent and skeptical daughter to Freud because of her hysterical symptoms. Instead of simply making the girl's symptoms disappear as the father wishes, however, Freud uncovers a sordid story of parental betrayal at the heart of Dora's distress. The father, having conducted a long-term affair with family friend Frau K., has attempted to appease the woman's husband by giving

Dora to him in exchange for his wife. In silent but effective protest, says Freud, Dora has conjured the symptoms of her illness. He boasts about his powers of observation:

When I set myself the task of bringing to light what human beings keep hidden within them, not by the compelling power of hypnosis, but by observing what they say and what they show, I thought the task was a harder one than it really is. He that has eyes to see and ears to hear may convince himself that no mortal can keep a secret.[44]

Yet while Freud inherits the objective and scientific viewing position of Victorian psychiatrists, he also allows his personal and private insecurity to show. Unlike earlier psychiatric texts, Freud's text leaves unobscured the professional man's uncertainty. Visible in *Dora* is the effort that the observer must make to "convince himself" of his own penetration and masculinity.

In spite of his authoritative-sounding prescriptions for women's mental health, Freud's claims of professional objectivity are seriously undermined by the autobiographical style in which he records the case. Boasting of his powers of observation ("When I set myself the task of bringing to light what human beings keep hidden within them . . . "), he calls attention to *himself* as subject of the text. Shifting to the third person (as Hartright does in the preface to *The Woman in White*), Freud attempts to universalize his assertions, but comes off as falsely modest about his vaunted achievements ("He that has eyes to see . . . "). In concluding my discussion of subjectivity and realism, I want to analyze the meaning of this shift in style from objective to openly, if defensively, subjective. To what extent does Freud's revelation of his own subjectivity while looking at his patient allow for the deconstruction of the masculine/feminine opposition upon which Victorian realism is built? To what extent is Freud's use of "I" a new technique for maintaining the distinctions of bourgeois realism and an early example of "how frequently male subjectivity works to appropriate 'femininity' while oppressing women"?[45]

The professional, distanced relationship between doctor and patient is a fiction demanded by a culture organized around difference, a fiction that must be cast aside if the social construction of subjectivity is to be exposed and examined. Psychoanalysis, Freud writes, does not create transferences in which the patient attempts to recreate past psychological relationships by engaging with the analyst: "It merely brings them to light, like so many other hidden psychical factors" (139). But as Juliet

Mitchell and Jacqueline Rose have remarked, the work of Lacan exposes the analyst as subjective and psychologically involved with the patient as well: "['Intervention on Transference'] calls into question the way psychoanalysis is instituted by revealing the irreducible difficulty, or impasse, of the intersubjective dialogue within which its clinical practice operates."[46] While Lacanians may look at the analytic scene and see two equally subjective beings, Freud, although acknowledging his own erring self, is loath to see himself in the same "light" as he sees his patient. His limited acceptance of his own feminine-identified subjectivity allows him to claim that his text is more truthful and realistic than its novelistic and psychiatric predecessors. At the same time, Freud, concerned with establishing his own professional identity, manages to maintain a professional viewing position similar to that of the Victorian psychiatrists. The modern reality of *Dora* resembles the old Victorian kind more than Freud likes to admit.

As I discussed earlier, the construction of the subject as feminine and lacking objectivity is not the discovery of Lacan but the open secret of nineteenth-century industrial capitalism. Thus Neil Hertz goes further than Lacan in identifying Freud not with Dora's father or Herr K., but with Dora herself:

Suppose what went wrong between Freud and Dora was not just a matter of unrecognized transferences (and countertransferences) but also of an unrecognized – or refused – identification? Suppose what Freud missed, or did not wish to see, was not that he was drawn to (or repelled by) Dora, but that he "was" Dora, or rather that the question of who was who was more radically confusing than even nuanced accounts of unacknowledged transferences and countertransferences suggest?[47]

Feminist psychoanalytic critics have celebrated the blurring of the boundaries between doctor and patient, man and woman, using Freud's theories about the social construction of the subject to demonstrate that women's place at home and as the object of the gaze is not a mandate of nature but a historical phenomenon. But it is important to remember that there is nothing *inherently* liberating in Freud's exposure of his own subjectivity. Freud's modern realism – his improved observation and analysis of Dora's hysterical symptoms – can and very often does allow for a new form of masculine, middle-class, professional authority. As does Freud, modernist writers (Henry James comes to mind here; so does James Joyce) coopt irrational and feminine subjectivity as a truth-telling strategy in order to assert their own masculine power in the sphere of high art, maintaining the separation between masculine and feminine, high and low, even as they destroy the objective/subjective opposition that characterizes the nineteenth-century relationship between middle-class men and women.[48]

In form, *Dora* sometimes resembles the reliable and complete nineteenth-century novel, and sometimes the self-conscious, modernist depiction of a fragmented reality. Yet as Toril Moi remarks, while he shuttles between ideas of completeness and fragmentation, "Freud here totally undermines any notion of a fundamental opposition between fragment and whole: it would have been impossible to write down a *complete* case history. The fragment can be presented as a complete book; the complete case history could not."[49] Making a virtue of necessity, he claims that his incomplete text is more truthful than a complete text would be:

I am aware that — in this town, at least — there are many physicians who (revolting though it may seem) choose to read a case history of this kind not as a contribution to the psychopathology of neuroses, but as a *roman à clef* designed for their private delectation. I can assure readers of this species that every case history which I may have occasion to publish in the future will be secured against their perspicacity by similar guarantees of secrecy, even though this resolution is bound to put quite extraordinary restrictions upon my choice of material. (23)

In order to validate a narrative of interiority as history, Freud points to its antinovelistic gaps and absences. Yet his text is not so much a demystification of nineteenth-century novelistic realism as a remystification. In *Dora*, the Victorian belief in the authenticity of private life is transmuted into the modernist belief in the authenticity of limited, subjective vision.

In his most remarkable denial of his text's genealogy, Freud trumpets his representation of Dora's desire for Frau K: "This element would rightly fall a sacrifice to the censorship of the writer, for he, after all, simplifies and abstracts when he appears in the character of a psychologist. But in the world of reality, which I am trying to depict here, a complication of motives, an accumulation and conjunction of mental activities — in a word, overdetermination — is the rule" (77). Freud claims to include Frau K. in his story *because* she does not fit into the conventional plot of the domestic novel. "The world of reality," of which Frau K. is presumably a part, is distinct from the world of fiction, which would exclude her. And yet, just as quickly as she is conjured as a badge of Freud's truthful professionalism, she is dropped. In her place, Freud puts first Herr K. and then the engineer, plotting Dora's story along the same lines as her mother's: "You told me yourself that your mother was engaged at seventeen and then waited two years for her husband. A daughter usually takes her mother's love-story as her model" (129). With the disappearance of Frau K., Dora's story becomes a conventional tale of the road to proper object choice. An alternate story is told only in the margins. In a long but necessarily subordinate footnote in Freud's postscript, he reintroduces Dora's desire for Frau K. as the reason for her hysteria, raising the possibility of a different story while telling the same old tale about love and marriage. Interruptive style, rather than the replacement of the old plot with a new one, ultimately distinguishes Freud from his predecessors.

In a modern-sounding rejection of Victorian values, Freud redefines the domestic woman's efficient management of home and personal relations as "housewife's psychosis."[50] At the same time, he appropriates undomesticated, irrational femininity as a valuable diagnostic tool. In *Dora*, it is the patient who is rational and objective while the doctor is irrational and subjective. Ironically, the doctor's embrace of his own irrationality is not so much a break with the Victorian need for professional objectivity as it is the new mark of his authority. Thus Freud can refute Dora's logic as part of her problem. When she rationally (and correctly) analyzes the behavior of her father and Herr K., Freud pounces on her reasoning as a sign not of her sanity but of her repression:

When the patient brings forward a sound and incontestable train of argument during psychoanalytic treatment, the physician is liable to feel a moment's embarrassment, and the patient may take advantage of it by asking: "This is all perfectly correct and true, isn't it? What do you want to change in it now that I've told it you?" But it soon becomes evident that the patient uses thoughts of this kind, which the analysis cannot attack, for the purpose of cloaking others which are anxious to escape from criticism and from consciousness. (51)

Freud maintains his professional dignity by discarding Dora's reasoning. The analyst, not bound by the rules of argument, is able to refute the patient's logic with a discourse outside of logic.

In this modern scheme, women are barred from education and the public life not, as they were in the nineteenth century, for fear that their intellectual exertion would cause their reproductive organs to atrophy but because study and public life distract them from the project of getting to know themselves. Dora's studiousness is transformed into avoidance of personal relationships that would enhance her self-knowledge: "She tried to avoid social intercourse, and employed herself — so far as she was allowed to by the fatigue and lack of concentration of which she complained — with attending lectures for women and with carrying on more or less serious studies" (38). The rejection of medical advice is not a sign of healthy skepticism, as it was in *The Woman in White*, but a sign of unhealthy repression:

> The child had developed into a mature young woman of very independent judgement, who had grown accustomed to laugh at the efforts of doctors, and in the end to renounce their help entirely. Moreover, she had always been against calling in medical advice, though she had no personal objection to her family doctor. Every proposal to consult a new physician aroused her resistance, and it was only her father's authority which induced her to come to me at all. (37)

While Freud attempts to distance himself from the scheming father, clearly they are involved in similar projects. Both use psychoanalysis to reinforce Dora's position as a domestic, self-absorbed, feminine subject.

With the second dream, Freud and Dora struggle over the interpretation of visual images and evidence. Through the dream analysis, he attempts to make her see herself his way. Freud remarks about the dream that " 'pictures' was a point of junction in the network of her dream thoughts" (116). In the dream, the town through which Dora roams resembles the pictures sent to her by the engineer: "At Christmas she had been sent an album from a German health-resort, containing views of the town; and the very day before the dream she had looked this up to show it to some relatives who were stopping with them" (115). The views in the album carry certain associations. Not only are they a gift from the man who wishes to marry her, but they also come from a health resort, the backdrop against which her father has attempted to exchange her for Frau K. Dora's dream re-vision of the views can be read as a reasonable rejection of the social structures that would control both her looking and her self-presentation. In the dream, Dora uses the pictures to imagine a place where she lives alone and away from the pressure to conform to her father's and society's view of her. But Freud reads Dora's reinscription of the views as an unhealthy avoidance of a position that she should naturally desire. In her new house, she finds a letter from her mother about her father: " 'Now he is dead, and if you like you can come' " (114). While Freud comes to agree with Dora that her father has treated her as exchangeable property, he cannot grant her dream of living alone the status of reality. He reads the letter as Dora's repressed desire for revenge against her father, a desire that must be acknowledged and exorcised before she can regain her health and marry the engineer.

Freud connects Dora's dream wandering to her refusal of a relative's offer to guide her through the Dresden gallery, having decided that she would rather look at the pictures by herself:

Another cousin of hers, who was with them and knew Dresden, had wanted to act as a guide and take her round the gallery. *But she declined, and went alone,* and stopped in front of the pictures that appealed to her. She remained *two hours* in front of the Sistine Madonna, rapt in silent admiration. (116; emphasis in text)

Dora's self-determined looking demands interpretation: "What was evident was that in this first part of the dream she was identifying herself with a young man" (116), the engineer. Freud can only see Dora's solitary search in oedipal terms. A wandering, observing woman does not conform to the structures of vision governing his definitions of mental health. Freud's delight in his interpretation is cut short by an unimpressed Dora, who informs him that she is quitting analysis: "At the end of the second sitting, when I expressed my satisfaction at the result, Dora replied in a deprecatory tone: 'Why, has anything so very remarkable come out?'" (126). It is no wonder that Dora greets Freud's reading with so little surprise. He has simply read back into the dream the structures of vision controlling the movements of her waking life.

Freud's narrative has a double ending, signifying its utopian possibilities but also its ties to both Victorian and modernist brands of realism. The first ending resists novelistic closure by refusing to align Dora's surfaces with her depths:

It is surprising, and might easily be misleading, to find that the patient's condition shows no noticeable alteration even though considerable progress has been made with the work of analysis. But in reality things are not as bad as they seem. It is true that the symptoms do not disappear while the work is proceeding; but they disappear a little while later, when the relations between patient and physician have been dissolved. The postponement of recovery or improvement is really only caused by the physician's own person. (137)

Freud says that at this moment reality must be read in opposition to, rather than as following from, Dora's visible symptoms. But while Freud rejects Victorian psychiatry's belief in the visibility of states of mind, he claims to make Dora's mind visible to us through his penetrating observation and writing. His explanation of Dora's appearance exposes, without itself abandoning, the nineteenth-century construction of feminine illness in relation to the male professional gaze.

The second ending satisfies the Victorian demand for closure:

> Years have again gone by since her visit. In the meantime the girl has married, and indeed — unless all the signs mislead me — she has married the young man who came into her associations at the beginning of the analysis of the second dream. Just as the first dream represented her turning away from the man she loved to her father — that is to say, her flight from life into disease — so the second dream announced that she was about to tear herself free from her father and had been reclaimed once more by the realities of life. (144)

Reality here is defined as submission to the novelistic plot. Thus Freud can ignore Dora's desire for Frau K. as unreal even though he has acknowledged that it exists. Ultimately, the "reality" of psychic life must be aligned with "reality" as defined by the gendered, middle-class structures of the nineteenth-century novel in order to be accepted and believed.

Freud's self-conscious text, no less than *The Woman in White*, depends on the presence of a symptomatic woman in representing and managing "real," irrational bourgeois life. His admission of his own fallible vision and selfishness serves, paradoxically, to reinforce his identity as authority on subjectivity. In being more "honest" about his own motives and blind spots, Freud is able to tell the same "truth" about women's interiority as did his psychiatric and novelistic predecessors. By appropriating undomesticated, irrational femininity for himself, he is able to maintain more effectively and convincingly than Victorian psychiatrists and sensation-novel heroes a public and authoritative persona.

The gender-inflected distinction between "real" private life and "false" public life still helps to rationalize the contradictions of capitalist culture today. The case of Woody Allen neatly demonstrates the middle-class professional man's enduring need to distinguish between public and private, phony and authentic, via the diagnosis of a domestic woman, even as postmodern media blur the boundaries between genders and spheres in ways unimagined in the nineteenth and early twentieth centuries. Allen's presentation of himself as a private, feminized subject underwrites his success in the public sphere as a professional man. But instead of destroying the moviegoing public's illusions about the authenticity of private life and the essential nature of gender difference, his confusion of public and private, masculine and feminine tends to reinforce nineteenth-century beliefs in the reality of the private and the superior judgment of middle-class men.

Throughout his career, Allen has constructed his public image as that of a private person. *Time* critic Richard Corliss describes Allen and his long-time companion Mia Farrow as publicly domestic:

Mom and Dad lived the city's most public private lives. *Tout* New York was their movie set, Madison Square Garden their all-star playground, the chic eatery Elaine's their kitchen. Central Park was their shared backyard. From their respective apartment windows on opposite sides of the park, they would wave love at each other.[51]

It is easy to feel that we can know the "real" Allen. The films are family affairs, using the same cast of friends and relatives over and over again. Allen plays roles guaranteed to remind us of his own real-life role as an entertainer and interpreter of culture — comedian (*Annie Hall*), documentary producer (*Crimes and Misdemeanors*), and English professor (*Husbands and Wives*). The comic realism of Allen's most popular films resides not simply in their mimetic recreation of a certain up-scale urban lifestyle but also in their ability to make us believe that they are revealing the psychic reality of their creator (The deadly serious and fantastic works are routinely rejected by fans and critics as Allen's attempts to be Bergman or Fellini instead of himself.) The films collectively create the image of Allen as a neurotic but essentially rational person. His credibility as an artist and professional is inextricably linked with the idea that he is making his private self public — that his work is not related to the money-making, dehumanizing public sphere but that it is part of his private search for self-knowledge.

The public was suddenly forced to readjust its beliefs when it was revealed that Allen had secretly been conducting an affair with Farrow's twenty-year-old adopted daughter Soon-Yi, and that Farrow was alleging that Allen had sexually abused their seven-year-old adopted daughter Dylan. The reporter Steve Kroft describes our surprise: "It's a story we've done before on *60 Minutes*, but this one is different because everyone knows the parents, at least from the movies." We thought we knew the details of Allen's and Farrow's private life from the movies; somewhere along the way we were deceived. His image threatened, he has attempted to tell his side of the story to the press. In public disclosures about his private life he demonstrates a strategy frequently deployed in his films:

while claiming his own irrationality as an alibi ("The heart wants what it wants. There's no logic to those things"), he frames and diagnoses the woman in his life as "really" crazy ("What happened was crazy behavior . . . you know, terrible rage, death threats. Look . . . if this is not irrational to you — I mean, she accused me of child molestation").[52] Mia Farrow's irrational behavior demonstrates her mental instability, but Allen's irrational behavior demonstrates his self-knowledge. As with Freud and Dora, sanity and objectivity are still the privileges of the middle-class professional man, even when — or especially when — he represents himself as slightly crazy.

The sensational image of the unhinged mother — familiar from *Lady Audley's Secret* if not from *The Woman in White* — comes in handy in representing Farrow's "irrational" response to the affair. About her own attempt to represent visually the events in question, Allen says,

She sent me a Valentine card . . . I opened it up, and there was a very, very, very chilling Valentine, meticulously worked on. I mean, I — one hesitates to say psychotically worked on — you know, a Victorian Valentine and photo of the family, and through all the kids was thrust needles and a steak knife stuck through the heart of the thing.[53]

As in Dora's case, Farrow's disturbing re-vision of events is used by Allen, in his overlapping roles as father and analyst, to efface his part in the destruction of the family.

Allen has more difficulty managing interpretations of the nude Polaroids of Soon-Yi discovered by Farrow in his apartment. When he is asked about them, words fail:

We were sitting around in this room, as a matter of fact, talking about her modeling career and she said would I take some nude pictures of her. I'm not a person that knows much about cameras; I mean I'm not good at that. And I, I took a small amount and left them out, and . . . and that was the, um, the origin of . . . I mean, there's nothing more to say about that.[54]

In a feeble renunciation of responsibility, Allen disingenuously claims that he does not know much about cameras and that Soon-Yi directed him to take the photos. Allen is not quite believable in the role of innocent accomplice, after years of styling himself as a meticulous, controlling director of the women in his life.

Allen self-righteously appropriates melodramatic, feminine self-denial in all of his statements to the press, proclaiming on "Sixty Minutes," for example, that "if tomorrow the entire world said to me: you're a dreadful and evil man, and you cannot do any more films, you know, it would mean zilch. I would simply stay home and write, and be very happy, just as long as I'm doing the best thing for my children."[55] (He could be playing the repentant mother Isabel Vane in *East Lynne*.) In contrast, he accuses Farrow of parading the children to the press as part of her scheme to win a big cash settlement from him. Why would a person who does not care about career and reputation, and who values privacy above all else, talk to the press at all? If Allen were really ready to give up career for children and a retired private life, he could just sit back and let the courts hear the evidence. But clearly his press interviews are carefully orchestrated attempts to salvage his professional identity and public image as a good guy who exhibits essentially truthful versions of himself for a living.

Of course, this is not to answer the questions of what really happened between Allen and Dylan, whether or not his relationship with Soon-Yi is really incestuous, and whether or not he really is a good father. It is simply to say that Allen's attempt to represent the reality of his story inherits its structures from Victorian definitions of gender, self, and sanity.

NOTES

I would like to thank Margaret Homans for reading drafts of this essay and for her very constructive criticism.

1. Patrick Brantlinger, "What Is 'Sensational' about the 'Sensation Novel'?" *Nineteenth-Century Literature* 37 (1982): 27.
2. See Eli Zaretsky, *Capitalism, the Family, and Personal Life* (New York: Harper Colophon, 1973), 73: "On one side the objective social world appeared, perceived at first as 'machinery' or 'industry,' then throughout the nineteenth century as 'society'. . . . In opposition to this harsh world that no individual could hope to affect, the modern world of subjectivity was created."
3. See Nancy Armstrong, *Desire and Domestic Fiction* (New York: Oxford University Press, 1987), on the nineteenth-century feminization of subjectivity and private life.
4. Michel Foucault, *Madness and Civilization* (New York: Vintage, 1965), esp. 64, 157–58, 181–82, 198.
5. W. F. Bynum, Roy Porter, and Michael Shepherd, eds., *The Anatomy of*

Madness: Essays in the History of Psychiatry, vol. 1 (New York: Routledge, 1988), 9.

6. Elaine Showalter, *The Female Malady* (New York: Pantheon, 1985).

7. Richard Sennett, *The Fall of Public Man* (New York: Knopf, 1977), 22.

8. Jonathan Crary, *Techniques of the Observer: On Vision and Modernity in the Nineteenth Century* (Cambridge: MIT Press, 1991), 113.

9. Ibid., 24.

10. Sennett, *The Fall of Public Man*, 25.

11. See James Krasner, *The Entangled Eye: Visual Perception and the Representation of Nature in Post-Darwinian Narrative* (New York: Oxford University Press, 1992), 5, on the problematic use of physiological vision as a figure for scientific observation in the nineteenth century.

12. Henry Maudsley, *Body and Mind*, rev. ed. (New York: Appleton, 1875), 58.

13. Hugh Diamond, "On the Application of Photography to the Physiognomic and Mental Phenomena of Insanity," in *The Face of Madness: Hugh W. Diamond and the Origin of Psychiatric Photography*, ed. Sander Gilman (New York: Brunner/Mazel, 1976), 20.

14. Michael J. Clark, " 'Morbid Introspection,' Unsoundness of Mind, and British Psychological Medicine, c. 1830–1900," in *The Anatomy of Madness*, vol. 3, ed. Bynum, Porter, and Shepherd, 81.

15. Charles Darwin, *The Expression of the Emotions in Man and Animals* (1872; New York: Greenwood, 1955), 154.

16. Ibid., 364–65.

17. Darwin, *Expression of the Emotions*, 264. In *Repression in Victorian Fiction* (Berkeley: University of California Press, 1987), 2, John Kucich argues that repression and self-control do not stifle individuality but help define and maintain the discrete and private self threatened by the public sphere. For a discussion of Darwin's work in relation to Victorian psychiatry, see Janet Browne, "Darwin and the Face of Madness," in *Anatomy of Madness*, vol. 1, ed. Bynum, Porter, and Shepherd.

18. See Jenny Bourne Taylor, *In the Secret Theatre of Home: Wilkie Collins, Sensation Narrative, and Nineteenth-Century Psychology* (New York: Routledge, 1988), 37: "With the development of the medical and psychiatric professions, the figure of middle-class feminine domestic virtue becomes the epitome of rationality and self-management, just as domesticity acquires new kinds of *homely* connotations; this is set against the differently pathologized imaginary excesses of upper- or working-class sexuality, of hysteria or of mania. The madwoman of every class is cured through learning to be a middle-class gentlewoman."

19. Samuel Tuke, *A Description of the Retreat* (York: Alexander, 1813), 141.

20. For a discussion of the Quakers' role in the treatment of insanity, see Fiona Godlee, "Aspects of Non-Conformity: Quakers and the Lunatic Fringe," in *The Anatomy of Madness* vol. 2, ed. Bynum, Porter, and Shepherd, 75.

21. Showalter, *Female Malady*, 68.

22. In *The Expression of the Emotions*, 295, Darwin relates this information, from

his correspondence with an asylum superintendent: "[Crichton Browne] has
sent me photographs of two women, taken in the intervals between their
paroxysms, and he adds with respect to one of these women, that the state of
her hair is a sure and convenient criterion of her mental condition."

23. For examples of this see Thomas S. Szasz, *The Manufacture of Madness* (New
York: Harper and Row, 1970); Andrew Scull, *Museums of Madness: The Social
Organization of Insanity in Nineteenth-Century England* (New York: St. Mar-
tin's, 1979).

24. Charlotte Mackenzie, "Social Factors in the Admission, Discharge, and Continuing Stay of Patients at Ticehurst Asylum, 1845–1917," in *The Anatomy of
Madness*, vol. 2, ed. Bynum, Porter, and Shepherd, 159.

25. Peter McCandless, " 'Dangerous to Themselves and Others': The Victorian
Debate over the Prevention of Wrongful Confinement," *Journal of British
Studies* 23 (1983): 84–104.

26. See Judith Walkowitz, *City of Dreadful Delight: Narratives of Sexual Danger in
Late-Victorian London* (Chicago: University of Chicago Press, 1992), 171–89,
for a discussion of Weldon's life and writing.

27. Clark, " 'Morbid Introspection,' " 92.

28. See Crary, *Techniques of the Observer*, 148, on psychoanalysis "as another
operation of relocating the 'interior' contents of the unconscious onto a field
where they can be formalized in linguistic terms, however imprecisely."

29. Jeffrey Masson, ed., *The Complete Letters of Sigmund Freud to Wilhelm Fliess*
(Cambridge: Belknap/Harvard University Press, 1985), 398.

30. Sigmund Freud, *The Standard Edition of the Complete Works of Sigmund Freud*.
Vol. 2, *Studies in Hysteria*, trans. James Strachey (London: Hogarth Press and
the Institute for Psychoanalysis, 1953–1974), 160.

31. For the historical links between British spiritualism and psychoanalysis, see
Janet Oppenheim, *The Other World: Spiritualism and Psychic Research in England, 1850–1914* (Cambridge: Cambridge University Press, 1985), 249–56.

32. Martin Stone, "Shellshock and the Psychologists," in *The Anatomy of Madness*,
vol. 2, ed. Bynum, Porter, and Shepherd, 245.

33. D. A. Miller, *The Novel and the Police* (Berkeley: University of California
Press, 1987), 157.

34. Wilkie Collins, *The Woman in White* (1860; New York: Bantam, 1985), 1.
Further citations will be incorporated in the text.

35. Unsigned review, *Guardian* (29 August 1860): xv, 780–81. Reprinted in Norman Page, ed., *Wilkie Collins: The Critical Heritage* (Boston: Routledge &
Kegan Paul, 1974), 91.

36. Henry James, from an unsigned review titled "Miss Braddon," *Nation*, November 9, 1865, i, 593–95. Reprinted in Page, *Wilkie Collins*, 123.

37. See in addition the famous passage in which Walter is shocked when his
preliminary judgment of Marian Halcombe is confounded by new visual
evidence: "The easy elegance of every movement of her limbs and body as
soon as she began to advance from the far end of the room, set me in a flutter
of expectation to see her face clearly. . . . She approached nearer – and I said

to myself (with a sense of surprise which words fail me to express), The lady is ugly!" (24). Walter's description is an attempt to control the threatening female figure as she advances. Defining her as ugly, just in time, he neutralizes the horror she represents — the spectacle of his own lack of power as an emasculated employee of the Fairlies.

38. Laurie Langbauer, "Women in White, Men in Feminism," *Yale Journal of Criticism* 2 (1989): 226, writes of both Walter Hartright and "men in feminism": "What men write on the blank tablet of the hysteric comes to seem the hidden truth revealed, brought to light by analysis."

39. Jenny Bourne Taylor's book, *In the Secret Theatre of Home*, takes as its subject Collins's appropriation of contemporary psychiatric discourse. She argues that in *The Woman in White* Collins plays with the discourse of moral management in order to elicit in the reader the very anxieties and fears that moral management aimed to treat.

40. Miller, *The Novel and the Police*, 166.

41. My argument here follows Joseph Litvak, *Caught in the Act: Theatricality and the Nineteenth-Century English Novel* (Berkeley: University of California Press, 1992), 131: "One might argue that Fosco's greatest crime, the one for which he must die, is the flamboyance with which he theatricalizes, and thereby compromises, panoptic power."

42. Tamar Heller, *Dead Secrets: Wilkie Collins and the Female Gothic* (New Haven, Conn.: Yale University Press, 1992), 140.

43. Many feminist critics have discussed the well-defined looking relations of psychoanalysis. For an account of Dora in particular, see Sharon Willis, "A Symptomatic Narrative," *Diacritics* 13 (1983): 46–60.

44. Sigmund Freud, *Dora: An Analysis of a Case of Hysteria* (1905; New York: Collier, 1963), 96. Further citations will be incorporated in the text.

45. Tania Modleski, *Feminism without Women: Culture and Criticism in a "Postfeminist" Age* (New York: Routledge, 1991), 7.

46. Juliet Mitchell and Jacqueline Rose, eds., *Feminine Sexuality: Jacques Lacan and the Ecole Freudienne* (New York: Norton, 1982), 62.

47. Neil Hertz, "Dora's Secrets, Freud's Techniques," in *Dora's Case: Freud-Hysteria-Feminism*, ed. Charles Bernheimer and Clare Kahane (New York: Columbia University Press, 1985), 225.

48. See Steven Marcus, "Freud and Dora: Story, History, Case History," *Representations: Essays on Literature and Society* (New York: Random House, 1975), 263–64, on *Dora*'s resemblance to a modernist novel.

49. Toril Moi, "Representation of Patriarchy: Sexuality and Epistemology in Freud's 'Dora,' " in *Dora's Case*, ed. Bernheimer and Kahane, 185–86.

50. See Armstrong, *Desire and Domestic Fiction*, 235, on this reversal: "It must have come as a shock to be told that all this was a mechanism of repression, that the real depths of the female did not reside in her maternal instincts, her affection for female friends, her domestic duties, or her concern for the weak and the poor."

51. Richard Corliss, "Scenes from a Breakup," *Time*, August 31, 1992, 54.

52. Interview in *Time*, August 31, 1992, 61. "Sixty Minutes" broadcast interview, CBS, November 22, 1992.
53. Ibid.
54. Interview in *Newsweek*, August 31, 1992, 55.
55. Ibid.

Memoirs from a German Colony: What Do White Women Want?

Marcia Klotz

This essay is part of a larger project investigating how the colonial campaign served as a productive imaginative field in which a racialized feminine identity began to take shape in Germany around the turn of the century. Germany's participation in the "scramble for Africa" contributed to the development of a racial discourse in Wilhelmine culture that allowed women to think of themselves not simply as women, but as *white* women. Despite the obviously conservative nature of a racial marking that always took place at the expense of the colonized, this development ironically had empowering consequences for women, opening up new avenues for women's political agency and expressions of erotic desire.

In the first decade of the twentieth century, the German government actively recruited women to travel to Southwest Africa, now Namibia, in order to reproduce German society there and hence preserve German hegemony. In 1910, a patriotic bourgeois women's group called the Frauenbund der deutschen Kolonialgesellschaft (Women's Auxiliary to the Colonial Society) formed with the explicit goal of promoting the travel of German women to the colonies. Its broader political goals included educating the public about the German colonies and fostering a stronger sense of patriotism in women. Within three years of its founding, this group boasted seven thousand members and published a weekly journal with one hundred thousand subscriptions. It quickly became one of the largest and most powerful women's organizations in the country. The
154

colonial campaign thus created a space in which nationalistic bourgeois women could take a very active part in the political arena.[1] Most of the German women who did travel to African colonies chose German Southwest Africa, now Namibia, as their goal, because it was the only German protectorate in which malaria was not a major threat. Some of these women wrote memoirs of their experiences, which were published in Germany and distributed by the Women's Auxiliary to the German Colonial Society. I will be examining three examples of such autobiographical writing here, from three settler women who lived in Southwest Africa around the turn of the century.

An examination of these women's histories must take its place within a much broader tradition, an ongoing discussion of the role of colonist women in a number of different settings, coming from a number of European countries. For the most part, scholars have assumed that such women responded differently to colonial society than did European men, or, as Mary Pratt states it, that there was a "specifically female relationship to North European expansionism."[2] Until recently, many historians have framed the particular nature of women's colonial involvement according to what it meant for European men in the colonies, viewing colonist women as inhibitors to the sexual relations between these men and colonized peoples. James McAuley, writing in 1961 about his experiences in New Guinea in the forties, states this position succinctly:

> While European men went out to Asia and Africa and the Pacific without wife and family, they entered into a different sort of relationship, socially and sexually, with the people. When the wife came out all was inevitably different.... The white woman is perhaps the real ruin of empires. If New Guinea had become a mulatto society it would be a slatternly, but more colourful and easy-going society, with the minor vices of concubinage and sloth, rather than the major respectable vices of coldheartedness and hypocrisy.[3]

This view has found a number of proponents, including most recently Ronald Hyam, who, in a book published in 1990, describes colonist women as a "fatally advancing feminine frontier."[4] Such historical accounts reiterate the views of many male colonists themselves — that white women came to the colonies with the Victorian ethics of Europe in tow, intent on putting an end to the sexual adventures of their men overseas. According to such accounts,[5] when left to their own devices, colonist men had enjoyed relatively free sexual access to the bodies of the colonized (under conditions generally left unstated). With the arrival of European women, however, this life of uninhibited sexuality, assumed to be indicative of more harmonious racial relations, came to an end, replaced by new policies of segregation and color bar. White women demanded these social strictures, according to the argument, not only because they feared rape at the hands of colonized men but also out of jealousy of sexual rivals among the colonized women. This resulted in a general deterioration in race relations and, some would go so far as to say, ultimately in the failure of the colonial enterprise.

Several feminist historians have recently taken issue with this account. Ann Lora Stoler, for example, argues that European women did not demand segregation, but rather were imported into colonial settings as a stabilizing measure, an excuse to justify segregation policies that had been planned before their arrival. Others argue that colonial women were if anything more compassionate in their actions and less racist in their attitudes toward the colonized populace than their male counterparts.[6] Mary Pratt, for example, finds in women's travel writing attempts to resist the dominant form of colonial perception. While male travelers and colonists adopt what Pratt terms a "monarch-of-all-I-survey" approach to the lands they pass through, the female colonists and travelers of Pratt's sources repeatedly refuse such an attitude, resisting the mastery of looking, often ironizing and parodying the travel narratives of their male counterparts (Pratt, 208–16). Martha Mamozai, in contrast, arrives at precisely the opposite conclusion, discussing many examples of colonist women's complicity in the inhuman crimes committed in the name of empire.[7] In a discussion of white German women's activities in colonial Africa, Mamozai concludes once and for all that sisterhood is far from global.

In each of these instances, colonialism serves to stage various debates on broad-reaching assumptions about gender. The questions that frame these studies have the most general implications: Do women inhibit men's ability to prove themselves in the world (here, to colonize successfully), or are women simply instrumentalized as scapegoats once a masculine enterprise fails? To what extent are women to be viewed as historical agents — even in unsavory political projects — and to what extent are women innocent objects, manipulated by the men in power? And, following that question, to the extent that women *were* active participants in the colonial endeavor, were they complicitous in racist crimes or were they resistant? Did women side with power, taking their place alongside colonist men, or did they rather see similarities between their own victimhood within a patriarchal society and that of the natives within a colonial one? Were there possibilities or instances of solidarity?

These questions are enticing because they seem to hold forth a promise of insight, whether by way of analogy or by way of genealogy, into the tangled complexities of race and gender and how we imagine them to be interrelated today. Evocative as such questions may be, however, they hold little promise of ever finding definitive answers. The historical record is filled with inconsistencies and contradictions, disallowing any monolithic description of European women's role in the colonial campaign. One can no more think of colonial women as a unified whole than one can conceive of colonial society in general as a homogeneous group. On this point, Ann Lora Stoler offers a useful critique of those studies that have framed the colonizer/colonized dichotomy as an easy split. There are differences not only among the colonized but among the colonizers as well, Stoler points out:

Colonizers ... were neither by nature unified nor did they inevitably share common interests and fears; their boundaries ... were never clear. On the contrary, I argue that colonizers live in what has elsewhere been called "imagined communities" — ones that are consciously created and fashioned to overcome the economic and social disparities that would in other contexts separate and often set their members in conflict. Racism is the classic foil to mitigate such divisions and is thus a critical factor in the casting of colonial cultures. (Stoler, 137)

Stoler's view allows for a more fluid interrogation of the historical record, based on a reformulation of the questions with which one approaches women's involvement in the colonial campaign. One might ask, for example, what *kinds of conflict* are being mitigated within a given account, or precisely *how* racism is instrumentalized within a specific context. Strategies are likely to change from one situation to the next, which makes room for contradictions within and between texts.

Moreover, as Jenny Sharpe admonishes in the introduction to her excellent book on the Indian Mutiny of 1857, one must be careful to distinguish racial oppression from gender subjugation, rather than imagining that the two function as a singular whole. Sharpe argues against

treating race and gender as interchangeable functions — which means that race cannot be theorized from the functioning of gender hierarchies. The task is not to resolve the problems of white femininity by mapping race onto gender but to maintain those problems as sites of textual and theoretical production. A place to

begin addressing this concern is with a dismantling of the victim-villain opposition. We need a critical model that can accommodate, on the one hand, female
power and desire and, on the other, gender restrictions and sexual subordination.[8]

Such an approach moves beyond the finger pointing of those studies
that seek to establish the (relative) guilt or innocence of European women
as historical agents. It is not enough to establish *whether* white women
were complicitous in or resistant to the crimes committed in the name of
colonialism without asking *what they stood to gain* from these actions, and
why they acted as they did. What, precisely, did these white women want?

In contrast to texts written by colonist men, which generally focus on
political and economic issues and relate first-person experience only when
recounting military exploits, women's memoirs tend to focus on the day-
to-day life of the domestic sphere.[9] Particularly for those living on farms,
this was dominated by interactions with African servants. Hence, whenever historical accounts of German colonial rule in Southwest Africa turn
to speculations about the lived relations between the races, these women's
names appear frequently in the footnotes.[10] This might seem a kind of
back-door victory for feminist historiography, as these written accounts,
written by women about their own daily experience, are accorded value
and included in the historical record. Yet such handling of the material
raises serious methodological questions. Joan Scott warns against granting
"experience" a fundamental status as a category of historical sources:

> We need to attend to the historical processes that, through discourse, position
> subjects and produce their experience. It is not individuals who have experience,
> but subjects who are constituted through experience. Experience in this definition
> then becomes not the origin of our explanation, not the authoritative (because
> seen or felt) evidence that grounds what is known, but rather that which we seek
> to explain, that about which knowledge is produced.[11]

Paraphrasing Denise Riley, Scott calls for a scholarship that does not treat
women as a unified mass, but that pays attention to how "agency is made
possible, the ways in which race and sexuality intersect with gender, the
ways in which politics organize and interpret experience — the ways in
which identity is a contested terrain, the site of multiple and conflicting
claims" (Scott 31).[12]

A line of intersection comes into being at the place where gender and
race meet in colonial discourse, where "whiteness" becomes a category of

empowerment. Margarethe von Eckenbrecher's depiction of the 1904 Herero uprising illustrates how this category functions. While her husband was away, a Herero man named Geert Afrika had come to her home to trade with her, Eckenbrecher writes, accompanied by a group of Herero men. Geert Afrika then followed her into the house and tried to lock her in, but she escaped, rebuking him with these words:

"You come to do business with me, yet you don't know how to treat the white woman? Make way, you rogue!" I walked right past him to the door.... If my husband had been there, they would certainly have killed him without mercy. But for me they must have had a little respect [Scheu], and they thought twice about carrying out their plan.[13]

In this moment of profound crisis, Eckenbrecher speculates that her life is spared because she, "the white woman," inspires awe. In fact, the Herero were very deliberate in sparing the lives of German women and children during the uprising, taking only German men as their victims — possibly, as the historian Horst Drechsler speculates, in retribution for sexual abuses perpetrated by German men against Herero women.[14] Eckenbrecher's account, however, eclipses the political decision of the Herero and thereby truncates any speculation as to why German men were chosen as the unique targets of violence. She reduces African political agency to a psychological motivation ascribed to her singular interlocutor, Geert Afrika, whose very name identifies him as an African "everyman." Moreover, she does not passively adopt the role she believes he has assigned her but addresses him with the attitude of an insulted queen, the fearsome "white woman" she imagines herself to be — as seen through the eyes of the colonized Other.

Eckenbrecher's text offers this identity as a gift to the female reader in Germany, who might very well picture herself in the same situation and see her own life being spared, all for the sake of her whiteness, while German men, who for some reason do not commend the same kind of respect, are slaughtered. This fantasy is not without a certain appeal, displacing the disadvantages of being a woman in the patriarchal society of Wilhelmine Germany with the imagined privilege of being a white woman in colonial Africa. Race thus takes on a new meaning in the writing and the reading of this narrative, compensating for gender as a category of identity construction.

Sexuality is a third important register, framing the ways race and gender intersect within the German white woman's colonial text. Within the contemporaneous ideological discourse, of course, sex motored women's participation in a campaign that sought their compliance for the sake of their bodies as a means of reproducing whiteness in the dark continent. This sexual project is not articulated within the memoirs themselves, however, in which there is not a single reference to the joys of serving as a kind of breeding cow for the nation. Settler women also devote very little ink to expressing outrage at the sexual relations between European men and African women, though most do mention, at least tangentially, that such relations are widespread.

If these, the desires attributed to colonist women by men, are not articulated within the women's texts, do settler women have an erotic agenda of their own? How are their desires constituted within the colonial setting, and how do they serve in the subject construction of the authors not simply as women, but as white women?

To interrogate these texts with such questions in mind is to take a deliberately literary approach to what have otherwise been considered historical documents. If women's memoirs are used as evidence to determine what really happened in Southwest Africa at the time, they can only offer a fragmentary and very questionable picture. If one reads them as narrative and rhetoric, however, attending to their many ruptures, inconsistencies, and multiple meanings, one arrives at an understanding of that history in which the boundaries between questions of power and desire become less rigid. This is the approach I will be taking here, reading these memoirs not as "evidence" of some preexisting factual history that lies outside the texts themselves, but rather as gendered articulations of a discourse that both constitutes and responds to German imperialism. This hermeneutical approach is not intended to supplement more empirical histories, but is meant as a challenge to them. No historical account of German colonialism in Southwest Africa can ever be objective, because all rely on any number of subjective first-person accounts, each of which lies open to myriad different readings. What I offer are three such readings, approaching what have hitherto been read as historical documents according to the flows of desire that move through them.

MARGARETHE VON ECKENBRECHER: "WHAT AFRICA GAVE AND
TOOK FROM ME: EXPERIENCES OF A GERMAN WOMAN IN
SOUTHWEST AFRICA"

In 1902, Margarethe von Eckenbrecher set out with her husband and
infant son to establish a home in the Herero territory of Southwest Africa.
At the time of her arrival, the Herero people were mired in a deep crisis
occasioned by both natural and political causes. Five years previously, a
rinderpest epidemic had destroyed 90 percent of their cattle herds, while
1898 had seen a typhoid epidemic that claimed over ten thousand Herero
lives. This was followed by a locust invasion and a severe drought, which
destroyed grazing and crop lands (Drechsler, 98). For the most part,
German settlers in the region had viewed these natural catastrophes with
optimism because they weakened Herero autonomy, forcing the Herero
to work for wages on German farms and to sell their land and cattle. This
same period was marked by economic expansion among the German
colonists, who were able to immunize their herds against the epidemic.
Unfair trade and the seizure of Herero cattle had also contributed to the
settlers' ability to secure a growing portion of the natural resources of the
region, and thereby a greater control over the Herero.

Eckenbrecher's memoirs reflect a discomfort with living in relative
prosperity among people who are literally starving. Although she admits
to using the whip on workers she believes to be stealing food from
her, she generally tries to portray herself as a somewhat reluctant good
Samaritan. She will go out of her way to care for the ill when asked, for
example, but she stresses the fact that she never volunteers her services:
"Whenever I thought I could relax, I was called on to visit the sick. . . .
My main resources consisted of quinine, calomel, and opium, with which
one can make some very nice treatments. If there were internal diseases, I
could sometimes help; most of them were starving, in which case they
received food for a time" (Eckenbrecher, 93).

In Africa, Eckenbrecher has found a place where she can play doctor, a
game that satisfies a number of narcissistic desires. She is completely
independent in her role, with no medical training and no need for assistance from her husband or anyone else. She is also desired; the people
come for her, but she has no need of them. Moreover, this role allows her
to repress the immediate political reality; she can mend the wounds

inflicted by German colonial policy without taking responsibility for what has happened. Starvation has nothing to do with the profit she draws from land that may have benefited her patients just a few years before, appearing in the context of "internal diseases," depoliticized and reversible, at least temporarily, because of the author's goodwill and medical prowess.

As she describes her doctoral duties, Eckenbrecher spends considerable time relaying a particular anecdote, ostensibly to exemplify "the terrible superstition and the stupidity of the people" (Eckenbrecher, 94). The story concerns a child who suffers from very serious burns. The author bandages the wounds and is initially surprised at how quickly they seem to be healing. But one day, as she goes to visit her patient, she finds the door to the child's *pontok*[15] barred. No one responds to her knocks, although she can hear the child moaning inside. That evening, Lydia, the child's grandmother, tells Eckenbrecher that she is no longer welcome; the child's mother is afraid of her medicine. Then, two days later, Lydia awakens Eckenbrecher in the middle of the night to beg her to come to the child, who is dying. An extended quotation relaying what happens when the author then returns to the *pontok* follows:

The door of the pontok was closed. I bent down and entered. There was a fire in the center, but a biting, smouldering smoke filled the pontok, making me tear so much that I couldn't see at first. Six or seven women squatted about. The little creature lay next to the fire; I immediately saw that it would not survive the night. I first tried to clear the smoke by holding the door open. Then an ancient, totally naked, hideous woman sprang at me, stretching her leathery hands toward me and screeching curses at me. Neck, breasts, arms, legs, and hips were covered with strange amulets. I told her to be quiet; she could tell me what she wanted later, outside. Lydia stood before me wringing her hands: "Oh, dear God, Ma'am, be careful. You're insulting our greatest magician, the wise woman who has come from far away to heal the child in exchange for a cow." – "And could she do it?" – "No, she said another power was working against her, for which reason the child must die. That power is your practice." – "Then I'll leave." – "No, your practice is more powerful than hers; you must help." – "I can do no more. Before the moon stands above the Huk (corner) of the river, the child will be dead." The first thing I did was look after the fire. . . . I then lit the lamp I had brought and looked at the child. The skillfully wrapped gauze dressing was gone. In its place, the child had been smeared with rancid butter, cow dung and a kind of pounded root. . . . Nothing more could be done. . . . [Lydia] apologized: "Ma'am, they wouldn't listen to me; will the child die?" – "Yes, tonight. But give it a try anyway and wash the magic potion off." But the little creature only whimpered weakly;

why should I torment it further. I did what was in my power to make its dying easier, and before the moon sank, the child was dead. (Eckenbrecher, 96)

This story, in which science is ultimately stymied by superstition and the author's philanthropic labor is brought to nought, may in fact depict how the child died that night. But it is also possible that the author might have interrupted a ritual in which the shaman woman was performing last rites for a dying child, or even, in the most cynical reading, that she might have inadvertently administered a lethal dose of opium to a recovering child. There is simply no way to tell. Eckenbrecher could offer whatever story she chose, relying on the strictures of colonial society to ensure that the other witnesses to the event would remain every bit as mute as the child now in need of burial.

If, however, we leave the question of veracity aside and examine the anecdote as textual narrative, two patterns of desire emerge, working in opposition to one another. On the surface, the author usurps a position of masculine authority as she, armed with the bright caduceus of science, opens up and penetrates the dark and smoky *pontok* to displace feminized powers of superstition. It is significant that all of the players in this story are female, with the possible exception of the wounded child, who is awarded neither name nor gender in the course of the narration. The stage for the action, the *pontok*, is also feminine and womblike, round with a single opening. It at first appears as a foreign, mystified obstacle; the cite of unknown magical practices, it frustrates the author's desire to enter and disallows her wish to see the child within. When she later penetrates the enclosure, the interior space immediately establishes itself as both hostile and feminine; she is dimly aware of squatting women as smoke attacks her eyes. She struggles against her disgust and her blindness in this foreign space, violating the enclosure in an attempt to clear the smoke and thereby reestablish the mastery of her own look. But this only provokes another wave of resistance, as the old healing woman flies at her, screeching.

The narrator then enters into a contest with this shaman, staging the familiar colonial battle between "enlightened" science and "dark" superstition. As the two women occupy opposing positions in the narrative structure, the wild inscrutability of the old woman finds its negation in the rational discourse of European science, to which the author herself lays claim. If the naked, amulet-bedecked Herero woman who shrieks nonsensical curses epitomizes the hysteric, Eckenbrecher, by setting herself in opposition to this figure, frees herself from any such designation, thereby escaping the stigma attached universally to women at the turn of the century.

One might read this as an appropriation of the medical establishment's triumph over midwifery, but it is here a white woman who steps into the powerful masculine position of the speculum-wielding doctor. The colonial context is crucial in the staging of this fantasy, as Africa provides the mysterious spaces of female interiority that then become available for Eckenbrecher's specular penetration. Confident in the superiority of European conceptions of the body, Eckenbrecher casts her gaze as a man of science, securing that it will be she, and not those squatting naked women, who will deliver the child from the hostile womb.

The child will be stillborn in any case, of course; Eckenbrecher is no more able to save the patient's life than was her rival. This brings me to a second movement within the text, one that does not pit the author against the healing woman but develops an identification between the two. If the author cannot rely on the patient's ultimate recovery to demonstrate the superiority of a European technology of the body, then the contest between the two women can only be decided by their relative abilities to manipulate words and images — by playing one form of magic off against another. Eckenbrecher's triumph over her rival lies only in Lydia's confession of faith: "Your practice is more powerful," in itself nothing more than a magical incantation. She follows suit with a prophecy, delivered in a style that is noticeably incongruous with the rest of her narrative ("Before the moon stands above the Huk [corner] of the river, the child will be dead"). This sentence is emphasized by the fact that she does not simply paraphrase her own speech for the reader, but quotes herself directly. Yet these, her own words as she reproduces them, are already quoting someone else, imitating what she considers to be — or tries to pass off as — authentic native speech. She signals this by marking time according to the passage of the moon across the sky, rather than by reference to the movement of hands across the face of a clock, and leaves a marker of the linguistic barrier that separates her speech from theirs in the Dutch word "*Huk*" (corner), for which she must offer her readers a translation. This leads into a hall-of-mirrors game of mimetic regression, with Eckenbrecher quoting herself as she imitates native speech, which is to say, she imitates the Herero's imitation of her own speech, with a single mock-native word thrown in, actually a reproduction of African speech reproducing the voice of a different colonizer. Yet it is through the very multiplicity of mimetic mediations that the statement dialectically tries to appropriate the authenticity of a magical language. As Homi Bhabha suggests, "The desire to emerge as 'authentic' through mimicry — through a process of writing and repetition — is the final irony of partial representation."[16] Substantively, these words mark the point at which the author abandons all hope of saving the child's life. It is significant that she proceeds to care for the patient anyway, again according to a logic of mimetic magic. Just as the old woman had removed her bandages, so she now washes off the magic salve. Each woman simply negates the work of her predecessor. This completed, there is nothing left but to "make the child's death easier," with which act the narrator fulfills her own prophecy — and she makes a point of telling us that the child dies before the moon goes down. She thus proves herself to be the more powerful magician, usurping the identity of the shaman she has ejected from the *pontok*.

In this anecdote one sees a feminized version of two tropes that appear quite often in colonial texts written by men. In her role as representative of European medicine, Eckenbrecher personifies the civilizing mission, bringing the power of European knowledge to superstitious natives as she penetrates, opens up, and illuminates the mysterious spaces of African darkness. And in her role as healing woman, she discovers a feminized version of the quest for regeneration in the colonies. In more masculinist examples of colonial discourse, this quest generally pertains to the opportunity to prove soldierly courage in battle with rebellious natives.[17] Lieutenant Stohlmann, a German officer in the Herero war, provides a good example of such masculine rhetoric: "I was convinced over there that the German soldier, despite the long period of peace, hasn't lost his courage, and that the softening influence of modern civilization has not yet harmed the mass of our people. . . . it was worthwhile to show all of those people who lack faith in the army, who don't believe in its courage and put down its representatives, that our sword is still sharp."[18]

Colonial rejuvenation here means an opportunity to display the phallic potency of male military prowess. Eckenbrecher discovers a different, woman-specific regeneration in the irrational, magical power of the healing woman and the feminized space of the *pontok*, both of which she imagines to be available for her appropriation. The author has it both ways in this story, miming the phallic identity of the man of science while claiming as her own the authentic identity of the woman of magic.

The contradiction between these two fantasies is repressed, or displaced, perhaps, onto the dying child, whose body is caught and suspended between the two poles of Eckenbrecher's desire. There is a return of the repressed at the end of the story, however, as the child is to be buried: "The churchbells rang as shrilly as execution bells, and the little creature was delivered to the earth. Now the funeral procession appeared at my house: 'Ma'am, you cared for the child; you gave the coffin and the gravecloth; now give us coffee and sugar for the wake.' One can imagine that I often lost my patience with things like that" (Eckenbrecher, 96–97).

The shrillness of these church bells closes the anecdote on an ambiguous note, for whose execution does Eckenbrecher imagine is being tolled? A child for whom death came too soon? Or a medical quack whose ineptitude demands punishment? Do the bells chime an accusation, or do they ring in a threat of vengeance, auguring, perhaps, the coming rebellion of the Herero? In any case, they indicate that something in this story is not as it should be, and that the author's "loss of patience" might well be mixed with both guilt and fear — the price of her own conflicted narcissistic fantasy.

ADA CRAMER: "WHITE OR BLACK? YEARS OF SUFFERING AND APPRENTICESHIP OF A FARMER IN SOUTHWEST AFRICA IN THE LIGHT OF RACIAL HATRED"

The tone of Ada Cramer's memoirs[19] is very different from that of Eckenbrecher's, attributable in part to the fact that they were written in a later period in Southwest Africa's history, the time following the Herero and Nama uprisings. Although only five years lie between Ada Cramer's 1907 arrival in the country and Eckenbrecher's, a massive transformation in the political and social structures of the protectorate had taken place in that brief time. German colonists had responded to native resistance with a war policy aimed at total extermination, eventually abandoning this goal only out of concern that a needed source of labor might be completely annihilated. Genocidal war then gave way to a forced labor policy, in which many native Africans could not own property or cattle and were forced to live in internment camps. These camps provided a ready supply of labor to German settlers at a minimal price. Most workers on German farms were severely underfed, and physical abuse of workers was rampant. If a laborer were so malnourished or injured as to be unable to work, replacements were always readily available from the camps. Flogging was officially sanctioned as a means of "educating" workers, and police patrols were vigilant in returning runaways either to their employer's or to the labor camp.

Ada and Ludwig Cramer used this system to great advantage in procuring workers for their farm in the province of Gibeon. The author's husband apparently used the whip quite indiscriminately, ignoring laws that set a limit of twenty-five lashes a day and prohibited the flogging of women. A police patrol on a routine visit to the Cramers' farm found that both male and female workers were covered with festering wounds. Ludwig Cramer was eventually tried and convicted on eight counts of assault and battery (seven against women, one against a man). According to the testimony of farm workers, Cramer's floggings led to the deaths of two women, and his beatings of pregnant women twice resulted in miscarriage (Drechsler, 235).

The text I will examine here was written by Ada Cramer in defense of her husband, both to explain his actions and to protest the fact that he had ever been brought to trial. She justifies her husband's violence as a matter of self-defense, arguing that the workers on their farm were trying to poison the two of them, along with their livestock. She alleges that some of their workers had been in contact with the San ("Bushpeople" is the term she uses), from whom they had purchased poisoned arrows. She describes in detail how she and her husband suffered from a protracted, nearly fatal illness, only to learn from one of the workers in the following year that this was the result of such a poisoning. The arrows, they are told, were the property of July, a Herero man, who used them personally to shoot Ada Cramer. They learn this story from Maria, a reliable source indeed, no less than July's own wife (and one of the two women who would later die of infected wounds from Cramer's lashes). The description of the arrows is quoted in Maria's own voice. When she explains that a poisoned arrow had been shot into Ludwig Cramer's hand, he interrupts her:

Up to this point my husband had quietly let the woman talk. She explained everything in namaqua and the kafir Hiweib translated it into German. Now he interrupted her and said excitedly: "You're lying; do you think I'm stupid enough to believe such a story? If Pitt had shot me, I would have noticed it, no matter how small the arrow is." . . . Now Hiweib got involved. "Baas," he said, "you don't understand that. Just as I don't understand the business with the white doctor, you don't understand the poison business with the bushpeople. Bushmen's arrows are Satan's business. You get shot and you don't notice a thing." (Cramer, 113)

This testimony is crucial to Cramer's argument, for she justifies her husband's brutality as a defense against this magical poison. The credibility of this account is therefore extremely important, and she guarantees it with direct quotation, citing the voice of an authentic native informant and including a full description of the translation process. To further allay any doubts, she invokes the voice of Hiweib, a second authentic informant. The words marking his passage from the function of translator to that of corroborator ("Nun mischte sich Hiweib ins Mittel" − literally, "Now Hiweib mixed himself into the potion") metaphorically mime that magical process ascribed to the San − the mixing of poison. Hiweib's testimony will make her story more believable, the venomous hatred of her propaganda more effective.

Like Eckenbrecher, Cramer works on two levels here, simultaneously appropriating the magical potential of poison for her text while superficially condemning it. She is also working within the same binarism as Eckenbrecher, opposing European science ("the business with the white doctor") to African magic. But there the similarity ends. Eckenbrecher had appealed to the reader's common sense to cast the medicine woman's magic in a ridiculous light; everyone knows, of course, that cow dung and rancid butter will not heal burns. Cramer, in contrast, presents Africa as a world in which common sense holds no sway, portraying an exotic landscape in which arrows indeed can kill without the victim ever becoming aware of having been hit.

Moreover, while primitive magic is encoded as distinctively feminine in Eckenbrecher's text, it is men here who practice the magic of poison on both the author and her husband. The female workers on the farm also make use of poison, but only to kill livestock. This would not seem as serious a crime, yet Ada Cramer seems to hold a special fear of and contempt for these women. She explains her dislike for them according to a belief held among many settlers that Herero women, who had fought alongside the men in the recent war against the Germans, had tortured and killed wounded soldiers in battle. Ada Cramer claims that some of these "war women" are working on their farm: "They were the kind of women one could imagine turning into hyenas in war. Better to die than to fall into those hands!" (Cramer, 89). This imagined past returns to haunt her as she and her husband prepare to search Maria and Konturu, two Herero women, for poisoned arrows:

I was dreadfully afraid; I wouldn't put anything past the malice of these women and swore to my husband that I would tie the women's hands behind their backs for the investigation. I would not even allow them to free their hands to take their blouses off; the horrible anguish of the past flashed before my eyes as vividly as if in the present. Never again would we allow something like that to happen! I got a pair of scissors and cut through Konturu's blouse. The excitement overpowered my husband; he stood next to me, trembling all over, and was unable to search the woman for the poison. Since I did not want to completely undress Konturu, I felt her and discovered three fat purses full of silver hidden under her skirt. (Cramer, 115–16)

The author participates in the staging of a sadistic fantasy here as she cuts through Konturu's blouse to expose the breast to her husband's uncontrollably excited gaze, then gropes under Konturu's skirt. The fatal poisoned arrows she hopes to find there invoke the "rifle-woman" who appears repeatedly, according to Klaus Theweleit, in the fantasies of many male protofascists, a figure whose skirt conceals a deadly knife or gun.[20] In Theweleit's sources, this phallic woman initially inspires terror, but this quickly gives way to fantasies of reducing the threatening woman's body to a bloody mass. Cramer's text repeats this pattern. After the inconclusive search, the author watches as her husband flogs the women. The next day, when three more calves show signs of poisoning, she fantasizes about killing the Herero women herself: "If I were a man, I would have shot all the women down. I had stood trembling and afraid as my husband, with the whip in his hand, had demanded the poison from the women; now I wanted to rip it from their criminal hands with superhuman strength. Those whom my husband had beaten were no longer human; I no longer felt pity" (Cramer, 119). Here the narrator's faith is restored; she may not have been able to find those arrows under the women's skirts, but they were there all along, and she now dreams of castration, tearing the things away "with superhuman strength." This is contingent, however, on occupying a masculine position herself ("If I were a man . . ."). Having granted the Herero women a deadly phallus, she is free to fantasize about adopting one herself, transforming herself into a superman who could castrate Herero women and shoot them down.

Theweleit's "male fantasies" may not be so exclusively male, after all. When men fall under her husband's whip, a similar blurring of gender identity occurs in Cramer's text. July, for example, who stands accused of having shot the author in the back with a poisoned arrow, appears repeatedly in the narrative, always mentioned by name and with the masculine pronoun – until the time comes when he is to be flogged: "He [Ludwig Cramer] pulled the beast *[die Bestie]* from her cage and demanded the poison from her, and hit the beast with a riding whip when she would not give over the poison" (Cramer, 111–12). If Cramer were to describe July as "*das Tier*" (the animal) in this passage, she could effectively *neuter* him with the pronoun "*es.*" She goes a step further, however, with "*die Bestie,*" invoking Biblical images of the Antichrist while granting July a specifically *feminine* gender. I will return to this point shortly. The flogging was quite severe, and in the following days the narrator grew concerned for July's recovery:

On Monday morning I went to my husband and asked him if I could cool July's wounds with lead water. My husband . . . looked at me with astonishment and was surprised that I would feel compassion for a poisoner like that. Man and woman are different from one another and must act according to their natures. One shouldn't say that I did the right thing; it would be sad if the feminized sensitivities of so many men should progress even further. (Cramer, 113–14)

This passage is thoroughly inconsistent, for if the author acted as she had to according to her nature as a woman and yet did what her readers should determine to be the wrong thing, in order to halt the progression of men's "feminized sensitivities," then she is holding herself to an ethical standard that is not appropriate to her own sex. Her gender seems to slide back and forth from one sentence to the next.

July's gender is every bit as slippery as Ada Cramer's own. When he is later hospitalized, his wounds are photographed as evidence to be used in the trial. Ada Cramer has this to say about the photos: "I haven't seen the pictures, but I can imagine how effectively the rosy flesh might contrast against the black skin on a photograph" (Cramer, 122). The adverb is notably ambiguous, leaving unclear whether the "effect" this image inspires is one of revulsion or of pleasure. Rosy flesh and black skin were also of great interest to Felix Bryk, a German anthropologist who traveled through western Africa in the 1920s. In a study that, under the guise of anthropological research, recounts his sexual exploits in Africa, Bryk claims that white men will find black women to be very interesting sex partners because of the "marked relief" of pink vaginas as they stand out against black skin.[21] This same chromatic contrast, as it appears in conjunction with a fantasized photographic image, aestheticizes the wound as it vaginalizes the man who carries it.

Not even the author's fourteen-year-old daughter seems able to keep hold of her gender in this narrative, where everything is up for grabs. When mother and daughter leave the farm to drive into town after Ludwig Cramer's arrest, the girl dons men's clothing before taking the reins.

In the hardest days, God let a staff and a support grow up for me in my child. I wasn't able to help her. . . . With manly prudence the wagon was packed. . . . The sun sank behind threatening, black storm clouds as we boarded the open horsecart. Two women, all alone through night and storm. My daughter sat next to me in man's clothing; a broad-rimmed army hat covered her thick braids. With a strong will she took the reins in her hands and we rode off into the breaking night. (126)

With her husband absent, Cramer discovers a desired phallic "staff" in her daughter, relieved to find such "manly prudence" in her offspring at a time when she feels unequal to the challenges facing her. Daughter and mother masquerade as man and wife as they ride into town, allowing the daughter to usurp her father's position in the household, opening up a space for incestuous desire between the two women.

It is only the backdrop of a menacing, ongoing racial war that allows Ada Cramer the justifying framework in which to situate such polymorphously transgressive fantasies. Sadism, homocroticism, and incest all appear insignificant in a world where whiteness must hold its own against a blackness that threatens to engulf the author and her family. Here, the gathering storm into which the mother-daughter couple rides signifies this danger, constituting the rationale for their incestuous disguise. As they pass a distant light, this menacing darkness takes on metaphysical dimensions: "Far in the distance, a light shone from the deepest darkness. How miserable I seemed to myself as we drove past the light. All lights had been extinguished in my life's path . . . . Dark powers had come and tried to put out the flame of our hearth fire which we had kept holy for almost a whole generation. Tears rolled down over my face; . . . I belonged to those who had been cast out from the light" (Cramer, 127).

As the Cramer family is broken apart, these ominous "dark powers," no longer limited to the dark bodies of their workers, expand to include the police officials and the colonial legal system – anything, in fact, which the author views as antagonistic to her family. With the guilty verdict, the enveloping blackness finally closes over their heads, only to open up again in a vision of redemption as the Cramers find support and solidarity among the community of German settlers:

The judgment was spoken to throw us into night and despair, but instead of casting us in chains, it burst our shackles. The hard-working people of Windhuk placed themselves like a protective wall in front of my husband; unknown people came up and shook his hand; my husband had never been greeted with such respect as on the day of this case. . . . The human judge had condemned us; the hard-working people had acquitted us. The voice of the people is God's voice! (Cramer, 141)

Indeed, public pressure was probably the determining factor in an appellate court's later decision to commute Ludwig Cramer's original sentence from one year and nine months to only four months with a fine. The Cramer case brought people in the settler community together, uniting them, on the one hand, against administrative authorities from Berlin, whom they believed to be fundamentally ignorant of the realities of colonial life and lacking in "racial awareness," and, on the other, against the native population. The judge and prosecuting attorney in the case repeatedly pathologized the Cramers, calling their references to the workers' poison an "idée fixe." The colonists who rallied to their cause, in contrast, may well have taken the stories of poison very seriously, which is not to say that they were necessarily *convinced* by the Cramers' account. As Peter Horn notes, "Statements of colonial ideology aren't believed because they are 'logical' or because they can be proven 'empirically'; they are believed because they make domination possible."[22]

But this only defers the question – if there is a need for an ideology that justifies such brutality, what purpose does the brutality itself serve? An economic response will not suffice here; it is obviously counterproductive to try to extract labor from a worker by beating that worker to death. In *Shamanism, Colonialism, and the Wild Man*, Michael Taussig addresses a similar issue as it relates to the rubber boom of the Putumayo region in Colombia around the turn of the century. The rubber companies employed such ruthless tactics in attempting to procure Indian labor to harvest rubber from the Putumayo jungles that their efforts showed every sign of ending in total genocide, exterminating the very workers on whose labor they depended. The rubber companies generally legitimated the persecution by claiming that the victims were cannibals. "Perhaps," Taussig speculates,

it was neither the political economy of rubber nor that of labor that was paramount here in the horrific "excesses" of the rubber boom. Perhaps, as in the manner strenuously theorized by Michel Foucault in his work on discipline, what was paramount here was the inscription of a mythology in the Indian body, an engraving of civilization locked in struggle with wildness whose model was taken from the colonist's fantasies about Indian cannibalism. "In the 'excesses' of torture," Foucault gnomically writes, "a whole economy of power is invested." There is no excess.[23]

Colonial fantasies of wildness are certainly operative in Cramer's text, too; if we substitute "African" for "Indian" and "poison" for "cannibalism," this passage applies to her writing equally well.

The Foucauldian economy of power, which Taussig employs to make sense of the financially nonsensical practices of the rubber companies, is relevant not only to what happened on the Cramer farm but also to the entire political economy of Southwest African farms at the time. While the Cramer case may present a relatively extreme example, it was by no means unique. There were a number of similar trials of settlers from 1910 to 1912, and the contemporaneous political discourse surrounding these cases indicates that such practices were so widespread that only a very small fraction of actual incidents ever came to trial.[24] Physical abuse of Africans was an accepted practice, the norm rather than the exception. If, on the surface of it, Ada Cramer's text appears to document one woman's — or perhaps one family's — descent into paranoia and sadism, this larger historical context calls for a different reading. She is not simply articulating the paranoia of a single pathological individual, but is writing a text that must be seen as a symptom, the kind of narrative that both constitutes and is constituted by a political system of terror.

CLARA BROCKMANN: "THE GERMAN WOMAN IN SOUTHWEST AFRICA: A CONTRIBUTION TO THE WOMEN'S QUESTION IN THE COLONIES" AND "LETTERS OF A GERMAN GIRL FROM SOUTHWEST AFRICA"

Unlike Margarethe von Eckenbrecher and Ada Cramer, Clara Brockmann considered herself a writer; she is, in fact, one of the few women who traveled to Southwest Africa with the explicit intention of publishing

an account of her experiences there.[25] She was the official colonial representative of the Women's Auxiliary to the German Colonial Society and
contributed numerous articles to its publication. Also in contrast to the
other two writers, she spent her time in the cities, primarily Windhuk,
where she held a job as a civil servant, occupying a small estate on the
outskirts of town.

In the introductory comments to her *Briefe eines deutschen Maedchens
aus Suedwest* (Letters of a German Girl from the Southwest; hereafter
LGGS), she articulates her political motivations for this project:[26]

Many books about Germany's colonies have gone out into the world in recent
years. . . . Through these, this piece of Germany in the "dark continent," which
was won with much noble blood, has been brought closer to home. And yet the
real, day-to-day life, the customs and habits over there, have remained unknown to
most circles at home. . . . [It is my desire] that these simple sketches will serve as
instructive lectures to the general populace and will find a home in the German
house, in the German family. For this is the nourishing ground of all love for the
fatherland, without which an interest in our possessions overseas isn't possible;
here nationalism, which is synonymous with love for our colonies, takes root and
ripens. (LGGS 5, 7; Brockmann's italics)

By highlighting her own gender in the very title of the text, she
implicitly draws attention to a gendered division of labor in colonial
writing; if the previous accounts that have brought the political, economic, and military aspects of the German presence in Southwest Africa
to the domestic audience have been written mostly by men, it is a "German girl" who will write about daily life in the colonies. Yet this is far
from an apology, for the "day-to-day" is also "the real" in her description.
She is not trying to tempt other women to follow her example in seeking
adventure on distant shores, but dedicates her text to the domestic sphere,
where national identity is reproduced. This nicely exemplifies the ironic
function that Roger Chickering attributes to the bourgeois women's colonial movement, which "reinvigorated the ideology of domesticity by ex-
porting it."[27]

While Eckenbrecher and Cramer emphasize the hardship of life in the
colonies, Brockmann attempts to portray Southwest Africa as very much
like home. Her location in the cities, along with her upper-class status,
facilitate this depiction. While visiting Swakopmund she writes,

We live here in the larger towns of the colony just like in Germany, and whoever
doubts this assertion should listen to the events of my day. I took a nice ride along

the coast at seven in the morning, then bathed in one of the small bays of the glittering blue sea, far from any human being, breakfasted, and read the most recent mail from Germany. For lunch, a black Herero woman brought me roast beef with horseradish sauce, plum-compot, chocolate pudding and coffee with cake. . . . At four o'clock I went to a singing audition for a concert, and later to my tailor, who is working hard to make me a real Queen Luise dress. (LGGS 202)

The colonial city combines all the comforts of home with a sense of unlimited mobility; it is a place where one need not forego chocolate pudding to enjoy uninhibited rides through a limitless wilderness. The serenity of the coastline and the sparkling seclusion of the bay in which she bathes contrasts starkly to the threatening landscapes portrayed by Eckenbrecher and Cramer. (Eckenbrecher, for example, anthropomorphizes all of Southwest Africa and assigns a hostile intent to it: "All of Southwest Africa has something mean and stubborn about it. It's as if nature itself were resisting the civilization which we whites are forcing on it" (Eckenbrecher, 73).

Brockmann's description of her home life is also marked by a sense of security that is lacking in the other women's texts. This manifests in a playful tone, as in descriptions of interactions with the women she hires to do household chores for her: "I had all of the different nations in my employment. The first black girl I got for my personal service was Susanne. Her name was actually Omangerere, but I, following an aesthetic feeling, gave her the chambermaid's name Susanne, although it certainly made a comic impression. She was a prisoner of war" (LGGS 102). The tangential comment that Omangerere is a prisoner of war bears reference to the fact that Brockmann's domestic servants are made available by the same forced labor system that procured workers for the Cramers' farm. The preconditions of Omangerere's employment do not appear in the text, of course, having been bracketed out, along with her Herero name, for the sake of an "aesthetic feeling." Despite her thorough satisfaction with Omangerere's service, Brockmann fires her in order to see how well representatives of other ethnic groups perform in the same function — "for the sake of science," she says. She soon hires a Bergdamara woman to take Omangerere's place:

The next morning a young Kafir woman named Emma appeared at my house. I immediately taught her that from now on she was a Susanne. . . . Even in the first days I noticed the difference in cleanliness between Hereros and Kafirs. Susanne # 1 had spoiled me in this regard; her replacement was a little piglet. Susanne 2 was also quickly replaced with a third. She told me one day that her family had grown, and brought me her so-called sister. . . . I took Elli into my service. I kept her name just for fun, because it fit so little to her burly physique that it always put me in a good mood. (LGGS 103)

And so on. Elli leaves when the author slaps her in the face for keeping her own comb on the same tray as her mistress's toiletries, while her replacement, a twelve-year-old girl, is fired when the white men of Windhuk begin to show sexual interest in her as she reaches puberty, thereby corrupting her — at least in Brockmann's view. In each instance, the maid is taken as a representative of her ethnic group, allowing the author to judge the groups' relative merits as domestic workers. Yet there is a fundamental lack of seriousness about this project, which distinguishes it from similar accounts written by German men comparing, for example, the relative abilities of Herero and Nama workers in the arts of animal husbandry.[28] By relating how she renamed her household workers "Susanne 1" and "Susanne 2," while allowing "Elli" to keep her name because she found it humorous, she underscores the fact that the hiring and firing of these women serves less as a source of information on how to run a colonial household than as a source of her own amusement. When she tires of the topic, she simply dismisses the differences among Herero, Bergdamara, and Nama and moves on: "What more should I say of the natives? I had the same experience with Hottentots, Hereros, Kafirs: on the one hand, an enthusiasm for learning, a hunger for knowledge, dexterity, even devotedness to a certain degree — on the other hand, deceptiveness, faithlessness, gluttony, indolence" (LGGS 111). The contradiction between this statement and that quoted above is hardly of note in this mock ethnography. Difference or sameness — the question is of no more interest to Brockmann than are the names of the individual women who pass through her household. The native people of Southwest Africa melt into an indistinguishable mass, any one of whom can be chosen out at random, given a name for a period of time, and then discarded back into the mass when the author grows bored or irritable.

And yet it is perhaps because there is so little at stake for Brockmann in her relations to the Africans she encounters in Southwest Africa that her views on native issues are generally more liberal than those of her contemporaries. At times she expresses doubt about the beneficial nature of German colonial policy, for example, wondering if the Africans might have been better off if the Europeans had simply left them alone. Such thoughts come to her when, while stopping at a water hole on a trip, she watches a group of Ovambo people passing by and cannot resist the temptation to move in for a closer look:

Driven by curiosity I approach them. . . . Never in my life have I been examined more critically and with more astonishment and curiosity. Many of them had probably never seen a white woman before. They are beautiful, symmetrically built figures, not exactly overburdened with clothing — if there's anything at all it's just half a sack. They carry all their worldly goods — usually just food in bundles — tied to long sticks over their shoulders. A happy people — or should one take pity on them because they're so poor and simple? We of course proudly beat our own chests when we think of how we've brought them civilization. Civilization? Yes — an increase in their needs. (LGGS 138–39)

Such musings stand out in the field of German colonial writing from Southwest Africa. Most debates at the time centered on how Europeans could best motivate Africans to work for them, and how best to insure that no indigenous social structures would threaten German hegemony in the region. Those who expressed any interest in the well-being of the Africans generally assumed that indolence had corrupted the souls of the Africans and threatened their very survival as a race.[29] For those who held redemption to be possible (and there were many who did not), there was a general consensus that this could only be achieved if Europeans taught Africans the superiority of hard work and a higher standard of living over less work in a life of poverty. Brockmann's speculations represent an unusual break with the dominant view.

Yet if one looks more closely at how this incident is framed — how Brockmann's own inquisitive stare is met by an equal curiosity on the part of the Ovambo, many of whom she imagines "might never have seen a white woman before" (despite the fact that they address her in Dutch), one finds the pleasure of an encounter that the author can construct as an incident of first contact. Moreover, her emphasis on *aesthetic* elements in this description of the Ovambo as "beautiful, symmetrically built figures" speaks to an interest in preserving the primitive status of these people less for the sake of their own well-being than for the beauty they add as a mobile element within the panorama she enjoys. She is a tourist passing through an enchanting, exotic landscape, one that would certainly lose a major part of its appeal if these splendid, half-naked figures were not also traveling through it.

Romanticism figures prominently in Brockmann's texts, not only in her description of the people and the scenery of Southwest Africa but also in her descriptions of her personal relationships. In *Die deutsche Frau in Suedwestafrika* (The German Woman in Southwest Africa; hereafter GWSA),[30] she describes a very pleasant evening, for example, spent with a female friend who, imagining a ravine near the author's home outside of Windhuk to be "highly romantic" by night, had insisted on visiting it on the next full moon. The two women make their plans accordingly and set out on their expedition, but before they can even get out of Brockmann's yard they are overcome by gales of laughter:

We . . . armed ourselves with steaks, red wine, and cognac bonbons. Then we took off, but just a few steps beyond the horsestall we were overwhelmed by the comical side of the situation and laughed so hard we couldn't go on, so we set our brimming plates down on the ground. When we came to our senses, we noticed that the two dogs that were accompanying us had eaten the steaks, which sent us into new hysterics. (GWSA 44)

The cause of this giddy hilarity remains unexplained, but it has a tone of pleasurable abandon to it — the giggling of two schoolgirls who are not yet burdened with the responsibilities of the adult world, or the pleasant tension of erotic attraction. When they reach the ravine, this laughter eventually gives way to a mood of sentimentalism:

When we got to the ravine we climbed over the huge, wild cliff boulders and looked for a spot fairly high up where we could sit down comfortably and eat our cognac bonbons — our melted dinner. When they had been eaten, a sentimental mood gradually came over us. We became susceptible to the wonderful magic of the African moonlight; . . . it ruled over the entire scene. . . . All around, the dreamy silence of the night. A fairy-tale magic spins itself around us. We look into the moon and feel that it's the only thing that unites our feelings with those of our loved ones in Germany; it is the meeting place of our thoughts. . . . We remain sitting next to each other for a long time, marveling at strange human destinies. (GWSA 44)

This is romanticism in its purest form, as the exotic African night overwhelms them, mystically joining them to those in Germany — and, by extension, to each other. The tropes are familiar, even clichéd; from the flirtatious laughter to the unifying magic of moonlight, the description holds to the conventions of the bourgeois romance. But what is the significance of the fact that this experience is shared between two women? Might the "strange human fates" that the two women ponder together long into the night be their own?

Lesboeroticism is never explicitly thematized in Brockmann's text. In fact, in the introduction to "A German Woman in Southwest Africa," she sets the political goals of her text within an overtly heterosexual framework. German women should come to Southwest Africa for four reasons, she argues: (1) to prevent miscegenation; (2) to marry and help their husbands run successful farms and businesses; (3) to establish German homes in Southwest Africa, making the new country more "homelike"; and (4) to educate the next generation, maintaining their connection with German culture (GWSA 26). Her message to women is clear: marry, have children, and keep a good German home. But this imperative could not be further removed from her own experiences in Southwest Africa. German men are mentioned so infrequently in both of her texts that their very presence in the colony seems to have been almost deliberately excised. Moreover, there are times when she must remind herself not to be overly enthusiastic in celebrating the pleasures of unmarried life: "Sundays are generally spent on pleasant riding excursions, or on trips in the eight-mule wagon, and a picnic in the African wild has tremendous charm. In such pursuits, the life of a young girl who has decided on living independently in the Southwest flows by. But I by no means want these descriptions to serve as propaganda to convince single ladies to go to the Southwest" (GWSA 47). The final sentence reads as an afterthought, for the author, after all, is such a single woman who has set out for Southwest Africa alone, and she seems to be in no hurry to find a husband there.

Most of Brockmann's female friends in the colony seem to have no more interest in marriage than she. Two such women have purchased a farm together, for example; she mentions them repeatedly in both of her works, and always with a tone of great admiration. Her own attraction for one of them is hardly disguised when she first introduces her to the reader: "I met her at a ball at the governor's house, and had remembered her as a tender, shy creature in a white muslin dress. How surprised I was later when someone told me that he had met her in short riding pants and a floppy-brimmed hat, smoking tobacco from a short pipe as she was taking her cattle from one station to another" (GWSA 38).

Conventions of bourgeois love again predominate when Brockmann describes how the two women met: "After a while she met her better half, her soulmate. That was a lady, about the same age as she, who had come to Africa with the same plan. . . . They were also compatible in their favorite idea: the desire to own a farm. I can see a time not far off when both of them, joined together in peace, will live on their own common ground and property" (GWSA 40). There is nothing to indicate that Brockmann finds anything unusual in a woman discovering her "better half" in another woman. If there is any reference to the couple's break with convention, it is associated with their nonconformity to gender norms rather than with resistance to a social order founded on what Adrienne Rich terms "compulsory heterosexuality."[31] The woman Brockmann had first befriended, for example, at one point confides in the author, "I know that my relatives think of me as being a little different. If I write home asking for knick-knacks, clothes and expensive soap, I'd get it all, but if I ask for spades, scales and machines, I meet with resistance and preconceived notions" (GWSA 40). If her relatives might also think it a bit strange that she is running the farm with another woman rather than a man, neither she nor the author makes reference to the fact. Brockmann follows this comment with a simple argument that some settler women are more capable farmers than many German men, and that the colonial administration should make land available to such women on the basis of their abilities. The prejudice both women perceive and against which they protest is thus related only to gender, while the question of sexual preference remains unarticulated.

In the introduction to *Nationalisms and Sexualities*, the editors write, "Certain sexual identities and practices are less represented and representable in nationalism. Until recently, for example, lesbianism has been far less visible than male homosexuality in Euro-American civic discourses."[32] It may be that the rhetoric of nationalism — with its focus on the (often eroticized) fraternal bonds between men and on allegories of women that reduce femaleness to motherhood — renders the love between women invisible. If so, Brockmann may be using nationalist discourse as a camouflage that renders the lesboeroticism of her text invisible. The patriotic call for women to come to Southwest Africa to marry and raise children serves in her text as a foil for a description of the colony as a place where women can actually make it on their own, or even, if they choose, with other women.

CONCLUSION

The three examples discussed here demonstrate the difficulty in arriving at any monolithic depiction of women's involvement in the colonial campaign. Yes, the women who participated in the colonial campaign *did* have an agenda of their own — both erotic and otherwise — or rather, they had many different agendas, as many, perhaps, as there were women colonists. Moreover, while colonial women obviously occupied a different position within colonial society than men, I would disagree with Pratt's contention that there was a "specifically female relationship to North European expansionism" (Pratt, 170). The importance of gender in determining the writers' position within colonial society is evident in each of the works examined here; it is because she is a woman that Margarethe von Eckenbrecher stays home to care for the sick while her husband attends to farm business, and it is likewise because of her gender that Ada Cramer is not charged with beating her workers, while her husband goes to jail. The frivolousness of Brockmann's description of the various "Susannes" who work for her is also connected to her gender; she does not take women's domestic labor seriously enough to merit a more earnest discussion, nor does she expect her readers to be offended.

But these differences in the specific position of the writers as women within colonial society do not indicate a more deep-seated internal difference in their relationship to expansionism. There are certainly elements of the "sovereign-of-all-I-see" genre in Brockmann's description of her early morning ride along the shore to the bay that lies waiting to offer her a private swim, or in her romanticized portrayal of the beautiful bodies of the traveling Ovambo. In a more insidious form, the "sovereign-of-all-I-see" approach also finds its way into Eckenbrecher's text, as she insistently exposes the interior of the *pontok* to her own prying view. Colonial women may at times have resisted the temptation to see with "imperial eyes," but to argue that women *always* did so, that such resistance constitutes a natural (even if culturally determined) female response to colonialism, is to essentialize gender.

There are other tropes common to male colonial texts that are exemplified in these three women's writings, as well. Eckenbrecher, in her attempt to bring science to the savages, is performing the familiar role of emissary of the "civilizing mission." But in taking on this role *as a woman*, she is also mimicking the role of the masculine doctor and exercising a male prerogative, thereby destabilizing European gender roles. Colonial privilege thus allows for a gender empowerment, for she can only adopt the role of masculine doctor by assuming that her untrained practice of medicine will be more beneficial to her patients than their own ways of healing.

Ada Cramer, in contrast, adopts a position closer to Conrad's Kurtz in *Heart of Darkness*. She "goes native," indulging in numerous constellations of transgressive desire, allowable only because they exist in response, or so she imagines, to the savagery around her. Her title, translated as "White or Black? Years of Suffering and Apprenticeship in the Light of Racial Hatred," does not bear reference to her own hatred of Africans, but rather to theirs of her. There are no limits to what is allowed in defending herself against the contempt and malice she imputes to them — anything goes.

Clara Brockmann, in yet a different vein, writes of the colonies as a site of romance and adventure, a place where one can get away from it all. Moreover, she presents colonial society as a utopian place, offering a freedom unavailable in Germany. Her "Letters of a German Girl from Southwest Africa," after all, was published in 1910, the year that also saw an attempt to expand paragraph 175 of the German Penal Code, which had previously prohibited homosexuality between men, in order to criminalize sexual acts between women as well.[33] The Southwest Africa of Brockmann's text promises a place of freedom where women can pursue whatever romantic interests they wish — but without needing to make an overt political statement about it.

What do white women want? Many things — a civilizing mission, a quest for rejuvenation, to go native, flight from the fast pace of modern life to a romanticized primitive landscape, sexual freedom. These are some of the most popular themes of colonial discourse as it is associated with some of the more familiar, masculine personages who occupy the history of empire. The tropes are inflected differently here by the gendered position of the authors, but they remain easily recognizable.

Within this familiar field, however, there are tremendous differences in the positions taken by each woman. Why does Eckenbrecher adopt the rhetoric of the civilizing mission while Cramer goes native and Brockmann seeks a romantic adventure? While personal, subjective differences among the three writers are not to be dismissed, there are also significant aspects to the different specific historical positions each woman occupies within colonial society that contribute to the variance among their approaches. In the pre-Herero war period, when Eckenbrecher was living in Ogombahe, interactions between the settlers and the Africans functioned according to a logic of trade. The Germans offered European commodities in exchange for cattle and land, and as an enticement to work for wages on German farms. No matter how unfair the trade practices were, settler discourse at the time is dominated by the notion that this trade was of benefit to the natives, whose lives would be improved by their access to the material goods of European civilization. Eckenbrecher's anecdote takes its place within this discourse, as the impotence of the old woman's magic demonstrates the Africans' need for Western medicine – and, by extension, for the other European goods that the settlers traded.

Cramer's narrative responds to different elements within German colonial discourse. Following the Herero and Nama uprisings, the fiction that the Europeans brought good things to the natives was no longer operative, once African cattle and land had been appropriated and native labor was secured by means of a system of blatant physical coercion. The poisoned arrows of Cramer's narrative, with their rarefied origins in the impenetrably wild, hidden world of the San and their magical ability to kill while remaining invisible, serve an important function within this discursive context. These arrows instantiate the fiction of ongoing, inscrutable native resistance, thus justifying the systematic use of terror with which many settlers maintained the pass law system.

Brockmann, despite the fact that she and Cramer are writing about the same period in the history of Southwest Africa, does not live on the frontier, but occupies the space of the colonial urban center. She thus inhabits a colonial setting that has been thoroughly pacified, for which reason her interactions with natives are not charged in the same way that those of Eckenbrecher or Cramer are. African bodies are not the primary focus of her attention; they are reducible to aestheticized elements within a landscape, or items of amusement within her home. They function as mobile props in a romantic, exotic theater in which the roles of the main characters have been reserved for German women.

In conclusion, it is clear in each of these texts that the author's gender has left its mark on the text. Yet one would be hard put to generalize even from these three limited examples to arrive at any larger notion of how white women's desire functioned within the colonial setting. There are no absolute, predictable predicates that could be ascribed to women's colonial writing as a whole, or that might distinguish it from men's colonial writing. Yes, gender does make a difference, but it makes a *different* difference in each particular instance, contingent on the historical specificity of the author's subject position and on the colonial structure at the time and place of her writing.

NOTES

I would like to thank all of those whose comments on earlier versions of this paper greatly strengthened it, including Leslie Adelson, Russell Berman, Erin Carlsten, Miranda Joseph, Leerom Medovoi, Andrew Parker, Benjamin Robinson, Ruth Starkman, and Heather Zwicker, and the editors of *Genders*.

1. Roger Chickering discusses the paradoxical nature of this group's political activity. The women who participated in this campaign did not consider themselves "feminists" in any sense of the word, generally holding the rhetoric of women's rights to be fundamentally at odds with the patriotism they espoused. Nevertheless, they took advantage of this campaign in order to win considerable political power for themselves. See Roger Chickering's article on the irony of this empowerment: "Casting Their Gaze More Broadly: Women's Patriotic Activism in Imperial Germany," *Past and Present* 118 (February 1988): 156–85.
2. Mary Louise Pratt, *Imperial Eyes: Travel Writing and Transculturation* (London and New York: Routledge, 1992), 170. Further references to this work will be included parenthetically in the text.
3. James McAuley, "My New Guinea," in *The Grammar of the Real: Selected Prose, 1959–1974* (Melbourne: Oxford University Press, 1975), 171–72.
4. Ronald Hyam, *Empire and Sexuality: The British Experience* (Manchester: Manchester University Press, 1990), 175.
5. Ronald Hyam is only the most recent advocate of this view. Ann Laura Stoler offers a detailed discussion of various other proponents in an excellent refutation of the argument: "Rethinking Colonial Categories: European Communities and the Boundaries of Rule," in *Comparative Studies in Society and History* (Madison: University of Wisconsin Press, 1989), 135–59. Further references to this work will be included parenthetically in the text.
6. See, for example, Susan L. Blake, "A Woman's Trek: What Difference Does Gender Make?" *Women's Studies International Forum* 13, no. 4 (1990); Helen Callaway, *Gender, Culture, and Empire: European Women in Colonial Nigeria* (London: Macmillan, 1987); Claudia Knapman, *White Women in Fiji, 1835–1930: The Ruin of Empire?* (Sydney: Allen and Unwin, 1986); Mary Ann Lind, "The Compassionate Memsahibs," *Contributions in Women's Studies* 90 (1988);

and Nupur Chaudhuri and Margaret Strobel, ed., *Western Women and Imperialism: Complicity and Resistance* (Bloomington and Indianapolis: Indiana University Press, 1992).

7. Martha Mamozai, *Schwarze Frau, weisse Herrin: Frauenleben in den deutschen Kolonien* (Black Woman, White Mistress: Women's Lives in the German Colonies) (Reinbek: Rowohlt, 1982); and *Komplizinnen* (Women Accomplices) (Reinbek: Rowohlt, 1990).

8. Jenny Sharpe, *Allegories of Empire: The Figure of Woman in the Colonial Text* (Minneapolis and London: University of Minnesota Press, 1993), 11.

9. In these general discussions of women's memoirs from the German colony of Southwest Africa, I am thinking not only of the texts I will be analyzing here but also of Margarethe von Eckenbrecher, Helene v. Falkenhausen, Stabsarzt Dr. Kuhn, and Oberleutnant Stuhlmann, *Deutsch-Suedwestafrika: Kriegs- und Friedensbilder* (German Southwest Africa: Images of War and Peace) (Reinbek: Berlin, Leipzig, 1907); Helene v. Falkenhausen, *Ansiedlerschicksale: Elf Jahre in Deutsch-Suedwestafrika, 1893–1904* (Settler Fates: Eleven Years in German Southwest Africa, 1893–1904) (Berlin: Reimer, 1906); Else Frobenius, *Dreissig Jahre koloniale Frauenarbeit* (Thirty Years of Colonial Women's Work) (Berlin: Reichskolonialbund, Department 4, 1936); Lydia Hoepker, *Um Scholle und Leben: Schicksale einer deutschen Farmerin in Suedwest-Afrika* (About Clods and Life: The Fates of a German Woman Farmer in Southwest Africa) (Minden: Köhler, 1927); Hedwig Irle, *Wie ich die Herero Lieben lernte* (How I Learned to Love the Herero) (Guetersloh: Bertelsmann, 1909), Maria Karo, *Wo sonst der Fuss des Kriegers trat: Farmerleben in Suedwest nach dem Kriege.* (Where Else the Soldier's Foot Trod: The Farmer's Life in Southwest after the War) (Berlin, 1911); Else Sonnenberg, *Wie es am Waterberg zuging: Ein Beitrag zur Geschichte des Hereroaufstandes* (What Happened on Waterberg: A Contribution to the History of the Herero Uprising) (Berlin: Suesseroth, 1905); Aenne Trey, *Tausend Kilometer im Ochsenwagen durch Suedwestafrika* (A Thousand Kilometers through Southwest Africa in an Ox Wagon) (Barmen, 1926); and *Unsere Aya* (Our Aya) (Barmen, 1926).

10. I am referring here to such historical accounts as Helmut Bley, *South-West Africa under German Rule: 1894–1914*, trans. Hugh Ridley (Evanston, Ill.: Northwestern University Press, 1968); Horst Drechsler, *Let Us Die Fighting: The Struggle of the Herero and Nama against German Imperialism (1884–1915)*, trans. Bernd Zöllner (London: Zed, 1980); Peter Duignan and L. H. Gann, *South West Africa — Namibia* (New York: American African Affairs Association, 1978) and *The Rulers of German Africa, 1884–1914* (Stanford: Stanford University Press, 1977); Horst Gruender, *Geschichte der deutschen Kolonien* (History of the German Colonies) (Paderborn: Schoning, 1985); Woodruff Smith, *The German Colonial Empire* (Chapel Hill: University of North Carolina Press, 1978); Uwe Timm, *Deutsche Kolonien* (German Colonies) (Munich: Verlag Autoren Edition, 1981); and Wilfried Westphal, *Geschichte der deutschen Kolonien* (History of the German Colonies) (Munich: Bertelsmann,

1984). Further references to the works of Bley and Drechsler will appear parenthetically in the text.

11. Joan W Scott, "Experience," in *Feminists Theorize the Political*, ed. Judith Butler and Joan W. Scott. (New York: Routledge, 1992), 26. Further references to this work will appear in parentheses in the text.

12. Denise Riley, *Am I That Name? Feminism and the Category of Women in History* (Minneapolis: University of Minnesota Press, 1988).

13. All citations for Margarethe v. Eckenbrecher's *Was Afrika mir gab und nahm: Erlebnisse einer deutschen Frau in Suedwestafrika* (What Africa Gave and Took from Me: Experiences of a German Woman in Southwest Africa) (Berlin: Mittler, 1940) are taken from the eighth edition of this work, reprinted, and certainly rewritten from earlier versions, in 1940. I could not locate an earlier edition. All translations for this and other citations originally in German are mine. Further references to this work will appear in parentheses in the text.

14. Drechsler cites repeated Herero complaints that the Germans had ignored the promises made in article 3 of the Treaty of Friendship and Protection with the Herero, in which the Germans agreed to respect Herero customs. Although records show that Herero leaders repeatedly complained that Germans were raping Herero women and girls with impunity, not a single case of rape came before the German courts before the uprising because "the Germans looked upon such offences as mere peccadilloes" (Drechsler, 133).

15. A *pontok* is an igloo-shaped dwelling made of mud and sticks, usually with only a single door for an opening.

16. Homi Bhabha, "Of Mimicry and Man: The Ambivalence of Colonial Discourse," *October* 28 (1984): 126–33, at 129.

17. Hugh Ridley, who describes rhetorical justification of imperialism as a means of regenerating masculinity in some detail, calls it "the most common cliché of colonial fiction: the idea that colonies were a proving-ground for national manhood, a 'providential asylum' for educating younger sons" (*Images of Imperial Rule* [New York: Saint Martin's, 1983], 104).

18. Oberleutnant Stuhlmann, "Aus dem Kriegsleben in Suedwest-Afrika" (From War Life in Southwest Africa), in *Deutsch-Suedwestafrika: Kriegs- und Friedensbilder* (German Southwest Africa: Images of War and Peace) (Berlin: Reinbek, 1911), 61.

19. Ada Cramer, *Weiss oder Schwarz? Lehr- und Leidensjahre eines Farmers in Suedwest im Lichte des Rassenhasses* (Berlin: Deutscher Kolonial-Verlag, 1913). Subsequent references to this work will be included parenthetically in the text.

20. Klaus Theweleit, *Male Fantasies*, vols. 1 and 2, trans. Stephen Conway (Minneapolis: University of Minnesota Press, 1987), 1, 63–79.

21. Felix Bryk, *Neger-Eros: Ethnologische Studien ueber das Sexualleben bei Negern* (Negro Eros: Ethnological Studies of the Sex Life in Negroes) (Berlin: Marcus und Weber, 1928).

22. Peter Horn, "Die Versuchung durch die barbarische Schönheit" (The Temp-

tation of Barbaric Beauty), *Germanisch-Romanische Monatsschriften* 35 (1985): 317–49, at 317.

23. Michael Taussig, *Shamanism, Colonialism, and the Wild Man: A Study in Terror and Healing*, (Chicago and London: University of Chicago Press, 1987), 27. Taussig is referring, of course, to Michel Foucault, *Discipline and Punish: The Birth of the Prison*, trans. Alan Sheridan (New York: Vintage, 1979).

24. In those cases that did come to trial, for instance, the witnesses, whether white or black, appeared to presume all present to be familiar enough with the practice of flogging that no explanation was necessary. Details of especially severe abuse, such as a mention that leather whips were studded with bits of iron, did not provoke comment (Bley, 262).

25. I am greatly indebted to Lora Wildenthal, who has also written an article on Clara Brockmann, for much of the information and many of the citations in this section. See Lora Wildenthal, " 'She Is the Victor': Bourgeois Women, National Identities, and the Ideal of the Independent Woman Farmer in German Southwest Africa" *Social Analysis* 4 (1993). Special Issue: "Nation, Colony, Metropole."

26. *Briefe eines deutschen Maedchens aus Suedwest* (Letters of a German Girl from Southwest Africa) (Berlin: Mittler, 1912).

27. Roger Chickering, "Casting Their Gaze More Broadly: Women's Patriotic Activism in Imperial Germany," *Past and Present* 118 (February 1988): 168.

28. See, for example, Karl Dove's lengthy descriptions of the various uses and relative abilities of different ethnic groups in Southwest Africa. Karl Dove, *Die deutschen Kolonien* (The German Colonies), 4 vols. (Berlin: Mittler, 1909), vol. 4, *Suedwest-Afrika* (Southwest Africa), 56–68.

29. J. M. Coetzee offers an insightful examination of this topic within the colonial discourse of the Cape in "Idleness in South Africa," the first chapter of *White Writing: On the Culture of Letters in South Africa* (New Haven and London: Yale University Press, 1988).

30. Clara Brockmann, *Die deutsche Frau in Suedwestafrika: Ein Beitrag zur Frauenfrage in den Kolonien* (The German Woman in Southwest Africa: A Contribution to the Woman Question in the Colonies) (Berlin: Mittler, 1910).

31. Adrienne Rich, "Compulsory Heterosexuality," *Signs* 5 (1980): 631–60.

32. Andrew Parker, Mary Russo, Doris Sommer, and Patricia Yaeger, *Nationalisms and Sexualities* (New York: Routledge 1992), 6–7.

33. Lillian Faderman and Brigitte Eriksson, trans. and ed., *Lesbian-Feminism in Turn-of-the-Century Germany* (Iowa City: Naiad, 1980), 5.

SEVEN

(Dis)Locating Gender Space and Medical Discourse in Colonial India

Sandhya Shetty

There are three histories of obstetrics and gynecology. Or so we are told.[1] First, the profession presents a picture of scientific beneficence in which heroic male obstetrical experts, struggling against the prejudices of their male colleagues — and the uncontrolled free market of childbearing help — achieve professional respectability and monopoly in the latter half of the nineteenth century.[2] A powerful feminist rewriting of this optimistic self-portrait focuses primarily on the elimination of the traditional midwife, a positively connoted development in the first account, and on the undue medicalization of female "patients," particularly in childbirth.[3] And the third history, focusing on the changing mechanisms of power, lays bare "the nature of professional power, how it was acquired by obstetrics, and how it was retained through its reformulation."[4] I offer this outline as a way of pointing schematically to the paradigms of a now-canonical issue, the critique of obstetrics/gynecology, within metropolitan inquiries into the development of biomedical disciplines and discourses. What is striking about the various strands of inquiry outlined above is that they all appear to share one feature in common, notwithstanding their noticeably conflicting agendas: a "sanctioned ignorance" or theoretical oversight of the colonial reach of metropolitan medical enunciation.[5]

No postcolonial critique of obstetrical/gynecological discourse can, however, forget that the European consolidation of this medical specialty coincided with the global deployment of Western scientific knowledge and power in the interests of empire.[6] This invocation of the colonial

188

field is not simply a call for a geographical extension of ongoing investigations into the history of obstetrics/gynecology. Rather, it underlines the fact that these investigations still need to grasp obstetrics/gynecology's insertion into the colonial project of subject constitution and to inscribe its colonial detour as part of the discourse's European history.[7] By citing a more "global" field of emergence for obstetrics/gynecology, this essay seeks to initiate the task of dislocating the received West-centered histories of medical discourse from their self-contained metropolitan habitat. More specifically, it takes on the task of complicating current renditions of obstetrics/gynecology's location and address by focusing on the discourse's transformative workings as a gendered site of colonial subjectification in British India.

In 1929, writing the history of women's medical work in colonial India, Margaret Balfour and Ruth Young, two doctors in the Women's Medical Service (WMS), credit zenana missionary women with being the first white women to testify to the "fatal and almost unspeakable tragedies which were common events in the zenanas [women's domestic quarters] they visited."[8] Balfour and Young reconstruct this "fatal" prehistory of Western biomedicine in the lives of Indian women in the following images:

They saw their zenana pupils dying in childbirth without any advice other than that of the dirty and ignorant old dai. They saw the precious babies snatched away by pneumonia or dysentery, untreated, because their mothers could not take them to a male doctor. They saw the women sinking into chronic ill health and fatal disease unrelieved, but when advised to go to the hospital, holding up their hands with horror at the idea of consulting a man.[9]

All the chief players in the performance of Western obstetrics/gynecology in colonial India take their bow here: invisible and helpless zenana women, the unscientific, indigenous *dai* (midwife), irrelevant male doctors, unvisited hospitals, and, less obviously, the disembodied, all-seeing "they," white women with privileged access to the sight and knowledge of native babies' and mothers' sufferings. In this tableau of distress, I would like particularly to point to the veiled female characters — "the dirty and ignorant old dai" and the zenana or purdah woman — as the key "originary" figures around which obstetrics/gynecology's colonial performance came to be constituted and legitimized as a womanly scientific practice. In what follows I reconstruct in detail certain scenes, characters, and spectators that formed the staples of an orientalist mise-en-scène constructed by Western obstetrics as the difficult locus of its colonial practice. It appears that the conditions of obstetrics/gynecology's deployment in colonial India varied greatly according to region. My discussion is limited to the discourse and practice in the northern parts of British India in the late nineteenth and early twentieth century.[10]

In reading obstetrics/gynecology otherwise, the following study addresses at least two broad questions: Western medical enunciation in the colonial sphere, on the one hand, and the problematics of gender and medical practice, on the other.[11] These two sets of concerns are braided together in an analysis that clarifies the productivity of obstetrics/gynecology's discursive strategies and effects in late colonial India, specifically its creation of particular subject positions for colonial women, indigenous and European. Indeed, what was most remarkable about the deployment of obstetrical knowledge in India (from about the 1860s on) was the active solicitation and empowerment of women as the proper, even exclusive, subjects of scientific medicine. This reinscription of the relation between sexual categories and scientific knowledge/practice is particularly significant if we remember that it happens at a time and in a medical specialty whose metropolitan practitioners had come increasingly to be defined as male.[12] I argue that it is the harnessing of the general imaginary of orientalism to the scientific practice of obstetrics/gynecology – particularly the intermesh of the two discourses around the focal metaphor of (un)veiling – that may have played a key part in this noteworthy colonial reordering of gender in medical practice.

Focusing first on the ignorant and dirty *dai* and then on the zenana image of Indian femininity, this essay provides a set of readings of these crucial topoi on which the practice of Western obstetrics/gynecology took place in colonial India. In the case of the zenana particularly, obstetrics/gynecology came to articulate the belief that the purdah woman had to be "unveiled" in order to be helped. The obsessive repetition of images of the secluded "native" female and of insanitary zenanas in colonial medical discourse signals this desire to bring the hitherto barred, out-of-sight space of unregulated "native" homes and female bodies into visibility. The exposure and liberation of zenana women's bodies from their enclosed infirmity into the open field of a curative vision could not, however, be a straightforward or final matter for a medical practice predicated on purdah women's remaining inveterately purdah. Hence it was through repetitive enactment or simulation of orientalist truths about purdah and the zenana in discourse that women doctors attempted to guarantee their own more or less exclusive access to veiled "native" women. While solicitous of the sentiments of an imaginary zenana, such hybridizing reenactments, we shall see, produced a stammer in the articulations of Western scientific medicine. Particularly as the sections on the *dai* and the Zenana Hospital demonstrate, it was in an interstitial space between scientific critique and strategic assimilation of indigenous practices that obstetrics/gynecology in colonial India was compelled to stage its ambivalent project of "supplying medical aid by women to the women of India."[13]

CONSTRUCTING CONTEXTS, ARTICULATING SITES

The articulation of colony and metropole into a single field of analysis constitutes a larger analytic task that any critique concerned with Western biomedicine's colonial interventions must address. This section attempts to repair the split between these two sites, a split that overdetermines Western feminist histories' theoretical oversight of the colony as a field of biomedical intervention and as a space for Western women's construction of an authoritative professional voice in relation to colonial subjects. One of the chief consequences of this analytical and ideological lag that severs colony from metropolis has been the asymmetrical valuation of the costs and effects of biomedicine's intervention in the labor processes, knowledges, and bodies of women in colony and in metropole. To cite but one example, the skeptical Euro-American feminist perception of the tendentiousness of representations of female midwives in Europe ("filthy women mercifully replaced by antiseptic ob/gyns") has not been extended to the evaluation of similar representations of Indian *dais* in the discourse of colonial physicians. The representation of the filthy, brutal, and grotesque ministrations of the Indian midwife in the writings of European medical women, where it has been noted at all, has been uncritically accepted as truth.[14] My point is that bringing metropole and colony into a single analytical field should theoretically enable us to rectify such blindnesses and open up another perspective. From this perspective, it might become possible to see the part played by obstetrics/gynecology in the reinscription of native bodies, and also, more significantly, the ways in which as a colonial discourse it may have functioned constitutively for metropolitan women, assigning them positions of professional legitimacy and authority. The uncontested vilification of indigenous *dais* in colonial obstetrical literature may then be read as a crucial part of the same process of subject production whereby middle-class women (European and Indian) acceded to the status of "lady doctor." Thus, the specific analytic advantage to be gained by reconstructing the context of study in this way is the possibility of tracing the mutual traffic, even constitution, of spatially disjunct cultural processes: gendered professional conflicts within medicine and women's liberal emancipatory discourses in the metropolis, on the one hand, and, on the other, a parochial colonial medicine that in effect seemed to have conceded the regulation of indigenous women's productive and reproductive labor to European female subjects of biomedical knowledge.

In this connection, the "indigenous *dai*" and the "purdah patient" in the writings of colonial-women physicians must be read as more than just imaginary figures structuring white women's testimony of the appalling conditions of childbirth in India and the redemptive practices organized around such testimony. In Balfour and Young's historical account, they also point critically, although obliquely, to the practical inattention of colonial health policy with regard to indigenous women and children. Contemporary historians of colonial medicine have also suggested that before the last quarter of that century, the labors of colonial doctors, whether in research or practice, were dictated by the priorities of conquest and mercantilism (and therefore narrowly confined to a European civil and military constituency).[15] David Arnold has written that it was only at the close of the century, when imperial "economies and administrative systems . . . sought a more comprehensive hold over the lives and labour" of the colonized, that a newly confident Western medicine began to play a key if belated colonial role.[16] But even then, considerations of political economy seem to have constrained colonial medicine's therapeutic measures, selection of constituencies for medical relief, and formulation of research problematics; consequently, its knowledge and effects were erratically distributed across colonial civil society.[17] Large subaltern constituencies — women, children, rural and tribal populations — in effect remained outside the threshold of colonial medical work in tropical disease research, epidemiology, and sanitation. It must, however, be noted that medical missionaries had attempted much earlier and more energetically to establish a far wider circle of influence for Western medicine, taking "Christ and surgery" to the far-flung corners of the Indian Empire — the forbidden space of zenanas in town and city as well as the "wild" frontiers of the Afghan border — where the colonial state in the first half of the nineteenth century had itself feared to tread.[18]

Speaking of the official neglect of indigenous women's health by the state and its professional arm, the Indian Medical Service, Dr. Mary Scharlieb, lecturer on midwifery and diseases of women at the University of Madras at the turn of the century, points to the too-close hitching of medical work to imperial policies and concerns as a reason for these gender inequities. In her foreword to Balfour and Young's history, Scharlieb writes of the colonial medical profession that "even doctors are almost obsessed by their great mission to take up the White Man's burden."[19] Consequently, the assimilation of medicine (almost exclusively defined as "general sanitation and the scientific control of epidemic and endemic disease") to imperialism's public ameliorative projects produced the exclusionary gendered structure for colonial medicine that sanctioned neglect of such "domestic" matters as "mother and child welfare" (and consequently of the obstetrical/gynecological branch of medicine). Because the "less insistently clamant ills of anaemic mothers and starved infants" were unassimilable to the white man's burden, they, writes Scharlieb, were abandoned, to be "redeemed by the skill and sympathy of women doctors."[20] Thus it was that obstetrics/gynecology as the Western "science of woman" seems to have become, in the late nineteenth century, in more places and ways than one, the white woman's burden.

Scharlieb's account of an imperialized medical service for which "anaemic mothers and starved infants" were unassimilable "wastes" works powerfully to question colonial medical ethics on behalf of indigenous women. But her inscription of the field of imperial medicine suggests that the task of medically redeeming indigenous women's bodies fell by default to women doctors, a suggestion that might lead one to miss the systematic and overdetermined nature of the processes by which "women doctors" came to "shoulder responsibility" for treatment of Indian mothers. For what gets obscured in this critique of the sexual division of colonial medical labor is the structuring of the relatively new category of "women doctors" itself and, most importantly, the implication of metropolitan processes — medical specialization and gendered professional identification — in the history of "native" women's constitution as subjects within the imperialist project.

In late colonial India, the work of constituting "native" women as subjects and objects of Western medical science appears to have been taken up by the newly emergent "science of woman," mediated by a variety of institutional means and methods.[21] Located in the field of maternity and child welfare services (rather than identified with strictly clinical practice or knowledge production), the sites from which obstetrical and gynecological discourse worked included secular and missionary women's teaching hospitals, women's wards of general hospitals in British and princely India, midwife training classes, maternity and welfare centers, health training schools, home-visiting activities by Health Visitors, exhibitions and conferences, and scholarship and aid funds. Of these latter, the Victoria Memorial Scholarships Fund (1905) and the Countess of Dufferin Fund, established in 1885 under the direct patronage of Queen Victoria, appear to have been the most prominent of the centralizing administrative bodies overseeing the various local (and let me stress highly uneven and contested) insertions of obstetrics/gynecology into the lives and labor of Indian women.

Annexed thus by medical missions of various denominations and a plethora of lay funds, agencies, and committees and operating primarily in the "domestic" sites of colonial civil society, obstetrics/gynecology as a "womanly" division of Western science invited gendered colonial subjects into the stratified domain of medical discourse as "patient," "trained medical worker," and "lady doctor." Such work in the interstitially located lives of indigenous women may never have been as celebrated or publicized as work in the "manly" fields of sanitation, epidemiology, or tropical-disease research. Nevertheless, I want to suggest that obstetrical/gynecological discourse may have played a key role in establishing the cultural hegemony of "scientific" medicine in domestic spaces otherwise inaccessible to Western medical interventions.[22] By bringing into the purview of scientific medicine these invisible spaces of zenana women's "lives and labor," obstetrical/gynecological practice functioned to extend not only Western medicine's but also empire's visibility. But, as we shall see, this may have occurred at the price of its own visibility in the broader public domain of colonial medical practice.

As Balfour and Young note, the systematic and coordinated efforts of private agencies and medical missions to rationalize birthing practices among women in late-nineteenth-century India were seriously handicapped by the unavailability of qualified women practitioners of Western scientific medicine.[23] The availability of professionally qualified women in colonial India, required primarily for obstetrical/gynecological work, was largely contingent upon the vicissitudes of the women's medical movement, driven by such women as Sophia Jex-Blake, Elizabeth Garrett Anderson, Edith Pechey, and others in England. There can be little doubt (although the specifics still need to be worked out) that the colonial deployment of obstetrical/gynecological knowledge welded the disputes and conflicts shaping obstetrics/gynecology in the metropolis to the lives and labor of Indian women in the last quarter of the nineteenth century. Although some colonial women, like Mary Scharlieb herself, were permitted by the government of Madras to study with male students at the Madras Medical College as early as 1875, the "Medical Mission of Women to India was" quite clearly "the early and excellent fruit of Mrs. Garrett Anderson's gallant endeavour to secure medical education, training and success for women in England."[24]

In England, the opening of the London School of Medicine in 1877 more or less ensured the entry and presence of increasing numbers of British women in the medical profession.[25] For at least forty years before this event the question of women's relation to medical science, education, and practice had been sorely debated in England and America. As Western feminist histories of obstetrics/gynecology inform us, male physicians directed their contrary ire first against untrained midwives and subsequently against women aspiring to be trained as qualified midwives and doctors. This continued until 1877, when male monopoly was virtually broken. Nevertheless, the point to note here is that despite these developments supervisory control of the medical profession and its resources, certainly of its obstetrical/gynecological arm, still remained fully under male jurisdiction.[26]

Contrasted with this, the profession's late-nineteenth-century transformation at its colonial Indian site presents a curious difference. Perhaps the most striking feature, as suggested above, is that women, indigenous and European, were actively interpellated as subjects of scientific obstetrical/gynecological knowledge and practice. Although for a number of reasons the ratio of Indian women physicians to white women doctors was extremely low, right from its inception the professional discourse had consistently sought to hail "a better class" of Indian women as knowing subjects of scientific medicine. Obstetrics/gynecology's success in addressing "native" elite women as professional subjects may be gauged from the memoirs of the few women doctors of the time. The best example is of course the much-publicized access to medical education of Dr. Anandibai Joshi of Poona, the first Indian woman to graduate, in 1886, from the Women's Medical College in Philadelphia, an institution that was regularly applied to for American women physicians who would serve in Indian hospitals.[27] As evidenced in Dr. Joshi's appointment papers and elsewhere, the mundane control of material resources, too, where and in whatever form these existed, appears to have been in the hands of colonial women doctors.[28] The precise modes and strategies by which Western-trained medical women attempted to establish such control over the field are elaborated in subsequent sections of this essay. Suffice it to say here that even as childbirth was being wrested out of women's hands in the West, in colonial India it was being successfully claimed as a female branch of qualified medical practice. The gendered subject of an increasingly "manly" metropolitan science was, in an uncanny movement of doubling and reversal, being transformed into a "womanly" colonial science.[29] Thus, while in the European and American case the establishment of the medical model has been critically read as a male takeover of the birthing process, the struggle to medicalize childbirth and women's bodies in colonial India demands a more complicated reading. For here, the struggle to medicalize was also the struggle to Westernize indigenous practices, in the context of the civilizing mission; and it was mainly European women (as much as or even more than men) who appear to have been empowered by the structure of colonial authority to carry out these interventions.

THE INDIGENOUS *DAI*

Representing itself as the only rational mode of managing maternity and childbirth, modern obstetrics at its colonial site of enunciation turned its disciplinary gaze obsessively on the hereditary *dai*.[30] It is not surprising that the earliest and most strenuous efforts of medical women were invested in the scientific training and supervision of the indigenous *dai*, identified as the root cause of maternal and infant mortality. But in addressing the *dai* as a professional subject, Western obstetrics traversed a set of cultural practices around childbirth, informed by an elite caste discourse of ritual pollution and purity. Within this discourse, childbirth, like menstruation and death, was an occasion that produced a condition of *sutika* (impurity), and anyone or anything in direct contact with the parturient mother became polluted and polluting. The hereditary *dai*, as the socially designated attendant at childbirth, who not only delivered the child and cut the cord but often also performed associated menial tasks for the mother, was clearly positioned within this Hindu discourse of purity and pollution as a ritually unclean person.[31] With the insertion of modern obstetrics into this symbolically charged ritual structure of childbearing, however, the *dai* came to be repositioned athwart two discontinuous discourses, both converging on the management of confinement and postnatal care.

This section focuses on the *dai*'s (dis)location within a scientific medical discourse. Displaced from the register of caste and pollution onto a medical register, the *dai* was recontextualized within professional obstetrics, where, as a strategic site of difference, she could function productively for a colonial discourse of modern midwifery. Constructed as the epitome of all surgical and sanitary abominations, "the superstitious, ignorant, and dirty midwife" provided Western obstetrical science its professional raison d'être, its occasion to speak and to be. But as professional obstetrics' self-consolidating other, the *dai* in her new location within medical discourse also marked, as I shall be demonstrating, the limits of Western obstetrical practice in colonial society. Indeed, "the widespread chain of indigenous relief in the hereditary dai class . . . fully trusted by the people" constituted the single most impervious barrier to the rationalization of "native" birthing under the scientific aegis of medical women.[32] In their professional writings, the *dai* therefore emerges as a linchpin figure, a crucial part of a ritual-bound process of home delivery wherein parturient women, ignorant of the first principles of hygiene and sanitation, and their female relatives, who supervised the entire superstitious process, were all equally blocked from obstetrics' scientific, reforming eye.[33] "They can only be reached," laments one Dr. Marion Wylie of the United Free Church of Scotland Mission in the town of Nagpur, "through the *dai* — the invariable attendant at the function of childbirth."[34] Produced in this way within the discourse as a professional rival, the hereditary, low-caste *dai* thus came to embody all that was heterogeneous to Western biomedical knowledge systems and practices, all that had to be either expelled and replaced or negotiated by science on its way to the barred central space of physical and cultural reproduction within indigenous society.

It is to the professional writings of colonial medical women that I now turn to witness the discursive transformation of the indigenous *dai*, a process that moved her from "legitimate" marginality within caste-structured conditions of childbirth to illegitimate marginality within a system of pathological knowledge. The repeated unveiling of the *dai*'s intervention in labor and delivery constitutes the central ritual enactment of this system of knowledge production. And not surprisingly, what we find to be the particular "discovery" of the scientific medical eye is the gruesome consequences of the *dai*'s inexpert attendance at obscure, superstition-governed native births. The following account is particularly striking as much for the viewing and naming of damaged female body parts, a compulsive ritual of truth in the discourse of scientific midwifery, as for the inadvertent avowal of the gratuitousness and excess in such representations:

> It is in the cases of delayed labor that so much mischief is done by interference. It is unnecessary here to cite instances such as we have all met with, of foetal arms pulled off, rupture of the uterus, lacerated cervix . . . partial or complete atresia of the vagina. . . . It is enough to say that . . . the dai is called on to make several vaginal examinations. . . . This she does with hands unwashed and anointed with some unaseptic lubricant. . . . When the delivery is over . . . she does not hesitate to plunge her hand into the uterus.[35]

But of course, as will be apparent to any reader of this literature, it is never "enough to say . . ." Rather, repetition works with great effect/affect in this discourse to fix and circulate a repertoire of abject images of the *dai*. The typical scenario of the forced extrication of the placenta by the *dai*'s dirty hands inserted into orifices of the maternal body discloses authoritatively the invasive violence of the *dai*'s unhygienic and unscientific intervention in the process of home delivery. But, perhaps less obviously, there is something gratuitous about the proliferation of these images of vaginal insertions and of inventive lists of substances so inserted (presumably as per the requirements of native superstition): melted butter, cow dung, plugs of spider's web, *huldi* (turmeric), seeds, and bejeweled hands, to name only a few.[36] The accumulated excess of such images of filthy insertions and body-boundary breaking in the writings of Western-trained obstetricians demands another explanation that would account for their density, abundance, and repetitiveness. I want to argue that these masterly unveilings of the *dai*'s ignorance and filth and compelling revelations of scientific procedures and rational prohibitions uncover a terrain of abjection.[37] Surely we are in this terrain when the subject obsessively repeats the "same old stories," hovering in horror and disgust over what should be outside the body — dirt, filth, hands and feet, seeds, hollyhock roots — but is half inside, out of place, blurring the body's borderlines. In terms of the *dai*'s re-assignment to a new subject position, as professional rival, such investments of affect mark out that position; moreover, as a dangerous and dirty figure, the *dai* works as a charged site of difference where two competing species of abjection converge: Hindu caste horror of the unclean and Western sanitary revulsion for the dirty and unhygienic.

Let us consider another detailing of professional horror, this by Dr. Katherine O. Vaughan, superintendent of the Jubilee Zenana Hospital in Srinagar, as she offers "cases typical of the sort of thing every medical woman practising in this country encounters":

A summons comes and we are told a woman is in labor. On arrival . . . we are taken into a small, dark and dirty room. . . . On the floor is the woman. With her are one or two dirty old women. Their clothes filthy . . . their heads alive with vermin. They explain that they are midwives . . . and they cannot get the child out. . . . On inspection we find the vulva swollen and torn, they tell us, yes, it was a bad case and they have had to use both feet and hands in their efforts to deliver her. . . . Then chloroform is given and the child extracted with forceps. We are sure to find hollyhock roots . . . inside the mother, sometimes . . . a dirty rag containing quince seeds in the uterus itself.[38]

The *dai*'s brand of midwifery is here represented as the work of some ghastly bricoleur; she uses whatever comes to hand to bring on birth (hands, feet, string, rags, whatever is most inappropriate), confounding the whole(some)ness of the body by infecting and disarticulating its parts. Such witnessing of the *dai*'s loathsome personal habits and criminally ignorant techniques of delivery might be double edged, however.

On the one hand, we might read this account of the *dai*'s practice as a strategic inversion of clean, expert hospital delivery. In the passage above, for instance, the signs of European technological advances ("chloroform," "forceps") clearly define the subject of Western obstetrics against the technically inferior ("dirty rag," "feet and hands") and downright ghastly makeshift methods of the untrained native subject of midwifery. But it is precisely at the point where the *dai*'s practices are represented as a repellent bricolage that we might trace an other scene of abjection. At this level, the indigenous *dai* as a bricoleur figure seems so abjecting — so impossible to master — perhaps because she returns to "scientific" obstetrics a distorted image of its own practice and history as a stigmatized, traditional female occupation.[39] In the process of marking (and jettisoning) the culturally and scientifically subordinate, the discourse offers, in effect, not so much an opposition but an inversion whereby the *dai*'s tactics become the negative of modern obstetrics' own practice as a form of bricolage — the work of a skilled technician who resorts to "standard procedures" or the tools of the trade — chloroform, forceps, surgical incisions, mechanical manipulations of the body, and other "scientific," hence appropriate, applications that control birth.[40] Thus it might be that these obsessive records of the hereditary *dai*'s loathsome activities, so crucial to the enunciation of colonial obstetrics' own authority, also silently demand an expulsion or "cleansing" of what is possibly "native" to Western midwifery itself. As a "low," gendered practice, metropolitan midwifery, we must recall, remained through much of the nineteenth century in an ambiguous and shifting relation to "science," requiring formal training, on the one hand, and to "the manual aspect of medicine," associated with women's work and experience, on the other.[41] Strategically produced as a subject of difference by colonial medical power, the indigenous *dai* might also be read as the alienated double that a professional "womanly" obstetrics had to disavow in order to preserve its own scientific authority.

Thus, on the one hand, the representation of the *dai* as the embodiment of filth and barbaric ignorance works strategically as a warrant for legislative and medical-administrative means to exterminate her in the name of science, modernity, and life itself; on the other hand, the intensity of the abjection, repeatedly demanded by the ever-expanding repertoire of abhorrent images, seems to call for another dimension in our reading. In the gratuitous proliferation of images of either viscera and sepsis or the grotesque uncleanliness of the *dai*'s person, it must be noted that the discursive production of the native midwife as the subject of difference is the effect of a continual and necessary enunciation and solicitation of affect. The horror and disgust solicited by the polluting *dai* works to separate and ground the female Western "self" as the clean and proper subject of medical knowledge and hygienic practice. As an ontological justification for the gendered colonial subject of scientific discourse, the *dai* as a disgusting, racialized subaltern figure is all that "must be thrust aside" in order for that bourgeois subject to be. Hence, it was around the *dai*'s evacuation that a female-dominated scientific obstetrics had to constitute itself as a violently cathartic discourse in ceaseless pursuit of (self-)purity. As hinted earlier, what is most significant about this "scientific" pursuit of purity is that it points up Western obstetrics' cathexis with the *dai* as a species of abjection, a ritual outcasting. I have argued that the iteration of disgust as an aspect of the *dai*'s discursive constitution works performatively to establish the boundaries of women physicians as Western, scientific subjects, but it is also important to grasp the obsessive citation of the *dai*'s unclean practice as a crucial dimension of obstetrics' transformation of indigenous women into subjects of modern medical knowledge. Even here, the instrumentality of the repugnance solicited by obstetrics' representation of the unclean *dai* as a dangerous practitioner worth eliminating for the sake of safe delivery should be sufficiently clear; the production of the *dai* as dirty and dangerous presses "natives" into "good citizenship" within the new regimes of medical truth. What, however, still remains to be clarified is the epistemological significance, for colonial subject constitution, of obstetrics' own ritual enactment of dirt avoidance in relation to the *dai*.

We have already noted the convergence of two forms of pollution behavior on the figure of the *dai*: Western scientific and caste Hindu.[42] While both seem to display the same ritual(istic) avoidance of the unclean, there is of course this difference: dirt is known as unhygienic and pathogenic within modern medical knowledge structured by the scientific episteme. It is only when we understand this regime of knowledge that the full violence of the representation of the *dai* in colonial obstetrical discourse becomes apparent. Consider Dr. Agnes Scott's 1918 paper on methods of dealing with the hazards occasioned by the *dai*, which presented "clearly and concisely, a tabular form such as the following . . . valuable for impressing the main facts":

Water-borne diseases...............................	Enteric, Cholera, dysenery, etc.
Diseases spread by flies and dirt...............	Infantile diarrhoea, ophthalmia
Diseases spread by the indigenous *dai*	Puerperal sepsis, tetanus, gonorrhoea, etc.[43]

To make the point about how scientifically ignorant Indians needed to be apprised of the *dai* as a bearer of contagion (as opposed to a potential source of ritual pollution), Dr. Scott's "scientific" representation resorts to the extreme of establishing the *dai* as a disease vector on the same plane as dirt, polluted water, and insects. As a phobic object, equivalent to dirt and germs, the indigenous *dai* here more than anywhere else signals the violent taxonomic shift whereby obstetrical discourse sought to recast the hereditary *dai* — a human source of symbolic pollution within indigenous social structures — as a pathogenic organism within a rationalizing medical discourse.

At this level, then, obstetricians' own "pollution behavior" cannot adequately be read only in terms of professional anxiety; more fundamentally, it is assimilable to Western medicine's larger struggle to overhaul the episteme within which "native" notions of pollution and purity counted as knowledge. And in the domestic sphere of indigenous civil society, the *dai* constitutes the site of this displacement, the discursive topos where obstetrics/gynecology could negotiate the "scientific" status of Western ideas of contagion and purity (wherein dirt is dominated by pathological knowledge) over against native notions of dirt and uncleanness, which, because of their alleged grounding in the sacred, were no longer to count as knowledge. The "success" of colonial subject production within medical discourse may be gauged from the statements of G. K. Devadhar of the Poona Seva Sadan Society, one of many social service organizations to crop up in the late nineteenth century and after:

> The modern demand for Health Visitors or trained nurses and midwives is the outcome of the growing knowledge of the laws of hygiene and sanitation which has set many an earnest mind athinking and created a new hygienic or sanitary conscience. The development of this thought has given rise to a spirit of enquiry ... in the direction of preventing human suffering, diseases, etc., to a considerable extent. This line of thought has created the need of a class of women workers.[44]

If the shifting of the native subject from one episteme to another involved the reconstitution of hereditary *dais* as "these dangerous women," as pathogenic even, then the logical consequence of such shifts would have to be calls for their extermination.[45] As various reports and papers from the early twentieth century demonstrate, doctors spent a good deal of their professional energy, in the absence of formal legislation, in devising ways and means to prevent untrained *dais* from attending births. A particularly energetic Medical Officer of Health, presenting a paper at a conference organized by the Lady Chelmsford All-India

League for Maternity and Child Welfare in 1927, noted the good work in surveillance that resulted in the fact that "we know every dai practising at Simla." He goes on to say, "In November 1926 we had six untrained dais in the town . . . they cannot be trained and the only alternative is to wait for their disappearance by natural causes. In November last the registration clerk gleefully announced that untrained *dai* Mariam of Kaithu had died. Her name was removed from the list of untrained dais" (132). For those unlucky enough to survive, however, incarceration was not deemed inappropriate as a way to "prevent them from practising in the town." "One such untrained dai is under our care at Simla and I could relate many amusing incidents connected with her, but space does not permit," writes Major Webb of the IMS.[46]

Such acts of straightforward domination were, however, complicated by more strategic attempts to negotiate a willing submission to the "superior" methods of Western obstetrics.[47] For at the same time as medical practitioners called for the *dai*'s extermination, they continued to argue that through bribery or sympathy a friendly science could and ought to bring the resistant *dai* around. In these accounts, the *dai* even cuts an enviable figure, in possession of cultural authority and the people's trust and goodwill.[48] A Mrs. K. M. Bose, for example, argued, at the same conference attended by Major Webb in February 1927, that the village *dai* could be a useful part of a modern women's health care system and that "there is something in indigenous practises which can be expanded and utilized."[49] Also to be considered is the fact that the *dai* class must indeed have afforded a "widespread chain of relief" not only to thousands of indigenous women but also potentially to the inadequately funded and staffed voluntary agencies at the turn of the century advocating the virtues of scientific obstetrics over ignorant and superstitious "native" methods. Not surprisingly, the Victoria Memorial Scholarships Fund initiated by Lady Curzon in 1901–1902, operating with a clear view of the problem of scale, established that the object of the fund should be the imparting of "a certain amount of practical knowledge to the indigenous midwife (dais)," thus reversing the precedent set by the Countess of Dufferin Fund in 1885, which sought to "train up midwives of a superior class."[50]

Thus, in a sort of travesty of T. B. Macaulay's educational theory of filtration (designed to produce an indigenous, male, Western-educated elite), medical women came to devise something of a farcical subplot in the course of their attempts to appropriate the *dai* for modern midwifery.[51] In this subplot, the subaltern figure of the *dai* was to be harnessed to science, given "a course of training and allow[ed] to continue her practice." Reinscribed as colonial subject, the trained hereditary *dai* would then, it was imagined, serve as an intermediary agent of safe, scientific midwifery among millions of ignorant native women, "patients" whose pathologized bodies and reproductive processes would in turn be subject to/of Western biomedical knowledge and professional control. As the "Rules and Regulations and Objectives" section of the *VMSF Report* published in 1903 put it, "Whatever they [indigenous midwives] learn will spread over a far wider area than can be reached by means of a superior class of midwives" (162). The class fix of the trained hereditary *dai* as colonial subject is made apparent by the parallel but differentiated production of the "superior class of midwives" and the "lady doctor" as enlightened bourgeois subjects whose interpellation as such within Western medical discourse marks the stratified production of gendered professional subjects within the more general process of indigenous class formation under territorial imperialism.

Thus faced with the immense prospect of assimilating the recalcitrant *dai* that medical women's discourse had represented to itself, the professional text of reform seemed to oscillate between two representations of the hereditary *dai* as a teachable and reliable figure of cultural authority on the one hand and as incorrigible and filthy on the other. However, this impasse proved discursively productive, for it was precisely here at this point of oscillation that obstetrics was able to proliferate a galaxy of new positions to be occupied by subjects in various stages of approximation to full-fledged obstetrical legitimacy: the hereditary *dai*, the trained hereditary *dai*, the indigenous but nonhereditary trained *dai*, trained in the vernacular, the nurse *dai* trained in English at Dufferin or mission hospitals, the Sarkari *dai*, the Tehsil Head Midwife, the reporting *dai*, etc.[52] Occupying these multiple, minutely discriminated, and overlapping positions, the partially reformed subject of modern midwifery thus circulates ambivalently as object of supervision in the vigilant discourse of colonial women physicians. " 'A little knowledge is a dangerous thing' — I have seen dais with a rudiment of hospital training giving large doses of Ergot early in labor, with consequent tetanic uterine contractions."[53] Hence, according to Dr. Dagmar Curjels of the Woman's Medical Service, the necessity for "constant supervision of the dai's afterwork." Notwithstanding, under the disciplinary eye of scientifically based training, these reformed objects seem to maintain rather than to yield their intransigent heterogeneity; splitting and thus eluding total conscription by the regime of Western knowledge systems and practices, the trained *dai* remains a duplicitous figure in the texts of obstetrical reform: "The dai is rarely an appetising figure when seen at her work, her clothes are filthy rags and her body unwashed. Even when a dai comes up prepared for inspection by a medical woman, in outwardly clean apparel, a request that she would loosen her outer garments, usually reveals her everyday dirty clothes underneath."[54]

Outwardly clean but dirty underneath, the trained *dai* emerges here as a perverse dissembler, and as such she signals medical discourse's imbrication with a more extensive system of cultural representation; indeed, as an example of native criminality and unreliability, requiring constant medical policing, the partially reformed *dai* may be taken as colonial obstetrics' contribution to stereotypical orientalist knowledge of native duplicity.[55] But what concerns me more centrally here is the function and effect of obstetrics' creation of the reformed midwife as a split subject of Western knowledge (neither wholly trained nor wholly untrained).[56] Even when redeemed from filth and ignorance and prepared for inspection, the trained *dai*, an advanced specimen of Western pedagogy, betrays a fatal difference; close examination reveals that her "clean apparel," which should properly be an unambiguous sign of the intelligent assimilation of hygienic practice, is only an improper camouflage: "outwardly clean apparel" that hides her "everyday" dirtiness. This duplicitous construction of the trained *dai* produces her as an enlightened subject of scientific midwifery even as it continues to support Western-trained obstetricians' continuing pedagogical investment in (the stereotypical knowledge of) the native as untrustworthy and incorrigible.[57] It is in fact this difficulty of keeping the clean uncontaminated by "the dirty" once and for all (of preventing the in-mixing evident in the trained midwife's beguiling cleanliness) that authorizes her continued subjection to unceasing inspection and regulation.

Similarly, the trained or "advanced *dai*" as the appropriate object of medical regulation disturbs the rules and order of scientific midwifery not only when she is clean but also when she is "right." Consider, for instance, doctors Balfour and Young's claim about the difficulties of rational pedagogy devoted to turning out unified subjects of knowledge. Insofar as the *dai* is concerned, they observe, "anyone who has ever attempted the task [of training] knows how fatally easy it is to secure the lip response which conveys the right answer to a question without the slightest real response on the part of the mind."[58] Her "lip response," which splits sound from original sense, disturbs the singularity and identity of scientific knowledge, repeating Western knowledge and hygienic practice with a difference that disrupts their integrity and whole(some)ness. The *dai*'s "right answer" — which the discourse constructs as neither the "real response" nor the wrong answer — in confounding the production of unified colonial subjects of scientific knowledge, gestures toward a perverse third space. What is noteworthy about this observation is that it highlights the productive nature of the process whereby the *dai*, when neither simply excluded nor fully appropriated, gets shaped anew within medicine's disciplinary project as a hybrid site of difference.

In sum, one might argue that within the attempt to signify science as Western in colonial India, this "lip response" of the duplicitous Oriental midwife, along with the "outwardly clean apparel" of Dr. Dagmar Curjels's report, enacts a productively contradictory process. As Gyan Prakash urges in his study of science in colonial India, what is therefore required is a rethinking of our customary understanding of the colonial discourse of scientific modernity as producing "nothing other than domination."[59] That this is indeed the case is powerfully suggested by the "lip response," which might be read both as the effect of obstetrics' negotiation of its own singular and unending authority and as the sign of the trained *dai*'s production as an actively knowing subject of scientific midwifery who articulates a new knowledge and practice. Furthermore, it is possible to argue that in constituting the *dai* as a crucial subject of its pedagogical and therapeutic practices, colonial obstetrics and gynecology did both more and less than establish its discursive authority. This view opens up the possibility for analyses that might claim the "perverse third space" or "new knowledge and practice" as the site of another subaltern knowledge that stubbornly contests correction undertaken in the name of Western rationality. The unlicensed toll exacted by this new hybrid form of subalternity on the hegemonic process whereby biomedicine attempted to hail "the native woman," obscurely located in the private domains of native life and labor, remains to be conceptualized.[60]

THE PURDAH WOMAN: UNVEILING DISEASE, ORIENTALIZING MEDICINE

Recent feminist investigations of Western women's location in imperialism have convincingly established the deep complicity of British feminist arguments with the ideological imperatives of the civilizing mission, despite their sometimes dissonant relationship with the voice of male colonial authority.[61] Gayatri Spivak's attempt to critique "feminist individualism in the age of imperialism" in her reading of *Jane Eyre* first worked out for us a theoretically powerful interpretation of the relationship between "the subject-constitution of the female individualist" and the "native female as such (within discourse, as a signifier)."[62] The manipulation of the sign of the "veiled native female" in the process of medical women's consolidation of their position as subjects of scientific knowing is the focus of this section. I want to begin by pointing out the interesting fact that the diseased Indian woman in purdah, Western obstetrical/gynecological practitioners' "discovery" at the colonial site, is also present at the heart of metropolitan professional debates in the latter half of the nineteenth century. Here, in English women's contested discourse on their right of entry into professional medical practice, the zenana and the veiled figure of the "native" woman are pressed into rhetorical service as cross-cultural tropes of female confinement. Consider the famous essay "Women in the Medical Profession" by Sophia Jex-Blake, pioneer of the medical women's movement in England. In her plea, Jex-Blake draws forcefully on images of suffering Indian zenana women, then circulating in the English press, in feminist journals, and in the reports of missionaries on furlough to bolster her argument about the need for women as physicians.[63] Jex-Blake cites a number of these contemporary accounts, one of which presents the following picture of "native ladies" in diseased confinement:

In many parts of India – I think I may say in most parts – native ladies are entirely shut out from any medical assistance, however great may be their need, because no man who is not one of the family can enter their apartments or see them; and although thousands thus die from neglect and want of timely help, yet nothing can be done to assist them until we have ladies willing and able to act in a medical capacity.

Jex-Blake's strategic staging of this medically impenetrable colonial scene makes clear that the discursive field of imperialism did not just nourish Western medicine's colonial projects; it also clarifies the constitution of "native ladies" as a signifier mobilized to legitimize liberal feminist causes in the context of intraprofessional rivalries in the metropolis as well. Specifically, it is veiled other woman as signifier that partly sets in motion the liberal narrative of women's uninhibited and equal access to medical qualifications and recognition in England. Thus, whichever site one looks at, the "native" female body confined in the veiled space of the zenana structures, to a lesser or greater extent, medical women's professional narratives in metropolis and colony.

In colonial Indian discourse, purdah, viewed as an Oriental infraction of Western conjugal and social normativity, embodied every kind of deviancy from "the civilized norm" in sexual, domestic, and social relations between the sexes. As a signifier of an absolutely other realm of Oriental sexuality, it was also metonymically linked to a vision of India's absolute sociopolitical difference, materialized in the degenerate and diseased condition of the native body (politic). Read as cause or symptom of Indian social and political pathology, purdah in colonialist reform discourses gave rise to a normative intention and practice, most earnestly imprinted in missionary and secular educational narratives on the mental and moral state of Indian women.[64] In colonial medical discourse, however, purdah registered itself as the exotic social form of the pathogenic element in "native" life. The desire for a clinical narrative that could unveil the pathological truth of purdah repeatedly engendered a fantasmatic zenana in colonial medical literature. As the locus of an insalubrious gathering and scattering of infections, superstitions, diseases, and deformities, the zenana haunts a range of texts on Hindu physique, tuberculosis, building, sanitation, and any number of "health" issues.

The potent influence of this custom is directly responsible for a great deal of the insanitary property in the native quarter of the city. To secure privacy, efficient lighting and ventilation are absolutely disregarded, the zenana or women's apartments being usually the most insanitary part of the house. No wonder that tuberculosis, which thrives in damp, dark, airless corners, plays havoc in the zenanas.[65]

Or again:

It is as I have reason to know a common practice in some circles for the same "burqa" to be used by various members of the one family. The "burqa" used perhaps by one daughter going to the hospital with advanced phthisis will be used immediately afterwards by another when going on an errand to the bazaar. The serious danger of infection resulting from this practice must be obvious to everyone.[66]

In these texts that medicalized purdah, veiled "native ladies" function as ideological figures that set in motion the desire for clinical exposure and regulation (unveiling). The purdah woman and alternately the ze-nana, as a gendered space of confinement and infection, thus give rise to a normative intention that would logically and ideally restore the patho-logical to healthy (read: civilized) normality. But while the fantasmatic space of the Indian zenana that haunted a range of medico-political representations incited such an explicit normative intention, the condi-tions of possibility for a narrative that would stage a clinical encounter with the veiled and diseased female body were limited by the very terms of a politico-erotic discourse on purdah as a system that banned such encounters. Within this discourse, the female body in purdah could not occupy the position of "the patient" except in a highly constrained and carefully choreographed clinical encounter.[67] Only a "womanly" medical science that could negotiate the prohibitions encircling any encounter with the native female body could position that body as an object of clinical intervention. And it was obstetrics/gynecology that took up the task not only of linking pathology with a particular version of Indian femininity but also of exploiting and negotiating rather than dismissing the notions of visibility/invisibility that structured the available represen-tation of "Oriental" women. Colonial Indian obstetrics/gynecology would thus come to produce a contradictory discourse that sought both to extend colonial medicine's rationalizing (super)vision of embodied sub-jects managed by scientific regimens and to interrupt that vision by relocating the female body within an economy of veiled labor based on orientalist notions of confined and suffering native women.

It should be clear that it is the orientalist imaginary that makes "the purdah woman" available as a constitutive element of obstetrics/gynecol-ogy at its colonial site. What needs elaboration is the reason "veiling" or visibility/invisibility should have become so crucial a metaphor to the practice of colonial obstetrics/gynecology. While individual medical women in colonial India recognized that purdah was a region-, religion-, caste-, and class-specific social practice, that knowledge was also strategically disavowed and displaced by an essentializing orientalist representation of women and gender relations in Indian society — representations around which obstetrics/gynecology organized its exclusionary practice.[68] Certainly, in the interests of naming women, indigenous and European, as sole subjects of obstetrical and gynecological practice — that is, in constructing a professional zenana in the patriarchal house of colonial medicine, shall we say — obstetrics/gynecology's imaginings came to be heavily invested in the zenana image of Indian femininity.

Thus most contemporary accounts of women's medical work in colonial India as well as the medical writings of obstetrical/gynecological "experts" themselves unfailingly and obsessively circle around the figure of the *purdahnashin* or "zenana lady," who obstructs vision and hence promotes disease, the *dai*, and fatalities. Documenting the history of medical aid for Indian women, doctors Balfour and Young, for instance, confidently construct a taxonomy of purdah women that is curiously only just this side of certainty:

In those days it may be said that there were three classes of Indian women — the strictly purdahnashin who under no circumstances, or almost no circumstances, would see a man; respectable women of all classes who would never consult a man for childbirth or diseases peculiar to women, but who were not debarred from doing so for other diseases; and very low class or disreputable women who did not mind whom they consulted. Even the second and largest class was almost debarred from consulting men doctors owing to the principle so prevalent in India, that women should not mix with men at least unless their husbands accompany them. Hence the Government hospitals were almost unattended by women.[69]

As the type of Indian femininity with which rational medicine would have to contend, the figure of the *purdahnashin* attained a charged status as "a ritual of truth" in the ambivalent ethnographic discourse of and on colonial women doctors. My contention is that obstetrics/gynecology's self-constitution had to rely on, further elaborate, and circulate this popular representation of indigenous womanhood as veiled womanhood, so that the conditions of its emergence as a "womanly" colonial science could be shaped. Hence nowhere was the alleged ubiquity of the "purdah spirit" among Indian women more insistently represented than in the writings of colonial women doctors.[70]

As suggested earlier, for tropical medicine and public health discourses, the body of the strict *purdahnashin*, sequestered by indigenous patriarchy in spaces inaccessible to gaze or glance, remained serially enveloped in a domestic "inside" and hence obscurely situated in relation to its hegemonic cultural projects. Purdah unequivocally debarred even the male medical gaze, which in the context of Oriental sexuality could only be interpretable as an erotic one. Thus, this "last" hidden outpost, the zenana, constituted an invisible frontier along which only a "womanly" medical practice could set up clinical camp; the *purdahnashin* could be made to unveil and yield herself only to a de-eroticized female clinical gaze. The task of encountering and "unveiling" the bodies of zenana women — that is, of illuminating them with the light of rational medical discourse — thus "naturally" devolved on women obstetricians/gynecologists, midwives, and nurses and on the several strictly women's or zenana dispensaries and hospitals that emerged after midcentury. In sum, the indigenous woman, by virtue of her designation as pathological, is at the origin of a medical narrative seeking to norm the "native" female body; by virtue of her alleged negation of the male clinical gaze, the patient-as-purdah-woman is also at the origin of the professional narrativization of women obstetricians' and gynecologists' unique authority and expertise in colonial India.

At this stage one can hardly wait to ask the question, what were the promises and pleasures incited by obstetrical and gynecological discourse around purdah?[71] And what in fact did this enlightening discourse make visible, or was the fulfillment of the promise of visibility — lifting purdah   continually deferred as a vital underlying principle of the profession's survival as a female domain? For to unveil the *purdahnashin*, to bring her out for the sake of her health — the ostensible goal of medicalizing her body — would also mean to negate the purdah woman's negation of the male gaze — in other words, the end of the profession as it was constituted. Obstetrical/gynecological work, as therapy and pedagogy, thus came to articulate a necessarily, and let me add productively, contradictory belief: purdah must go (the native female body must be brought into the visual domain); purdah will prevail (the native female body must inevitably remain invisible). It is in the paradoxical space of this unending "striptease," in between these two enunciations, that colonial obstetrics and gynecology set up its profoundly ambivalent project of "supplying medical aid by women to the women of India."

Neither the task of unveiling the diseased body of "native" women nor the self-arrogated professional privilege of this unveiling by women doctors remained uncontested, however. In contemporary medical women's accounts, we sense, among other tensions, the tension between professionalizing women and their male counterparts. The male Civil Surgeon, firmly anchored in the official echelons of the Indian Medical Service, unlike most women doctors, appears as a paternalistic rival with little "experience of the management of women workers, or gynecology, while she [the medical woman] had become something of an expert in both directions."[72] Not surprisingly, the question around which "friction most commonly occurred" was purdah. Holding herself responsible for the strict observance of purdah in the hospital wards where male Civil Surgeons appeared to make inspections, the medical woman insisted that notice always be given of such visits, so that "purdah women could be hidden out of sight." Apparently, Civil Surgeons were apt to make surprise visits and this made the medical women, "who had perhaps persuaded some purdah lady to enter the hospital . . . [feel] the matter keenly." Speaking for colonial women doctors, Balfour and Young inform us that male doctors usually "thought the medical women were imagining or exaggerating the strength of the purdah system."[73]

Clearly this insistence on patients' seclusion and refusal to see male doctors should be considered as a strategic move deriving from professional women's investments in an inaccessible, native female body. Colonial women doctors' heavy investment in making this body visible to scientific medicine on the one hand and their solicitude for the conservatisms of purdah on the other signal the status of purdah as the site of a complex negotiation among bodies, power, and knowledge within the institution of colonial medicine. Here let me emphasize that obstetrics/gynecology's double and contradictory investment in discovering and scientifically treating the "native" female body and in re-covering it "out of sight" not only structured its conditions of possibility but also its limits as a "feminine" branch of medical discourse in colonial India.

For, so great and contagious was this purdah spirit in the practice of obstetrics and gynecology that, in effect, it confined obstetrical/gynecological practitioners to a professional zenana, located in the obscure interstices of colonial Indian society. What can on one count be read as an assertive feminization of professional power and practice can on another be viewed as a highly dubious gain in the context of a patriarchal colonial culture that valorized and materially bolstered the public and spectacular acts of the civilizing mission: the heroic "masculine" activity of scientific epidemic control, sanitation, and endemic tropical-disease research. The feminization of colonial Indian obstetrics/gynecology, which secured professional control for women physicians, paradoxically riveted in place the sexual division of colonial medical labor, sequestering the "womanly" colonial science in a private, despectacularized space — "the stricken fields," as Dr. Mary Scharlieb called it, of indigenous women's diseased lives and labor. The very conditions of possibility for colonial obstetrics/gynecology's emergence as a female domain constituted the limits of that domain beyond which it could not stray. By and large obliged to neglect all objects of colonial medical discourse outside this domain, medical women, in an uncanny repetition of zenana life and labor, were to be "experts" only in those pathologies and abnormalities consequent on sexual difference and the excesses of native male desire as that came to be "read off" from purdah (and other "sexual barbarisms").[74] In this sense, obstetrics/gynecology seems to have facilitated the "natural" displacement of sexuality and sexual difference from the realms of public medical discourse (tropical medicine and public health) to the private, eroticized realm of women's diseased confinement. The female subject, both patient and doctor, was thus effectively (re)positioned within the confining limits of an Orientalized discursive, clinical, and spatial structure.

THE HOME AND/IN THE HOSPITAL

Perhaps the Purdah or Zenana Hospitals that began to emerge in colonial Indian cities in the 1860s best exemplify the orientalized clinical and spatial structures within which the new confinement of obstetrics/gynecology's domain of discursive objects as well as of its own technologies and practices were located. The process of moving the purdah woman, the emergent gendered subject of obstetrical/gynecological discourse, from the space of domestic seclusion to a clinical space of visibility was not just a question of her subjection and recontainment in a modern economy of medicalized health care provision and consumption dominated by the hospital. The unveiling of pathological pregnancies and birthing within an orientalized medical discourse also required in effect that the Western subject of colonial obstetrical and gynecological practice go into seclusion, orientalize and veil itself out of sight. For, as we have seen, Western medical science's project of rendering visible the bodies of zenana women living in the diseased confinement of Indian homes could not simply be (at the literal or metaphoric level) a question of a straight-forward unveiling. Even though exposure was inevitable if the female body were to be moved under the light of medical surveillance and rational therapy, treatment had somehow to take place without exposure; the unveiling of the purdah patient had to be carried on, but "out of sight." What was required was some material spatial inscription of this interplay of visual-perceptual structures (visibility/invisibility) that could house the process of scientifically renovating indigenous practices around the sick, pregnant, or parturient body. The Zenana, Purdah, or Women's Hospital, as it was variously called, seemed to provide a fortuitous archi-tectural answer to this colonial medical quandary.

The very first women's hospitals in colonial India appear to have been established only after the 1850s, although government and municipal general hospitals and dispensaries (open to both sexes) were founded as far back as the end of the eighteenth century.[75] In the 1860s and 1870s, medical mission women in different parts of India set about organizing makeshift clinics and dispensaries and even small hospitals for women. Later, in the 1880s, as qualified medical women, newly turned out by medical schools recently opened to women in England, came out in increasing numbers, several of the earlier clinics and hospitals were dis-placed or incorporated into modern-style teaching hospitals. By the 1920s we hear in contemporary accounts, particularly with regard to mission hospitals, that medical women arriving in India found "organized hospi-tals, with full beds, trained staff, competent assistants and usually excellent operating rooms, instruments and medicine."[76]

Interestingly, however, the organization of medical aid, particularly the clinical experience of purdah patients, appears in these contemporary accounts to be governed less by the quality of the relationship between doctor and patient than by the monumental structure of the women's hospital building, viewed as the architectural apotheosis of medical work as a womanly profession. Far from mere backdrop, this gendered space of Western-trained medical women's work also functioned as the place of indigenous woman's liberation and entry (as both objects and subjects of knowing) into the field of light and visibility, of medical knowledge and modernity, all materialized in a triumph of colonial architectural hybridity. The women's hospital thus registers itself primarily as an impressive building or built space that supports an emancipatory narrative wherein woman doctor and patient become "free" subjects and objects of modern medical knowledge and hygienic practices. In this section, I attempt to sketch a reading of the purdah hospital as housing, as an artifact of colonial medical culture uniquely constructed to rehabilitate indigenous female bodies and subjectivities. Like the *dai*, the hospital functions as a crucial site for Western medicine's production of difference as a strategy of power through which both the positioning and regulation of native subjects and the renegotiation of its own authority could be effected. One key facet of the women's hospital highlighted in this section is its domestic address. Contemporary Englishwomen's accounts afford the best glimpses of the strategic workings and discursive effects of this emphatically domestic inflection in purdah hospital planning, layout, and administration. By way of tracing the thematics of cleanliness, unveiling/veiling, and segregated confinement in this transformative discourse of women's hospital administration, I will draw on two such accounts, one by Frances Ward Billington, published in 1895, and the other by Edith Craske, written after a four-month medical-inspection tour of Indian mission hospitals in the late 1920s.[77]

Embedded in the story of the colonial women's hospital as told by Billington and Craske, we may sight another imaginary scene: the domestic routine of native women's daily lives and labor in their sequestered, unsanitary homes. That the narrative disposition of the purdah hospital is deeply haunted by the imagined arrangements of its architectural double, the zenana home, is particularly well demonstrated in Billington's late-nineteenth-century account, wherein discussion of medical work among Indian women quickly and imperceptibly shades off into representation of a built space — the women's hospital, its building style, layout, and floor plan. The reader is informed that, directed by "native architects and advisers" (91), and unlike government civil hospitals, the homelike setting of the professional work space of colonial women's hospitals is scrupulously attuned to the least niceties of purdah, caste, and other daily regimens of Indian women's domestic life — nursing arrangements, cooking arrangements, and arrangements for religious worship. The most stringent of these arrangements, ignored by government hospitals, which were consequently unattended by women, were of course the purdah arrangements that "exclude those not of position or undoubted respectability," so that "the most jealous husband, father, or brother knows that the patients are absolutely secured against intrusive male eyes" (91). A spatial installation of caste, religion, class, and sex hierarchies, the purdah hospital thus architecturally inscribes an orientalist sociology of Indian domesticity, grafting it onto the secular administrative regimen of a modern institution run on strictly sanitary and scientific lines. But, it must be noted that more than anything else, it is the knowledge of purdah, the notion of a necessary confinement, that produces the women's hospital's forked discourse.

Similarly fascinated by the colonial hospital's reinscription of Western technologies and "native" prejudices, Craske's *Sister India* lingers long on a description of the then-famous Ludhiana Women's Christian Medical College and Memorial Hospital.[78] From a ten-room school building in 1894, the medical school and zenana hospital had become at the time of Craske's visit "a large women's hospital of 200 beds, with extensive college buildings, having 250 Indian students of whom 98 are medicals, the remainder being in training as nurses, dispensers and midwives" (Craske, 42). When the reader is first brought up to the threshold of the Memorial Hospital for Women, the text holds up a sign of colonial evangelical medicine's triumphant adaptability that reads, "a monument to the value of respecting prejudices without sacrificing principles" (15). This claim at the very outset of Craske's tour of the hospital's interior is of interest because it returns us to the problematic of purdah that operates an orientalized obstetrics/gynecology's discursive negotiations with the conditions of childbearing in India. Craske's declaration, on the hospital's behalf, of its admirable accommodation goes over in an easy stroke the incoherences and fractures that mark "the zenana hospital" as a productive sanitary-architectural practice supportive of Western medicine's negotiated insertion into the private sphere of colonial civil society.

As the narrative round of the hospital unfolds, the hospital — its buildings and wards — as part of the spatial technology of Western colonial power presents itself as something more and something less than "an original itself," whether English or Indian — as something peculiarly colonial. That the colonial hospital is an uncanny, hybrid presence is made clear by Craske, our hospital tour guide, who warns that the eye of the English visitor receives "horrid shocks" (53) if "all recollection of a British hospital, with its spotless wards and double row of snowy beds" is not "put away" (53). The almost-jesting reference to "horrid shocks" identifies a mimesis of "the English hospital-as-authoritative norm," which is how-

ever displaced and even rendered grotesque by the difference established
by this colonial reproduction. Craske's surveying eye is here confronted
by a returning gaze of difference in the colonial women's hospital, where
the double row of snowy beds is indeed "put away" and in their stead we
find charpoys – string beds without mattresses or pillows – not only in
the wards but also in the verandahs onto which they open and under the
trees in the large courtyard onto which the verandah looks.

Here, besides the charpoys are also to be found by day scores of
"relations, children and crows disport[ing] themselves" (52). The uncontrolled proliferation of charpoys and the multiplication of nonprofes-
sional, nonpatient bodies also unsettles the precision of the quantified
description of hospital resources encountered earlier: two hundred beds,
two hundred and fifty students, ninety medicals, etc. This use of hospital
space by purdah patients and the female relatives who accompanied them
turns objects of medical knowledge into active negotiators whose own
habits, proclivities, and ideas about the hospital make equivocal the relations of power inscribed in its regimented ordering of space. Craske's text
provides several such fascinating moments that we might read for
glimpses of patients' renegotiation of hospital procedures or even refusal
of its accommodation, in both senses of the word: "There are epidemics
of patients running away, often before treatment is begun, as a result of a
sudden attack of homesickness."[79] We hear, moreover, that

frequently women come and bargain on the doorstep that they will on no account
submit to an operation, and even after protestations that the hospital is not a
prison, that all who come are free to go again if they wish, that it is impossible to
operate on an unwilling patient, still, it is difficult to persuade them to come in
for treatment. Even more pathetic are those who come too late . . . and beseech
the doctors to operate on them, and will not take "No" as a final answer, but
clutch their [the doctors'] feet and offer fees if only they may be cured. (54)

Offered as an account of medical practice's noncoercive efforts or "invitation" to female patients, this passage speaks to the contested nature of the
women's hospital's self-representation as a "free" place and, even more,
to its incomplete authority, which leads to the pathologizing move that
rewrites a putative freedom to come and go as (home)sickness and epidemic.

Sister India also helpfully furnishes a photograph of a minute scale
model of the Memorial Hospital that helps the reader reconstruct the
physical and perceptual configuration of this purdah hospital's spatial and

visual field. The model plan reveals to an omniscient gaze from above a large hollow oblong space with Muslim, Hindu, private, and surgical wards all around opening onto arched verandahs that overlook a large, inner courtyard with trees. The private wards, however, have their own small private courtyards that open onto the road. By this ingenious arrangement the wealthy Indian men who insist on a stricter purdah than that available in the already-strict purdah of the general wards (and who paid heavily, as Billington informs us, for their insistence) are provided entrances and exits onto the road to ensure, in turn, that they "can come and see their womenfolk without invading the sanctity of the hospital" (55). In this eminently discreet process of hiding and being hidden, of seeing and not seeing or being seen, everybody, it would seem, at some point or place needs to be made invisible or blind — except perhaps those narratively hailed as "the doctor," "the English inspector," and "the reader."

The spatial arrangement of the oblong hollow, turned in upon itself, ensures that "no masculine eye can peep into the enclosure" even as the discourse of the hospital is explicitly devoted to "exposure" as it ushers the inspector/reader into a mobile vantage point from where can be enjoyed, in addition to a great many other things, "an undisturbed view of endless little domestic scenes connected with the patients' toilet carried on in full view of all comers without concern" (53). Clearly, the dominating strategy in confining and unveiling the diseases of women is not prohibitive. "Accommodation," as we have seen, is the word, the strategy that allows sex, religious, and caste prejudices full play so that native women may be "loosed from [their] infirmity" even as they are bound to it. Thus, as a discourse of reform, the most powerful boast of the women's hospital seems to have been that it was as purdah as women's own homes and yet "so truly sanitary" — an additional clause that emphasized that "public," medically managed birthing could now occur without the dangers of exposure to male eyes on the one hand or to the invisible regimes of dirt, disease, and the *dai* on the other.

Reminiscing in the mid-twentieth century, one colonial doctor observed of hospital practice that "Indian houses were a subject that deeply affects our work in the Hospital."[80] This certainly seems true of the women's hospital as a clinical discourse that constituted itself not only as an architectural but also as a hygienic retort to the domestic living conditions of Indian women. In attempting to plot the necessary move of maternity and childbirth from the private precincts of the zenana home to the clean and commodious "public" space of the hospital/clinic, the narrative of the women's hospital turned crucially on the concept of "diseased confinement." But confinement in hospitals could only be positively inflected if what the hospital was replicating for tactical reasons — the seclusion of the zenana home — could also be represented as what the hospital was not. Dislodged from their "natural" setting, the filthy, germ-laden corners of the Indian house where the superstitious *dai* reigned, zenana women were to be reconfined for medical reasons, but in large, airy, well-equipped, and sanitary hospital conditions. The exchange of a licentious, recklessly unsanitary, diseased confinement for a virtuous, clean, and curative one could only have an edifying effect. For even as the purdah hospital would "respect prejudices," it would also silently castigate them by patients' confinement in and subjection to the hospital's modern, good-neighborly, and sanitary administrative regimens.

"The Indian home" was widely represented in colonial discourse as a disordered and unsanitary space requiring some form of regulation that would sculpt it according to Western aesthetics and sanitary norms. Throughout the late nineteenth and early twentieth centuries, a new domestic and sanitary science had sought to induct notions of beauty, utility, and cleanliness into the new type of Indian woman, who would transform the physical (and moral) interiors of "native" homes.[81] Colonial obstetrics/gynecology's own medical and sanitary strictures against the *sutikagraha* (confinement rooms) in Indian homes entangled it within these larger pedagogical projects of domestic and sanitary reform wherein the gendered colonial subject was being recast. In women physicians' writings, for example, the problem of "the patient's house," frequently linked to the "*dai* question" and the need for her supervision, looms large: "The conditions in a patient's house are very different from those in a hospital, and they teach the dais to make use of what they find at hand."[82] Again, Western obstetricians caught in the imaginary spectacle of the native home devised odd experiments to figure out ways of popularizing "the custom of going into hospital for the birth of a child."[83] One such experiment involved the bait of painless delivery and projected the women's hospital as a unique place specializing in and guaranteeing methods of eliminating pain during childbirth. Reporting on experiments with the "twilight sleep" method conducted in the labor ward of the Rainy Hospital in Tondiarpet, Madras, a Dr. Campbell writes that Indian women are attracted to dark rooms at the time of confinement:

It gratifies her instinctive desire to hide herself at such a time. In her own home this leads to the darkest and dirtiest room in the house being selected, often with a fatal result as sepsis is induced. Still the contrast between what she would have at home and the blaze of light in a hospital labor ward is so great that she shrinks from the latter. To prepare our Labor ward . . . for twilight sleep, we painted dark green the upper part of the walls. . . . As soon as a twilight sleeper came in, the room was darkened . . . and she slept peacefully till the event was over.[84]

Unmistakably it is the Indian home (the feature of the "darkened room" in this case) that fuels the knowledge and practices of hospital-based colonial obstetrics. As a repetition of the spatial and social regimen of the Indian home with a significant rational-sanitary difference, the purdah hospital thus placed itself on the threshold of a public/domestic divide, a space where a spick-and-span zone of monitored visibility and regulated openness ("the blaze of light in a hospital ward") doubles for the pathogenic, dirty privacy of the zenana home. What is interesting here is that while it is precisely this "twilight" status that the purdah hospital as a technology of power aims to achieve, it is also that which it must, as a discourse of colonial authority, seek to deny. For after all, liminality as the purdah hospital's modus vivendi troubles the clear opposition between "zenana home" and "women's hospital" on which the hospital's scientific authority was ostensibly founded.

Yet, the strategic construction of the home-in-the-hospital, like the construction of the *dai* as a site of difference, seems part of a necessary enactment through which obstetrics/gynecology's multiple and stratified assignation of subject positions could proceed. The foregoing essay has tried to understand this enactment and the ensemble of situations through which obstetrics/gynecology sought to establish and consolidate its colonial subjects and practice. What has, hopefully, also emerged is a recognition that the deployment of the indigenous *dai*, the purdah patient, and the home in/and the hospital, as productive sites for obstetrical/gynecological medicine's authoritative negotiations and subject-constitutive strategies, cannot be adequately understood without a prior analytic adjustment. Such an adjustment, I have argued, rectifies the theoretical oversight eliding obstetrics/gynecology's "global" dispersal in the age of imperialism. In emphasizing the colonial enunciation of obstetrics/

gynecology, largely ignored by Western feminist critiques of biomedicine, the essay has attempted to grasp both medicine's (en)gendering of
colonial subjects and the knotted togetherness of metropolitan medical-
professional developments and this process of colonial subject constitution. It is within the context of such an articulation of colony and metropolis that colonial obstetrics/gynecology's importance as a site of transformation can be most richly apprehended.

NOTES

I gratefully acknowledge the support provided by a Rockefeller Foundation Fellowship, awarded by the Institute of Culture and Consciousness in South Asia,
University of Chicago, and the Clarence Gustafson Fellowship, awarded by the
Center for the Humanities, University of New Hampshire, which made possible
travel to India and time off for research and writing. I would also like to thank
Gyan Prakash, Itty Abraham, Lalitha Gopalan, Parama Roy, and R. Sethuraman
for the valuable comments and support they provided at various stages in the
preparation of this essay. Thanks are also due to the anonymous reviewers for
Genders for their suggestions.

1. See William Arney, *The Power and Profession of Obstetrics* (Chicago: University
   of Chicago Press, 1982), 1–10.
2. For a good example of such portraiture, see Walter Radcliffe, *Milestones in
   Midwifery* (Bristol: Wright, 1967). As Ornella Moscucci points out, beginning
   with James Hobson Aveling's *English Midwives* (1872), the history of obstetrics in England has been seen mostly through the eyes of male accoucheurs.
   See *The Science of Woman: Gynecology and Gender in England, 1800–1929*
   (Cambridge: Cambridge University Press, 1990).
3. A vast literature critical of "scientific" obstetrics and gynecology and its
   professional development in England and America now exists. For some of
   the more important and influential discussions, in addition to Moscucci's (see
   n. 2), see Adrienne Rich, *Of Women Born: Motherhood as Experience and Institu-
   tion* (New York: Norton, 1976); G. J. Barker-Benfield, *The Horrors of the Half-
   Known Life: Male Attitudes toward Women and Sexuality in Nineteenth-Century
   America* (New York: Harper & Row, 1976), esp. 61–71, 80–90; Mary Poovey,
   " 'Scenes of an Indelicate Character': The Medical 'Treatment' of Victorian
   Women," in *The Making of the Modern Body*, ed. Catherine Gallagher and
   Thomas Laqueur (Berkeley: University of California Press, 1987), 137–68;
   Paula Treichler, "Feminism, Medicine, and the Meaning of Childbirth," in
   Body/Politics: Women and the Discourses of Science, ed. Mary Jacobus, Evelyn
   Fox Keller, and Sally Shuttleworth (New York: Routledge, 1990), 113–38;
   Jean Donnison, *Midwives and Medical Men: A History of Inter-Professional*

Rivalries and Women's Rights (London: Heinemann, 1977), 62–158; Regina Markell Morantz-Sanchez, *Sympathy and Science: Women Physicians in American Medicine* (New York: Oxford University Press, 1985); Barbara Ehrenreich and Deirdre English, *Complaints and Disorders: The Sexual Politics of Sickness* (New York: Feminist Press, 1973) and *For Her Own Good: 150 Years of the Experts' Advice to Women* (New York: Doubleday, 1978); Ann Oakley, *Women Confined: Towards a Sociology of Childbirth* (New York: Schocken, 1980); Mary Daly, *Gyn/Ecology: The Metaethics of Radical Feminism* (Boston: Beacon, 1978), 223–92.

4. Arney, *Power and Profession*, 2.

5. The phrase "sanctioned ignorance" is Gayatri Spivak's. See her "Can the Subaltern Speak?" in *Marxism and the Interpretation of Culture* (Urbana-Champaign: University of Illinois Press, 1986), 271–313.

6. David Arnold, "Introduction: Disease, Medicine, and Empire," in *Imperial Medicine and Indigenous Societies*, ed. David Arnold (Delhi: Oxford University Press, 1989). See Sara Tucker, "Opportunities for Women: The Development of Professional Women's Medicine at Canton, China, 1879–1901," *Women's Studies International Forum* 13 (1990): 357–79. Tucker's is one of the few attempts to globalize the question of biomedicine's institutionalization and intervention in women's lives. Her focus is on American missionary medicine and its facilitation of medical education among Chinese and American women.

7. Edward Said and Gayatri Spivak are only two of the many postcolonial critics who have insisted on drawing attention to the shared histories of East and West by pointing to the global production of "Europe." See Said, "Intellectuals in the Post-Colonial World," *Salmagundi* (Spring-Summer 1986): 44–64; and Spivak, "French Feminism Revisited: Ethics and Politics," in *Feminists Theorize the Political*, ed. Judith Butler and Joan Scott (New York: Routledge, 1992), and "Can the Subaltern Speak?" See also Dipesh Chakrabarty's "Postcoloniality and the Artifice of History: Who Speaks for 'Indian' Pasts?" *Representations* 37 (Winter 1992): 1–26.

8. Margaret Balfour and Ruth Young, *The Work of Medical Women in India* (London: Oxford University Press, 1929), 14. The Women's Medical Service was established in 1914 and attached to the Dufferin Fund. For a detailed account of the service, see Balfour and Young, 50–74.

9. Ibid., 14.

10. For the most part, my sources pertain to those regions where purdah was practiced among certain classes and groups. "Purdah," of course, has a complex signification. An Urdu term, it can designate both the institution of women's seclusion and veiling and the veiling material itself (veil or curtain). The black gown worn by a purdah woman when she leaves the house is the *burqa*. "Zenana" refers to the women's quarters of the Indian home, Muslim or Hindu, in which purdah is observed. The zenana should not be confused with "harem" and its eroticized orientalist significations although colonialist texts sometimes used the word interchangeably. See Hanna Papanek,

"Afterword – Caging the Lion: A Fable for Our Time," in *"Sultana's Dream"* *and Selections from "The Secluded Ones,"* trans. and ed. Roushan Jahan (New York: Feminist Press, 1988), 62–67; and Shahida Lateef, *Muslim Women in India: Political and Private Realities, 1890s-1980s* (London: Zed, 1990), 16–94.

11. Homi Bhabha's reflections on colonial representation in terms of repetition, mastery, and authority also provide a useful way of thinking about Western medical enunciation in the colonial sphere. See, for instance, his "The Other Question: Difference, Discrimination, and the Discourse of Colonialism," in *Literature, Politics, and Theory: Papers from the Essex Conference, 1976–1984*, ed. Francis Barker, et al. (London: Methuen, 1986), 148–72; and "Signs Taken for Wonders: Questions of Ambivalence and Authority under a Tree outside Delhi, May 1817," in *"Race," Writing, and Difference*, ed. Henry Louis Gates, Jr. (Chicago: University of Chicago Press, 1986), 163–84. Gyan Prakash works out and brilliantly extends some of Bhabha's ideas in relation to the colonial deployment of science in "Science 'Gone Native' in Colonial India," *Representations* 40 (Fall 1992): 153–78.

12. See Donnison, *Midwives and Medical Men*; Poovey, " 'Scenes' "; Treichler, "Feminism, Medicine, and the Meaning"; Barker-Benfield, *Horrors*; and Arney, *Power and Profession*, 34–38.

13. This was also the prolix name taken by the Countess of Dufferin Fund, established by the then Vicereine Countess of Dufferin at the request of Queen Victoria in 1885. For a more detailed account of the work of the Countess of Dufferin Fund, see Balfour and Young, *Work of Medical Women*, 33–53; Major-General E. W. C. Bradfield, *An Indian Medical Review* (Delhi: Government of India Press, 1938), 264–69; Sir Patrick Hehir, *The Medical Profession in India* (London: Frowde, Hodder & Stoughton, 1923); and Frances Ward Billington, *Woman in India* (London: Chapman & Hall, 1895).

14. I am not arguing principally about the truth value of Western feminist or colonial physicians' accounts. Nor am I concerned to establish the comparative superiority or effectiveness of Western and indigenous practices. There is no "good" *dai* grounding my critique. See Mary Daly's *Gyn/Ecology* for an instance of the effects of conceptually severing metropole and colony in feminist critique of male obstetrical/gynecological power and practice. Daly's text, despite the global reach of its critique of "planetary patriarchy," is stunningly blind to the contradiction of excoriating Anglo-American medical representations of the female midwife's filth and ignorance while at the same time warmly approving representations of the Indian *dai* by colonial women physicians and in Katherine Mayo's notoriously problematic text, *Mother India*. Compare, in Daly, 113–33, 438–39, and the chapter and notes on "Indian Suttee" with 223–92, the chapter on "American Gynecology."

15. For historical accounts and analyses of colonial Indian medicine, see David Arnold, "Medical Priorities and Practice in Nineteenth-Century British India," *South Asia Research* 5 (November 1985): 167–83, esp. 170–72; Mark Harrison, "Towards a Sanitary Utopia? Professional Visions and Public Health in India, 1880–1914," *South Asia Research* 10 (May 1990): 19–40; John

Chandler Hume, "Colonialism and Sanitary Medicine: The Development of Preventive Health Policy in the Punjab, 1860 to 1900," *Modern Asian Studies* 20 (1986): 703–24; Roger Jeffery, *The Politics of Health in India* (Berkeley: University of California Press, 1988), 19–20, 74, 93–102; Radhika Ramasubban, "Imperial Health in British India, 1857–1900," in *Disease, Medicine, and Empire: Perspectives on Western Medicine and the Experience of European Expansion*, ed. Roy Macleod and M. Lewis (London: Routledge, 1988), 38–60. David Arnold's *Colonizing the Body: State Medicine and Epidemic Disease in Nineteenth-Century India* (Delhi: Oxford University Press, 1993) came to my notice after this essay had been completed.

16. See Arnold, "Introduction: Disease, Medicine, and Empire," 17.

17. Ibid., 14–16. I might add that sometimes medical policy, whether in its practical or in its research dimensions, was also influenced by imperialist/ nationalist rivalries and on occasion by international sanitary opinion that delivered itself in times of cholera and plague epidemics. See I. J. Catanach, "Plague and the Tensions of Empire: India, 1896–1918," in *Imperial Medicine and Indigenous Societies*, 149–71; Jeffery, *Politics of Health*, 94; Ramasubban, "Imperial Health," 44–45.

18. For a sampling of medical-mission literature, see "Pioneers of C.M.S. Medical Missions: India and the Far East," *Church Missionary Review* 66 (May 1915); A. Carless, "Fifty Years of Medical Missions," *Church Missionary Review* 66 (July 1915); Dr. T. L. Pennell, *Among the Wild Tribes of the Afghan Frontier: A Record of Sixteen Years of Close Intercourse with the Natives of the Indian Marches* (London: Seeley, 1909); Dr. A. C. Lankester, "The Medical Missionary Motive," *Church Missionary Review* 65 (February 1914); T. Howard Somervell, *Knife and Life in India: The Story of a Surgical Missionary at Neyyoor, Travancore* (London: Livingstone, 1940); John Spencer Carman, *Rats, Plague, and Religion: Stories of Medical Mission Work in India* (Philadelphia: Judson, 1936); Dr. R. H. Western, *Some Women of Sindh: In Home and Hospital* (London: Church of England Zenana Missionary Society, n.d.).

19. See Scharlieb's foreword in Balfour and Young's *Work of Medical Women*, xii; see also ibid., 123–25, where Balfour and Young themselves address this point.

20. Ibid., xii.

21. In the first half of the twentieth century, maternity and child welfare work, given a fillip by eugenic sentiment and an emergent nationalist "physical culture," was marked by a proliferation of new positions and sites from which obstetrical and gynecological discourse could operate: new systems of record keeping, municipal child welfare centers, leagues and associations for maternity and child welfare, health training schools, Health Visitors who did "home visiting," statistical studies of maternal and infant mortality, societies for the promotion of scientific knowledge, baby weeks and baby welcomes, resolutions of the Women's India Association and, later, of the All-India Women's Conference, and health exhibitions "where models of sanitary dwellings and wells and labour rooms can be shown with great advantage." See *Report:*

Maternity and Child Welfare Conference (Delhi: Lady Chelmsford All-India League for Maternity and Child Welfare, 1927); Ruth Young, *Maternity and Infant Welfare: A Handbook for Health Visitors, Parents, and Others in India* (Calcutta: Superintendent Government Printing, 1922); Hamid Ali, "Maternity and Welfare Work in India," and Dr. J. Jhirad, "Some Aspects of Medico-Social Work in India," both in *Women in Modern India*, ed. Evelyn Gedge and Mithan Choksi (Bombay: Taraporevala, 1929), 132–43; *Social Service Quarterly* 11, no. 2 (October 1925).

22. For a discussion of the influence of Western modes on *bhadralok* birthing practices in Bengal, see Meredith Borthwick, *The Changing Role of Women in Bengal, 1849–1905* (Princeton, N.J.: Princeton University Press, 1984).

23. See Balfour and Young, *Work of Medical Women*, 14–16, for an account of the situation before medical education became regularly available to women in England and in India.

24. Ibid., 22.

25. See Donnison, *Midwives and Medical Men*, 83–87, for a detailed account of Sophia Jex-Blake and the movement that led to the establishment of the London School of Medicine. See also Sophia Jex-Blake's own *Medical Women: Two Essays* (Edinburgh: Oliphant, 1872), and Morantz-Sanchez, *Sympathy and Science*, for details of the story of women physicians in America.

26. See Mary Scharlieb's review of medical women's struggles with their "professional brethren" in Balfour and Young, *Work of Medical Women*, ix.

27. See Caroline Healey Dall, *Life of Anandibai Joshee* (Boston: Roberts, 1888). This memoir of Anandibai's life and education in America is a fascinating source of letters and other material from which we can glean some sense of the determinations within which this elite Indian woman was assigned a professional subject position and also of her own negotiations with the structures that produced her as a professional.

28. See Balfour and Young, *Work of Medical Women*, 72. Doctors Balfour and Young, comparing conditions of employment in the Women's Medical Service, India (formed in 1914), and those under other colonial governments, write that "in the Indian Service, medical women have complete professional control of their hospitals." I submit that this may have been equally true in a comparison of medical women's professional positions in colonial India and in England.

29. See Moscucci, *Science of Women*, 73; and also Poovey, " 'Scenes' "; Donnison, *Midwives and Medical Men*; and Treichler, "Feminism, Medicine, and the Meaning" for excellent discussions of how issues of gender and sexuality — "disputes about power, authority, and professional competence and domains" — shaped the growing pains of obstetrics and gynecology in England and America.

30. The attack on the indigenous midwife was ubiquitous and systematic. The most influential of lay attacks was undoubtedly Katherine Mayo's in *Mother India* (New York: Harcourt, Brace, 1927), 90–110. For professional representations, see *Report: Maternity and Child Welfare Conference*; Hehir, *The Medical*

Profession in India, 125–30; Dr. J. Jhirad and Mrs. Hamid Ali, in *Women in Modern India*; Carman, *Rats, Plague, and Religion*, 165–97; and, most importantly, the *Victoria Memorial Scholarship Fund Report: Improvement of the Conditions of Childbirth in India* (Calcutta: Superintendent Government Printing, 1918). Several medical papers solicited from Anglo-American women physicians and "qualified midwives" in India were included in this influential special report on the work of the VMS Fund established by Lady Curzon in 1903.

31. When not engaged in delivering babies, the *dai* probably worked as *ayah* or *dhobi* (washerwoman) or at any number of other jobs unrelated to childbirth. In short, the indigenous midwife was not a "specialist" in the professional sense.

32. See Balfour and Young's account of the obstacles presented by the *dai* and by pollution beliefs circumscribing birth that prevented the progress of obstetrics and also of the solutions unendingly devised and abandoned (*Work of Medical Women*, 126–40).

33. See Borthwick, *Changing Role*, 152–64, for an account of indigenous birthing practices among Bengali *bhadralok* women. For an ethnographic account of birthing practices in North India in the postindependence period, see Roger Jeffery, et al., *Labour Pains and Labour Power: Women and Childbearing in India* (London: Zed, 1989). *Phaniyamma*, trans. Tejaswini Niranjana (Delhi: Kali for Women, 1989), by the Kannada writer M. K. Indira, provides a richly detailed representation of birthing practices structured by *madi* beliefs among Brahmin households in the Malnad district of the southern state of Karnataka.

34. See Dr. Marion Wylie, *Victoria Memorial Scholarship Fund Report*, 89. Henceforth *VMSF Report*.

35. *VMSF Report*, 85–86.

36. See, for examples, Borthwick, *Changing Role*, 155; and *VMSF Report*, passim.

37. Although she does not address the question of the abject and its relation to colonialism, I find Julia Kristeva's elaboration of the notion of abjection a compelling way of thinking through the horror and disgust produced in colonial discourse vis-à-vis "native" bodies and environments. See *Powers of Horror: An Essay on Abjection* (New York: Columbia University Press, 1982). Mary Douglas's work, *Purity and Danger: An Analysis of Concepts of Pollution and Taboo* (London: Routledge, 1963), on which Kristeva draws, is also useful here in conceptualizing the relations among filth, boundaries, and bodies.

38. Dr. Katherine O. Vaughan, *VMSF Report*, 99. The same passage is quoted and discussed in Katherine Mayo's much-publicized discussion of the conditions of childbirth in *Mother India*, which propelled the work of European women doctors in India into the international limelight in the late 1920s.

39. In the writings of Western-trained female obstetricians, the Indian midwife is frequently alluded to as a Sarah Gamp.

40. For a discussion of the machine metaphor in the development of Western obstetrics, see Emily Martin, *The Woman in the Body: A Cultural Analysis of Reproduction* (Boston: Beacon, 1987), 54–67.

41. See Moscucci's *Science of Woman* for a detailed analysis of such professional shifts in British obstetrics. See particularly 42–74.

42. See Mary Douglas's classic work on pollution behavior (*Purity and Danger*), to which I am here indebted. Douglas also looks upon Western notions of dirt as a form of pollution behavior.

43. Agnes Scott, *VMSF Report*, 91.

44. G. K. Devadhar, "The Health Visitor and Her Work," *Report: Maternity and Child Welfare Conference*, 66. Henceforth *Report: MCWC*.

45. See *Report: MCWC*, 145. The phrase is quoted from a paper entitled "Is the Time Ripe for Legislation to Authorize the Registration of Practising Dais?" by Miss R. Piggott, Secretary, Dais Improvement Scheme in Sind.

46. Major J. R. D. Webb, "The Dai," in *Report: MCWC*, 132–37.

47. See Gauri Vishwananthan for a discussion of British India's "checkered history of cultural confrontation [which] conferred a sense of urgency to voluntary cultural assimilation as the most effective form of political action" ("Currying Favor: The Politics of British Educational and Cultural Policy in India, 1813–1854," *Social Text* 7 [Fall 1988]: 85–104), 85.

48. See for example Dr. J. Jhirad's "Some Aspects of Medico-Social Work," in *Women in Modern India*, 25.

49. See *Report: MCWC*, 116.

50. *VMSF Report*, 161.

51. Here I am thinking of Macaulay's famous 1835 Minute on Indian education in which he argued for English as the medium of instruction and for the recreation of "natives" as Indian in blood and color but English in everything else.

52. See Agnes Scott's plans and charts in *VMSF Report*, 94.

53. Dr. Dagmar Curjels, *VMSF Report*, 69.

54. Ibid., 72.

55. See Katherine Mayo's *Mother India* and George MacMunn's *Underworld of India* (London: Jarrolds, 1933) for a sense of the *dai*'s appropriation by colonial popular discourse as a type of exotic criminality made possible by barbaric Hindu religious and social customs.

56. Here I am thinking of Homi Bhabha's now familiar but highly suggestive theoretical formulation regarding the production of hybridity and partial subjects in colonial discourse. See particularly "Signs Taken for Wonders."

57. I am grateful for the clarification on this point provided by the anonymous reviewer for *Genders*.

58. Balfour and Young, *Work of Medical Women*, 137–38.

59. See Gyan Prakash, "Science 'Gone Native,' " 172

60. This kind of analysis is beyond the scope of the present essay. It would require a theoretical and methodological shift as well as different kinds of sources than those employed here.

61. A great deal of work has been done on this question, but here I list only a few of the most recent books. For a literary-theoretical approach, see Laura E. Donaldson, *Decolonizing Feminisms: Race, Gender, and Empire-Building* (Chapel

228 SANDHYA SHETTY

Hill: University of North Carolina Press, 1992); Nupur Chaudhuri and Margaret Strobel, eds., *Western Women and Imperialism: Complicity and Resistance* (Bloomington: Indiana University Press, 1992). This is a useful collection of articles, primarily by historians, many of which have appeared elsewhere. See particularly essays by Dea Birkett and Leslie Flemming, which touch most closely the question of medicine, colonialism, and gender.

62. See Gayatri Spivak, "Three Women's Texts and a Critique of Imperialism," in *"Race," Writing, and Difference*, 262–80. See also Vron Ware, esp. the section "Britannia's Other Daughters," which concentrates on India, for another discussion of feminism in the age of imperialism in *Beyond the Pale: White Women, Racism, and History* (London: Verso, 1992), 119–66; and Antoinette Burton, "The White Woman's Burden: British Feminists and the Indian Woman, 1865–1915," *Women's International Studies Forum* 13 (1990): 295–321. (This essay can also be found in Chaudhuri and Strobel, eds. *Western Women and Imperialism*.)

63. See Jex-Blake, *Medical Women*, 42–45, and compare with Balfour and Young, *Medical Women*, 76–77. The extract below is from Jex-Blake, *Medical Women*, 42. See also Ware, *Beyond the Pale*, 129, 250.

64. Colonial Indian writing on purdah and zenana life is vast and it is impossible to document it exhaustively. See particularly Mayo, *Mother India*; Cornelia Sorabji, *The Purdahnashin* (Calcutta: Thacker, Spink, 1917); Dr. Rukmabai, "Purdah: The Need for Its Abolition," in *Women in Modern India*, 144–48; *The Key of Progress: A Survey of the Status and Conditions of Women in India*, ed. A. R. Caton (London: Oxford University Press, 1930), 115–23; "Purdah, or the Seclusion of Indian Women," in *Pice Papers on Indian Reform: Sanitation, Social, Moral, and Religious*, no. 7 (London and Madras: Christian Literary Society for India, 1897); George MacMunn, *The Underworld of India* (London: Jarrolds, 1933), 46–72; Mrs. Marcus B. Fuller, *The Wrongs of Indian Womanhood* (Edinburgh: Oliphant, Anderson & Ferrier, 1900), 76–99. For a less "typical" account that traces changes in the practice in relation to the growing women's movement in the early twentieth century, see Frieda Hauswirth, *Purdah: The Status of Indian Women* (London: Kegan Paul, Trench, Trubner, 1932); Vron Ware, *Beyond the Pale*, 129, 250. We have one powerful representation of purdah by an indigenous woman, Rokeya Sakhawat Hossain, who wrote against purdah in the early twentieth century, *Sultana's Dream and Selections from "The Secluded Ones."* For a recent elegant critical and historical essay on the Indian zenana and purdah, see Janaki Nair, "Uncovering the Zenana: Visions of Indian Womanhood in Englishwomen's Writings, 1813–1940," *Journal of Women's History* 2 (1990): 8–34; see also Geraldine Forbes, "In Search of the 'Pure Heathen': Missionary Women in Nineteenth-Century India," *Economic and Political Weekly* 21 (Women's Studies Suppl.; April 1986): 2–8; Hanna Papanek and Gail Minault, eds., *Separate Worlds: Studies of Purdah in South Asia* (Columbia, Mo.: South Asia Books, 1982).

65. Dr. Crake, Health Officer of Calcutta, quoted in Dr. A. C. Lankester, *Tuber-*

culosis in India: Its Prevalence, Causation, and Prevention (Calcutta: Butterworth [India] 1920), 144. The pathologizing view of purdah is particularly evident in Dr. Katherine O. Vaughan, *The Purdah System and Its Effect on Motherhood: Osteomalacia Caused by Absence of Light in India* (Cambridge: Heffer, 1928); and Katherine Mayo's *Mother India*, 111–22. See also Frances Ward Billington, *Woman in India* (London: Chapman & Hall, 1895), 86–111; Western, *Some Women of Sindh*; Somervell, *Knife and Life in India*, 119 27.

66. Lankester, *Tuberculosis in India*, 147. See also entire chapter 11.

67. The accounts of contemporary medical men and women are full of anecdotes on the ridiculous consequences of purdah in a clinical context. For a more recent fictional scene that repeats the hilarity reported of these clinical proceedings, see Salman Rushdie's narration of the medical encounters among Saleem's grandparents, Dr. Aadam Aziz, and Naseem Ghani, "the patient" in purdah examined through a perforated sheet. (*Midnight's Children* [New York: Avon, 1982], 19, 22–27).

68. See for example the extremely ambivalent, self-interrupting account of purdah in chapter 1 of Balfour and Young, *Work of Medical Women*. It must be noted that some women physicians even denied publicly the relevance of purdah to either the prevalence of disease or the problem of establishing Western obstetrics/gynecology's institutional hegemony in colonial India. See for example *VMSF Report*, 76–78.

69. Balfour and Young, *Work of Medical Women*, 34.

70. The phrase "purdah spirit" is Mary Frances Billington's (*Women in India*, 90).

71. In this connection Billington's quotation from a "private letter written to [her] by the editor of one of the leading newspapers of India is interesting. Speaking of medical women's assistance for the sick in purdah, this editor remarks, 'The chief value in my eyes of the movement has always lain in the promise and hope it at last afforded of at last invading the seclusion of the zenana' " (*Women in India*, 110). The violent, sexually inflected language of "reform" around purdah signals the entire dimension of desire that the present study has only lightly touched upon. The question of how desire and whose desire is played out in the scopic field structured by metaphors of visible/invisibility and movements of concealment and exposure warrants a different essay that would explore in greater detail the clinical context of the nexus of desire in which the gendered colonial subject is caught.

72. Balfour and Young, *Work of Medical Women*, 44.

73. Ibid., 44. For their defense against allegations that women physicians encouraged the continuance of purdah by making such concessions to it in their administration of medical aid, see Balfour and Young, *Work of Medical Women*, 35. Contra this defense, consider Borthwick's argument in *Changing Role of Women* that in the case of Bengal the accuracy of the assertion that women would not see male doctors was doubtful (216–19). In addition, see also the complaints of a Major A. J. H. Russell of the Indian Medical Service, Madras, who, speaking of the organization of maternity and child welfare

work in India and the monopoly of voluntary, non-official organizations, argued that mother and child welfare cannot be "entirely the province of women" (*Report: MCWC*, 13).

74. See Mayo, *Mother India*, for a detailed if sensational interpretation of Hindu social customs like child marriage and purdah as sexual barbarisms, consequences of what she refers to as the exaggerated sexual life of Hindus.

75. See Jeffery, *Politics of Health*, 87; and Balfour and Young, *Work of Medical Women*, 14–15, for accounts of the development of hospitals in colonial India.

76. Balfour and Young also categorize three types of women's hospitals that subsequently came to be established in the Punjab: mission hospitals, nonmission or Dufferin hospitals, and women's blocks or wards of government civil hospitals. See their extended discussion of hospitals and hospital administration in *Work of Medical Women*, 161–69.

77. Billington, *Women in India*; and Edith Craske, *Sister India: One Solution to the Problems of "Mother India"* (London: Religious Tract Society, 1930). Further references to these works will be included parenthetically in text.

78. For another contemporary account of this famous institution see Christine Tinling, *India's Womanhood: Forty Years' Work at Ludhiana* (London: Lutterworth, 1935).

79. Another glimpse into the appropriative use made by patients housed in these hospitals is afforded by Western's suggestion in *Some Women of Sindh* that often women "did not come for medicine at all, but as one might to see a circus or menagerie, with the simple wish to see something extraordinary" (137). In *Sister India*, Craske also comments on the outcome of the hospital's accommodation to caste "prejudices" of Hindu patients, which necessitated a Brahmin cook who "must be allowed to have her own sweet will in most of her methods.... Never for an instant must we draw near, lest our dread shadows ... defile the meal" (58). The Western doctor here becomes herself a source of pollution whose touch required submission to rituals of purification.

80. Somervell, *Knife and Life in India*, 80.

81. See Chakrabarty's discussion of the "Indian" home as a colonial construct in "Postcoloniality and the Artifice of History," 11–17; Borthwick, *Changing Role*, esp. 186–227. For a specific illustrative text, see the stories collected in Western's *Some Women of Sindh*. Here "the Indian home" emerges, in a specifically medical context, as crowded, chaotic, and dirty and Indian women as lacking in basic notions of home management. See particularly the tale "Confidence Lost and Won," 11–24.

82. *VMSF Report*, 73.

83. Ibid., 120.

84. Ibid., 121–22.

PART THREE

Dream Girls and Boys

The Third Sex: Figures of Inversion in Djuna Barnes's *Nightwood*

Andrea L. Harris

Dr. Matthew O'Connor, the voluble storyteller of Djuna Barnes's 1937 novel, *Nightwood*, spins tales on the subjects of woman's sexuality, homosexuality, desire, and love, spouting wild anecdotes, bitter laments, and intricate theories in a series of densely metaphorical monologues addressed primarily to a woman. By means of the figure of the doctor, a transvestite gynecologist, and his theories, the novel conceives of gender identity as an open-ended range of possibilities rather than a strict choice between masculine or feminine. Matthew bases his theories of gender and sexuality on two ambiguously gendered characters — Robin Vote, "a girl who resembles a boy," and himself.[1]

Matthew's gender ambiguity has a strong impact on his position as a storyteller and on his narrative authority. On the one hand, Matthew is an authoritative male speaker who aims to explain the intricacies of inversion to Nora Flood, Robin's lover. That is, Matthew speaks with the authority of his masculine subjectivity and his status as a doctor. Yet these traditional bases of authority are blatantly undercut by the fact that he is a would-be woman and an unlicensed quack.[2] By portraying Matthew as a transvestite gynecologist/theorist, Barnes creates a biting parody of the figure of the sexologist whose aim is to define the nature of female inversion. The theorist's interest, however, is found to be more than theoretical: Matthew studies women in order to satisfy his desire to be a woman. Matthew's own ambiguous gender position allows him to ques-

233

tion the gender binary and to construct more complex models of fluid gender identifications on the wide-ranging gender spectrum.

Matthew devises several theoretical models for inversion or homosexuality that throw both masculine and feminine radically into question. The gender of "the third sex" or the homosexual consists of a vacillation between masculine and feminine, regardless of her or his biological sex. By making the relation between sex and gender asymmetrical and indeterminate, the text denaturalizes the supposed congruence between sex and gender that is promoted by means of the gender binary. The invert thus provides a way of breaking open the closed and symmetrical binary opposition between masculine and feminine and challenging the idea of the binary opposition on which gender has been understood to rest. In a textual doubling of sexual inversion, the invert is inscribed in the text by means of the rhetorical figure of the chiasmus, a figure that consists of a double inversion.[3] Matthew attempts to determine the truth of inversion in these formulae, but the shifting, unstable nature of his own formulae undoes his quest for the truth. What happens to gender in this process? Matthew's figures of inversion rely to some extent on the gender binary at the same time that they question and undo it, an ambiguity that I will explore below. Matthew thus becomes a kind of deconstructive theorist of inversion, but at the same time he is a parody of the sexologist whose discourse relies upon and confirms the gender binary. This ambiguity can be seen especially in Matthew's transvestism. While on the one hand Matthew is sophisticated in his reading of gender ambiguity, particularly its manifestations in inversion, on the other hand he is very literal in his use of transvestism as a means of arriving at an end — being a woman. Other strands of the text also work to question this reliance upon the masculine/feminine opposition. First, Robin Vote, as a representation of the feminine, escapes any attempt to pin her down.[4] Finally and most importantly, not only do Matthew's own figures for inversion undermine the truth of inversion, in that the gender of the invert is left undecidable and indeterminate, but they also render undecidable the truth of gender — the simple binary scheme upon which gender is based. The constructed nature of gender in the invert is not just a special case of gender ambiguity; instead, it points to the constructed and ambiguous nature of all gender identity.

DISCONNECTING GENDER FROM SEX

In *Nightwood*, gender is a free-floating range of possibilities: one is neither masculine nor feminine, but both masculine and feminine to varying degrees and in various combinations. This sounds like a utopian description of androgyny, which is hardly the situation sketched by the novel. When gender is conceived not as fixed, certain, and consistent with sex and desire but as unstable, shifting, and inconsistent with sex, this situation sometimes causes conflict and pain, as it does for Robin and Matthew.[5] In *Nightwood*, Matthew and Robin, who typify the difficulties of those whose gender identities are compound and multiple, are seen struggling against the culturally constructed meanings attached to their sexed bodies, which are in conflict with their gender identifications. Their conflict is caused by the act of disconnecting gender from sex. This is the first, necessary step in refiguring the relation between masculine and feminine. If anatomy (or sex) is not seen as destiny, then gender need no longer be conceived as equivalent to sex; in other words, femaleness does not presuppose femininity. This allows the body to be cut loose from culturally prescribed meanings, yet this does not result in the return to a precultural, natural, and, therefore, nongendered state, for that would be impossible. Once cut loose from these prescribed meanings, newly gendered meanings may be devised for the body. Some of these new inscriptions of gender are embodied in Matthew's figures of inversion.

Several passages typify the divide between sex and gender that predominates in the novel, one being Robin's experience of pregnancy. When Robin becomes pregnant early in the novel, she thinks of her pregnancy as "some lost land in herself" (45). At this point, she begins to wander far from home, a habit that becomes characteristic over the course of the novel and that underlines her similarity to animals. When Robin gives birth, the event is described in this way:

Shuddering in the double pains of birth and fury, cursing like a sailor, she rose up on her elbow in her bloody gown, looking about her in the bed *as if she had lost something*. . . .

A week out of bed *she was lost*, as if she had done something irreparable, as if this act had caught her attention for the first time.

One night, Felix, having come in unheard, found her standing in the centre of the floor holding the child high in her hand as if she were about to dash it down, but she brought it down gently. (48; my emphasis)

At first, the child she is about to have is represented as "a lost land" within her, in the sense that it occupies a body that had formerly been hers entirely. Robin then experiences giving birth as the loss of "something": the "land" within her that was lost to the child (in other words, her uterus, which held the fetus) now seems doubly lost since she has given birth. This double loss is then further compounded: it becomes the loss of herself ("a week out of bed she was lost"). The "fury" and "despair" that mark Robin's feelings about having a child lead to her "cursing like a sailor" during childbirth, an act that underscores her masculinity even during this most feminine of acts. Her despair is then transmuted into the rage that nearly leads her to kill the child. Threatening to dash the child to the floor is a gesture she repeats with the doll that she gives to Nora; in the second instance, she actually does throw the doll/child to the floor. Robin's pregnancy is figured as a loss rather than as a gain or a "gift" of life, and this indicates her refusal of motherhood as an intrinsic trait of femininity and even of femaleness. Robin rejects the necessity of the link between motherhood and femaleness because maternity is not an expression of her gender identity. Robin does not possess the intrinsic femininity that is supposed to follow from her sex. Rather, maternity becomes a means by which Robin understands her distance from femininity.[6]

The refusal to be constrained by anatomical sex is shared by Matthew, the novel's other invert. Inversion in Matthew's case involves the desire to possess a different sex in order to possess a different gender. Since Barnes does not see anatomy as a constraint upon gender, however, Matthew can mime women and thereby become a woman in a man's body. While Robin rejects motherhood, Matthew longs for it, in an inversion of traditional gender roles that is typical of the novel.[7] Matthew often refers to himself as a girl or a woman ("am I not the girl to know of what I speak?" [90]) and bemoans the fact that although he is anatomically male, he is psychically feminine. Matthew explains the dilemma of his gender that is at odds with his sex in this way:

No matter what I may be doing, in my heart is the wish for children and knitting. God, I never asked better than to boil some good man's potatoes and toss up a child for him every nine months by the calendar. Is it my fault that my only fireside is the outhouse? (91)

Matthew longs to have the body of a woman and a woman's capacity to reproduce, but instead he must dress as a woman and mime the sex that he can never possess "naturally." Matthew is unable to have a home or a "fireside," which is something that he sees as a luxury attained only by those with a legitimate sexuality. His only home is the outhouse or kiosk, a place for cruising men.

Although Barnes trumps up Matthew's authority and uses him to mock the male fascination with women, his "gender trouble," to use Judith Butler's term, is not mocked. Rather, his gender trouble actually makes his theories of the invert or "the third sex" more believable because these theories are informed by experience. Matthew's love for men has been thwarted because he was born a man. He tells his tale of thwarted desire in terms of past lives:

In the old days I was possibly a girl in Marseilles thumping the dock with a sailor, and perhaps it's that memory that haunts me . . . am I to be blamed if I've turned up this time as I shouldn't have been, when it was a high soprano 1 wanted, and deep corn curls to my bum, with a womb as big as the king's kettle, and a bosom as high as the bowsprit of a fishing schooner? And what do I get but a face on me like an old child's bottom — is that a happiness, do you think? (90–91)

Matthew's image of the woman he was meant to be is a transvestite's fantasy. She is a hyperbole: he/she would have the highest voice, the longest hair, the deepest womb, and the highest bosom. Transvestism involves taking the prominent features of one sex and inflating them with hyperbole. These features are then put into even sharper relief by their appearance on a person of the opposite sex. The result is that Matthew's fantasy of himself as the "real" woman he was meant to be is an exaggeration of the features of stereotypical femininity. Femininity seems less natural as a result of the transvestite's image of it: drag makes evident the cultural construction of all gender roles.[8]

The shifting, unstable nature of Matthew's gender emerges clearly in his many asides on himself. In "Watchman," winding up for his account of the first meeting of Robin and Jenny, Matthew explains to Nora, "It was more than a boy like me (who am the last woman left in the world, though I am the bearded lady) could bear, and I went into a lather of misery watching them and thinking of you" (100). Matthew's gender is put into question the moment it is established by virtue of the way in which the subject of speech in these remarks is predicated: the "boy" underscores his undeveloped masculinity and his helplessness as a witness of this fateful meeting; the "last woman" suggests that he alone retains some vestige of true femininity compared to those who are anatomically female. And perhaps the most apt description is the "bearded lady," for he is an anomaly, a strange confusion of masculine and feminine. Matthew's misery is caused by the thought of Nora's pain, and his close identification with her may lead in part to his identification of himself as a woman in these remarks. In another instance where his ambiguous gender comes to the fore, Matthew refers to himself as "the other woman that God forgot" (143). He explains Nora's confession to him in this way — naturally she would come to him, for he is the woman that God forgot, or "the girl that God forgot," as he also calls himself (73). Not only is he a woman in a man's body (and thus God has forgotten him), but also he is an exceptional woman, the most womanly of women, as he establishes in the passages mentioned above. This endows him with a knowledge of the love of woman for woman, and of another special case like Robin, who may be, in a similar way, the last boy that God forgot. Just as Matthew, a man, is "the girl that God forgot" precisely in that he is a man and yet a girl, Robin is "the boy that God forgot" in that she is a woman and yet a boy. These complex formulations indicate the complexity of the relations among sex, gender, sexual practice, and desire in the novel. A question that arises about Matthew's gender ambiguity is, if Matthew is "the girl that God forgot," what does this mean for his role as the theoretician of sexuality and gender?

THE THEORETICIAN OF SEX AS BEARDED LADY: DR. MATTHEW O'CONNOR

Before we examine *Nightwood*'s theories of homosexuality, the theorist behind the theories should be discussed. "Dr. Matthew-Mighty-grain-of-salt-Dante-O'Connor" is a theorist as well as a priest figure who hears confessions (80). As a storyteller and theorist, Matthew carries great weight in the novel, but his full title (he is "mighty" but not worth "a grain of salt") seems to suggest that he is a mockery. Matthew is a figure of masculine discursive authority in the novel, and his monologues occupy so much of the novel that he sometimes seems a second narrator. But his apparent discursive authority in the text should be questioned, not taken at face value. To question Matthew's authority is to question the masculine prerogative to know in general, and to know in particular the truth of woman. Nora approaches Matthew with questions — "What is Robin?" and "What is the love of woman for woman?" — that are versions of the age-old question — "What is woman?" Men have always attempted to answer this question, but have always "knocked their heads against it," as Freud complained.[9] Matthew is a figure of Freud, of Ulrichs and other sexologists, and also of the male modernist artist who seeks to usurp the place of the feminine subject for his own.[10] By questioning Matthew's apparent discursive authority, we are merely following Barnes's lead, for she has made him a mockery of the authoritative male theorist: he is a frustrated transvestite and a quack doctor who envies women bitterly because he is not and cannot be one.

One way to question his authority in the novel is by considering his "profession" — gynecology. Many critics note that Matthew is a quack, but few find his specialty worth mentioning, though it is significant. Matthew is a gynecologist, and an "unlicensed practitioner" who practices with license at that (35). Throughout the novel, the only occasion on which he "practices medicine" is when he makes his house call on Robin in "La Somnambule," if throwing water on a woman who has fainted can be called medicine. The other references to his profession in the text are some details about his medical instruments. Matthew's oath, "May my dilator burst and my speculum rust, may panic seize my index finger before I point out my man" (37), seems to have come true by the time Nora goes to see him in his rooms in "Watchman, What of the Night?" for his tools are rusted and he, if not his index finger, is in a panic about being discovered in drag by Nora. In this passage, while Nora takes in the sight of Matthew in gown and curls, the narrator describes his surroundings, dwelling on the assortment of objects on Matthew's dresser:

On a maple dresser . . . lay a rusty pair of forceps, a broken scalpel, half a dozen odd instruments that she could not place, a catheter, some twenty perfume bottles, almost empty, pomades, creams, rouges, powder boxes and puffs. From the half-open drawers of this chiffonnier hung laces, ribands, stockings, ladies' underclothing and an abdominal brace which gave the impression that the feminine finery had suffered venery. (78–79)

The reader's shock is as great as Nora's when she makes this house call. The tools of Matthew's medical arts are sure to maim any woman who comes under them: the forceps are rusty and the scalpel broken. It is difficult not to see Matthew as a misogynist after reading this passage. Why does the text provide this exhaustive catalogue of objects? First, this description provides a backdrop for the heavily rouged man lying in bed in his nightgown. The specific objects on the dresser are significant, however.

The description of Matthew's dresser top is a catalogue of mismatched objects: women's makeup bottles lie next to rusty medical instruments; lacy "ladies' underclothing" lies next to a man's abdominal brace. Just as Matthew's sex, gender, and sexuality are incongruent — they form no logical, intelligible order — so is the assortment of objects in his private space incongruent. The result of this confusion of objects — feminine/masculine, cosmetic/medical, whole/broken — is that the privileged objects are contaminated by the very nearness of the others. And what is privileged here is the feminine finery, for it corresponds with the rouged and wigged man lying in bed. In private, Matthew plays at being a woman, and these objects enable him to carry out his fantasy. Although the masculine objects correspond to Matthew's "real" gender and his public persona, for Matthew, these are not real, but a false and inescapable condition. We can see this tension between the privileged feminine objects and the loathed masculine objects in the description of the masculine brace whose proximity sexually taints the women's lingerie: it "gave the impression that the feminine finery had suffered venery." Matthew's collection of feminine adornments constructs femininity as a pose, a facade created by the application to a blank surface (the woman) of a series of coverings: rouge, powder, perfume, hair combs, clothing, and so on. Matthew is deprived of a "natural" femininity, yet Barnes suggests through this concept of femininity as a facade or a masquerade that femininity does not exist in a natural state. Thus, it is available to Matthew to the same degree that it is available to any woman.

Through this description of objects, the text not only constructs femininity as a masquerade, but it also brings together Matthew's public persona and his private persona.[11] In private, Matthew is a transvestite, and the perfume, pomade, stockings, and lace indicate his attempt to play a woman since he is not one. In public, on the other hand, Matthew is Dr. O'Connor, the great storyteller and unlicensed but skilled doctor. His choice of gynecology seems arbitrary until we discover that Matthew longs to be a woman, for being a gynecologist helps relieve Matthew's frustration at being a man. Since he cannot be a woman, he can at least attempt to control women by means of his authority as a doctor. Since his desire to be a woman is thwarted and impossible to realize actually, he cultivates and studies women's bodies — both their internal parts and their diseases — as well as the external finery used to adorn their bodies. What is the effect of this characterization of Matthew — as a quack who practices gynecology because of his envy of women — on his position as the authority on sexuality in the novel?

Some critics see Matthew as the narrative foundation of the novel. Elizabeth Pochoda, for example, asserts that Matthew controls the novel's language, as if he, rather than Barnes, has written the novel. For this reason, she claims that the chapter entitled "The Possessed" is a stylistic failure and an "anticlimax" because it is not propelled by Matthew's storytelling abilities.[12] Pochoda does not consider that Barnes has silenced him; rather, she insists that his silence is Barnes's silence. By displacing the female author and replacing her with a male character, Pochoda blocks a feminist reading of the gender ambiguity that Barnes has put into play in her portrayal of Matthew. Although Pochoda denies Barnes authorial control, in a gesture suggestive of the poststructuralist notion of "the death of the author," she grants it fully to Matthew. Charles Baxter also attributes the control of the novel to Matthew, suggesting that "the novelist continues to write as long as O'Connor can talk."[13] For Alan Singer, the monologues bear such weight that he mistakenly attributes certain passages in the novel to the doctor when in fact it is the narrator speaking.[14] This tendency to privilege Matthew to the point of erasing the actual narrator is a common feature of the criticism up until the feminist revival of Barnes in the 1980s. In recent criticism, Matthew's ambiguous authority is noted by Jane Marcus, for example, who also sees him as a parody of Freud. Donna Gerstenberger sees his narrative power as contained by that of Barnes. She is correct to note that although his "stories often seem to exist for their own telling," they are "nonetheless inscribed within Barnes's narrative purpose."[15] In a text that does much to undermine all hierarchies, it is difficult to maintain that a figure such as Matthew holds such overwhelming discursive authority that he usurps the actual narrator's position.

Through these details of Matthew's portrayal — his quackery, his falling silent in a drunken heap in "Go Down, Matthew," his envy of women, and his self-mockery — Barnes creates a ridiculous figure, one who evokes laughter more than reverence. Yet some critics see in Matthew a masterful prophet, a reading that is possible only when his sexuality is misread, as Baxter misreads him in his equation of homosexuality with narcissism.[16] Baxter's traditional view of masculine authority would be undercut com-

242 ANDREA L. HARRIS

pletely were the critic to acknowledge Matthew's femininity. Ignoring
this, Baxter depicts him as a figure of monolithic authority — a prophet, a
character who steals the novel. Yet, if the surface of this character is
scratched, one sees that Barnes trumps up his authority and undercuts it
at every turn. In doing so, she inscribes a male figure who tries to usurp
the feminine role but who nevertheless holds on tight to his masculine
prerogatives. The nod to nineteenth-century sexologists only makes the
parody more biting. Through her transvestite gynecologist/priest/psycho-
analyst, Barnes reveals some very interested motives behind the masculine
discursive fascination with women. Matthew devises his theories of "the
third sex" in order to explain Robin to Nora, but also to come closer to
an understanding of woman for himself. The undecidability of both of
these figures — the invert and woman — undermines Matthew's own authority, making him a still more ambiguous figure. Yet this ambiguity
may better qualify him as an authority on subjects that by their questionable status undermine authority.

SEXUAL/TEXTUAL INVERSIONS: THE "PRINCE-PRINCESS"

Matthew responds to Nora's questions about the night and about Robin
with a series of compelling rhetorical figures for the invert, figures that
operate by means of syntactical inversion. What is the status of masculine
and feminine before inversion takes place? Barnes is writing both within
and against a dominant tradition in which discourse is organized around
binary oppositions rooted in the man/woman couple. *Nightwood* centers
around a series of privileged terms that are traditionally associated with
the feminine in the history of Western culture: the night, the irrational,
and the unconscious.[17] Although the feminine is privileged rather than
the masculine, the gender binary prevails, for the hierarchy has simply
been overturned. Barnes goes further in questioning this hierarchy, however, with her figures of inversion. Because of the complex, shifting nature
of gender in the invert, neither masculine nor feminine can be said to
predominate, as in a hierarchical binary structure. Matthew uses the term
"invert" to describe a state of vacillation — a blurring and confusion of
genders within the subject — not a simple predominance of feminine over
masculine or masculine over feminine. Since masculinity and femininity
are not eradicated but proliferated through inversion, the gender binary
is at the same time assumed in these figures and questioned and disrupted

through them. Inversion involves the figuring and refiguring of gender, for inversion consists of a merging and confusion of genders within the subject. For example, when female sex is joined to masculine gender identity and desire for women, to simply name the gender of this subject "feminine" or "masculine" is inadequate and misleading. This complex gender identity cannot be designated by these terms, yet it does not exist outside this binary; rather, it is an offshoot of the binary.[18] Masculine and feminine are propagated and proliferated in such a subject, one that *Nightwood* designates variously as the third sex, the invert, the prince, and the doll.

Matthew's first theory of the origin of homosexuality is prompted by Nora's remark about Robin's masculine appearance: "I, who want power, chose a girl who resembles a boy" (136). Matthew picks up this thread of androgyny and weaves a tale about love for the "same" sex, but this is clearly not love for the "same" sex, pure and simple, for Robin's resemblance to a boy is the mark of her difference.[19] According to Matthew, the love for the "invert" arises from childhood, specifically from childhood reading of romances and "fairy" tales. The passage reads:

What is this love we have for the invert, boy or girl? It was they who were spoken of in every romance that we ever read. *The girl lost, what is she but the Prince found?* The Prince on the white horse that we have always been seeking. *And the pretty lad who is a girl, what but the prince-princess in point lace* — neither one and half the other, the painting on the fan! We love them for that reason. (136; my emphasis)

What we find in this discussion of inverts is a series of inversions, both syntactical and logical. The figure for female homosexuality is the prince: "the girl lost," the lesbian, is "the Prince found." The term for the female homosexual is the prince, which is also the term for the male homosexual in the rest of the passage, which will be discussed below. It seems at first that the figure for the female invert is based upon the male and derived from it secondarily. This is a familiar scheme, common in Freudian theory. But when we turn to the discussion of the male invert, we find that there is no stable referent in the passage whatsoever — no referent that is primary. The only referents for the male homosexual are the girl (he is "the pretty lad who is a girl"), yet the girl is the prince. The second referent for the male homosexual is the prince-princess: the male invert — "the pretty lad who is a girl" — is "the prince-princess in point lace." In other words, the figure for the male invert refers to the figure for the

244 ANDREA L. HARRIS

female invert, and vice versa. There is no way out of this closed circle of reference, for we are never told exactly what the prince is. This figure becomes still more mysterious in this description: "The girl lost, what is she but the Prince found? The Prince on the white horse that we have always been seeking." We have always sought the prince, for he is a desirable object, but once we find him, it is only to discover that the prince is female — he is "the girl lost." This type of young masculinity and bravado turns out to be a boyish woman in drag, and "the girl lost," when we find her, is a feminine and boyish prince. In each case, our expectations are confounded by gender ambiguity, so we must continue our search, for what we have found is not what we were looking for. This search is also endless because these fairy-tale figures are fictional and therefore elusive. We may search the world over, but we will not find them, for they imprinted themselves upon our imaginations in childhood, and this childhood realm is their only locus.

To return to the figure for the male invert: he is described early in the passage not just as the prince but as "the prince-princess." This formulation suggests an androgyny that the male invert possesses but not the female invert. This figure is adorned in "point lace," a detail that calls to mind Matthew's feminine finery, spilling lavishly out of his dresser drawer when Nora arrives at his room at the beginning of "Watchman, What of the Night?" Why is the gender ambiguity of the female invert apparently captured by the comparison to the prince ("the girl lost" is "the Prince found"), while that of the male invert is not adequately described by the comparison to the prince? In other words, why the asymmetry in the figures for the two inverts, while other parts of the passage suggest that inversion is inversion, regardless of the invert's sex? Matthew seems to need to use a bigendered term to convey male inversion. As a male invert, Matthew has a stake in the formulation of this figure. What his dual term does is to assert both the masculinity and the femininity of the male invert while the femininity of the female invert is completely eradicated: she is simply a prince. The result is that masculinity is predominant over femininity in the invert. As an authoritative male speaker, Matthew wants to retain his masculine privilege, a privilege outside the domain of princesses. As we will see in the continuation of this passage, the invert is more prince than princess. Although the princess enters the scheme here, she does so only in the composite figure of the "prince-princess," and she is absent from the rest of Matthew's musings.

Yet what are the implications of the absence of the princess from the rest of the passage on the prince as the invert? Perhaps the pertinent question is not why the princess is omitted later in the passage but why it is added early in the passage. The "prince-princess in point lace" may be read as an intrusion into the text of the mark of transvestism — Matthew's mark. Just as Matthew's lacy lingerie peeks from his drawer in "Watchman," further exposing him for what he is or longs to be, so this distinctly feminine image of the princess peeks through and bursts in upon his otherwise predominantly masculine figures of princes. In other words, femininity, excessive with respect to discourse, as Irigaray has shown, shows its face here.[20] And this femininity is the mark of Matthew — the invert of inverts — that overt transgressor of the gender binary, the transvestite. Yet if transvestism entails a transgression of the gender binary, how is it that Matthew believes he can capture femininity by means of transvestism? Matthew fails to see that because the trappings of womanhood are transferable — they may be worn on men as well as women — they do not convey stable, essential femininity, but instead they point to unstable, constructed femininity — femininity as masquerade. Although he is well aware of the instability of gender identity and the incongruence between sex and gender in himself, Matthew regards cross-dressing not as the subversion of the gender binary, which it is, but as a means to capturing and claiming true femininity for himself.[21]

Despite the one conspicuous appearance of the princess, the overall emphasis of the passage is on princes. This emphasis on masculinity escalates when the princess is dropped from the rest of Matthew's musings. Matthew goes on at first to stress the origin of desire in childhood reading and fantasy: "We were impaled in our childhood upon them as they rode through our primers, the sweetest lie of all, now come to be in boy or girl" (136–37). The basis of object choice in childhood reading shows the grounding of desire in fantasy. Barnes has chosen the sort of fairy-tale figures that usually form the basis for heterosexual fantasies. Yet the gallant prince on the white charger is not only the rescuer of Sleeping Beauty and Cinderella but also the desirable object for the male invert and the model for both the male and female invert. Matthew calls this childhood fixation on the characters of children's storybooks "the sweetest lie of all." Why is the love for these characters a lie? Since these characters are fictional, they are ideal creatures whom we seek, but never find. This love is the "sweetest" lie of all in part because Matthew is a lover of princes himself. But more importantly, this lie is "sweetest" because desire in *Nightwood* is firmly rooted in the imagination and is best kept there — desire, once realized, is no longer desire but failed love.

This passage about inversion employs a rhetorical figure based on syntactical inversion; thus, textual inversion doubles sexual inversion. The last phrase in the passage contains a chiasmus, typically a symmetrical structure, although this one is asymmetrical: "In the girl it is the *prince*, and in the boy it is the *girl* that makes a prince a prince and not a *man*" (137; my emphasis).[22] If this were a symmetrical chiasmic reversal, the phrase would read, "In the girl it is the *prince*, and in the boy it is the *princess*." Yet this version of the phrase is impossible because Matthew has removed the princess from the model entirely because the princess signifies not just femininity but the transvestite's version of femininity, and transvestites are a special case of inverts. Another symmetrical variation of the phrase is, "In the girl it is the *boy* and in the boy it is the *girl*." The girlish aspect of the boy makes him a prince, but the princely aspect rather than the boyish aspect of the girl makes her a prince in Matthew's version of the model.[23] The prince is also the model for the invert, male or female, for the girl and the boy are treated as one here: "In the girl it is the prince, and in the boy it is the girl that makes a prince a prince and not a man." The statement explains what causes *both* boy and girl to become princes. In other words, the female invert and the male invert are described by means of the same figure — that of the prince. Another asymmetry in the text involves the girl again. Matthew states that it is the prince in the girl and the girl in the boy that creates inversion or "makes a prince a prince and not a man." The male invert (prince) is "not a man," as stated by the text; by the same token, the female invert (prince) is not a woman. Yet the text only implies that the female invert is not a woman; it does not state it. The asymmetry here is so great that it is as if the conclusion of the phrase were lopped off: the fact that the female invert is not a woman is simply omitted from the passage. But perhaps this asymmetry is not the result of Matthew's privileging of the masculine model. Barnes may be suggesting that a female homosexual is still a woman in a way that a male homosexual cannot be a man. "Womanhood" is not threatened by homosexuality as "manhood" is, because of the historical privilege and status of the latter. The omission of the statement that the female invert is not a woman may also suggest that women have a fundamental bisexuality, as Freud argued.

Why is the male the primary referent in Matthew's discussion of the invert? There are two factors that cause the text's blind spot concerning the girl. First, a boy who is like a girl and a girl who is like a boy are essentially the same creatures — androgynous, "third-sexed" creatures. Second, an androgyny in which masculinity is slightly more predominant seems to be privileged in *Nightwood* by means of Matthew's focus on Robin; therefore, the prince is the predominant model, not the "prince-princess." We see this in Robin's un-self-conscious androgyny (she is "a girl who resembles a boy" [136]), which is privileged in the novel, whereas Matthew's transvestism, which rests on a belief that he is truly a woman, makes him a parodic figure.[24] Because both male and female inverts have the same origin (in childhood fixations on androgynous characters) and because they have the same qualities (an androgyny in which masculinity is slightly more pronounced and same-sex love), Matthew uses the same term to refer to both female and male homosexuals — they are "the third sex" or "the invert." The use of the same term for female and male homosexuals also works to undo the binary opposition between male and female: "the third sex" questions the hierarchy between the first and second sex.

The asymmetry of the syntax in the passages describing the prince is not merely an aberration of a classically symmetrical figure of speech. The symmetrical versions described above are dependent upon the diametrical or binary opposition between masculine and feminine. To posit the male and female homosexual as diametrical opposites would be in effect to recreate the masculine/feminine opposition that the text is attempting to undo by means of the figure of "the third sex." This figure is inscribed as a third term precisely in order to question the legitimacy of a strict opposition between masculine and feminine. In *Nightwood*, the masculine is inhabited by the feminine, and vice versa: all of the text's inverts are not merely inverted; rather, they live out the tension between masculine and feminine and are in some way both masculine and feminine. Their state is not one of the simple inversion of gender positions, but rather of the constant vacillation between them (or among them).

Take, for example, Robin's complex gender identity. "She" is not simply a woman who, seeing herself as masculine, wants to be a man, which would imply a resolution of the conflicts among sex, gender, and desire. Rather, Robin is, in the terms of the novel, a girl/prince: a female (her sex) who resembles a feminine male — the prince (her gender) — and who loves women (her desire). These incongruous identifications exist side by side, and the tension among them is never resolved in a simple formula such as, "Robin is a man in a woman's body."[25] Robin is *not* a man in a woman's body, but a woman who loves women, who seems masculine, and whose very body and self-presentation also seem masculine. A passage from Butler describes the kind of intricately gendered being that Robin is:

It is possible to become a being whom neither *man* nor *woman* truly describes. This is not the figure of the androgyne nor some hypothetical "third gender," nor is it a *transcendence* of the binary. Instead, it is an internal subversion in which the binary is both presupposed and proliferated to the point where it no longer makes sense.[26]

Robin is indeed a being whom neither "man" nor "woman" describes adequately. Yet, while I have followed Barnes in describing Robin as a member of "the third sex," Butler cautions that this type of gendered being is something other than the androgyne or the "hypothetical 'third gender.' " While the notion of "the third sex" was first coined to describe the idea of the man trapped in a woman's body and has also been understood as an androgynous state beyond gender, Barnes's "third sex" is a radical reconceptualization of this idea.[27] Her vision of "the third sex" is much closer to contemporary notions of the socially constructed, performative nature of gender. By means of this third term, which would undermine the binary opposition between masculine and feminine, Barnes's text refuses simple binary opposition or symmetry in its articulation of gender. This third term will be more explicitly theorized in Matthew's other model for inversion, discussed in the next section, where Matthew names this third term "the third sex."

"THE THIRD SEX"

Matthew's second model for homosexuality — the doll — is similar to that based on the prince: it is lifeless, yet lifelike; it derives from childhood; and it is androgynous. Matthew offers his second theory in response to Nora's story of the doll that Robin has given to her. Nora regards a doll given to a woman by her lover as a replacement for, or a representation of, the child they cannot have: "We give death to a child when we give it a doll — it's the effigy and the shroud; when a woman gives it to a woman, it is the life they cannot have, it is their child, sacred and profane" (142). As a gift from a woman to her lover, the doll is a stand-in for the child the women cannot have, indicating the attempt to model their life after a heterosexual relationship, an attempt that necessarily fails. In a sense, the doll is a sign of this failure, yet Nora is nevertheless attached to the doll as a gift from Robin.[28] Thus, when Robin throws and "kills" the doll in a fit of rage, the action devastates Nora. This incident takes place when Robin returns home after wandering the night streets, a habit that underscores the distance between the lovers. Nora attributes Robin's violent treatment of the doll to the fact that "she was angry because for once I had not been there all the time, waiting" (148). For Nora, the doll is a mediator between Robin and herself: it is a replacement for the connection that is lacking between them.

The doll resembles the figure of the prince as invert not only in its relation to childhood fantasy but also in the way that it is inscribed in the text: both models appear as chiasmic reversals. After discussing Robin's sense of herself as the doll, Matthew likens the doll explicitly to the invert:

The last doll, given to age, is the girl who should have been a boy, and the boy who should have been a girl. The love of that last doll was foreshadowed in that love of the first. The doll and the immature have something right about them, *the doll because it resembles but does not contain life, and the third sex because it contains life but resembles the doll.* (148; my emphasis)

In this passage, the origin of homosexuality is located again in childhood, or rather in a regression to childhood ("the last doll given to age" is the doll that an adult might give to another adult, as Robin gives Nora a doll and Felix a baby). More important, the "last doll" is a metaphor for the homosexual: "the girl who should have been a boy and the boy who should have been a girl." The love that they inspire was "foreshadowed" in the love of the first doll of childhood, just as the love of the prince was foreshadowed, or actually inspired by, the love of the figure of the prince in fairy tales. The model for homosexuality is again a replica of a person that children endow with a name, a character, and so on, like the princes of childhood readers. Children may project their desires onto such figures; they may perceive them as doubles of themselves. In short, the doll and the prince may be transformed into whatever the child wants them to be because they are purely fictional. Similar to the function of the doll for Nora, the prince is also a beloved yet lost object that is introjected and incorporated through melancholia. In the same way, Nora loves Robin because Robin's lack of identity at first allows her to be transformed into anything. In this sense, the doll and the invert are both inanimate figures that can be animated.

Again, the structure of the passage is that of a chiasmus — this time, a double chiasmus. The first sentence contains a simple symmetrical chiasmus: "the girl who should have been a boy, and the boy who should have been a girl." The sentence beginning "the doll and the immature" forms another symmetrical chiasmus: "the doll because it resembles but does not contain life, and the third sex because it contains life but resembles the doll." As in the passage on the prince, the text construes sexual "inversion" as syntactical inversion. The symmetry of these inversions at first seems to imply a simple acceptance of a binary scheme for gender: homosexuality is the result of being misplaced in one's anatomical sex. But this simple inversion — the invert is the girl who should have been a boy and the boy who should have been a girl — is subverted by the language of the rest of the passage.

There Matthew describes the doll's face as a composite of two sexless beings: "The blessed face! It should be seen only *in profile*, otherwise it is observed to be the conjunction of the identical *cleaved halves* of sexless misgiving!" (148; my emphasis). In other words, the doll's face is neither masculine nor feminine, and for this reason in particular he uses the metaphor of the doll for the homosexual. Matthew's image relies on the idea of the splitting in two (as implied by "cleaved," "halves," and "profile") of something that we expect to be whole (the face). Yet "cleave" also refers to a joining together, as in the biblical reference to marriage. The face is that part of the body traditionally thought to convey identity, a concept that implies wholeness and unity. The face of the invert, however, is divided, torn asunder, and therefore the only way to convey the impression of the whole (an idea that is implicit in the meaning of the face) is to look at only one half — the profile.

One word stands out in this passage that seems to work against the predominant note of division and disunity. That word is "identical": the face is "observed to be the *conjunction* of the *identical* cleaved halves of sexless misgiving." Though the face of the doll/invert is divided, its parts are identical to each other. The two identical halves of the doll's face could be read as masculine and feminine, conjoined: each half consists of a blend of masculine and feminine.[29] Thus, gender confusion is conceived not as a simple case of a man trapped in a woman's body (or a woman trapped in a man's body) but as a complex case of both genders inflecting one body.[30] The halves referred to in the passage are not only the parts of the face; they are also the "cleaved halves of sexless misgiving." That is, the division is caused by the uncertainty of the doll/invert about its sex, which results in a state of "sexless misgiving." On the other hand, the sex of the invert has been "mis-given," or given wrongly: Matthew's image also implies that inversion is the result of an incorrect assignment of sex. Since the conjunction of masculine and feminine in one person is perceived as gender uncertainty in our culture, the invert seems a sexless creature, suspended in a state of uncertainty or misgiving. The text's careful delineation of the self-division of the doll/invert is what works against the seemingly simple binary scheme of these particular chiasmi. The self-division indicates that the doll/invert is made up of both masculine and feminine characteristics: so the formula "the girl who should have been a boy" then represents a girl/boy, not a boy in spirit and in sexuality who is at war with her female body.

These analogies between the invert and lifeless dolls or fairy-tale figures emphasize on one level the idea that gender and sexuality are not necessarily consistent with anatomical sex, because the connections between them are constructed through the psyche, language, and culture, and are not natural. Although homosexuality is often construed as a false miming of the "natural" genders found in heterosexuality, what Barnes is trying to get at here is the way in which "the third sex" makes explicit the performative nature of all gendered behavior.[31] A glance at a passage on "the third sex" as the "Sodomite" reveals that this is one of the reasons for the placement of the invert in the realm of the fictional as opposed to the real. In "Watchman," Matthew turns to the subject of loving a "Sodomite" after introducing the night to Nora.

> "And do I know my Sodomites?" the doctor said unhappily, "and what the heart goes bang up against if it loves one of them, especially if it's a woman loving one of them. What do they find then, *that this lover has committed the unpardonable error of not being able to exist - and they come down with a dummy in their arms.* God's last round, shadow-boxing, that the heart may be murdered and swept into that still quiet place where it can sit and say: 'Once I was, now I can rest.' " (93; my emphasis)

Although the term "Sodomite" historically refers to male inverts, Matthew is clearly using it to refer to female inverts as well, since he speaks of what happens when a woman loves one of them, and Nora clearly loves a female invert. Just as he merges male and female homosexuals under the terms "prince" and "invert," so he uses the masculine term "Sodomite" to refer to both sexes. While Matthew's aim in describing the prince and the doll was theoretical, his aim in describing the sodomite here is existential. The doll and the prince were devised to show the origin of homosexuality in childhood and to describe the qualities of this other sexuality. These figures were also devised in order to theorize the complex gender identity of the invert. Here, on the other hand, he explains to Nora what *happens* when one loves a sodomite. He speaks, that is, of his painful experience: "And do I know my Sodomites?" refers not to his encyclopedic knowledge of the species invert but to the basis of his knowledge — his own life as an invert and his frustrated desires. His subject, as he goes on to say, is "what the heart goes bang up against if it loves one of them."

The invert's inability to exist causes pain and anguish to those who love inverts. But why does Matthew claim that the invert is "not able to exist"? Once again, the novel likens the invert or "Sodomite" to that which is lifeless — in this case, a "dummy," which, like the doll, is an imitation of life. Matthew's prince similarly was "a lie" — a desirable object that was always sought but never found, because it did not exist in the real. Although the prince exists, at least in the imagination, he/she is unattainable because he/she is absent from the real. But the lifelessness of the sodomite as dummy seems more dramatic than that of the prince or the doll: the doll "does not contain life," according to Matthew, while the sodomite is *"not able to exist."* The invert's habitat is the night, and consequently, the invert is associated with the novel's central terms — the anonymous, the unconscious, nonreason — which are associated with death and nothingness.[32] For this reason, in part, the invert "is not able to exist." The invert is also one of the many abject, outcast characters that populate this novel: as Marcus argues, *Nightwood* is a tale of Jews, blacks, lesbians, and transvestites, oppressed others who resisted the authoritarian domination that typified European politics in the 1930s.[33] The invert, like other oppressed people — like other "others" — lives on the margins of society, which is figured as the night in this novel, a space that is privileged yet still marked as outside. In other words, "the third sex" is a term that subverts binary oppositions by being a conjunction of masculine and feminine: the very term "the third sex" poses a challenge to the structure of binary opposition that shores up the world of the day, discourse, and structures of power.

"THERE IS NO TRUTH" OF GENDER

In attempting to resolve the question of the degree to which *Nightwood*'s figures of inversion rely upon the gender binary even as they deconstruct the truth of inversion, I will close by considering a remark of Matthew's that may be read as a self-reflexive comment on his own status as a speaker. Matthew describes to Nora the mistake involved in imposing a formula on love: "There is no truth, and you have set it between you; you have been unwise enough to make a formula; you have dressed the unknowable in the garments of the known" (136). In order to understand her love for Robin, Nora goes to Matthew for an explanation of the truth about Robin, the truth about homosexuality, and the truth about the night. But these truths — or formulae — do not exist and this is something that Matthew also tries to teach Nora. Although Matthew's voice in the novel is endowed with authority, his authority is also ambiguous: while admitting that there is no truth and that he only tells lies, he nevertheless presents Nora with several accounts of inversion that sound like attempts to speak the truth. Yet rather than reveal the truth, as Matthew sets out to do, he only reveals the inadequacy of his own formulae.

While focusing on Nora's desire for the truth, this remark of Matthew's is also self-reflexive in that he is aware that he himself has "dressed the unknowable in the garments of the known." As a self-professed theorist of sexuality, Matthew has devised models for the invert that do precisely this: they take an unknowable entity and explain it by means of familiar terms that the invert itself puts seriously into question. Matthew has taken the person whose gender is an indeterminable amalgamation of masculinity and femininity and given it a name (or several names), an origin, and a history. But for Barnes, "the third sex" is fundamentally undecidable, and any attempt to formulate it is bound to miss its mark. The characters Robin and Matthew, as well as Matthew's theories of the invert, have shown that masculine and feminine are not easily distinguishable, do not neatly coincide with male and female, and that gender is not a simple choice between two options. Although *Nightwood* has ventured a theory of "the third sex," it undoes its own attempt precisely to show that there is no certain truth of either inversion or gender. "The third sex" is the mark of this uncertainty.

Matthew's metaphor of "dressing the unknowable in the garments of the known," as formulaic as it may seem, brings together all the uncertainty and undecidability surrounding gender in this text. First, it is a self-conscious remark in that it refers to his own transvestism in an almost literal way. Although Matthew claims that it is an error to "dress the unknowable in the garments of the known," isn't this what he himself attempts to do by means of his transvestism? In his desire to be a woman, he takes the costumes and cosmetics that are cultural markers of femininity — "the garments of the known" — and uses them to "dress the unknowable." But what is the unknowable in this instance — the woman Matthew longs to be or the ambiguous gender that he possesses? In his eagerness to be a true woman, or a woman in truth, Matthew has mistaken the feminine masquerade for the essence of woman. Removing the "garments" of femininity from Matthew would simply reveal an aging man, not the beautiful young woman he longs to be. In a similar way, his ambiguous gender, "the third sex," is unknowable (in the sense of being indeterminate and in flux) and undecidable, and no garment could ever take the shape of its strange contours. The text seems to suggest then that "the third sex" is fundamentally "unknowable." Although via Robin the text also represents the feminine as mysterious, enigmatic, and unknowable — and in this way, she resembles an essential feminine — it also moves toward a recognition of femininity as construct or masquerade. The scene in which Nora finds Matthew in drag, surrounded by "feminine finery," indicates the impulse in the text toward this other view of transvestism: instead of garments failing to convey the truth of woman, garments — the masquerade — themselves constitute femininity. In this sense, Matthew may be read both as a parody of the nineteenth-century sexologist and as a prescient sketch of a contemporary gender theorist. While *Nightwood* anticipates the theorization of gender as performance, there still lingers in this rich text a belief in an essential, fundamental gender difference lurking beneath, as it were, the garments of culturally constructed, multiple gender differences.

NOTES

I am grateful to Stacy Hubbard, who commented on several early versions of this essay. I also thank the anonymous reviewers at *Genders* for their helpful suggestions on a later revision.

1. Djuna Barnes, *Nightwood* (1937; rpt. New York: New Directions, 1961), 136. Further references to this work will appear in the text.
2. Given the fact that *Nightwood* is a modernist text, it may be that Matthew's femininity actually provides, rather than undercuts, his narrative authority. Gayatri Chakravorty Spivak writes that the masculine displacement of the feminine subject position provides deconstruction with its discursive power ("Displacement and the Discourse of Woman," in *Displacement: Derrida and After*, ed. Mark Krupnick [Bloomington: Indiana University Press, 1983], 169–72). Alice Jardine has also examined the valorization of the feminine as a means of exploring the meaning of modernity in twentieth-century male-authored writing (*Gynesis: Configurations of Woman and Modernity* [Ithaca, N.Y.: Cornell University Press, 1985], 25). I read Matthew similarly, as a male theorist who masquerades as a woman in order to displace his own subjectivity.
3. These figures must be read both thematically and stylistically, for issues of gender and style cannot be separated in the study of women modernists' texts, where gender experimentation is tied closely to stylistic experimentation. Style was the primary focus of criticism on Barnes until the late 1980s, when Sandra M. Gilbert and Susan Gubar, Shari Benstock, and Frann Michel brought attention to the centrality of gender within Barnes's texts, while also examining style. See Gilbert and Gubar, *Sexchanges*, Vol. 2 of *No Man's Land: The Place of the Woman Writer in the Twentieth Century*, 2 vols. to date (New Haven, Conn.: Yale University Press, 1989); Shari Benstock, *Women of the Left Bank: Paris, 1900–1940* (Austin: University of Texas Press, 1986); and Frann Michel, "Displacing Castration: *Nightwood, Ladies Almanack*, and Feminine Writing," *Contemporary Literature* 30, no. 1 (1989): 33–58. One notable early study of gender and style in *Nightwood* is Carolyn Allen's 1978 essay, " 'Dressing the Unknowable in the Garments of the Known': The Style of Djuna Barnes's *Nightwood*," in *Women's Language and Style*, ed. Douglas Butturf and Edmund L. Epstein (Akron, Ohio: University of Akron Press, 1978), 106–18. Recent feminist readings of the novel that continue the study of gender and style and that I will discuss below are essays by Judith Lee and Jane Marcus in Mary Lynn Broe's *Silence and Power: A Reevaluation of Djuna Barnes* (Carbondale: Southern Illinois University Press, 1991). See Lee, "*Nightwood*: 'The Sweetest Lie,' " 207–18; and Marcus, "Laughing at Leviticus: *Nightwood* as Woman's Circus Epic," 221–50. In my focus on Matthew as a storyteller/theorist, I am returning to one of the tendencies of 1970s and

early 1980s Barnes criticism. The critics Charles Baxter, Elizabeth Pochoda, and Alan Singer, whose work I will examine below, tended to emphasize Matthew's discursive power and narrative authority, which they saw as eclipsing Barnes's authorial power. I would like to reread Matthew's narrative authority and the focus of his narrative — inversion and gender — in light of some of the insights of feminist Barnes studies on the text's inscription of gender.

4. For convincing readings of Robin as a representation of the feminine, see Michel, "Displacing Castration," 41–42, and Lee, "*Nightwood*," 210–11.

5. I am using Judith Butler's definition of gender identity as "a relationship among sex, gender, sexual practice, and desire" (*Gender Trouble: Feminism and the Subversion of Identity* [New York: Routledge, 1990], 18).

6. While Robin rebels against both pregnancy and motherhood, and thus in some sense she rejects her gender role, her possibilities for complete rejection are more limited than those of Matthew, who rebels against masculinity through dressing as a woman. Matthew can refuse to engage in masculine sexual behavior, while Robin's reproductive capacity is a constant fact of life.

7. Gender role is defined as "a set of expectations about what behaviors are appropriate for people of one gender" (Suzanne J. Kessler and Wendy McKenna, *Gender: An Ethnomethodological Approach* [New York: Wiley, 1978], 11).

8. On the denaturalization of gender in drag performance, see Esther Newton, *Mother Camp: Female Impersonators in America* (Chicago: University of Chicago Press, 1979), 103, 107.

9. Sigmund Freud, "Femininity," *The Standard Edition of the Complete Psychological Works of Freud*, trans. James Strachey, 28 vols. (London: Hogarth, 1964), 22:113.

10. Marcus comments on Matthew as a scathing parody of Freud, or of sexologists in general. See "Laughing at Leviticus," 233–34, 245. For discussions of the masculine displacement of the feminine subject position, see note 2 above.

11. The masquerade of femininity, first theorized by Joan Riviere, designates the deliberate putting on of femininity — according to Luce Irigaray, the "affirmation" of traditional connotations of the feminine. See Riviere, "Womanliness as a Masquerade," in *Psychoanalysis and Female Sexuality*, ed. Hendrik M. Ruitenbeek (New Haven, Conn.: College and University Press, 1966), 209–20; and Irigaray, *This Sex Which Is Not One*, trans. Catherine Porter (Ithaca, N.Y.: Cornell University Press, 1985), 76. This affirmation allows for a transformation, or a "transvaluation," of the feminine itself because it is the feminine's potentially subversive qualities that are privileged. See Naomi Schor, "This Essentialism Which Is Not One: Coming to Grips with Irigaray," *differences* 1, no. 2 (1989): 48. The feminine's multiplicity, undecidability, and excess are self-consciously emphasized as a way of setting loose their subversive potential. For other feminist discussions of masquerade and the related term "mimesis," see Mary Ann Doane, "Film and the Masquerade:

Theorising the Female Spectator," *Screen* 23, nos. 3–4 (1982): 81–82; and Butler, *Gender Trouble*, 47–53.

12. Pochoda writes, "The novel has already jettisoned language; O'Connor has exited, and really there is no way to rescue the end of the story from the melodrama it has eschewed so far" ("Style's Hoax: A Reading of Djuna Barnes's *Nightwood*," *Twentieth Century Literature* 22 [1976]: 188). The style of "The Possessed" is spare and monosyllabic not because Barnes has reached her limit in previous chapters, but because language has been such an obstacle to Robin and Nora that they attempt silence as a last resort. Moreover, the novel's resources are not depleted; rather, Matthew's resources are depleted because the misery that he experiences in telling stories on subjects that others are "keeping hushed" leads him to choose silence over speech as well. See *Nightwood*, 162–63.

13. Charles Baxter, "A Self-Consuming Light: *Nightwood* and the Crisis of Modernism," *Journal of Modern Literature* 3 (1974): 1177.

14. Alan Singer, "The Horse Who Knew Too Much: Metaphor and the Narrative of Discontinuity in *Nightwood*," *Contemporary Literature* 25, no. 1 (1984): 75, 82.

15. Donna Gerstenberger, "The Radical Narrative of Djuna Barnes's *Nightwood*," in *Breaking the Sequence: Women's Experimental Fiction*, ed. Ellen G. Friedman and Miriam Fuchs (Princeton, N. J.: Princeton University Press, 1989), 136.

16. Baxter, "A Self-Consuming Light," 1180.

17. For a discussion of the masculine/feminine hierarchy, see Hélène Cixous, "Sorties," in *New French Feminisms*, ed. Elaine Marks and Isabelle de Courtivron (New York: Schocken, 1981), 90–91. My discussion of the status of the masculine/feminine opposition in *Nightwood* is informed by Michel's convincing argument that the feminine in Barnes's texts closely resembles the feminine within the work of Hélène Cixous, Luce Irigaray, and Julia Kristeva. See Michel, "Displacing Castration," 34–39. For the connection between the night and the destabilization of identity, an issue too involved to be addressed adequately here, see *Nightwood*, 81–83, 88.

18. Butler's notion of the relation between stable and destabilizing gender provides a clear framework for Barnes's notion of the third sex as I am formulating it, and I am indebted to Butler here: gender is destabilized "through the mobilization, subversive confusion, and proliferation of precisely those constitutive categories that seek to keep gender in its place by posturing as the foundational illusions of identity" (*Gender Trouble*, 34).

19. Pamela L. Caughie critiques the tendency to read androgyny as a transcendence of gender in criticism on Virginia Woolf. For example, in Gilbert and Gubar's reading of androgyny in women's modernist fiction, they negate the very gender categories they seek to maintain by construing androgyny as a state "beyond gender." See Gilbert and Gubar, *Sexchanges*, 332, 361–62. Following Caughie, I argue that the ambiguously gendered "third sex" enacts or deploys gender, rather than transcends it. See Caughie, "Virginia Woolf's

Double Discourse," in *Discontented Discourses: Feminism/Textual Intervention/ Psychoanalysis*, ed. Marleen S. Barr and Richard Feldstein (Urbana: University of Illinois Press, 1989), 46, 51.

20. Irigaray, *This Sex*, 78.

21. See Butler, *Gender Trouble*, 136–38, for a reading of drag as a subversive practice that creates gender confusion and proliferation.

22. My reading owes much to Andrzej Warminski's reading of an asymmetrical chiasmus in Nietzsche's *Birth of Tragedy*. The metaphor in question that undergoes a chiasmic reversal involves the opposition of Apollo and Dionysos, light and dark, blinding and healing. Warminski's text dwells on this figure for some thirty pages and cannot be paraphrased here. However, the thrust of his reading is that Apollonian light is found to result in the same nothingness that the Dionysian night presents to the senses. And this nothing is "radically unknowable" in terms of binary opposition. This is the reason for the figure's bursting the boundaries of a tidy symmetrical reversal. I would suggest that similarly, for Barnes, gender and sexuality cannot be contained or even suggested within the confines of a scheme of thinking based on binary opposition. See *Readings in Interpretation: Holderlin, Hegel, Heidegger* (Minneapolis: University of Minnesota Press, 1986), xxxv–lxi.

23. For a convincing gloss on this passage, see Michel, "Displacing Castration," 42. She points out that the female invert "contains the difference that she is" — the difference of inversion — while the male invert "becomes an invert by containing the difference of the feminine." According to Michel, Matthew's figures of inversion thus reaffirm the gender binary in that difference is located "on the side of Woman" in these figures. Yet Michel argues that another of Matthew's descriptions of the invert "disrupt[s]" the "binary structure of gender." She reads the description of the invert as "neither one and half the other" as stressing otherness and difference and thus disrupting the gender binary (*Nightwood*, 136). While I agree that Matthew's figures rely on the gender binary to a certain degree, I argue that the asymmetry of the figures, as well as the complex interplay among all components of gender identity in the text's inverts — sex, gender, sexual practice, and desire — result in the disruption rather than the reaffirmation of the gender binary.

24. While Robin's androgyny is described as a natural trait, it is also deliberate in that she dresses like a boy, perhaps to enhance her masculinity.

25. The idea of a woman trapped in a man's body is put forward by Gilbert and Gubar, an idea that the language of the text does not bear out. See their *Sexchanges*, 216–17.

26. Butler, *Gender Trouble*, 127. Emphasis in original.

27. "The third sex," the term that best conveys *Nightwood*'s inscription of inversion, is a term coined by the nineteenth-century sexologist Karl Heinrich Ulrichs to designate the concept of the homosexual as a man trapped in a woman's body. This concept, also known as the "man-woman," was further theorized and popularized by better-known sexologists such as Richard von Krafft-Ebing and Havelock Ellis. See J. E. Rivers, "The Myth and Science of

THE THIRD SEX 259

Homosexuality in *A la recherche du temps perdu,*" in *Homosexualities and French Literature,* ed. George Stambolian and Elaine Marks (Ithaca, N. Y.: Cornell University Press, 1979), 265–66. Benstock provides important commentary on the effects of such theories in the sociocultural realm for women writers of the 1920s and 1930s (*Women of the Left Bank,* 49–52).

28. The doll stands in for the loss of Robin: in a response to Robin's refusal of love, Nora displaces her love onto a stand-in, the doll. Nora in this way resembles the melancholiac of Sigmund Freud's "Mourning and Melancholia." See *General Psychological Theory,* ed. Philip Rieff (New York: Collier, 1963), 164–66. Butler's reading of the incorporative structure of melancholy in the formation of gender identity is also suggestive in relation to Nora, but this issue is too involved to take up adequately in this essay. See Butler, *Gender Trouble,* 48–53.

29. This is but one of a series of metaphors in *Nightwood* that involve the joining and merging of halves and that indicate the overcoming of opposition. See 38, 69, 138.

30. Not only does Barnes subvert the opposition of masculine and feminine by means of this metaphor of the face, but she also subverts the opposition of spirit and body an opposition that is congruent with the masculine/feminine opposition. The face is seen as conveying identity and yet it is a part of the body: it conjoins the internal (the soul) and the external (the body) on the level of the body.

31. Butler's theorization of gender as performative and constructed sheds new light on gender in *Nightwood.* On the question of the relation of heterosexuality and homosexuality to gender identity, Butler writes that "the replication of heterosexual constructs in non-heterosexual frames brings into relief the utterly constructed status of the so-called heterosexual original. Thus, gay is to straight *not* as copy is to original, but, rather, as copy is to copy. The parodic repetition of 'the original' . . . reveals the original to be nothing other than a parody of the *idea* of the natural and the original" (*Gender Trouble,* 31). This denaturalization of the so-called natural basis of gender and sexuality (their supposed basis in anatomical sex) through parody and mimicry is what is behind the placement of the prince, the doll, and the invert in the realm of fiction. Fiction, like mimicry and parody, is in the register of rhetoric and performance.

32. Allen was the first critic to recognize the subjects of *Nightwood* as "the power of the night, of irrationality and the unconscious; and the nature of love, particularly love between women," and to suggest the connection between the night and inversion (" 'Dressing the Unknowable,' " 107).

33. Marcus, "Laughing at Leviticus," 221.

Boys' Own Stories and New Spellings of My Name: Coming Out and Other Myths of Queer Positionality

Robert McRuer

MYTHS OF QUEER POSITIONALITY

In *The Beautiful Room Is Empty*, Edmund White's nameless narrator envisions a day when gay people will claim the right to define themselves: "Then I caught myself foolishly imagining that gays might someday constitute a community rather than a diagnosis."[1] This exhilarating thought comes to White's protagonist as he finds himself in the middle of an uprising at the Stonewall Inn Bar in Greenwich Village on the night of June 27, 1969. Drawing on civil rights rhetoric, the protagonist and his friends reclaim and reposition their own experiences with chants such as "Gay is good" and "We're the Pink Panthers."[2] Although White's is a fictional account, these riots outside the Stonewall Inn are generally considered the beginning of the contemporary gay liberation movement, and they did indeed usher in a decade of redefinition by lesbian and gay communities: within weeks, the Gay Liberation Front (GLF) had formed, employing the slogan "Out of the Closets and into the Streets!"; within a year, the Radicalesbians, influenced by both gay liberation and the women's movement, had presented feminists with the "woman-identified woman," a position from which to construct a challenging, politicized identity; by 1974, activists had successfully worked to remove homosexuality from the American Psychiatric Association's list of mental disorders. In short, the new names and identities embraced by White's protagonist and his friends were high on the agenda for the early gay liberationists.[3]

These newly available gay and lesbian identities were claimed, and proclaimed, through the act of "coming out." This act, as it was understood by the early gay liberationists, provided lesbians and gay men with positions that could serve as starting points for radical political action. Indeed, the very slogan of the gay liberationists (and the title of a 1972 essay by Allen Young), "Out of the Closets, into the Streets," suggests not simply that one claims a position ("out of the closet"), but rather that one moves from that position to effect radical social change. Young writes, "Of course, we want to 'come out.' . . . But the movement for a new definition of sexuality does not, and cannot, end there. . . . The revolutionary goals of gay liberation, including the elimination of capitalism, imperialism and racism, are premised on the termination of the system of male supremacy."[4] Similarly, "woman-identification," according to the Radicalesbians, can be "develop[ed] with reference to ourselves, and not in relation to men. This consciousness is the revolutionary force from which all else will follow."[5] Like the identity positions (pro)claimed by all the "new social movements," the identities into which gay and lesbian activists "came out" were meant to generate radical social change based on new and different ways of understanding the world.[6]

"Coming out," as an organizational strategy, does not have the same radical edge for the new generation of queer activists that it had for their gay liberationist forebears. On the contrary: coming out, along with its product — one's "coming-out story" — has been thoroughly critiqued by many contemporary lesbian and gay writers. In particular, theorists have critiqued coming-out stories for their emphasis on the discovery of an individual and essential gay identity, unmarked by other categories of difference, such as race or class. The first section of this essay will take these and other criticisms into account, but I will nonetheless attempt to lay the theoretical groundwork for a reclamation of coming out's radical potential. In the final two sections, I want to consider — through readings of two works of contemporary gay and lesbian fiction — whether a feminist-informed and antiracist analysis might be able to (re)claim coming out as a myth of what I'll call queer (op)positionality.

Through the term "(op)positionality," I intend to invoke both the "opposition" to established and oppressive systems of power that was voiced by the GLF, the Radicalesbians, and members of all the new social movements, and "positionality" theory as it has evolved in recent feminist writing. In feminism, standpoint theorists argue for a nonessentialist "position" from which to forge coalition-based political action. Linda Alcoff, for example, argues,

> If we combine the concept of identity politics with a conception of the subject as positionality, we can conceive of the subject as nonessentialized and emergent from a historical experience and yet retain our political ability to take gender as an important point of departure. . . . Being a "woman" is to take up a position within a moving historical context and to be able to choose what we make of this position and how we alter this context. . . . [in order that] women can themselves articulate a set of interests and ground a feminist politics.[7]

Similarly, Donna Haraway's feminist redefinition of "objectivity" argues for an openly acknowledged, although partial, position or perspective. In "Situated Knowledges: The Science Question in Feminism and the Privilege of Partial Perspective," Haraway writes, "Feminist objectivity is about limited location and situated knowledge, not about transcendence and splitting of subject and object."[8] This *partial* perspective is necessitated since, not unlike Edmund White's narrator in *The Beautiful Room Is Empty*, with his concern about psychiatric diagnoses, Haraway confesses that she has occasional paranoid fantasies about so-called *impartial*, "objective" discourses that appropriate "embodied others" as "objects" of knowledge: "The imagined 'they' constitute a kind of invisible conspiracy of masculinist scientists and philosophers replete with grants and laboratories; and the imagined 'we' are the embodied others, who are not allowed *not* to have a body."[9] Because of these fears, Haraway's redefinition of "objectivity," like the rhetoric of gay liberation, gives preference to other ways of seeing, particularly those ways of seeing that emerge from what she calls the "standpoints of the subjugated." She writes, " 'Subjugated' standpoints are preferred because they seem to promise more adequate, sustained, objective, transforming accounts of the world."[10] Such standpoints are actually more "objective" because they do not claim to see simultaneously "everything from nowhere," or "to be," as Richard Dyer puts it in his analysis of the social construction of whiteness, "everything and nothing."[11] Such standpoints are more "transforming" because coalition politics are fundamental to what theorists of positionality envision; both Haraway and Alcoff, for example, place race, as well as gender, at the center of their projects: "I think this point can be readily intuited by people of mixed races and cultures who have had to choose in some sense their identity"; "['Women of color'] marks out a self-consciously constructed space that cannot affirm the capacity to act on the basis of natural identification, but only on the basis of conscious coalition, of affinity, of political kinship."[12]

Other theorists, recognizing the value of such coalition-based and self-reflexive "positionality," have attempted to link gay male and feminist standpoint theory. Earl Jackson, Jr., for one, begins his study of Robert Glück by acknowledging, "One of the most important things gay men can learn from feminist and lesbian-feminist discursive practices, is how to read and write from responsibly identified positions."[13] Nevertheless, there are drawbacks to an attempt such as mine to link, specifically, *coming out* to feminist theories of positionality; these drawbacks become evident from the critiques of coming out I alluded to earlier. The position "out of the closet," much more than the "standpoint" of recent feminist theory, has become in the past two decades a *mandated* position, for both men and women. In the process of forging the imperative to "come out," unfortunately, some lesbian and gay communities lost the sense that "coming out" was, as feminist theorists now argue about the feminist standpoint, only a beginning point from which to ground political action, the rallying cry "Out of the Closets, into the Streets" quickly became simply "Out of the Closets." Martin Duberman explains,

GAA [Gay Activists Alliance] had recently come into existence as a breakaway alternative to the Gay Liberation Front, and would shortly supersede it. . . . Whereas GLF had argued that sexual liberation had to be fought for in conjunction with a variety of other social reforms and in alliance with other oppressed minorities, GAA believed in a single-minded concentration on gay civil rights and eschewed "romantic" excursions into revolutionary ideology.[14]

Moreover, in addition to the dangers of quietism that Duberman foregrounds, "coming out" as a focus for gay and lesbian theory could also reinscribe a disturbing tendency toward an apolitical essentialism. The narrowing of vision Duberman recounts could, and often does, narrow even further, so that coming out comes to signify solely the simple assertion of one's (supposedly long-repressed) identity. This model of coming out, by itself, exhibits little concern for how lesbian or gay identities are socially constituted, for how they are intersected by other arenas of difference, or for what sort of collective political action might develop from an assertion of one's lesbian or gay identity. "Coming out" here becomes a suspiciously white and middle-class move toward "self-respect," not revolutionary social change, and many coming-out *narratives* might be seen as products of this shift toward individualism and essentialism.

Haraway too stresses that essentialism, in its many guises, is a pitfall for feminist theories of positionality, especially those, like hers, that foreground the "standpoints of the subjugated": "But here lies a serious danger of romanticizing and/or appropriating the vision of the less powerful while claiming to see from their positions. . . . A commitment to mobile positioning and to passionate detachment is dependent on the impossibility of innocent 'identity' politics." [15] Haraway's disclaimers suggest that these essentializing tendencies might not engulf feminist theories of positionality, but the tendency toward an "innocent 'identity' politics" in coming-out narratives has been thoroughly critiqued in gay and lesbian theory. Diana Fuss sees even in the Radicalesbians a "tension between the notions of 'developing' an identity and 'finding' an identity [and this tension] points to a more general confusion over the very definition of 'identity' and the precise signification of 'lesbian.' " [16] Biddy Martin discusses how, by the end of the 1970s, the imperative to come out evolves into a predictable (and white) narrative, and how "many of the coming-out stories are tautological insofar as they describe a process of coming to know something that has always been true, a truth to which the author has returned." [17] Jeffrey Minson takes this tautology a step further, suggesting that "far from constituting a break from a repressive, closeted past, coming out might be situated as the latest in a long line of organised rituals of confession. . . . Sexual avowal therefore is a mode of social regimentation." [18]

Finally, although Fuss's, Martin's, and Minson's criticisms might also be leveled at some feminist theories of positionality, coming out may be problematic for yet another, more mundane reason: the imperative to "Come Out!" is by now, for many, a worn-out refrain. "National Coming Out Day" is at this point televised yearly on the *Oprah Winfrey Show*, and encouragement, such as the exhortation in my own campus newspaper to "come out, wherever you are, and friends won't turn away" often sounds like pandering for heterosexual "sympathy." [19] Since coming out, according to this mainstream model, is virtually synonymous with a call to "respect yourself," many lesbian and gay people are understandably bored or irritated with the focus on coming out and its product, the coming-out narrative. David Van Leer, for example, after insisting that, for White, "coming-out [is] the quintessential gay experience," goes on to suggest, in a review of *The Faber Book of Gay Short Fiction*, that "in its preoccupation with the opinion of others, coming-out sometimes looks like a bid for heterosexual sympathy, even for absolution."[20] Sarah Schulman states more forcefully, "The coming out story should be permanently laid to rest. . . . It was a defining stage we had to go through, but it doesn't help us develop a literature true to our experience."[21] Although I have no doubt that "we" will never construct a literature "true to our experience," since that "experience" is multiple and that "truth" is always socially constituted and continually shifting, I am nonetheless sympathetic with Schulman's frustration over the primacy given the coming-out narrative, especially when this focus comes at the expense of attention to other queer stories. Richard Hall, in a review of White's *The Beautiful Room Is Empty*, is more tentative than Schulman, suggesting "not that the coming-out novel in its pristine liberationist form is dead. Maybe it's just weary. . . . Here is another coming-up-and-out story, taking the narrator into adolescence and young manhood."[22] Although Hall feels White's novel is told with "wit, humor and aphoristic elegance," his reservations about the coming-out novel are at this point standard fare in reviews of contemporary gay and lesbian literature.[23]

Thus, despite a possible affinity with recent feminist theory, as a myth of "queer positionality" coming out can be read as a worn-out concept. In the remainder of this essay, I want to explore more thoroughly why this is the case, but I also want to use the insights offered by feminist positionality theory to present an analysis that considers ways to revise or reclaim the coming-out story. Perhaps myths of queer positionality/identity need not be hopelessly lost on teleological journeys toward essential wholeness; perhaps "noninnocent" myths of queer positionality can be found in a "queer world" that is about "lived social and bodily realities [and] in which people are not afraid . . . of permanently partial identities and contradictory standpoints," as in the "cyborg world" Haraway envisions and argues for.[24] Through an examination of Edmund White's *A Boy's Own Story* and Audre Lorde's *Zami: A New Spelling of My Name* — both published in 1982, but concerned primarily with a single character's experience of America in the 1950s — I want to reclaim coming out as a myth of queer (op)positionality.[25]

QUEER OPPOSITIONALITY/QUEER (A)POSITIONALITY

Edmund White's *A Boy's Own Story* is the first novel in a planned three-novel series. In each text, White's goal is to trace the development of his nameless, faceless narrator. *A Boy's Own Story* focuses on this development during the 1950s; *The Beautiful Room Is Empty*, on this development during the 1960s. One novel as yet unwritten will carry the protagonist through the 1970s and 1980s. The "invisibility" used as a mechanism in these texts, of course, works as a metaphor for the pain the protagonist goes through as a gay youth in heterosexist America. Like many other lesbians and gay men, White's protagonist feels that none of the people around him knows who he "really" is, and that he must consequently wear a (heterosexual) mask. The young narrator of *A Boy's Own Story* muses, "What if I could write about my life exactly as it was? What if I could show it in all its density and tedium and its concealed passion?"[26] The point is, however, that he cannot, given the normative versions of gender and sexuality available to him, and hence "invisibility" works to under-score that the narrator is forced to "live a lie," at the same time as it works to stress more generally the pain and isolation of being marginalized in American society. As the narrator of Ralph Ellison's *Invisible Man* states, "I am invisible . . . because people refuse to see me."[27]

I mention Ellison at this point because White's use of the trope of invisibility in *A Boy's Own Story* is not unlike Ellison's use of the same trope in his 1952 novel. Indeed, White's narrators often see parallels between their experiences and the experiences of African Americans in the United States. In *A Boy's Own Story*, for example, the narrator finds himself pressured by his friends to accompany them to a whorehouse staffed by two black women and one white woman. As the protagonist sits in the waiting room, one of the black prostitutes engages him in conversa-tion. The narrator admits, "I felt sorry for her. I thought she might really need my ten dollars. After all this was Saturday night, and yet she didn't have any customers. Somehow I equated her fatness, her blackness, her unpopularity with my own outcast status" (183). White's narrator goes on to imagine a marriage in which the two "outcasts" could decide to face the world together, "she a Negro whore and I her little protector. . . . If this fantasy kept me a pariah by exchanging homosexuality for miscegena-tion, it also gave me a sacrifice to make and a companion to cherish. I would educate and protect her" (183).

The queer identifications here and elsewhere in White with African-American (and "fat" and "unpopular") identity are suspect for several reasons, and my main argument in this section will be that the construction of sexuality in *A Boy's Own Story* is in tension with the construction of race, and this tension preempts the possibility that the story might serve as a myth of queer (op)positionality. Although there are ways in which the novel might indeed be considered "oppositional," I will argue that any "oppositionality" is ultimately undercut by the "apositionality," or invisibility, of whiteness in the text.

Initially, White's novel may be read as "oppositional" for its disruption of what Kenneth Kidd describes as "a linear sexual development . . . which valorizes heterosexuality as maturity."[28] This disruption of heterosexual telos is underscored by the very form of the text, which re-presents the protagonist's story in a nonlinear fashion (he is fifteen in the first chapter, seven at the beginning of the third, fifteen again by the end of the sixth, and so on). Yet despite this "opposition" to heterosexual telos, White's novel does, nonetheless, teleologically represent his protagonist's coming to a racially unmarked, gay consciousness. Although overt acts of "coming out" into this new gay consciousness are deemphasized in the text (the narrator confesses to a friend that he is gay only once, offhandedly [88]), it is still clear throughout *A Boy's Own Story* that homosexuality is precisely and primarily what White's nameless narrator must confront. Indeed, he uses a homosexual encounter with and betrayal of a "straight" teacher at the very end of the novel to confront this identity, which, he says, is "at once my essence and also an attribute I was totally unfamiliar with. . . . this sexual allure so foreign to my understanding yet so central to my being" (198). In the end, the betrayal of his teacher finally allows White's narrator to work through the contradiction inherent in his "impossible desire to love a man but not to be a homosexual" (218). Thus, although *A Boy's Own Story* certainly disrupts the cultural mandate to develop heterosexually, it also institutes a "coming-out" narrative as necessary for understanding one's (essential) gay identity.

Lisa Duggan suggests that "any gay politics based on the primacy of sexual identity defined as unitary and 'essential' . . . ultimately represents the view from the subject position '20th-century Western white gay male.'"[29] In *A Boy's Own Story*, this unitary, essential subject position is achieved through the mechanism of "invisibility." Of course, this may come across at first as an unjust (mis)reading of White, since his narrator is "invisible" throughout the novel precisely because homosexuality is an identity that he cannot openly embrace. Yet the construction of sexuality here colludes with the construction of whiteness, which maintains its power precisely to the extent that it is able to remain hidden from view; as Richard Dyer argues, "White power secures its dominance by seeming not to be anything in particular."[30] What this effects in *A Boy's Own Story* is contradictory: on the one hand, the story is one of marginalization and oppression; on the other, the story is *representative*. Even the title, after all, suggests that this "boy's own story" is as much about any (gay) boy as about White's specific protagonist. Indeed, I was struck when I attempted to teach one of White's texts by a student's response to my very first question, "Why do you think White chooses to not give his narrator a name or face?" A Filipino-American student of mine responded, "So we can put ourselves into the story?"

My student was not "wrong," of course, to identify with White's protagonist; he is, in fact, like White's narrator, a gay man living in a homophobic society. Yet the interrogative inflection my student gave to his response suggests that he knew his resolution to my question might be a bit problematic. For White's character is not simply a representative "Everyboy": his mother and he play games with the classical radio station, guessing whether the composer is Haydn, Mozart, or early Beethoven (80); a (black female) maid, a (white male) therapist, and a private school are all part of his childhood; and he admits, however ironically, that "even as I made much of my present miseries I was cautiously planning my bourgeois future" (178). In short, aspects of the protagonist's identity are race and class coded, despite his "invisible" gay identity. Indeed, his gay identity is rendered representative precisely because the "naturalness" of his racial identity is maintained through White's "god-trick" of "invisibility."

The term "god-trick" is Haraway's, and she uses it to refer to seemingly "innocent" perspectives that claim to see the world more comprehensively while actually "being nowhere."[31] Again, this may seem to be an unfair charge to level at White's story of gay development, but it is harder to dismiss in the context of Dyer's analysis of whiteness. Dyer suggests that

white people . . . are difficult, if not impossible, to analyse *qua* white. The subject seems to fall apart in your hands as soon as you begin. Any instance of white representation is always immediately something more specific − *Brief Encounter* is not about white people, it is about English middle-class people; *The Godfather* is not about white people, it is about Italian-American people; but *The Color Purple* is about black people, before it is about poor, southern US people.[32]

Similarly, *A Boy's Own Story* is not about white people; it is about gay people — but *Zami* is the autobiography of a black lesbian, not of the gay community more generally.

The very landscape of *A Boy's Own Story* underwrites white apositionality. The story takes place, alternately, in Illinois, Michigan, and Ohio. This is not Toni Morrison's *Ohio*, however, in which racial divisions are graphically (and, in *Sula*, geo-graphically) represented. Like the protagonist, the various settings for the novel are unmarked: a "boy's own story," presumably, takes place in Anywhere, U.S.A. David Bergman argues that "the importance of Cincinnati . . . cannot be underestimated in White's fiction," but it is Bergman, not White, who actually *names* the "Queen City" that plays such a "prominent role in [White's] autobiographical novel *A Boy's Own Story*."[33] Of course, the Midwest has long had a reputation for being the blank "nonregion" of the United States, the land — as in Don DeLillo's *White Noise* — of supermarkets, station wagons, and "an expressway beyond the backyard."[34] This unmarked regional identity, however, does not preclude White, in his novel, from marking *other* parts of the country regionally: the protagonist and his sister make fun of "hillbillies" from Kentucky (73) and the protagonist himself dreams of escaping to the "charm" and sophistication of New York City (52–57).

As in DeLillo, certainly, the blankness of White's Midwest (as opposed to other parts of the country) might be read as simply a metaphor for the region's supposed cultural sterility. This interpretation would elide, however, the ways regional blankness underwrites racial "invisibility" in *A Boy's Own Story*. Like Kentuckians and New Yorkers, African Americans in White's Cincinnati are embodied as such, and throughout this text, the embodied "others" enable the protagonist *not* to have a regional/racial identity of his own. Beyond that, the "other," marked identities allow White's narrator to negotiate a problematic double gesture: he simultaneously appropriates "outcast" status for himself and effaces differences of race and region.

For example, in the second chapter, the protagonist admits,

As a little boy, I'd thought of our house . . . as the place God had meant us to own, but now I knew in a vague way that its seclusion and ease had been artificial and that it had strenuously excluded the city at the same time we depended on the city for food, money, comfort, help, even pleasure. The black maids were the representatives of the city I'd grown up among. I'd never wanted anything from them — nothing except their love. To win it, or at least to ward off their silent, sighing resentment, I'd learned how to make my own bed and cook my own breakfast. But nothing I could do seemed to make up to them for the terrible loss they'd endured. (36)

At first, this passage might be read as starkly exposing the mechanisms of power that enable and ensure white privilege: the unmarked and privileged white identity is depicted here as depending for its very existence on the labor of a marked and African-American identity. And indeed, events later in this chapter could underscore such a reading. When their maid's daughter survives a bloody fight and needs help, the protagonist's father takes him along on a journey to her home in the "dangerous" section of town. This journey forces the protagonist to confront the poverty of the African-American section of their town:

That had been another city — Blanche's two rooms, scrupulously clean in contrast to the squalor of the halls, her parrot squawking under the tea towel draped over the cage, the chromo of a sad Jesus pointing to his exposed, juicy heart as though he were a free-clinic patient with a troubling symptom, the filched wedding photo of my father and stepmother in a nest of crepe-paper flowers, the bloody sheet torn into strips that had been wildly clawed off and hurled onto the flowered congoleum floor. (50)

Nonetheless, this identification of an/"other" city is already appropriated by the end of the chapter to facilitate the protagonist's *own* developing sense of self. The very use of the name "Blanche" foreshadows the possibility that this scene could be as much about "White" as it is about the maid herself.[35] And indeed, when he is considering running away to New York City, the protagonist appropriates — without reference to Blanche herself — the rhetoric he had earlier used to identify her: "I'd go hungry! The boardinghouse room with the toilet down the hall, blood on the linoleum, christ in a chromo, crepe-paper flowers" (56). In this entire section, racial difference is not so much "exposed" and challenged as it is safely *contained* — in White's Cincinnati, in his novel, and ultimately in his own "outcast" protagonist. This is White's second chapter, and racial difference becomes a crucial factor only once more in the novel, when White's protagonist and his friends, in the final chapter, visit the whorehouse. Despite the reemergence of race, though, the relations of power that determine and maintain white power remain safely behind in chapter 2; what was earlier an identification *of* racial difference becomes at the whorehouse an identification *with* racial difference (White's protagonist, as I mentioned earlier, equates the woman's situation with his own). It is precisely the "invisibility" of the protagonist's racial identity (as well as the "blankness" of the regional scene upon which all of this is played out) that allows for this slippage and appropriation to go unnoticed. Since the narrator's regional and racialized body is "invisible," he can safely appropriate "other" identities for his own queer uses. Thus, I am reluctant to write off the blankness of the midwestern landscape and the "invisibility" of whiteness in *A Boy's Own Story* as simply metaphors for cultural sterility. Unmarked and dislocated racial and regional identities are exactly what enable this to be a "representative" story about *gay* people, rather than about white midwesterners.

Hence, "queer (op)positionality" in *A Boy's Own Story* is preempted by white appositionality. In other contexts, the ways in which the identity "Edmund White" is constructed replicates this pattern. For example, after White edited an anthology of gay fiction *(The Faber Book of Gay Short Fiction)*, which included one black writer (James Baldwin) and no women, the controversy was reported in a publication no less mainstream than *USA Today*. In the article, Kent Fordyce explicitly spells out the tension between sexuality and race: "I think Faber flubbed the title . . . I think it should be 'Edmund White's Anthology of White Short Story Writers.' "[36] *The book isn't about white people*, White himself seems to be saying when he explains that he "read dozens of stories by dozens of gay black writers and I didn't find anything too suitable. And I thought it was wrong to include them just because they were black."[37] His dismissal of race notwithstanding, in the foreword to *The Faber Book*, White continues to appropriate racial identity for its comparative value: "Do gays really constitute something like an ethnic minority? Does an author's sexuality represent a more crucial part of his identity than his social class, generation, race or regional origins?"[38] This persistent blindness to race (and other arenas of difference), except when he is appropriating it to talk about his own oppression, is surely what led Essex Hemphill to signify on White in his own introduction to *Brother to Brother: New Writings by Black Gay Men*, "When black gay men approached the gay community to participate in the struggle for acceptance and to forge bonds of brotherhood . . . we discovered that the beautiful rhetoric was empty."[39]

. . .

In her book *Essentially Speaking: Feminism, Nature, and Difference,* Diana
Fuss admits to implying throughout that "the adherence to essentialism is
a measure of the degree to which a particular political group has been
culturally oppressed."[40] And yet, in her chapter on lesbian and gay identity politics, Fuss spends only a page early on "exposing" the "essentialism" of the Combahee River Collective, Cherríe Moraga, and Barbara
Smith.[41] Although Lorde is mentioned in passing in an earlier chapter, no
other gay men or lesbians of color are engaged with in the chapter on
identity politics, or in the entire book, for that matter.[42] To me, this
hardly provides enough material to justify a sweeping statement the logical conclusion of which would be that lesbians of color are the *most*
essentialist of all. In fact, in contrast to Fuss, I feel that, at times, those
who are oppressed in only one facet of their identity stand the most
to gain from essentialism.[43] As Edmund White writes, introducing his
anthology of (white) gay short story writers, "Most gay men believe they
did not choose to be homosexual, that this orientation was imposed on
them, although whether by nature or nurture they have no way of knowing."[44] Of course White does not and need not speak for all white gay
men here, but it is worth pointing out that clinging to an essential and
essentially oppressed gay identity is exactly what allows White in *A Boy's
Own Story, The Faber Book,* and elsewhere to mask white and male power.

"One of the signs of the times is that we really don't know what 'white'
is," Kobena Mercer writes.[45] Whiteness, after all, maintains its hegemony
by passing itself off as no-thing. As *A Boy's Own Story* indicates, whiteness
is apositionality; it denies "the stakes in location, embodiment, and partial
perspective [and makes] it impossible to see well."[46] "Every gay man has
polished his story through repetition," White writes in the foreword to
The Faber Book, "and much gay fiction is a version of this first tale."[47]
Perhaps. Yet what White disavows in *A Boy's Own Story* and *The Faber
Book* are the mechanisms of power that enable him to transform *his* story
into "a boy's own." Denying its own racial situatedness, the novel fails as
a "non-innocent" myth of queer (op)positionality. Like the texts Biddy
Martin examines, White's understanding of the "story" "simply reproduces the demand that women [and men] of color . . . abandon their
histories, the histories of their communities, their complex locations and
selves, in the name of a [gay] unity that barely masks its white, middle
class cultural reference/referent."[48]

AN/OTHER MYTH OF QUEER POSITIONALITY

Edmund White's *A Boy's Own Story* is set in roughly the same time period as Audre Lorde's *Zami: A New Spelling of My Name*. At about the same time that White's protagonist is learning the difference between Mozart and Haydn, Audre, the persona at the center of what Lorde calls her "biomythography," goes to Washington, D.C., to celebrate her graduation from the eighth grade. Stopping at a Breyer's ice cream and soda fountain, Audre and her family are told they can get their dessert to "take out," but they cannot eat the ice cream on the premises. The bitter episode ends with Audre thinking, "The waitress was white, and the counter was white, and the ice cream I never ate in Washington, D.C. that summer I left my childhood was white, and the white heat and the white pavement and the white stone monuments made me sick to my stomach for the whole rest of that trip and it wasn't much of a graduation present after all."[49] In stark contrast to *A Boy's Own Story*, the mechanisms of white power are all too visible in *Zami*.

Clearly, despite nominal similarities (the 1950s setting, the 1982 publication date, the autobiographical elements, homosexuality), *A Boy's Own Story* and *Zami* are extremely different texts. Their publication history reflects this difference as well: whereas White's novel was published in hardcover by E. P. Dutton and in paperback by Plume, both divisions of New American Library, *Zami* was rejected by a dozen or more mainstream publishing houses, including, as Barbara Smith reports, a house known for publishing gay titles.[50] Smith explains, "The white male editor at that supposedly sympathetic house returned the manuscript saying, 'If only you were just one,' Black or lesbian."[51] To my knowledge, Lorde has not been interviewed by *USA Today*.[52]

Zami was, of course, eventually published by Persephone Press and the Crossing Press Feminist Series, and Donna Haraway, Katie King, and others have already noted *Zami*'s importance for feminist theory. Haraway includes *Zami* in her discussion of "feminist cyborg stories" that "have the task of recoding communication and intelligence to subvert command and control."[53] King is more specific, suggesting,

It is in this currently contested time/place [the lesbian bar of the 1950s] where "the passing dreams of choice" are mobilized that Lorde looks for the secrets of the making of her personal identity; the passing dreams of choice, where sexual identity is neither an existential decision nor biochemically/psychoanalytically programmed, but instead produced in the fields of difference individually *and* collectively.[54]

Taking Haraway's and King's observations as a starting point, I want to suggest further that, in these "fields of difference," where sexual identity is "produced . . . individually *and* collectively," *Zami* also allows for a "recoding" of the "coming-out" story, a "recoding" along the lines of what I'm calling queer (op)positionality. For *Zami* is not so much about coming out into a fiction of individualistic, isolated identity of the sort represented in *A Boy's Own Story*. Instead, *Zami* can be seen as an/"other" myth of queer positionality — not because Lorde makes, as White does, an attempt to construct her protagonist into an alienated, marked "other," but rather because *Zami* is concerned, as King notes, with collective identity. A humanist, unified self is not Lorde's objective, but rather a definition of "self" as defined in and through others, particularly those "who work together as friends and lovers" (255).

Already this goes against White's objectives in *A Boy's Own Story* (which ended, after all, with a betrayal that enabled the protagonist to self-define *as against* a lover) and problematizes Linda Alcoff's theory of positionality, which fears that "post-structuralism's negation of the authority of the subject coincides nicely with classical liberal views that human particularities are irrelevant."[55] Indeed, the fiction of identity Lorde constructs in *Zami* goes beyond the poststructuralism Alcoff fears, since a negation of the authority of the subject works here to underscore the *relevance* of human particularities. Taking its protagonist through approximately two decades of development, *Zami* is framed by a prologue and an epilogue that are meditations on the *particular* women Audre has loved. In the prologue, Lorde poses the question, *"To whom do I owe the woman I have become?"* (4), and proceeds to answer it by naming and describing those who have shaped her identity. Lorde concludes the prologue by apostrophizing:

To the battalion of arms where I often retreated for shelter and sometimes found it. To the others who helped, pushing me into the merciless sun — I, coming out blackened and whole.

To the journeywoman pieces of myself.
Becoming.
Afrekete. (5)

Of course, the penultimate stanza of the prologue might read like another teleological myth of essential wholeness, but Lorde immediately undercuts this with fragmentation and open-endedness ("pieces of myself," "becoming"). Moreover, even the "wholeness" into which Lorde "comes out" here is unlike the myth of identity represented in White. Particular "others" have helped to forge this identity, and the metonymic reference to baking serves to underscore Lorde's emphasis on the construction, rather than the discovery, of identity.

In the body of the text, Audre has a number of "friends and lovers," black and white, beginning with Genevieve, a girlhood friend who commits suicide while the two are still in high school. Audre emerges from this experience and, over the course of the text, has a series of lovers, eventually meeting Afrekete ("Kitty") at a party for black women. The identity of this final lover, however, is unstable and merges freely with others: not only does the epilogue explain what the prologue did not — that Afrekete is the name of a goddess and trickster — but also, even as Audre and Kitty make love, the scene shifts seamlessly from the present to memories of Genevieve, and the identity of the first lover hence ultimately reemerges in the identity of the last. Furthermore, in the epilogue, although "human particularities" (women's roles and names, both "real" and mythical) are present, "Audre," in her specificity as a named subject, is not. In fact, the "new spelling of my name" envisioned in the title is finally explained in the epilogue, and it turns out not to be about individuality at all: "*Zami. A Carriacou name for women who work together as friends and lovers*" (255).

Alcoff wants to reclaim an "identity," fictional as this may be, from which women can construct a feminist politics.[56] The queer position Audre/Lorde constructs for herself, however, is a position that effaces Lorde's individual identity. Sagri Dhairyam argues, "*Zami* . . . calls itself 'biomythography,' a description which explicitly recognizes that any interpretive act, whether of the writer or reader, (re)constitutes reality. 'Biomythography' recognizes the tactical uses of fictional identity, but refuses to grant the author primacy over the textuality of her life."[57] Indeed, this refusal to grant primacy to the individual author ensures that, in *Zami*, fictional identity and *nonidentity* alike are employed to construct "the very house of difference rather than the security of any one particular difference" (226). At the same time, this is not some White/white "god-trick" that disavows its own situatedness. It may be impossible to read "Audre" as a self-identical, unified individual, but the identities "black"/ "lesbian"/"woman" are all present in the identity "Zami." In a sense, Lorde's persona "comes out" into a fiction of nonidentity not unlike what Trinh T. Minh-ha envisions:

> A critical difference from myself means that I am not i, am within and without i. I/i can be I or i, you and me both involved. . . . "I" is, therefore, not a unified subject, a fixed identity, or that solid mass covered with layers of superficialities one has gradually to peel off before one can see its true face. "I" is, itself, *infinite layers*. Its complexity can hardly be conveyed through such typographic conventions as I, i, or I/i. Thus, I/i am compelled by the will to say/unsay, to resort to the entire gamut of personal pronouns to stay near this fleeing *and* static essence of Not-I.[58]

This, it seems to me, is queer (op)positionality at its best: an effacement of, and in-your-face-ment to, the liberal humanist God/Man/Subject. And, as much as *Zami* works as a realization of Trinh's unstable i/I/ Not-I, it also, pace Alcoff, maintains in its very self-definition a commitment to feminist political action; these are, after all, women actively working and loving together. *Zami* constructs a nonessentialist identity position from which to forge a coalition-based, and oppositional, politics. Indeed, King and Haraway both understand *Zami* in relation to Chela Sandoval's notion of "oppositional consciousness."[59] As Sandoval herself writes, "These constantly speaking differences stand at the crux of another, mutant unity . . . it is unity mobilized in a location heretofore unrecognized. . . . This connection is a mobile unity, constantly weaving and reweaving an interaction of differences into coalition."[60]

Lorde's *Chosen Poems* were published in 1982, the same year as her "biomythography," and I find the narrative she constructs about her life in this collection of poetry similar to the narrative she constructs in *Zami*. "Need: A Choral of Black Women's Voices," the final poem and one newly written for the collection, reproduces on a more urgent level the exploration of identity/nonidentity found in the epilogue to *Zami*. The poem has three speakers, "I," "P.C.," and "B.J.G.," the latter two speakers representing the voices of Patricia Cowan and Bobbie Jean Graham, two women murdered in Detroit and Boston in 1978 and 1979, respectively. As in *Zami*, naming is a central preoccupation in "Need." After P.C. and B.J.G. describe their own violent deaths, the "I" of the poem rages, "I do not even know all their names. / My sisters deaths are not noteworthy /

nor threatening enough to decorate the evening news . . . blood blood of my sisters fallen in this bloody war / with no names no medals no exchange of prisoners."[61] The three voices weave in and out in this prolonged meditation on violence and oppression, until the final stanza of the poem, when the "I" transforms into an "ALL": " *'We cannot live without our lives.'* / *'We cannot live without our lives.'* "[62] A footnote at the bottom of the page explains that the italicized quote is from a poem by Barbara Deming. The words are, therefore, Lorde's and not Lorde's, and the individual identities of Lorde/I/Patricia Cowan/Bobbie Jean Graham/Barbara Deming, along with all the women named and not named in *Chosen Poems*, coalesce as they do in the epilogue to *Zami* into a powerful, threatening collective identity that depends for its existence on the foregrounded positionality of the identity "black"/"lesbian"/"woman." The poem, once again, belies any notion of a unified, essential self, and indeed, in the face of such violence and destruction, such a notion seems not only unproductive but absurd. Nonetheless, the poem refuses to efface the mechanisms of power that produce or erase identity:

This woman is Black
so her blood is shed into silence
this woman is Black
so her death falls to the earth
like the dripping of birds
to be washed away with silence and rain.[63]

"Need" itself is a particularly useful example, even beyond the textual analysis I've attempted here, of the ways in which Lorde "comes out" into a myth of collective identity. As I said, Lorde's *Chosen Poems* were originally published by Norton in 1982. "Need," however, was reissued as a pamphlet in 1990 by Kitchen Table: Women of Color Press as part of their "Freedom Organizing Series." In the preface to this new, revised version of "Need," Lorde traces the poem's genealogy:

"Need" was first written in 1979 after 12 Black women were killed in the Boston area within four months. In a grassroots movement spearheaded by Black and Latina Lesbians, Women of Color in the area rallied. . . . My lasting image of that spring, beyond the sick sadness and anger and worry, was of women whom I knew, loved, and trembled for: Barbara Smith, Demita Frazier, Margo Okazawa-Rey, and women whose names were unknown to me, leading a march through the streets of Boston behind a broad banner stitched with a line from Barbara Deming: "WE CANNOT LIVE WITHOUT OUR LIVES."[64]

Lorde again attributes the words to Barbara Deming, but the overdetermined identity/nonidentity articulated in "Need" and in Lorde's genealogy of "Need" belies any unified authorial consciousness. Deming does
not become so much the "source" here as another element in the collective identity into which the women behind the banner "come out." This
collective identity is a powerful and threatening one, made more so by its
lack of fixity. Indeed, the reissuance of "Need" reaffirms and deploys that
lack of fixity: each pamphlet includes a button, "WE CANNOT LIVE
WITHOUT OUR LIVES," printed on top of the pan-African colors and
beside the symbol for female. Neither Lorde nor Kitchen Table Press
makes any attempt here to suture, within the reissued text, the identity
being articulated; on the contrary, the button and a "Resources for Organizing" section that follows the poem encourage women (and, presumably, men) reading the text to join and hence continually reshape this
collective identity.[65] Lorde herself, in fact, traces the 1990 revisions of
the poem to the ways in which it had already been used and reshaped by
others since its publication: "Alterations in the text since the poem was
originally published are a result of hearing the poem read aloud several
times by groups of women."[66]

*Then I caught myself foolishly imagining that gays might someday constitute a
community rather than a diagnosis.* White's protagonist's thoughts during
the Stonewall riots, with which I began this essay, apparently contradict
the points I have been making about White/white apositionality and *A
Boy's Own Story*, and appear to participate in a more productive myth of
identity, akin to those articulated in *Zami* and in "Need." This moment
of potentiality in *The Beautiful Room Is Empty*, however, is trumped by the
novel's notorious ending:

I stayed over at Lou's [one of the nameless narrator's friends. We hugged each
other in bed like brothers, but we were too excited to sleep. We rushed down to
buy the morning papers to see how the Stonewall Uprising had been described.
"It's really our Bastille Day," Lou said. But we couldn't find a single mention in
the press of the turning point of our lives.[67]

At the end of *The Beautiful Room Is Empty*, bittersweet isolation and
invisibility triumph over the possibility of community.
  Yet the story of Stonewall has been told otherwise. Martin Duberman's
historical overview, *Stonewall*, interweaves the stories of six people who

were active in lesbian and gay communities during the time of the Stonewall riots. Craig Rodwell was one of the men actually present when the riots broke out, and Duberman details his reaction: "Craig dashed to a nearby phone booth. Ever conscious of the need for publicity — for *visibility* — and realizing that a critical moment had arrived, he called all three daily papers, the *Times*, the *Post*, and the *News*, and alerted them that 'a major story was breaking.' Then he ran to his apartment a few blocks away to get his camera."[68] Rodwell's photographs never came out, but Duberman's "day after" is nonetheless not characterized by the existential alienation White's protagonist and his friend feel:

Word of the confrontation spread through the gay grapevine all day Saturday. Moreover, all three of the dailies wrote about the riot (the *News* put the story on page one), and local television and radio reported it as well. The extensive coverage brought out the crowds, just as Craig had predicted (and had worked to achieve). All day Saturday, curious knots of people gathered outside the bar to gape at the damage and warily celebrate the implausible fact that, for once, cops, not gays, had been routed.[69]

At Stonewall and in *Stonewall*, gay men and lesbians "come out" into a myth of collective identity, and the ramifications of that collective act are still being felt today.

During high school, the protagonist of *A Boy's Own Story* and Tommy, his current obsession, go slumming: "He and I had trekked more than once downtown . . . to listen, frightened and transported, to a big black Lesbian with a crew cut moan her way through the blues" (120–21). Of course, this exoticization of the "big black Lesbian" is only a minor incident for the narrator, unconnected to the larger project of coming to his own, individual, gay consciousness. And yet, the black lesbian singing the blues in *A Boy's Own Story* is not as out of place as she might at first appear. Teleological and essential (white) "boys' own stories" at this point offer feminism and queer politics little in the way of queer (op)positionality. Like the protagonist of *Zami*, whose "heart ached and ached for something [she] could not name" (85), the blues singer needs an/other myth of queer positionality. Coming out into an essential wholeness may be the myth that lesbians and gays are told they must embrace, but as Audre's teacher declares early on, when the young protagonist of *Zami* refuses to take dictation in the same manner as the rest of the class, Audre is "a young lady who does not want to do as she is told" (26). Lorde constructs a nonessentialist, non-self-identical "new spelling of my name"

in *Zami*, and only through this new construction is she able to envision a
queer and powerful community of women, whose new identities are
chosen and whose coalitions are conscious.

NOTES

My thanks to Amanda Anderson for her comments on an early draft of this essay,
and to Michael Bérubé, Robert Parker, and Lisa Duggan for their comments on a
longer version. Michael Stowe-Thurston, Bob Nowatzki, Jon D'Errico, and Elizabeth Davies have read and provided me with helpful comments on all the versions.
Tom Murray, Sagri Dhairyam, Steve Amarnick, Kenneth Kidd, and Will Harris
all provided me with insightful criticism and/or tremendous encouragement.

1. Edmund White, *The Beautiful Room Is Empty* (New York: Knopf, 1988), 226.
2. Ibid.
3. On the GLF, see John D'Emilio, *Making Trouble: Essays on Gay History,
   Politics, and the University* (New York: Routledge, 1992), 239–46. On Stonewall generally, see Martin Duberman, *Stonewall* (New York: Dutton, 1993).
   On the Radicalesbians, see Alice Echols, *Daring to Be Bad: Radical Feminism
   in America, 1967–1975* (Minneapolis: University of Minnesota Press, 1989),
   215–17, 232. The construction of the "woman-identified woman" enabled
   heterosexual feminists to identify more fully with their lesbian sisters, but it
   was in many ways a conservative move. Echols explains that it was "designed
   to assuage heterosexual feminists' fears about lesbianism" (215); consequently,
   it ended up desexualizing lesbianism.
4. Allen Young, "Out of the Closets, into the Streets," in Karla Jay and Allen
   Young, eds., *Out of the Closets: Voices of Gay Liberation* (New York: New York
   University Press, 1992), 10.
5. Radicalesbians, "The Woman-Identified Woman," in Karla Jay and Allen
   Young, eds., *Out of the Closets: Voices of Gay Liberation* (New York: New York
   University Press, 1992), 176.
6. I have already mentioned the re-presentation of civil rights rhetoric in
   White's fictional account of Stonewall. The name "Gay Liberation Front"
   itself was meant to give tribute to the liberation struggles in Vietnam and
   Algeria (Duberman, *Stonewall*, 217).
7. Linda Alcoff, "Cultural Feminism versus Post-Structuralism: The Identity
   Crisis in Feminist Theory," *Signs* 13 (Spring 1988): 433, 435. For a good
   overview of feminist standpoint epistemology, as well as "an archeology of
   standpoint theory" (76), see Sandra Harding, "Rethinking Standpoint Epistemology: What is 'Strong Objectivity'?" in Linda Alcoff and Elizabeth Potter,
   eds., *Feminist Epistemologies* (New York: Routledge, 1993). Harding explains
   that feminist standpoint theory emerges from an engagement with Marxism
   (53–54). See also Donna Haraway, *Simians, Cyborgs, and Women: The Reinven-*

tion of Nature (New York: Routledge, 1991), 186–87. By translating stand-point theory to a queer context, I am — in an attempt to further coalition building among theorists — agreeing in this essay with Harding's recognition that "even though standpoint arguments are most fully articulated as such in feminist writings, they appear in the scientific projects of all the new social movements" (54).

8. Haraway, *Simians, Cyborgs, and Women*, 190.
9. Ibid., 183.
10. Ibid., 191.
11. Ibid., 189; Richard Dyer, "White," *Screen* 29 (Autumn 1988): 45.
12. Alcoff, "Cultural Feminism versus Post-Structuralism," 432; Haraway, *Simians, Cyborgs, and Women*, 156.
13. Earl Jackson, Jr., "Scandalous Subjects: Robert Glück's Embodied Narratives," *differences: A Journal of Feminist Cultural Studies* 3, no. 2 (Summer 1991): 112. See esp. 121–22 for Jackson's discussion of Haraway and "situated knowledges."
14. Martin Duberman, *Cures: A Gay Man's Odyssey* (New York: Dutton-Penguin, 1991), 213–14.
15. Haraway, *Simians, Cyborgs, and Women*, 192–93.
16. Diana Fuss, *Essentially Speaking: Feminism, Nature, and Difference* (New York: Routledge, 1989), 100.
17. Biddy Martin, "Lesbian Identity and Autobiographical Difference[s]," in Bella Brodsky and Celeste Schenck, eds., *Life/Lines: Theorizing Women's Autobiography* (Ithaca, N. Y.: Cornell University Press, 1988), 89.
18. Jeffrey Minson, *Genealogies of Morals: Nietzsche, Foucault, Donzelot, and the Eccentricity of Ethics* (London: Macmillan, 1985), 37. See also Jeffrey Minson, "The Assertion of Homosexuality," *m/f* 6 (1981): 19–39.
19. Bill Behrens, "Come Out, Wherever You Are, and Friends Won't Turn Away," *Daily Illini*, October 10, 1990, 19. I am grateful to Steve Amarnick for helping me to sort out some of the issues I am working with here. I am not trying to dismiss the psychological importance of coming out, nor am I denying that Oprah Winfrey's sensitivity to coming out is empowering to thousands of gay and lesbian people. Rather, I am suggesting that the coming-out = self-respect model alone can be equally disempowering for many other lesbian and gay people who rarely see themselves represented in any other way.
20. David Van Leer, "Beyond the Margins," *New Republic*, October 12, 1992, 50.
21. Kenny Fries, "Fighting False Symbols: Sarah Schulman Searches for a Satisfying Lesbian Identity," *Lambda Book Report* 3, no. 8 (January-February 1993): 8.
22. Richard Hall, "Gay Fiction Comes Home," *New York Times Book Review*, June 19, 1988, 27.
23. Ibid.; For a counterexample, see John Preston, "Prognostications," *Lambda Book Report* 3 (January-February 1993): 39. Preston's defense of the coming-out story suggests that many critics have expressed their reservations about

the genre. Indeed, Preston's article is in the same issue of *Lambda Book Report* that includes Schulman's derisive comments about the coming-out story.

24. Haraway, *Simians, Cyborgs, and Women*, 154. See also Lisa Duggan, "Making It Perfectly Queer," *Socialist Review* 22 (January-March 1992): 25–26.

25. To my knowledge, neither White nor Lorde has identified with "queer" as it is deployed in this article. However, many of their readers can and do identify with the term. I am using White and Lorde here because this article is part of my larger work in progress (tentatively titled "Reading the Queer Renaissance"), in which I link the unprecedented outpouring of creative work over the last decade and a half (a "renaissance" of which Lorde and White are a part) to the rebirth, or "renaissance," of radical gay, lesbian, and bisexual politics (I am thus appropriating the term, yet attempting to critique its "transcendent" connotations by applying it to the "political" arena). In this context, the ways in which authors self-identify is less important to me than the ways in which readers do; my larger work is concerned with how members of the latter renaissance ("queers") can respond to the former.

26. Edmund White, *A Boy's Own Story* (New York: Plume-NAL, 1982), 41. Further references to this work will be included parenthetically in the text.

27. Ralph Ellison, *Invisible Man* (1952; repr. New York: Vintage-Random House, 1972), 3.

28. Kenneth Kidd, "Pederasty, Pedagogy, and the Rhetoric(s) of Childhood in *A Boy's Own Story* and *Ambidextrous*," paper presented at "Making It Perfectly Queer: The Second National Graduate Student Conference on Lesbian, Bisexual, and Gay Studies," University of Illinois, Urbana, April 3, 1992, 3.

29. Duggan, "Making It Perfectly Queer," 18.

30. Dyer, "White," 44.

31. Haraway, *Simians, Cyborgs, and Women*, 191.

32. Dyer, "White," 46.

33. David Bergman, "Edmund White," in Emmanuel Nelson, ed., *Contemporary Gay American Novelists* (Westport, Conn.: Greenwood, 1993), 387.

34. Don DeLillo, *White Noise* (New York: Viking-Penguin, 1985), 4.

35. I am grateful to Michael Stowe-Thurston for pointing out this connection to me.

36. Craig Wilson, "Gay-Fiction Anthology Opens Doors to Debate," *USA Today*, November 14, 1991, 8D. I am grateful to Harold Ivan Smith for bringing this article to my attention.

37. Ibid.

38. Edmund White, Foreword to *The Faber Book of Gay Short Fiction*, ed. Edmund White (London: Faber and Faber, 1991), xvii.

39. Essex Hemphill, Introduction to *Brother to Brother: New Writings by Black Gay Men*, ed. Essex Hemphill (Boston: Alyson, 1991), xix.

40. Fuss, *Essentially Speaking*, 98.

41. Ibid., 99.

42. For the Lorde reference, see ibid., 44.

43. Barbara Smith has made a similar point. See Elly Bulkin, Barbara Smith, and Minnie Bruce Pratt, *Yours in Struggle: Three Feminist Perspectives on Anti-Semitism and Racism* (New York: Long Haul Press, 1984), 75–76.
44. White, Foreword, ix.
45. Kobena Mercer, "Skin Head Sex Thing: Racial Difference and the Homoerotic Imaginary," in Bad Object-Choices, eds., *How Do I Look?: Queer Film and Video* (Seattle: Bay Press, 1991), 204.
46. Haraway, *Simians, Cyborgs, and Women*, 191.
47. White, Foreword, ix.
48. Martin, "Lesbian Identity and Autobiographical Difference[s]," 93.
49. Audre Lorde, *Zami: A New Spelling of My Name* (Trumansburg, N.Y.: Crossing Press Feminist Series, 1982), 71. Further references to this work will be included parenthetically in the text.
50. Barbara Smith, "The Truth That Never Hurts: Black Lesbians in Fiction in the 1980s," in Chandra Talpade Mohanty, Ann Russo, and Lourdes Torres, eds., *Third World Women and the Politics of Feminism* (Bloomington: Indiana University Press, 1991), 123.
51. Ibid.
52. To be fair, White's own publication history has at times been equally rocky (see Kay Bonetti, "An Interview with Edmund White," *Missouri Review* 13 [1990]: 101–2), and Lorde has been published by both small feminist and mainstream presses. I don't want to institute an argument here that implies too much about White's or Lorde's canonical or precanonical status. Indeed, the "canonicity" of either author is difficult to assess, since it would appear that both White and Lorde are fairly "canonical," but in different contexts. Lorde is more likely to be taught in college classrooms, but *Time* magazine declared White "America's most influential gay writer" (Leonard Schulman, "Imagining Other Lives," *Time*, July 30, 1990, 58). White, then, is quickly becoming ensconced as the gay author mainstream readers (but not necessarily academic readers) need to know. The Quality Paperback Book Club, "proud to announce the launch of Triangle Classics, a series of landmark books illuminating the gay and lesbian experience," includes one writer from the 1980s in their new series: Edmund White. The series includes one black author, James Baldwin. The Baldwin novel included, *Giovanni's Room*, is about Europeans. I am grateful to Stacy Alaimo for calling my attention to this series.
53. Haraway, *Simians, Cyborgs, and Women*, 175.
54. Katie King, "Audre Lorde's Lacquered Layerings: The Lesbian Bar as a Site of Literary Production," *Cultural Studies* 2 (1988): 332.
55. Alcoff, "Cultural Feminism versus Post-Structuralism," 420.
56. Ibid., 435.
57. Sagri Dhairyam, " 'Artifacts for Survival': Remapping the Contours of Poetry with Audre Lorde," *Feminist Studies* 18 (Summer 1992): 226.
58. Trinh T. Minh-ha, *Woman, Native, Other* (Bloomington: Indiana University Press, 1989), 90, 94.

59. See King, "Audre Lorde's Lacquered Layerings," 338; and Haraway, *Simians, Cyborgs, and Women*, 174.
60. Chela Sandoval, "U.S. Third World Feminism: The Theory and Method of Oppositional Consciousness in the Postmodern World," *Genders* 10 (Spring 1991): 18.
61. Audre Lorde, *Chosen Poems — Old and New* (New York: Norton, 1982), 112.
62. Ibid., 115.
63. Ibid., 111.
64. Audre Lorde, *Need: A Chorale of Black Woman Voices* (Latham, N. Y.: Kitchen Table: Women of Color Press, 1990), 3.
65. Though I myself am a white gay man, I am not particularly troubled by the fact that identity, as Lorde constructs it in *Zami*, "Need," and elsewhere often does not apparently include men or white people. As I hope the conclusion of my essay makes clear, I want my general argument to be for "other myths of queer identity" (versions of which might include men and white people, or might be shaped by men and white people), not for "zami" as *the* necessary corrective to versions of "coming out" such as White's. Moreover, Lorde often connects with men — particularly men of color/gay men — throughout her work. The only reason I overtly include men at this particular point in my own text is because the Kitchen Table Press version of *Need* seems to at least allow for male inclusion: the "Resources for Organizing" section that follows the poem includes the address for organizations such as NCBLG: The National Coalition of Black Lesbians and Gays, The National Black Men's Health Network, Men Stopping Rape, and the Oakland Men's Project (Lorde, *Need*, 16–17).

For some white gay male creative work that is more self-reflexive about whiteness or about positionality, respectively, see Allan Gurganus, *White People* (New York: Ivy-Ballantine, 1990), and Tom Joslin and Peter Friedman's 1993 film *Silverlake Life: The View from Here*. Gurganus's stories explore both gay and nongay white life in North Carolina, and Joslin and Friedman's film is a collective effort (often depending on who has the strength to work the camera) at documenting Joslin's and his lover Mark Massi's deaths from AIDS. The position from which the camera "sees" is repeatedly foregrounded and complicated. For a discussion of embodied and communal identity in the work of a white gay male author, see Jackson, Jr., "Scandalous Subjects." See also Douglas Crimp, "Right On, Girlfriend!" *Social Text* 33 (Spring, 1993): 2–18, for another consideration of the sort of relational, collective identity I discuss in this final section.
66. Lorde, *Need*, 3.
67. White, *The Beautiful Room Is Empty*, 227–28.
68. Duberman, *Stonewall*, 198; emphasis mine.
69. Ibid., 202.

In Formation: Male Homosocial Desire in Willa Cather's *One of Ours*

D. A. Boxwell

> In war everything is very simple but the simplest things are very difficult.
> — Clausewitz, *On War*

> War is the spectacle of the masculine bond; the stage where men can perform, for themselves and their "enemies," it is the ostentation of bonding.
> — Susan Jeffords, *The Remasculinization of America*

During the convulsively panicked response to Bill Clinton's efforts, early in his administration, to liberalize official policy on gays and lesbians in the military, the military's glorious tradition of "performing" gender incoherence was easily forgotten.[1] To take just one example from that tradition: in August 1918, enlisted men at the Newport (Rhode Island) Naval Training Station mounted a production of "H.M.S. *Pinafore*" in which the female roles were performed by American sailors readying themselves for the European theater of war. Interest in these performances warranted coverage by the *Providence Journal* and the navy's own local magazine, the *Newport Recruit*, which included the following caption to a photograph of a sailor in drag: "This is Billy Hughes, Yeo[man] 2nd C[lass]. It's a shame to break the news like that, but enough of the men who saw 'Pinafore' fell in love with Bill, without adding to their number." Thus (surprisingly) attuned to a camp sensibility, the *Recruit* went on to add that " 'Little Highesy,' as he is affectionately known, dances like a Ziegfeld chorus girl."[2]

285

Lest one think that such cross-gender masquerade was unique to the sailors at Newport, however, historians Allan Bérubé and George Chauncey have pointed out that female impersonation was a regular feature of navy shows during and immediately following World War I.[3] But the complicating factor in such travesty assumptions of cross-gender identity is that, as Chauncey notes, "the ubiquity of such drag shows and the fact that numerous 'straight'-identified men took part in them" served not only "to protect gay female impersonators" in the ranks from suspicion of being homosexual but also to symbolically blur the distinctions between straight and gay identity in the community of sailors at Newport and elsewhere.[4] Moreover, while this production of Gilbert and Sullivan's nautical operetta became a naughty "scandal" two years later during an official probe of "immoral conditions" at the training station, naval investigators learned that one of the gay men in the cast had been lent "corsets, stockings, shirt waists, [and women's] pumps" by the wife of the station's commandant.[5]

This incident crystallizes a moment in American military history when discourses about gender and sexuality began to attempt consciously to articulate identifiable standards of alterity and difference.[6] Army regulations, for example, did not fully codify and inscribe prohibitions against male homosexual identity until the eve of World War II, and it was only until October 1944 that directives specifically established lesbianism as a category of disqualification from the Women's Army Corps.[7] As Allan Bérubé notes, "If any homosexuals were rejected as such in World War I, it was because they had physiological disorders or had prison or insane asylum records as 'sex perverts,' not because they had homosexual personalities or tendencies."[8] So, during the great war, male homosocial communities in the military were less subject to pathologizing discourses that strictly normativized sexual identities and acts. As George Chauncey points out, medical discourse still played little or no role in the shaping of working-class homosexual identities and categories by World War I; furthermore, "medical discourse appears to have had as little influence on the military hierarchy as on the people of Newport."[9] Thus there were no official structures in place to "screen out" homosexuals in 1918. But the tacit acknowledgment of homosexual activity as a manifestation, or expression, of homosocial desire during the war quickly became intolerable after 1918. Indeed, we can see that the U.S. Navy finally came into congruence with other institutions in making "the homosexual," as Michel Foucault has succinctly put it, "a species."[10] This became clear in the vigorous prosecution of twenty sailors and sixteen civilians in Newport in the spring and summer of 1919, including some of the participants in the production of "H.M.S. *Pinafore*," as well as a prominent Episcopal clergyman, Samuel Kent, who was tried on charges of being a "lewd and wanton person."[11]

In general terms, at all events, traditional or conventional understandings of gender and sexuality, as Sandra Gilbert has argued at length, were thrown into complete disarray by the cataclysmic effects of the war itself. Uncertain identities and role reversals emerged triumphantly, if nothing else did, from the smoldering ashes of Europe's ruins. Feminized, emasculated, and hysterized men on the one hand and virilized women on the other (as well as every possible permutation in between) resulted because, Gilbert states, "the most crucial rule the war had overturned was the rule of patrilineal succession, the founding law of patriarchal society itself" in the wake of almost inconceivable losses.[12] In brief, never before was the male body seen to be so vulnerable. With specific reference to Newport, Chauncey contends that this series of trials marks a point in American social history when the effort to clearly demarcate a boundary separating homosexuality and homosociality began to collapse under the weight of its own fictionality. As a consequence of the Newport trials, "the men prosecuted by the Navy made it increasingly difficult for the Navy to maintain standards which categorized certain men as 'straight' even though they had engaged in homosexual acts with the defendants."[13] A distinctly male form of hysteria ensued as the navy's "decoys," who were tasked in the "sting operation" with initiating "pickups," were themselves suspected of deviant conduct (and homosexual identities) and so the case ended in 1921, in a state of confusion, when the Senate Naval Affairs Committee successfully urged the navy to retreat from its prosecutions. The whole affair was, as we might predict, hushed up to save the navy from further embarrassment, especially since the secretary of the navy at the time of the naughtiness at Newport was a rising politician by the name of Franklin Delano Roosevelt.[14]

For the purposes of this paper, I want to locate Willa Cather's novel *One of Ours* (written between 1918 and 1921, and published by Knopf in 1922) against this highly theatrical backdrop of gender confusion and sexual anxiety: a cultural event mixing elements of farce and melodrama. As for *One of Ours*, there may be no better work of fiction arising from the American involvement in the great war that addresses the ways in which culturally constructed sexual categories within a homosocial continuum are further complicated by shifting and unstable gender roles as they are assumed by combatants in war. As Eve Kosofsky Sedgwick's influential study *Between Men* establishes, the "homosocial" is contiguous with "desire" in ways that explain "the potential unbrokenness of a continuum between homosocial and homosexual."[15] This structure of men's relation with other men, and "its relation to women and the gender system as a whole,"[16] can provide an insightful way of interpreting issues of gender in the war novel. A continuum suggests blurring, merging, and indeterminate boundaries. That *One of Ours* was written by a lesbian who, in her teens, had scandalized her small town by dressing as a boy and calling herself "William" makes the riotous proliferation of permeable gender boundaries all the more delightfully problematic.[17]

To begin with, the circumstances of the text's creation deeply inhere in knotty questions of gender and authenticity. Cather undertook her commitment to writing a novel about the war from personal motives: she wished to commemorate the death of her cousin G. P. Cather, killed in 1918 at Cantigny. His death on the field of battle seemed, as Cather's biographer Sharon O'Brien puts it, transformative and heroic. Her cousin, "who had been a sullen, discontented country boy, seemed to her to have found dignity and purpose" in the trenches, and Cather thus produced "a novel that portrays the First World War as the arena" for her protagonist's "liberation, maturation, self-discovery, and heroism."[18] In short, Cather intended to inscribe a masculinist romance of death and transfiguration in war: the archetypal text about male experience in combat from Homer to Rambo. Susan Rosowski points out that Cather's male critics have regarded *One of Ours* as "an American version of Arthurian legend that sets a would-be knight in search of . . . an order he could join, and a chivalric ideal he could follow."[19] Yet in order to do this Cather had to "cross-dress" as a writer. It is tempting to see Cather, as Sandra Gilbert does, inscribing herself as a butch lesbian into a male-centered text. Cather's letters to her friend and confidante Dorothy Canfield Fisher bear witness to this assumption.[20] Her identification with her protagonist—G. P. Cather, now fictionally renamed Claude Wheeler (the initials of which form an inversion of her own)—became intense in the writing process. As O'Brien remarks, "Cather's [unpublished] letters to Canfield are filled with imagery of blurred boundaries and interpenetration, as if the emotional bond she shared with Claude, who was simultaneously self and other, legitimated the woman writer's foray into male literary and social territory."[21]

Quite predictably, however, many of the male reviewers in 1922 questioned and mocked Cather's presumption to cross gender lines in this way. Most notably, Ernest Hemingway derided what he saw as Cather's inauthentic, and sentimental, presentation of heroism in war. In 1923, two years before he attained success with his first collected work of fiction, *In Our Time*, he expressed professional envy of Cather's success to Edmund Wilson: "Look at *One of Ours* . . . [Pulitzer] Prize, big sale, people taking it seriously." Even in his satirical novel of 1926, *The Torrents of Spring*, Hemingway reiterated the derision of Cather's work first expressed in the letter to Wilson: "You were in the war, weren't you? Wasn't that last scene in the lines wonderful? Do you know where it came from? The battle scene in Birth of a Nation. [I] identified episode after episode, Catherized. Poor woman she has to get her war experience somewhere."[22]

In fact, as O'Brien's biographical work has convincingly demonstrated, *One of Ours* was meticulously researched after the war; it wasn't purely and simply a fantasmatic projection of herself as a "doughboy," however much her letters to Canfield reveal this aspect of the novel's inspiration. Cather read numerous soldiers' journals and letters and conducted detailed interviews with returning veterans in New York throughout 1919.[23] So the resisting reader of Hemingway, to use Judith Fetterley's famous phrase, might well ask, what was it about Cather's novel that threatened him, since he couldn't (or wouldn't) remain indifferent to it? To be blunt, his lasting vituperation might be explained in terms of homosexual panic.

What makes Hemingway's diatribe against Cather's "appropriation" of male experience and a traditionally male literary genre all the more relevant here is Hemingway's own troubled exploration of the blurred zone between the homosocial and the homoerotic. Aside from the crucial issue of Hemingway's personal experience as a transgendered child, which Kenneth Lynn and Mark Spilka detail at length, Hemingway's anxiety-laden working out of gender ambiguity and homosexuality in both his fiction and his life might well be described as obsessive. Lynn characterizes it as a "helpless fascination . . . with androgyny and sexual transposition,"[24] coupled with strenuous, compensatory homophobic assertions of

290 D. A. BOXWELL

conventional masculinity. Spilka and Lynn, among many other commentators, note how frequently the fiction ultimately both avows and disavows
"troubling" aspects of gender and sexuality. To take merely one example
relevant to the great war: the story "A Simple Enquiry," from the aptly
named collection *Men Without Women*. In this work, Hemingway articulates the ambiguities and terrors he sees inherent in the homosexual
proposition. The subaltern's response to an overture (the "enquiry" of the
title) made by a senior officer makes it clear that homoerotic desire in war
is often "unreadable." In contrast to Pinin's oblivious verbal response to
the coded language of the major's proposition, the soldier's body language
seems to indicate another story: "Pinin was flushed and moved differently
than he had moved when he brought in the wood for the fire."[25] The
answer to the "simple enquiry," as the final sentence of the story has it, is
rife with ambiguity and unfulfilled desire. "The little devil, [the major]
thought, I wonder if he lied to me."[26]

So Hemingway might well have been put on the defensive by Cather's
acute understanding of the problematic myth of the battlefield as a homosocial paradise, a zone where the concept of "brotherhood in arms" also
has forbidden erotic underpinnings, suggested in the multiple meanings
of the word "arms" — or, as Cather's novel suggests, a zone where the
distinctions between homosocial and homoerotic are very blurred indeed.
If, as Lynn suggests, Hemingway was continually compelled to prove his
"masculinity through flat denials of" his anxiety,[27] it is not surprising that
he displaced denial (as well as anger) onto Cather and her novel.

I wish to argue that beyond the traditional view of *One of Ours* as an
inauthentic, male-identified glorification of war, the novel expresses far
more ambivalence about men in war. While it is tempting to regard
Cather's novel, as Sandra Gilbert does, as a celebratory "vision" of her
"own release" from being gendered female,[28] Cather's *One of Ours* also
destabilizes and questions male identities and gender relations as they are
inscribed normatively in literature about war. Not simply a celebration of
male homosocial bonds and desires, *One of Ours*, I wish to argue instead,
reveals a profound awareness of male homosocial desire as a motivation
for war, but also the problematic nature of that desire in war. Moreover,
Cather's novel suggests that efforts to negotiate a way out of the double
bind of homosocial desire can only end in the kind of panicked silence,
avoidance, or denial that marked the Newport Training Station investigations of 1919–1920. The double bind of male homosocial desire — that it

is, as Sedgwick so perceptively puts it, "at once the most compulsory and the most prohibited of social bonds"[29] — becomes all the more intensified in war. As Sedgwick accurately notes, the military is "the most male-homosocial of institutions,"[30] and the one in which homosexual panic most visibly operates to regulate male homosocial desire and keep it within acceptable bounds. To reiterate Sedgwick: homosexual panic is the fear and loathing experienced by men that serves to structure and main-tain "definitional leverage over the whole range of male bonds that shape the social constitution" of all-male communities, sanctioning certain forms of homosociality and outlawing others. All men, except uncloseted homosexuals, are vulnerable to this panic, the result of a "coercive double bind," she asserts, in which men are socialized to be "men's men," and rewarded for doing so but in which being a "man's man" is separated from being "interested" in men "only by an invisible, carefully blurred, always-already crossed line."[31] "The deep structure of this double bind, the fact of profound schism based on minimal and undecidable differenti-ation, has persisted and intensified in the 20th century."[32] Trying to negotiate their way through this mine field, men in combat, Cather's novel suggests, are placed in tortuously bewildering, and often not fully knowable, forms of gender and sexual arrangements. I propose that Cather's significant deconstruction of gender and sexual identities in the novel was enough to throw Hemingway into a fit of defensive contempt for her acute understanding of the unstable, not to say incoherent, nature of male homosocial relationships, and the very real misogynistic base upon which those relationships rest.

But Cather's method of upsetting secure and stable male homosocial arrangements is indirect and subtle. From a narratological or formalistic standpoint, Cather is still insufficiently recognized as a modernist writer. The lack of textual experimentation in her works has deceptively lulled readers into thinking that she is merely a conservative traditionalist, and *One of Ours* had a strong appeal to a middle-brow readership in 1922. She didn't self-consciously call herself a modernist in any literary manifesto in the way that Ezra Pound, say, strenuously did. But as Jane Lillenfeld argues, "the centrality of traditional fictional forms — supple prose that deliberately avoids calling attention to itself, an omniscient author, and seemingly realistic characters and narratives" are, in reality, "as much disguises" in Cather's works "as are the wrenched syntax" and the elabo-rately allusive ludic strategies of James Joyce's.[33] Cather's prose style

enabled her to maintain a large and faithful reading public throughout
her career, and to garner a Pulitzer Prize for *One of Ours*, but also
to perform a degree of experimentation that was often unnoticed by
her readership.[34]

For example, *One of Ours* is somewhat unusual in Cather's oeuvre for
having not an unreliable narrator but, rather, a deceptively ingenuous
controlling consciousness, that of Claude Wheeler, as reported by the
third person omniscient narrator. This complex, layered, and modernist
form of conveying the narrative has given rise to much critical misinter-
pretation of the novel. Many of Cather's critics have elided the two
(narrator/consciousness), arguing that Cather identifies with Claude, failing to see the distance she maintains from her protagonist. In 1960, for
example, John H. Randall argued that "Claude is much too passive to be
credible as the romantic hero Cather makes him out to be."[35] In his 1951
study of Cather, David Daiches characterized Cather as a male-identified
writer when he asserted that "the sensibility at work here seems doggedly
masculine."[36] Even Sharon O'Brien, a preeminent feminist Cather
scholar, sees insufficient complexity in the novel when she argues that
Cather "saw in war and combat ... the apotheosis of masculinity, a
temporary refuge from social definitions of feminine identity, linked in
her mind with passivity and victimization."[37]

Yet none of these assertions accounts for what Cather stated in a 1921
newspaper interview, as she was completing the novel. To her interlocutor she said that she intended to create an unreliable central point of view,
as the world at war is filtered through Claude's naive and excessively
idealistic consciousness. She said, "I have cut out all [objective] descriptive
work in this book—the thing I do best. I have cut out all picture-making
because that boy does not see pictures."[38] Susan Rosowski, at least,
perceptively appreciates Cather's technique in *One of Ours*, pointing out
that Cather is critical of her protagonist's limited vision and faulty understanding of his own desires and aspirations. Claude embraces illusions as
a way of shielding himself from "threatening reality."[39] Indeed, the novelist's elaboration of Claude's stifled and thwarted desires in Nebraska
before the war, and his sense of fulfillment and redemptive death in the
trenches, occurs within the realm of the protagonist's (mis)perceptions
and (mis)recognitions. This narrative technique plays a crucial part in
Cather's representation of male homosocial desire. What Eve Kosofksy
Sedgwick calls the "complex and contradictory map of sexual and gender

definition"[40] can be drawn in the space created between the (unnamed) narrator and Claude's (lack of) consciousness.

Another indication of Cather's modernist sensibility comes in her 1922 essay, "The Novel Démeublé," written alongside the publication of *One of Ours*. This essay invites us to understand Cather's deployment of gaps, silences, fissures, and white space as narrative tactics that enable her to inscribe transgressively and evocatively of sexuality, as Sharon O'Brien has noted in her consideration of Cather as a closeted lesbian writer. These tactics certainly enabled her critical exploration of male homosocial desire in *One of Ours*. In a statement that rejected the crudely literal and overfurnished Balzacian work of realist fiction, Cather wrote in praise of "whatever is felt upon the page without being specifically named there . . . the inexplicable presence of the thing not named, of the overtone divined by the ear but not heard by it."[41] This allows for some remarkable textual slippage to occur in her works, and none of her novels is more suffused with the "thing not named" than *One of Ours*. As O'Brien nicely expresses it, sexuality is evoked in Cather's fiction as "an unnamed, absent presence," a constellation, as it were, of "complex or barely-sensed signifieds for which there exists no precise verbal signifier."[42] It is possible to read Cather's desire to evoke the unnamed in the light of Foucault's parallel assertion that in the history of human sexuality, "Silence itself—the things one declines to say, or is forbidden to name— . . . is less the absolute limit of discourse, the other side from which it is separated by a strict boundary, than an element that functions alongside the things said."[43] Cather's *One of Ours* exemplifies Foucault's dictum that silences "are an integral part of the strategies that underlie and permeate discourses."[44] In the permeable and mutable interstices of her text, along with its unreliable controlling consciousness, Cather can be seen to inscribe—or, rather, evoke—gender identities and identifications that proliferate beyond clearly established binary norms so comforting to Hemingway and the investigators at Newport.

Maureen Ryan has noted that Cather emphasizes "throughout the second part of the novel the camaraderie and community that the men experience with each other. In short Cather is attempting to create a quintessentially male experience."[45] Yet it should be noted that Claude's desire for close homosocial bonds exists in the Nebraska scenes as well. What Cather is elaborating in the first part of the novel is the extent to which young men seek to participate in war precisely because combat is the fullest realization of the tantalizing glimpses of perfect homosociality that civilian life also affords.

Prevented from attending the University of Nebraska by his pious mother and skinflint father, Claude, friendless and frustrated at the beginning of the novel, can only look longingly on the intensely homosocial environment of the university while he is attending a third-rate Bible college in Lincoln named Temple. There he is subject to dogmatic and puritanical lessons admonishing against pleasure in all its forms. His mother, Evangeline, frowns on the university, "where they give so much time to athletics and frivolity," and she warns him that "fraternity houses are places where boys learn all sorts of evil."[46] She goes on to suggest, without specific first-hand knowledge, "that dreadful things go on in them sometimes" (23). He is left to imagine what terrors they hold for young innocents. And, indeed, she may well intend to protect him from the anticipated dangers of heterosexual promiscuity, which she can more readily envisage; yet Cather's way of phrasing Evangeline Wheeler's fears leaves open the ambiguous possibility of more polymorphous ("all sorts") forms of "evil" in the reader's mind.

At all events, Claude's mother does her best to reassure him that he will "be able to study better in a quiet, serious atmosphere" (23). But he is skeptical and resentful of these warnings, without being able to voice his discontent. Even playing halfback on the Temple football team fails to satisfy his longings; his homosocial desire is only fulfilled after a game against the more worldly state university team, in which "he brought his eleven off with a good showing. The State men congratulated him warmly," a "proud moment" (35) in his life. The reader is left to imagine the backslapping and embracing with which men in team sports express their congratulations. It is at this game that he encounters Julius Erlich, the state quarterback, their friendship cemented "while they dressed after their shower . . . all in a few minutes" (35). Claude "was so astonished at finding himself on such easy, confidential terms with Erlich," in comparison to his feeling of shame and rage when Annabelle Chapin, one of his female acquaintances at Temple, effusively congratulates him after the game. To Claude she is "ridiculous in a sport suit of her own construction" and she "positively threw herself upon his neck. He disengaged himself, not very gently" (35). Erlich saves him from having to return to the stiflingly conventional and heterosexist atmosphere of Temple by inviting him to supper at his house, where, under the generous and unobtrusive presence of Mrs. Erlich, Julius says reassuringly to Claude, " 'We're all boys at home.' " Claude consents to this invitation *"before he had time to frighten himself by imagining difficulties"* (35; emphasis added). When he arrives at the Erlichs, he enters a liberatory, unconfined wonderland of male homosociality, "a rambling wooden house with an unfenced, terraced lawn" (36). Claude and Julius enter a big, book filled room "full of boys and young men, seated on long divans or perched on the arms of easy chairs," all talking "outspokenly and frankly" and smoking. He thinks that "they were all nice boys," with "easy, agreeable manners," and they welcome him warmly, he reassures himself. Claude looks at a "little plaster bust of Byron" on the mantel, around the neck of which one of Julius's brothers had put his dress tie "at a rakish angle" (36). "For some reason," which is not articulated, this costuming "instantly made him wish he lived" with the Erlichs (37).

This is one of several important points early in the novel wherein Cather establishes Claude's desire for homosocial contact and fulfillment. Yet there are some problematic elements here that alert the reader to the real nature of homosocial bonding, and the unstable ground upon which it is constructed. From Claude's perspective the football game (a seemingly self-contradictory, ritualized form of homosocial rivalry and bonding) and the dinner after it, afford an almost miraculously free and easy refuge from the pinched, impoverished social and intellectual life of Temple. Team athletics, communal bathing and dressing, and the replication of a junior version of the men's club at the Erlichs' all exert a powerfully attractive appeal on Claude. At the same time, however, there is something to fear in such intensely all-male social pursuits and environs. Claude's homosexual panic is indicated by the narrator's suggestion that he is capable of "frighten[ing] himself by imagining difficulties" involved in participating in homosocial arrangements. He can't dwell on the risks too long before accepting Julius's invitation. We can see Claude here sensing, although it is never actually stated overtly, that the Erlich household is uncertainly delineated terrain.

Yet in order for Claude to attain any degree of social authority in the world, he must step onto this terrain. As Sedgwick notes, "such compulsory relationships," which Cather represents in the novel, "as male friendship, mentorship, admiring identification" and both friendly and "heterosexual rivalry" all "involve forms of investment that force men into the arbitrarily mapped, self-contradictory, and anathema-riddled quicksands of the middle distance of male homosocial desire."[47] Sedgwick goes on to argue that the "small space" of this middle ground "may always, just as arbitrarily . . . be foreclosed": this is the double bind of male homosociality.[48] As a result of a man's accession to the "entitlement" of male homosociality, and the power and authority he can derive from it, he must also accede to the "acute manipulability, through the fear of one's own 'homosexuality,' of [other similarly] acculturated men."[49] Sedgwick perceptively notes the "reservoir of potential for violence caused by the self-ignorance that this regime constitutively enforces,"[50] feelings of violence that the military attempts to redirect against the enemy in war. With this in mind, the reader of *One of Ours* might well wonder what "difficulties" Claude is either imagining or repressing. He has been taught to suspect the lure of all-male environments according to his own socialization in rigidly puritanical and heterosexist institutions: the family, his schools, and his church. What are the potential dangers that lurk in the exciting world of "outspoken and frank" young men? What are the "evils" in all-male institutions in urban settings that his mother warns him of? The decorated bust of Byron signifies a world of effete dandyism and bookish overrefinement that Claude has been taught to find repellent. Yet at the same time, his "sensitive" nature has been carefully outlined by Cather's narrator in Claude's reaction against the coarse masculinity of his father and his father's farmhands, who tell crude jokes and function as despoilers of nature and aesthetic principles, who mistreat horses and chop down "beautiful" cherry trees (4, 26). His conflict arises because he senses that the Erlichs have social power and he is enticed by the world of possibilities, never fully defined, signified by the adorned bust of Byron. In response to the repeated, but never definitively answered, observation that "Claude knew, and everybody else knew, seemingly, that there was something wrong with him" (90, with variations on 104 and 193), he finds that the fulfillment of homosocial desire makes him "perhaps less tied-up in mind and body than usual" (35).

Another problem that Cather makes us see is that Claude's liberation and empowerment are achieved in all-male environments at the expense of women. At its core, male homosociality is an attempted flight from women. For Claude, the fascinating attraction of war is engendered by his fear of women and his inability to relate to them as equals. Sedgwick has shown how misogyny and gynophobia are coeval with homophobia in male homosocial desire: all draw on the male fear of the "feminine."[51] Advancing Sedgwick's conclusion still further, one can also assert that homosocial desire is predicated on an escape from the female body as well, especially in terms of men's imaginary perception of it as a powerfully engulfing or devouring entity.[52] Cather begins to signal this pernicious aspect of homosocial desire in the revealing moment after the football game when Claude is repelled by the violent assault upon him from Annabelle Chapin, and his disengagement—a word with apt military connotations—from her in order to rejoin the company of men. His forceful rejection of Annabelle's attention marks his distaste for women in general. The contrast provided by the Erlichs' household (all-male except for the overly idealized mother who knows enough to stay out of the library while the boys are in it) affords an opportunity to escape the demands of the "ridiculous" and aggressive young women who were experiencing a degree of liberation themselves in the modern period.

Women his own age are frighteningly liberated and strongly sexual agents in Claude's mind. There is Peachy Millmore, too, an art student at the university, for example, who objectifies him, coaxing him "to pose in his track clothes for the life class on Saturday morning, telling him that he had 'a magnificent physique,' a compliment which covered him with confusion. But he posed, of course" (50), since he seems powerless in the face of such demanding women. With the prompting of Julius Erlich, who informs him that Peachy's forwardness has made her the butt of frat-house jokes on campus, Claude drops her. "Her eager susceptibility presented not the slightest temptation to him," the narrator meaningfully notes (51). "He was a boy with strong impulses, and he detested the idea of trifling with them" (51). The narrator informs the reader that Claude has a "sharp disgust for sensuality," bred by the talk of his father's crude farmhands (51), but the unstated aspect of Claude's disgust is that it is only manifested around women his own age. Rather, Cather's text, in its representation of Claude around other men, invokes "the distinctive sensuality attributed to the male-homosocial romance, its extravagant loyalties aerated by extroversion, eye-hunger, and inexpressiveness," to quote Sedgwick's witty phrasing.[53]

Ultimately, a failed marriage is the spur to his enlistment in 1917. Compelled by his upbringing in a heterosexist culture to marry, Claude is no more successful at securing a stable position for himself in the sex/gender "system," in which women and men are not fully fixed as either "feminine" or "masculine" in the way he wants. In a disastrous and unconsummated attempt at marriage to a "local girl," Enid Royce, Claude finds himself outgunned by Enid's strong will. Enid, typically of her generation, drives, a fact of modern life that prevents men from fully containing women in the domestic sphere. Claude's neighbor Leonard Dawson remarks to him, "Having a wife with a car of her own is next thing to having no wife at all" (174). Claude doesn't disagree. In a revealing episode during their engagement, Enid takes over from Claude at the wheel during a thunderstorm, when he futilely argues that it's too dangerous to drive. She insists on driving to get home on time: she "could not bear to have her plans changed by people or circumstances" (117). Enid has social activist ambitions, however conventionally directed they may be toward mission work and membership in the Anti-Saloon League. Enid fails to live up to Claude's conventional expectations of her as a dutiful homemaker; she keeps a spotless house, but she's often out of it when Claude returns home from working his fields. The narrator remarks, ambiguously as usual, "Whether she neglected her husband depended upon one's conception of what was his due" (180). Dawson calls Enid "a fanatic," her activism more often than not leaving him at home "eating a cold supper by himself" (175). The local men can't forgive Enid for coming between Claude and his boyhood "chum," Ernest Havel, over Havel's drinking (176). The notion that women interfere with male homosocial bonding provides another reason for Claude's desire to flee. The effort to "renew their former intimacy" (195) fails and so Enid goes to China on a mission, and Claude is free to enlist in the army. The marriage has been doomed to fail, of course, since Claude idealizes and essentializes women, as he does all things, and no women of his own age measure up to his mother or the subject of his history thesis, Joan of Arc. He thinks, as the narrator reports, "Women ought to be religious; faith was the natural fragrance of their minds. The more incredible the things they believed, the more lovely was the act of belief. . . . A woman who didn't have holy thoughts about mysterious things far away would be prosaic and commonplace, like a man" (111). Modern women, he believes, are materialistic and insufficiently spiritual. Thus threatened by overpowering women with whom he has only unsatisfying relationships, Claude seeks refuge in the all-male environment of the army, however much he claims to do so from patriotic motives.

He announces his decision to enlist, before the draft, to his uncomprehending family members: " 'I'm going over to help fight the Germans' "
(201). But the advantage of "going over" is that, as Susan Jeffords points
out about all combat situations, only men do the fighting.

In her feminist study of gender and the Vietnam War, Jeffords perceptively notes that "collectivity fulfills the structural in Vietnam representation through the imagery and frame of the masculine bond."[54] Much of
her insight about male bonding in the Vietnam war pertains to representations of male experience in the great war as well.[55] Claude's intensely
homosocial experience in training and mobilization for war occurs among
soldiers from diverse class and ethnic (though not racial) backgrounds,
but the bonds they try to forge are masculine: to echo Jeffords, "At no
point are women to be included as part of this collectivity."[56] In fact, the
homosocial bonding that is crucial for organizational coherence and esprit
de corps "depends for its existence on an affirmation of difference — men
are not women."[57] Indeed, patriarchy thrives on war because the exclusion of women from war has, as Jeffords states, valorized "bonds between
men over those between women and within families."[58] As Cather's
Albert Usher, a Marine who befriends Claude on the voyage to France,
says, " 'Now the U.S. Marines are my family. Wherever they are, I'm at
home' " (241). Moreover, in such a context, as Jeffords puts it, "the female
must by necessity be excluded from the enactment and maintenance of
this masculine community."[59] Patriarchy has constructed, within this
framework, "female" as "representing the body, the appetitive, necessity,
the domestic, and the mundane," in "contradistinction to that which
["male"] presents itself as being: the abstract, the immortal, the unchanging, the public."[60] This conventional distinction between genders in war
also depends, as Sedgwick also points out, on fear of the "female" in any
form. In Cather's novel, Claude supposes — before actually arriving in
France — that "French girls haven't any scruples" when it comes to entrapping American "doughboys," and his friend Victor Morse responds,
" 'I haven't found that girls have many, anywhere' " (248).

Cather's novel, however, questions the military's ability to maintain
absolutely the "masculine" at the expense of the "feminine" in homosocial
collectives. As Sharon O'Brien and Frederick T. Griffiths argue in their
analyses of gender in *One of Ours*, Cather overturns notions of masculinity
and femininity, portraying men enacting roles that have traditionally been

300 D. A. BOXWELL

constructed as "feminine." As Griffiths succinctly puts it, Cather's novel establishes "a radical redefinition of sex roles which is nowhere acknowledged and everywhere felt."[61] Commentators have, for example, made much of Claude's nurturing, "maternal" leadership on board the *Anchises*, the plague-ridden troop ship that transports his unit to France. Griffiths, for example, has stated, "While being transported as a warrior [Claude] in fact turns himself into quite a good nurse and thereby develops nurturant qualities always frustrated in Nebraska."[62] Critics have also noted Claude's interest in making the battlefield a domestic refuge—his desire to tidy up and furnish the "comfortable little hole" in the trenches he shares with his closest friend in the war, the musician David Gerhardt (310).

By such gender role reversals, Cather represents male nurturance as it conflicts with an anxiety-ridden effort to uphold traditional norms of masculine identity and behavior. In the institutionalized absence of women, the enactment of "feminine" roles causes soldiers in war, or in preparation for war, to move uncontrollably around on the homosocial continuum, causing, as Sedgwick notes, ruptures in that continuum. Cather accurately represents the entire military superstructure's effort to erase the presence of women altogether in its attempt to foster homosocial desire. Claude is given a French phrasebook while he is at boot camp. It is "(made up of sentences chosen for their usefulness to soldiers, such as; 'Non, jamais je ne regarde les femmes')," the narrator parenthetically notes (209). In the double valence of the French word "*regarder*," the soldiers are being indoctrinated with a sense that women are not to be looked at, much less thought about; while "*jamais*" ("never") forcefully articulates the absolute nature of the army's prohibition against women, who were a "distraction" figured, in much military discourse during the war in terms of contamination and disease.[63]

Yet if women are not to be "looked at," the gaze is, by default, redirected toward the male body. Claude, while visiting some wounded men under his command at a Paris hospital, considers one victim of the Battle of Cantigny "fortunate" (288).

This young man is described by the doctor as a "star patient" but "a psychopathic case" (287). As Dr. Trueman tells Claude, " 'the fellow has forgotten almost everything about his life before he came to France. The queer thing is,' " Claude learns, " 'it's his recollection of women that is most affected' " (287). (The word "queer" in this context hardly requires my italicization for emphasis.) This "fortunate" patient can't remember his mother, sisters, or fiancée. Here is someone, Claude envyingly thinks, who has succeeded in escaping the entrapping bonds of women, even if he has become partially amnesic in order to do it. Claude, ever nurturant, pities the amnesiac: "He wished he could do something to help that boy" (288). More importantly, Claude entertains a potentially erotic fantasy of oblivion about this victim. The narrator reports that Claude expresses to himself a wish to rescue this wounded victim, to "help him get away from the doctor who was writing a book about him, and the girl who wanted him to make the most of himself; get away and be lost altogether in what he had been lucky enough to find." This encounter with "the lost American" ends with a description of Claude's cruising gaze as he walks though the streets of Paris: "All day, as Claude came and went, he looked among the crowds for that young face, so compassionate and tender" (288).

Claude still attempts to uphold proper "masculine" conduct, however nurturant he may be. In a telling scene on board the *Anchises* as it makes its way to France, he gently reprimands Private Fuller for crying in front of the English stewards on board the ship. After taking the young enlisted man's temperature ("Claude stuck a thermometer into his mouth") and sending the deck steward to bring him a comforting cup of tea, Claude enjoins the "blubbering" young man to remember the folks in Nebraska:

"Well, now what would they think of you, back there? I suppose they got the band out and made a fuss over you when you went away, and thought they were sending off a fine soldier. And I've always thought you'd be a first rate soldier. I guess we'll forget about this. You feel better already, don't you?" (252)

Fuller promises not to cry again, after Claude relies on the regulating ballast of all homosocial arrangements in the military: young men's shame at acting "feminine." " 'I know it's a little gloomy,' " Claude tells Fuller in the midst of a shipboard epidemic with a certain degree of delusional understatement, " 'but don't you shame me before these English stewards' " (252). In other scenes, Claude keeps faithful bedside vigil for Fanning and Tannhauser, two of his men afflicted with the contagious influenza that breaks out on the *Anchises*, measuring the time for giving medication with "the wrist watch which he had hitherto despised as effeminate and had carried in his pocket" (254), but that he now wears openly and finds "a very useful article" (254). Cather suggests that in male homosocial environments, especially in wartime, concealed "effeminacy" can also be displayed with impunity, and, in fact, may be vital and lifegiving. Yet Claude is oblivious to this, still mouthing the traditional and normative shibboleths about proper masculine conduct in the unit. Real men don't cry or wear wristwatches.

But they do "bond." Even before departing for France and receiving his commission, Claude burns "with the first ardor of the enlisted man" during his training at Fort R_____, its full name unrevealed by the narrator. He feels "ardor" not only because he feels he has a sense of purpose in his life for the first time but also because of "his friends at camp" (213) who comprise the first fully fledged male homosocial world he has experienced since the Erlich household. He idealistically believes that the other recruits are just like him, regardless of class and ethnic differences: "They all came to give and not to ask, and what they offered was just themselves," selves that Claude enumerates in terms of male body parts: "their big red hands, their strong backs, the steady, honest, modest look in their eyes" (213). He rhapsodizes about his fellow soldiers as they form a collective aboard the *Anchises.* "Taking them altogether the men were a fine sight as they lounged about the decks in the sunlight." Claude thinks that "seen in a mass like this . . . they were rather noble looking fellows" (240). Earlier, Claude had volunteered to help the medical examiner at the training camp, which presumably throws him into the midst of hordes of men in varying states of undress, although this is not stated as such. He assesses the homosocial bliss of his enlistment training: "Claude loved the men he trained with, — wouldn't choose to live in any better company" (214). When he returns home for one final visit from his bootcamp experience with his homosocial desire fully sated, Claude's father-in-law remarks, "rather childishly, 'It can't be that Claude's grown taller? I suppose it's the way they learn to carry themselves. He always was a manly looking boy' " (214). Cather is suggesting that patriarchal society values homosocial institutions and environments for their ability to augment "masculinity," but the oxymoronic juxtaposition here of "boy" and "man" makes us aware of the unstable nature of the product of such environments and institutions.

Insofar as the military functions as a homosocialization machine, masculine norms are fostered and reinforced not merely in spite of, but because of, a design flaw that always threatens to make the machinery break down. As Sedgwick describes it, in the military, "where both men's manipulability and their potential for violence are at the highest possible premium, the prescription of the most intimate male bonding and the proscription of . . . 'homosexuality' are both stronger than in civilian society—are, in fact, close to absolute."[64] Cather cannily draws on this pre/proscription double bind in the training and combat scenes in *One of Ours*, but she also reveals that male homosocial desire, as it is maintained and regulated by this double bind, is a remarkably tenuous and shaky construct. To take one instance of this, we can see Cather's acute understanding of the importance of the homosocial gaze whenever Claude is actually described looking at another man. On board the *Anchises* the Marine Albert Usher becomes the object of Claude's "eye hunger," to use Sedgwick's vivid phrase. Usher is described as "a young fellow, rather pale from his recent illness, but he was exactly Claude's idea of what a soldier ought to look like. His eye followed the Marine about all day" (240). And something ineffable or unnamed lies at the heart of this friendship:

Claude glanced sidewise at the boy's handsome head, that came up from his neck with clean, strong lines. . . . He could not have said exactly what it was he liked about young Usher's face, but it seemed to him a face that had gone through things,—that had been trained down like his body, and had developed a definite character. What Claude thought due to a manly, adventurous life, was really due to well shaped bones. (241)

Here is a perfect example of the way in which the protagonist's perceptions are undercut by the narrator. The narrator is again indicating Claude's romanticization of his fellow soldiers, an acceptably prescribed romanticization that has formed the heart of male homosocial desire since Achilles and Patroclus. Yet, at the same time, there is an inarticulable eroticization going on here that verges on the dangerously proscribed ("he could not have said exactly what it was he liked"). And this is one of many moments in the text where Cather portrays the contiguity of homosocial and (always potentially) homoerotic desire.

Thus does Claude's gaze begin to merge into the transgressively erotic and "feminized," the signal of proscribed "homosexuality." Yet Cather portrays Claude as being unable to fully distinguish between the prescribed and the proscribed, and nowhere is this more apparent than in the astonishing scene toward the end of the novel, just prior to his own death, when Claude rushes into a bedroom and bayonets, "in the back," a German officer who has been firing sniper shots at noncombatants in

Beaufort. Leaving aside the stark sexual symbolism of Claude's method of despatching the enemy (and the location of this event is also sexually significant), the text describes the German as "very handsome," with beautifully manicured hands ("his nails so pink and smooth"). He is wearing a pinkie ring "with a ruby, beautifully cut," and linen "as white as if he were going to a ball" (366). From Claude's point of view, he sees the German officer's "gorgeous silk dressing gown" on the bed and "a dressing case full of hammered silver" (367). Surrounded by all this luxurious finery, "This officer, Claude was thinking, was a very different sort of being from the poor prisoners they had been scooping up like tadpoles from the cellars" (367). The reader must attempt to discern how Claude is figuring difference here. The real marker of the German officer's sexuality is around his neck, where, "hung by a delicate chain," is a miniature "not . . . of a beautiful woman, but of a young man, pale as snow, with blurred forget-me-not eyes" (367). Claude's interpretive skills are lacking: "Claude studied it, wondering, 'It looks like a poet, or something. Probably a kid brother, killed at the beginning of the war' " (367).

Are we supposed to accept this misrecognition as ingenuous? Most of Cather's critics give credence to Claude's obtuseness about all the material signifiers of homosexuality present at the scene of the crime; but enough has happened in the text by this point to make an assuredly affirmative response to this question somewhat problematic. Claude doesn't interpret what he sees very definitively ("or something"). By contrast, the more worldly David Gerhardt "took it and glanced at it with a disdainful expression" (367) and, though his disdain signals his homophobia to the reader, Claude is reassured by David's own affirmative response to Claude's obtuse reading of the ostentatious visual texts of the scene before their eyes: "Probably." Again, Cather undercuts this because David touches Claude's shoulder in this scene, as "Claude noticed that David looked at him as if he were very much pleased with him, — looked indeed, as if something pleasant had happened in this room" (367). Significantly, as Frederick T. Griffiths points out, this is the only point in the narrative when the two friends are shown making any physical contact whatever, and "Claude's first kill has all of the sexual overtones that Hemingway will see in such archetypal scenes of exposure and violence," with one key difference — ironizing distance.[65] Echoing Sedgwick's assessment of homosociality in the military, I would go so far as to suggest that Claude's pleasurable penetrative act of initiation functions as his apotheosis as a homosocial being. He has entered into the ritual realm of pre-scribed conduct, that of killing other men designated "the enemy," which serves to channel a vast unspoken and unacknowledged reservoir of vio-lence arising from the self-ignorance and repression that have marked his own desire for male comradeship. Claude's desire is, as Cather percep-tively shows throughout the novel, fostered and exploited and rewarded by all the regimes of social acculturation that have formed the sex/gender/sexuality structures in which he is located. Claude's heroism is enacted against a figure otherized as an enemy not merely in terms of nationality or class but also in terms of sexuality and gender transitivity. The scene, while rife with ambiguity and duplicity, has the crucially important effect of cementing the homosocial bonds between Claude and David even further. "Just now he felt that Gerhardt . . . was in some way connected with him" (368). Hence a kind of homosocial climax has occurred in the act of killing an effeminate homosexual.

Cather's remarkable novel was published in the year after the army was, for the first time, persuaded by the psychiatric establishment to change its regulations to list "feminine characteristics among the 'stig-mata of degeneration' that made a man unfit for military service."[66] The revised standards implemented in 1921 provided the basis for follow on prohibitions against homosexuality and homosexuals during the next world war and thereafter. As Allan Bérubé states, "With these 1921 standards, the Army established its first written guidelines for excluding men who displayed feminine bodily characteristics or who were sexual 'perverts' or 'psychopaths.' "[67] These guidelines were characterized by predictably eugenicist ideas about physical degeneration as a marker of moral degeneration. According to the 1921 standards, "A young man with a 'scant and downy beard' or a 'female figure' was . . . to be closely observed for evidence of 'internal glandular disturbances' " and rejected for military service.[68]

Cather's representation of the furious, but not always conscious, effort to stamp out gender ambiguity and sexual transgressivity (here displaced onto a defeated and "corrupt" enemy bayonetted suggestively in the back) might well have induced a sense of unease, if not actual panic, in many of its male readers like Hemingway. Cather's *One of Ours* maps out and explores the intersection of thanatos and eros on the continuum of male homosocial desire, and on this terrain all sorts of unpredictable and inexplicable things happen in war. Men in war, as Cather suggests, lose control of self-understanding and, to echo Clausewitz (who was only thinking of military tactics), seemingly simple matters of gender and sexuality become very difficult indeed.

Cather's complex response to the spectacle of male-male desire encompasses both her ambivalent admiration for and her critical distance from a gendered experience that necessitated the exclusion, and even obliteration, of women (in corporeal form) and any behavior constructed and marked as "feminine." To echo Susan Jeffords's astute phrasing, Cather's staging of the spectacle of the masculine bond in both war and peace shows up male-male relationships for what they really are: anxiety-ridden, uncomprehending, and "irresolvably unstable,"[69] perhaps, as a male sailor of indeterminate sexual orientation in a dress singing, in the midst of a catastrophic war, "I'm Called Little Buttercup—dear Little Buttercup, / Though I could never tell why."

A coda: in one of my first-year honors classes at the military academy where I was teaching in 1991, one particularly outspoken male cadet volunteered, pace Hemingway, without any prompting from me (and to the uneasy chortling of his classmates), that Claude was a "queer." I asked him to substantiate this assertion in the light of textual evidence, especially since Cather does not depict Claude committing a homosexual act, much less overtly declaring erotic yearnings to another man. He was unable to do so, which is what Cather probably intended, I like to think. This led to a discussion, as I had hoped it would, about the concept of a continuum of male bonding. It was a perceptive female cadet who took the risk of alienating herself from her male classmates by saying that "if Claude was a queer, then so is every guy at the Academy." When all is said and done, female spectators, who are forced to watch, and expected to valorize, the ostentatious displays of male bonding at the military academies, have the best perspective—as "outsiders"—on the misogynistic and homophobic ideologies that interpellate military personnel.

NOTES

I wish to thank Elin Diamond, William Galperin, Carol Siegel, and readers at *Genders* for their insightful and enriching responses to this essay.

1. The epigraph above is from Susan Jeffords, *The Remasculinization of America: Gender and the Vietnam War* (Bloomington: Indiana University Press, 1989),

73. Jeffords provides a pertinent discussion of the military as performance arena.

2. George Chauncey, Jr., "Christian Brotherhood or Sexual Perversion? Homosexual Identities and the Construction of Sexual Boundaries in the World War I Era," in *Hidden from History: Reclaiming the Gay and Lesbian Past*, ed. Martin Duberman, Martha Vicinus, and Chauncey (New York: New American Library), 542.

3. Ibid; and Allan Bérubé, *Coming Out under Fire: The History of Gay Men and Women in World War Two* (New York: Free Press), 75.

4. Chauncey, "Christian Brotherhood," 297.

5. Ibid., 298.

6. For the purposes of clarity and consistency I want to avail myself of Eve Kosofsky Sedgwick's cogent differentiation among sex, sexuality, and gender in *Epistemology of the Closet* (Berkeley: University of California Press, 1990) while acknowledging, with her, that their "usage and analytical relations are almost irremediably slippery" (27). She defines "sex" as the irreducible biological difference between males and females of a species. Gender, she states, is the more elaborate and "the more fully and rigidly dichotomized social production of male and female identities and behaviors" (27). Sexuality, finally, is "the array of acts, expectations, narratives, pleasures, identity formations, and knowledges . . . that tends to cluster around certain genital sensations but not adequately defined by them" (29). For a full account of the process by which gays and lesbians became categorized as "excludable" from military service from 1921 onward, see Bérubé, *Coming Out*, 8–33, 128–74.

7. Bérubé, *Coming Out*, 32.

8. Ibid., 13.

9. Chauncey, "Christian Brotherhood," 313.

10. Michel Foucault, *The History of Sexuality*. Vol I, *An Introduction*, trans. Robert Hurley (New York: Random House, 1978), 43. We can begin to trace self-conscious and anxiety-ridden preoccupations about masculinity, and what constituted it, as far back as the 1890s, "as America began to assert itself as a world power with expansionist ambitions," according to David F. Greenberg, *The Construction of Homosexuality* (Chicago: University of Chicago Press, 1988), 393. Theodore Roosevelt, for one, asserted that extended peace was a danger that created "effeminate tendencies in young men" (quoted in Greenberg, 393). Cather's novel, contra Roosevelt, reveals that experience in war fosters all kinds of gendered behavior in young men.

11. Chauncey, "Christian Brotherhood," 295. It is especially revealing to look at this trial in the context of many other efforts to "purify" American society in the immediate aftermath of the great war, a period of extreme social anxiety: Prohibition; the rapid implementation of immigration quotas after 1919; the Sacco-Vanzetti arrests in 1920; and the attempt to crush the Industrial Workers of the World (the "Wobblies"), beginning in 1916, but reaching a climax in 1919, with the arrest of more than a thousand IWW members.

12. Sandra M. Gilbert, "Soldier's Heart: Literary Men, Literary Women, and the

Great War," in *Speaking of Gender*, ed. Elaine Showalter (New York: Routledge, 1989), 290. As Gilbert points out, by 1918, "when World War I was over, there were eight and a half million European men dead, and there had been thirty-seven and a half million male casualties" (302). Of course, in numerical terms, American losses were dramatically fewer (116,516 American soldiers and sailors died), but were sustained in a more compressed time frame (twenty months), which assuredly had measurable psychic impact on the nation.

13. Chauncey, "Christian Brotherhood," 305.

14. For a full account of this episode in American military and social history, see Chauncey's superb rendering in "Christian Brotherhood," 294–317.

15. Eve Kosofsky Sedgwick, *Between Men: English Literature and Male Homosocial Desire* (New York: Columbia University Press, 1985), 1.

16. Ibid.

17. See Sharon O'Brien's biography *Cather: The Emerging Voice* (New York: Oxford University Press, 1987), chapters 4–6, for a thorough rendition of Cather's adolescent experimentation in cross-dressing and local amateur theatrical performances in male parts.

18. Sharon O'Brien, "Combat Envy and Survival Guilt: Willa Cather's 'Manly Battle Yarn,' " in *Arms and the Woman: War, Gender, and Literary Representation*, ed. Helen M. Cooper, Adrienne Auslander Munich, and Susan M. Squier (Chapel Hill: University of North Carolina Press, 1989), 186.

19. Susan J. Rosowski, *The Voyage Perilous: Willa Cather's Romanticism* (Lincoln: University of Nebraska Press, 1986), 97.

20. O'Brien, "Combat Envy," 187.

21. Ibid., 190.

22. Ibid., 186. See also Stanley Cooperman, *World War I and the American Novel* (Baltimore, Md.: Johns Hopkins University Press, 1967), 136.

23. O'Brien, "Combat Envy," 189.

24. Kenneth Lynn, *Hemingway* (New York: Simon and Schuster, 1987), 533; Mark Spilka, *Hemingway's Quarrel with Androgyny* (Lincoln: University of Nebraska Press, 1990).

25. Ernest Hemingway, *Men without Women* (New York: Scribners, 1927), 166.

26. Ibid., 167.

27. Lynn, *Hemingway*, 318.

28. Gilbert, "Soldier's Heart," 297.

29. Sedgwick, *Epistemology*, 187.

30. Sedgwick, *Between Men*, 222.

31. Ibid., 89.

32. Ibid., 201.

33. Jane Lilienfeld, "Willa Cather," in *The Gender of Modernism*, ed. Bonnie Kime Scott (Bloomington: University of Indiana Press, 1990), 49.

34. Sharon O'Brien's essay, " 'The Thing Not Named': Willa Cather as a Lesbian Writer," *Signs* 9, no. 4 (Summer 1984), begins the necessary work of analyzing Cather's sophisticated textual strategies, especially in terms of the

novelist's interplay between figure and ground, as well as her subtexts and encodings. O'Brien's is a superb feminist and deconstructive analysis that resists simplistic or definitive interpretive solutions to the challenges of Cather's complex work.

35. Quoted in Maureen Ryan, "No Woman's Land: Gender in Willa Cather's *One of Ours*," *Studies in American Fiction* 18, no. 1 (Spring 1990): 65.
36. Ibid.
37. O'Brien, "Combat Envy," 184.
38. Quoted in Rosowski, *The Voyage Perilous*, 96.
39. Ibid., 105.
40. Eve Kosofsky Sedgwick, "Across Gender, across Sexuality: Willa Cather and Others," *South Atlantic Quarterly* 88, no. 1 (Winter 1989): 60.
41. Willa Cather, "The Novel Démeublé," in *The Gender of Modernism*, 55.
42. O'Brien, " 'The Thing Not Named,' " 576.
43. Foucault, *History of Sexuality*, 27.
44. Ibid.
45. Ryan, "No Woman's Land," 67.
46. Willa Cather, *One of Ours* (New York: Random House, 1971), 23. Further references to this work will be included parenthetically in the text.
47. Sedgwick, *Epistemology*, 186.
48. Ibid.
49. Ibid.
50. Ibid.
51. Sedgwick, *Between Men*, 20.
52. For a stunning analytical elaboration of this misogynistic component of male bonding in military institutions (here, specifically, the German Freikorps in the aftermath of World War I) see Klaus Theweleit, *Male Fantasies*. Vol. I, *Women, Floods, Bodies, History*, trans. Stephen Conway (Minneapolis: University of Minnesota Press, 1987).
53. Sedgwick, "Across Gender," 69.
54. Jeffords, *Remasculinization*, 59.
55. Consider the intensely homosocial romance of much of the now canonical "trench poetry," including Wilfred Owen's "Strange Meeting" (1918), in which the two dead German and British soldiers who address each other in tender and consolatory words achieve peaceful union in the suggestive ellipsis of the last line: "Let us sleep now . . . "
56. Jeffords, *Remasculinization*, 59.
57. Ibid., 60.
58. Ibid.
59. Ibid., 61.
60. Ibid.
61. Frederick T. Griffiths, "The Woman Warrior: Willa Cather and *One of Ours*," *Women's Studies* 11 (1984): 270.
62. Ibid., 276.
63. See John D'Emilio and Estelle B. Freedman's fascinating account of this in

310   D. A. BOXWELL

Intimate Matters: A History of Sexuality in America (New York: Harper and Row, 1988), 211–13. One example: "In December 1917, in response to a five hundred percent increase in VD rates among soldiers stationed at St. Nazaire, Pershing placed brothels and saloons in port cities of debarkation off limits to soldiers and stationed MPs around them" (212). A discussion of military police monitoring American soldiers' sexual conduct in France occurs in *One of Ours* (248).

64. Sedgwick, *Epistemology*, 186.
65. Griffiths, "The Woman Warrior," 267.
66. Bérubé, *Coming Out*, 13.
67. Ibid., 14.
68. Ibid.
69. Jeffords, *Remasculinization*, 10.

Shakespeare Out in Portland: Gus Van Sant's *My Own Private Idaho*, Homoneurotics, and Boy Actors

David Román

Gus Van Sant's 1991 film *My Own Private Idaho* (Fine Line Feature) participates in simultaneous constructions of "Shakespeare" and "homosexuality" that, while grounded in long and unstable historical narratives laden with anxieties about both Shakespeare and homosexuality, are seen to reach a crisis point in U.S. cultural politics by the fall of 1991. This crisis is played out in the film industry and in the popular culture—as it was in the theater and culture of early modern England—mainly around the issue of the (boy) actors.[1] Various competing agents, including the director, film critics, gay activists, and even the actors themselves, invest Keanu Reeves and River Phoenix, the two main actors in Van Sant's film, with indeterminate but nonetheless heavily politicized meanings. Such an epistemological chaos suggests at once what Greg Bredbeck succinctly states in his discussion of Renaissance sodomy when he claims that "sodomy does not create disorder; rather, disorder creates sodomy."[2] And whenever and wherever there is such disorder, Shakespeare—like Elvis[3]—is sure to resurface.

SHAKESPEARE AND THE ROAD BEFORE US

"I always know where I am by the way the road looks."

—*My Own Private Idaho*

311

If U.S. commercial film and television industries are any indication, the fall of 1991 was a good season for William Shakespeare.

If U.S. commercial film and television industries are any indication, the fall of 1991 was a good season for William Shakespeare. Not only were his plays quoted throughout the televised Senate confirmation hearings of Clarence Thomas, but also for weeks on end, two "Shakespearean" films—Peter Greenaway's *Prospero's Books* and Gus Van Sant's *My Own Private Idaho*—played side by side in mainstream movie theaters. Marjorie Garber, noted Shakespearean and cultural critic, aptly has argued that the current manifestation of the Shakespeare fetish in fashion these days "has come to stand for a kind of 'humanness' that, purporting to be inclusive of race, class, and gender, is in fact the neutralizing (or neutering) of those potent discourses by appropriation."[4] For Garber, and many other Shakespeare critics, "[Shakespeare] is—whoever he is, or was—the fantasy of original cultural wholeness, the last vestige of universalism: *unser* Shakespeare."[5] Garber cites some of the events in the late 1980s—Laurence Olivier's funeral, Secretary of Education Lynn Cheney's report on the humanities, and U.S. actor Sam Wanamaker's campaign to rebuild the Globe theater—to make her point, but the events of the fall of 1991 demonstrate that the Shakespeare fetish phenomenon continues, if not grows. The Senate confirmation hearings, with Alan Simpson of Wyoming acting as if he were the head of a doctoral defense, correcting Joseph Biden's mistaken allusion to Shakespeare and grilling Thomas on his recollection of *Othello*, only add to Garber's thesis that Shakespeare's uncanny recurring presence in our time materializes as a type of cultural assurance of civility and power, however ironic its staging may be.[6] That Simpson himself failed to recognize that the quote he cited to support Judge Thomas is actually spoken by the duplicitous villain Iago was ironic, but, by then, beside the point. That Shakespeare was introduced— inevitably and deliberately—placed Thomas's position in the arena of the universal, legitimate, true.

If, during the Thomas confirmations, Shakespeare is brought out by those in power in order to stabilize public anxieties regarding gender and race relations, in Gus Van Sant's *My Own Private Idaho* a different set of dynamics are at play that focuses on anxieties about (homo)sexuality. Set in Portland, the film retells the story of Shakespeare's Prince Hal, who, having slummed through the underbelly of England's social landscape, emerges triumphant in his transformation as King Henry V. Like Shakespeare's Henry IV plays, Van Sant's film only partially focuses on the political career of Scott Favor (Keanu Reeves), the delinquent son of the mayor of Portland. Both Shakespeare and Van Sant extend their stories beyond the lives of princes to comment on two very different cultures facing similar challenges relating to the shifting social ideologies of gender and sexuality. While the evocations of Shakespeare during the Thomas hearings remind us of Shakespeare's leverage in contemporary culture to legitimate the vulnerable positions of those in power—that is, to enact the Renaissance spectacle that Stephen Orgel calls "the illusion of power"[7]—Van Sant's film reminds us that the anxieties of Shakespeare's age find direct engagement in our own cultural moment as well. By looking at polemics around the issue of the (boy) actors in the 1590s and the 1990s, I hope to demonstrate how both Shakespeare's plays and Van Sant's film incite similar (albeit historically specific) cultural tensions that permeate the popular imagination and participate in the ideological shapings of the age.

SHAKESPEARE OUT IN PORTLAND: GUS VAN SANT'S MY OWN PRIVATE IDAHO

Gus Van Sant's film tells the story of the thwarted friendship between two male hustlers—one's gay, the other isn't—who embark on an odyssey in search of their identities that begins in Seattle, passes through Portland, moves through Idaho, arrives in Rome, and then returns to Portland, where their friendship finally dissolves. River Phoenix plays the part of Mike Waters, a disheveled narcoleptic hustler who falls in love with Scott Favor, the rebellious son of the ailing Portland mayor. Scott and Mike become fast friends; in many ways the film relies on the conventional structures of the buddy films and road films popularized in the 1960s. But the implicit homoerotics of male bonding of those earlier films are foregrounded in My Own Private Idaho with Mike's growing unrequited love for Scott, who travels in this crowd of hustlers, druggies, and petty thieves mainly to infuriate his patrician father. Much of their story is cast in the familiar frame of Shakespeare's Henry IV plays in which Hal slums in the taverns and brothels of Eastcheap in order to insure that his return to his father and the court will be all the more esteemed and dramatic. Like Shakespeare's Hal, Scott has a surrogate father in the figure of the coke-sniffing and boy-loving Bob, a stand-in for Falstaff, who eagerly awaits Scott's twenty-first birthday, only weeks away, so that he too can share in the money Scott stands to inherit. The film even includes a remarkable restaging of the Gadshill caper in which Falstaff is tricked by Hal's carefully choreographed pseudorobbery; the scene reminds the others involved that Prince Hal, or in this case, Scott, always wins out in the end. By the end of the film, Scott, like Henry V, marries a foreign woman and returns with her triumphant to his home turf, shunning his "riots past and wild societies."[8]

The intertextual markings between Shakespeare's plays and Van Sant's film have dumbfounded critics, who, while attempting to make sense of Van Sant's employment of Shakespeare, are left with few ideas on such a peculiar pairing. Vincent Canby, writing in the *New York Times*, goes so far as to advise that "too much should not be made of the free use of Falstaff, Hal, and the two Henry IV plays. It's a nervy thing to do," he claims, "and it works as far it goes."[9] But how far does it actually go? Many critics, disregarding Canby's suggestion, view the Shakespeare insertion as making some direct commentary on Van Sant's story of street hustlers in Portland. Placing Shakespeare out in Portland, for many of these writers, suggests that Van Sant himself was deliberately attempting to anchor his own agenda by locating it in the comforts of Shakespearean authority. Owen Gleiberman, the film critic for *Entertainment Weekly*, argues, for example, that "the updated Elizabethan dialogue is simply too much of a conceptual stunt. It's as if Van Sant, who's openly gay, felt some misguided need to prove that a movie about male prostitutes could be Art. He needn't have tried so hard."[10] Others see it as yet one more example of Van Sant's cryptic yet evocative style of mixing visual, aural, and thematic motifs that don't necessarily hold any meaning at all, as if this is what we've come to expect from independent filmmakers.

Van Sant himself offers little insight other than that he was drawn to the Falstaff/Hal relationship and Orson Welles's own 1966 appropriation of the story in the *Chimes at Midnight*. In an interview, the director explains his intent: "I didn't want the language to be so much Shakespearean as private and cliquish, the way people who are bonded in a group develop a special way of talking. I wanted it to be more of a symbol, even though it doesn't signal itself as such."[11] Yet, as Peter Bowen points out, what becomes interesting in the film is precisely how the Shakespeare doesn't signal culture. Rather than marking the hustlers' story in the elevated ranks of the official and socially sanctioned, Van Sant's use of Shakespeare "works more to destabilize our sense of historical continuity and cultural destiny than it does to affirm it."[12] While thematic and structural links between the two texts can be located and even compared, as Bowen demonstrates, I would like to offer a different approach. I suggest that the main affinity between Shakespeare's plays and Van Sant's film lies in the material conditions of early modern English theater and contemporary film, particularly surrounding the concern over boy actors.

BOY ACTORS AND OTHER EARLY MODERN ARTIFACTS

These goodly pageants being ended, every mate sorts to his mate, everyone brings another homeward of their way very friendly, and in their secret conclaves covertly they play the Sodomites or worse.

— Phillip Stubbes, 1583

Boy actors played all the women's roles on the English Renaissance stage, and as feminist Shakespeare critics have long argued,[13] the fact that the boy actor engendered such controversy in the period demonstrates deep cultural anxieties concerning both gender and sexuality. The all-male enterprise that defines Renaissance drama invoked an extreme antitheatrical rhetoric that pronounced the theater the corrupter of social values and cultural norms. The transvestism of the boy actor confuses male spectators, and as Dr. John Rainoldes, one of the primary players in the antitheatrical movement, claims in 1599, "is an occasion of wantonness and lust."[14] Renaissance cultural historian Lisa Jardine explains how for Rainoldes, "sexuality, misdirected toward the boy masquerading in female dress is 'stirred' by attire and gesture; male prostitution and perverted sexual activity is the inevitable accompaniment of female impersonation."[15] Yet as Alan Bray demonstrates in his groundbreaking study, *Homosexuality and Renaissance England*, discussions of sodomy in the Renaissance were for the most part contained in larger polemics against debauchery and licentiousness. Jonathan Goldberg, whose recent study of sodomy follows upon Bray's research, thus is able to claim that

although sodomy is, as a sexual act, anything that threatens alliance—any sexual act, that is, that does not promote the aim of married procreative sex (anal intercourse, fellatio, masturbation, bestiality—any of these may fall under the label of sodomy in various legal codifications and learned discourses), and while sodomy involves therefore acts that men might perform with men, women with women (a possibility rarely envisioned), men and women with each other, and anyone with a goat, a pig, or a horse, these acts—or accusations of their performance—emerge into visibility only when those who are said to have done them also can be called traitors, heretics, or the like, at the very least, disturbers of the social order that alliance—marriage arrangements—maintained.[16]

Goldberg's fundamental and indispensable contribution lies in a deconstruction of what he calls "sodometries, the relational structures precariously available to prevailing discourses."[17] By putting pressure upon these "sodometries," Goldberg demonstrates both the irrefutable instability of the term[18] and its strategic and lethal employment by various social networks of power. While sodomy may have been grouped with such transgressive social customs and practices as adultery, sorcery, prostitution, heresy, and even popery, the antitheatrical tracts of the period begin to convey some of the stakes involved around the issue of the boy actor as it pertains to the question of sodomy and the cultural investment in regulated norms.

In her study of the relationship between the antitheatrical literature written before 1600 and Shakespeare's drama, Jean Howard demonstrates how these tracts reproduce deep-seated fears about possible social disruptions and transgressions of the ruling ideological orders:

The tracts repeatedly connect the theater and theatrical practices with threats to established gender and class categories and hierarchies; . . . they demonize social groups presented as embodying these threats, and . . . are highly selective in their condemnation of theatrical practices.[19]

While Howard focuses her argument on the misogynist constructions of women in the tracts as the "duplicitous, inherently theatrical sex,"[20] her ideas about their highly political interest in policing and maintaining closed systems of the social order and in scapegoating those on the margins of it (mainly women and actors) or subordinate to it (mainly women), are useful when examining the diatribes against sodomy in the antitheatrical literature. According to Phillip Stubbes, whose *Anatomy of Abuses* was published in 1583, the theater institutionalizes the disruption of sexual and class differences evident in early modern fashion,[21] and furthermore, as my opening epigraph demonstrates, implicates the entire audience of the public theater in the "performances" of sodomy.

While cosmetics and excesses of finery in apparel (cork shoes and the like) dismantle long-standing restrictions within gender and class ideologies, assumptions of sodomitical performances in the theater trigger potential social upheavals of established sexual norms. For these reasons, Stubbes claims that the public commercial theater in England is evil, not only in its deliberate staging of class and gender transgressions but also because of its increasing reputation for the promotion of sodomy. In his attacks on the theater, Stubbes not only demonizes women and actors, as Jean Howard argues, but he also anticipates the cultural construction of homosexuality by scripting the actor as sodomite.[22] While individual actors and others affiliated with the public theater may not have identified themselves as sodomites, social conservatives were quick to label them as such. Stubbes's voice, it must be noted, was not alone. The theater's reputation for homosexuality and other sodomitical performances was also declared by Guilpin and Drayton.[23]

Moreover, the learned Puritan, Dr. Rainoldes, writing in 1592 on the problems of the theater and its association with sodomy, warns that such theatrical conventions as transvestism, boy actors, and even dancing are perversions of nature and morally dangerous. J. W. Binns's important study of the specific antitheatrical debate at Oxford in the 1590s contextualizes Rainoldes's objections. Binns explains that "in the marginal notes with which he supports his allegations, Rainoldes refers the reader to Biblical and classical examples of sodomy, homosexuality, homosexuality coupled with sadistic flagellation, cross-dressing, and male marriage."[24] The anxiety produced by the stage, coupled with the rhetoric of biblical condemnation, so apparent in these antitheatrical tracts, perpetuated the fantastic concept in the Renaissance of the actor as demonic sodomite. Yet as Bray so clearly points out, "What is missing is any social expression of homosexuality based on the fact of homosexuality itself."[25] Instead, what becomes apparent in these debates is how the socially marginal—in this case, the actor—is scapegoated as the disrupter and corrupter of social mores and how pronouncements about securing closed social systems are ubiquitous.

Renaissance boy actors were the embodied sites of these debates— debates that continue even now, albeit differently and with somewhat less vehemence, as demonstrated by the voluminous research by feminist, new-historicist, and cultural-materialist critics, who each argue competing positions regarding the ramifications of the cross-dressing boy actor.[26] While little consensus is voiced by current critics, such a line of questioning proves useful in contextualizing the ongoing concern of employing "boy" actors, particularly in relation to Van Sant's film.

BOY ACTORS AND OTHER POSTMODERN ARTIFACTS

"I don't think the part is risky; there's not a lot in the film about sucking dick and getting fucked. I think it's more about family and the lives out there. I mean it's *more.*"

— Keanu Reeves, *US* magazine, 1991

"We were driving in a car on Santa Monica Boulevard, probably on the way to a club, and we were talking really fast about the whole idea. We were excited. It could have been like a bad dream—a dream that never follows through because no one commits, but we just forced ourselves into it. We said, 'O.K., I'll do it if you do it. I won't do it if you don't.' We shook hands. That was it."

— River Phoenix, *Interview*, 1991

"It's a political act to do a film like this. They're handling it very well for being obviously straight."

— Gus Van Sant, *American Film*, 1991

Performing gay male sexuality, as Gus Van Sant suggests, is a political act; but rather than foreground his comment, I'd like to focus on how the (boy) actors in his film—whom he forecloses as "obviously straight"—perceive their own participation in the political ramifications of playing "gay," and how these responses are then appropriated by dominant ideologies that reconstruct the actors in a manner similar to the early modern period. Nearly four hundred years later, and in light of the makings of a modern homosexual identity initiated at least over a century ago,[27] male-male sexual activity remains a highly charged and hotly contested location of politically imbedded debates around the same issues of morality, transgression, and agency. Eve Sedgwick has noted that the fine line between the homosocial and the homosexual is tenuous indeed. The homoerotic bonds between men are laden with an anxiety that at once suggests the fear of difference and the fear of associative contagion, indicative of what I would call a "homoneurotics." Sedgwick underlines this tension when she writes, "For a man to be a man's man is separated only by an invisible, carefully blurred, always-already-crossed line from being 'interested in men.' "[28] "Homoneurotics," as I employ it, puts pressure upon the presumptive universalizing of modern regimes that normalize heterosexuality and homosexuality as an essential binarism. While "homoerotics" conveys the possible pleasures available within homosociality, "homoneurotics" names the individual and cultural anxieties regarding those very potential pleasures. Such a homoneurotic dynamic, available in any expression of same-sex bonding, solicits—at its worst—a type of "homosexual panic" that, at its worst, results in violent queer bashings, murders, and socially sanctioned (that is, official) homoneurotic practices contributing to the insidious oppression of lesbians and gays in governmental policies on AIDS, social liberties, and privacy matters.[29]

If the Renaissance saw the regulation of the theater and the theater's supposed complicity in the corruption of society as the polemical site of the shifting social ideologies of sexuality and gender, contemporary U.S. culture finds its own anxieties around these issues played out in commercial films.[30] Both River Phoenix and Keanu Reeves seem to notice the political stakes involved in performing gay male sexuality. River Phoenix's remarks in *Interview* convey the homoerotic bond the two actors needed to forge, on Santa Monica Boulevard no less, in order to guarantee that they themselves would be equipped to combat the inevitable innuendos concerning their own sexuality. And, if River Phoenix's description of their promise—"I'll do it if you do it, I won't do it if you don't"—sounds less like a bad dream and more like a wet one, Keanu Reeves's comments in *US* negate the sexual acts of male hustlers along with his own complicity in the homoerotics of male bonding by explaining that the film is about something else, and something "better," entirely: "I mean, its more." Throughout the film and in their own perceptions of their roles in the film, the boy actors in *My Own Private Idaho* embody the simultaneous arousal of homoerotic possibility and its homoneurotic disavowal.

In the film, this double discourse plays out primarily through the relationship between Scott and Mike. Throughout the film, Keanu Reeves's Prince Hal character calls attention to his nongay identity; he has little interest in sex with males other than as a means to upset his father and set up his climactic redemption at the end through heterosexual marriage.[31] River Phoenix's Mike, on the other hand, articulates homosexual desire and calls attention to both the homosocial and homoneurotic components of his encounters with Scott and the other Portland hustlers. Indeed, Mike goes so far as to speak of male-male love, in many ways suggesting that it is homosexual love and not sexual desire that enacts the ultimate social transgression. Throughout his performance, Phoenix evokes a gay subjectivity that counters Reeves's performance of heterosexual privilege. In a brilliant sequence, Van Sant encapsulates this dialectic: the camera swoops through a porno shop as the viewer, following a cowboy-hatted number inside, is led to a gay porno display of such mags as *Homo on the Range, Joyboy, Male Call,* and *G-String.* Once in this nebulous male space, Van Sant displays his boy actors on the covers of these skinmags as the pinups they indeed are—suggesting that in contemporary U.S. culture, the road from *Teen Beat* to *Beat Meat* is not quite as long as one might think.[32] Objectifying and commodifying— indeed, marketing—the sex appeal of both Reeves and Phoenix, Van Sant has his cover-boy stars come to life. The pinups exchange glances and engage in cross-rack chatter as if they were on the opening credits of *The Brady Bunch* or *Hollywood Squares.* Despite such campy invocations, this moment demonstrates the operative dynamics of the homoneurotics engendered by boy actors. As hustlers, these pinups articulate their views of their profession; yet these discussions soon come down to the central differences between Mike and Scott. Scott explains that, unlike Mike, he never gives away his body for free. Such a claim distinguishes for Scott the line imagined between straight and gay identities, an arbitrary distinction that Mike doesn't quite understand:

SCOTT: It's when you start doing things for free that you start to grow wings and become a fairy.
MIKE: Huh?

Later in the film, Mike challenges Scott's ignorance when, in the campfire scene Phoenix is credited by the director for rewriting, he asks Scott to hold him. Mike and Scott are sitting alone at night by a campfire in the desert somewhere, presumably in Idaho. "What do I mean to you?" Mike asks, declaring his love for Scott, who is at a loss as to how to respond. Scott's earlier distinction of what is gay and what is not, defined for him by an economic transaction, is upset by Mike's insightful comment: "I love you, and you don't pay me."[33] In interviews, Van Sant details the revisions of this scene, which in his initial script had Mike less gay identified and even less capable of being in love. "River made the character more gay," Van Sant affirms. "I think that was a political act on his part."[34]

If Scott and Mike—as male hustlers—need to explain themselves, as they do in the porno shop scene, where they grace the covers of pornotrade publications, Keanu Reeves and River Phoenix—as actors paid to play these roles—need to enact a similar discursive strategy as they grace the covers of film-trade and mainstream entertainment publications.

While both River Phoenix and Keanu Reeves raised some initial concerns about playing these roles, their subsequent responses in the press reveal, for the most part, a playful and erotic friendship that seems less concerned with any fear of gay identification and more determined to estrange the homophobic perception that they should be anxious about their roles as male hustlers. In other words, it is the commercial milieu of U.S. film — press junkets, print publicity, interviews, marketing strategies, and the review process — that invokes homoneurotic anxieties relating to boy actors performing gay roles. One example, for instance, is evident from the comments of a production assistant on the set during the filming of the porno-mag fantasy sequence:

Both River and Keanu are taking this really well. . . . It may sound weird, but even though we're almost done with filming, we still sort of half-expect them both to wake up and realize what kind of movie they are in.[35]

In the *US* profile, readers are told that Van Sant is openly gay, as if we are supposed to know in advance what that may signify. In fact, the writer makes certain we do: Van Sant is "silent and brooding," "paternal," and "Peter Pan"-like. The boy actors in the film, on the other hand, are never identified as either straight or gay. Instead, they are described by their actions on the set. Keanu Reeves displays his scars from a motorcycle accident, listens to Jane's Addiction, and smokes pot between scenes, inscribing the actor with the cultural markings these attributes supposedly combine to signify as "straight." The actor, however, seems to refuse or at least confuse such clear categorizations of gender and sexual behavior. The instability or "utterly confused category" of sodomy in the early modern period resurfaces here as the limits of the categories available within modern regimes to regulate sexual practices and identities. At one point, homoneurotic panic surfaces when the writer describes Reeves's — for some — homoerotic actions on the set:

Shifting gears, the hyper actor gets into character, resuming his hustler prowl as he comes on to no one in particular. "Hey!" he shouts. "I know you want me. I know you want to do me. C'mon suck my dick for money!" This is not in the script, and so a few of the crew members get red-faced and giggle.[36]

In *Interview*, the two women paired up to interview the actors dwell on questions that focus on the actors' sexuality and image, so much so that at one point Reeves and Phoenix draw attention to the press's obsession with image, critical reception, and box-office receipts. Rather than discussing homosexuality, or AIDS—the always-hidden subtext of any discussion of gay male sexuality for mainstream media—the actors couch their parodic repartee around narcolepsy:

KR: Do you think this film will cause narcolepsy? I mean, should parents watch out for their children?
RP: I would definitely stress that viewers should all be very aware of the catching nature of narcolepsy.
KR: Should viewers wear special glasses?
RP: It's like the eclipse. If you look at it too long, you might get it.[37]

Gay critics writing in gay publications for mainly gay readers often go the other route. If straight publications go to great lengths to deflect the possible queerness of the actors, gay critics tend to cast doubt on their assumed heterosexuality. Notice how Warren Sonbert, writing in the *Bay Area Reporter*, focuses on the actors:

Reeves plays the Prince Hal figure as if his Hollywood reputation of macho masculinity depended on an intense Errol Flynn impersonation. With Phoenix on the other hand, one gets the impression from his remarkable (perhaps too remarkable) method acting à la James Dean that had Van Sant asked him to get gang raped in the middle of Times Square in broad daylight, the young actor would have jumped at the chance.[38]

While, overall, the review of the film is positive, the reviewer still cannot let go of his fetish for the boy actors, especially for Keanu Reeves:

Van Sant was disingenuous in an interview with me when he couldn't recall in the rapid fire gay three-way who was doing what to whom. I guess he didn't want to "compromise" Reeves' standing when it was pointed out to him—confirmed definitely on a repeat viewing—that Hans has his finger buried in Scott's butt . . . and he seems to be enjoying it—above and beyond the financial returns involved.[39]

What these mainstream publications and gay reviews end up fabricating in their discussions about the actors in *My Own Private Idaho* only duplicates the vexed and contradictory positions regarding gay male sexuality currently in circulation in the popular culture. While mainstream publications need to affirm the assumed heterosexuality of these actors in order to contain the neurotics of homosexual panic, gay publications assert the possibility of the actors' sexual indeterminacy. Yet rather than recognizing Judith Butler's argument for the enabling capacity of such an indeterminacy,[40] gay critics end up reinscribing a hetero/homo binarism by trying to claim the actors as really "gay." Van Sant's own ambivalence concerning his "gay" identity only contributed to this confusion when he explained in the *Advocate*—a gay and lesbian publication—that he'd "rather hang out with straight guys and not get any sex than hang out with gay guys and get sex."[41] It's no wonder then that the film and its related productions in the popular media have solicited such anxieties around sexuality, given that the boy actors and the film's director promote such equivocal performances of their own sexuality.

Moreover, there is another way to understand this dynamic, one that emerges from both Keanu Reeves and River Phoenix, though perhaps too early in either of their careers to make too much of too soon. There is, undoubtedly, the possibility that Reeves and Phoenix may be positioning themselves much like Hal and Scott have, rebelling against conventional heterosexual roles by playing gay, perhaps only in order to return at a later date to their normative heterosexualities in an elevated and restored state. As actors paid to play these roles, Reeves and Phoenix—like Scott and Mike on the porno-trade publications rack—humorously distance themselves in the popular press from the sex acts they perform. Scott's and Mike's playful distancing, indeed near misunderstanding (think of Mike's "Huh?"), of the pornography industry's production of commodified sexual personas only begs the question of Reeves's and Phoenix's own investments in Hollywood's economic productions of sexualities consumed by popular culture. At this point, however, both actors continue working with out gay directors and accepting gay roles. River Phoenix is set to star as French Symbolist poet Arthur Rimbaud in the film adaptation of Christopher Hampton's 1968 play *Total Eclipse*, about the passionate but tragic love affair between Rimbaud and Paul Verlaine. And Reeves, who has played serious gay roles before, including a community theater production of Martin Sherman's *Bent*, appears in Van Sant's latest film, *Even Cowgirls Get the Blues*.

STRANGE TONGUES AND GROSS TERMS; OR "HELLO, IS ANYBODY OUT THERE?"

The prince but studied his companions
Like a strange tongue, wherein to gain the language,
'tis needful that the most immodest word
be looked upon and learnt; which once attain'd

Your highness knows, comes no further use
but to be known and hated. So like gross terms,
the prince will, in the performances of time,
cast off his followers.

— Henry IV, part 2

Hello, is anybody out there?

— Michelangelo Signorile, 1991

Warwick's comments on Prince Hal's mastery of "strange tongues" and "gross terms" are offered to King Henry IV in an attempt to curb the king's anxiety that his son's activities at the seedy taverns in Eastcheap have no end in sight. Warwick recognizes what the king himself has not, that Hal's appropriation of Falstaff's world has little to do with the archetypal story of the prodigal son and should be seen instead as a princely exercise of power. Young Hal travels through Eastcheap to "study" and then "cast off" "gross terms," a process familiar in the early modern period.[42] This was, after all, the age of discovery, colonization, and nationalism, an age that introduced in Elizabethan England a wealth of oddities, trifles, strange things, and marvelous possessions.[43] But not everything rendered as strange or gross was necessarily a foreign import. Steven Mullaney convincingly argues that in the early modern period the popular stage "occupied the position of a strange thing itself"[44] and not merely because of its location at the outskirts of the city. Renaissance theater, Mullaney explains, "allows and even demands a full and potentially self-consuming review of unfamiliar things."[45] Renaissance theater in England was one of many social practices of the period that participated in what Mullaney brilliantly terms "the rehearsal of cultures," a process that allowed for a temporary suspension of constraint in order for the culture to define itself anew:

The popular stage [was] a collection of strange things, marginal pastimes, and subcultures, to be sure, but one that was itself lodged on the tenuous margins of its society, as much an object of ambivalent fascination as any of the other extravagant and extraneous cultural phenomena being maintained and, for a while, upheld by the period.[46]

Prince Hal's excursions through Eastcheap rehearsed gross terms in order to cast them off later, just as Renaissance audiences watching the Henry IV plays partook in a type of rehearsal all their own. Such a liminal moment, Mullaney argues, much like Prince Hal's own journey through the tavern world, provided Renaissance audiences an opportunity to appropriate its marginal social elements so that like Hal, the different, strange, and gross could be extracted, "consummately rehearsed and thus consummately foreclosed."[47]

In Shakespeare, this foreclosure was, of course, enacted by Hal's rejection of Falstaff at the end of Henry IV, part 2, and not surprisingly, finds its analogue in the film with Scott's dismissal of Bob. But as Mullaney makes clear, the issues involved here seem to have little to do with Hal and Falstaff, or for that matter Scott and Bob. Instead, these concerns indicate how the popular culture of the Renaissance, manipulated by the Privy Council, which called forth in 1597 — the year of Henry IV, part 1 — for new restraints against plays and the theater, was subject to continual surveillance. The early modern theater, as both Howard and Mullaney demonstrate, is imagined by those in power as holding the capacity to instigate confusion and social instability. Shakespeare's theater was itself laden with "gross terms," apparent, at the most basic level, by the spoken language of its characters and, moreover, by the presumed immoralities of the boy actors. The social space of the early modern theater populated with such subversive potential thus became a place for ceremonious cultural expurgations monitored and policed by the Privy Council in order to cleanse the culture of "gross terms" even as it paradoxically performed them.

I find it interesting that My Own Private Idaho, with its deliberate evocation of Shakespeare and the public's uncanny concern over its actors, enacts some of these same ceremonial expurgations for us now. Like Shakespeare, Van Sant guides us through some of our own "strange tongues and gross terms" — the argot of male hustlers, queer sexualities, gay desire. I suspect that, as in the early modern period, the film ultimately reenacts the consummate foreclosure that extracts difference. For popular audiences, Van Sant's film may provide the vicarious voyeurism of what is culturally construed as "gross" and thus dispensable. For queer audiences, this process is further exacerbated by what Goldberg terms the "desiring Hal" syndrome operative in the Shakespeare plays and reiterated and naturalized in Shakespeare scholarship and, to build on his point, in the film and its reception. Goldberg deconstructs this process by detailing the various identifications in the Shakespeare plays and criticism, identifications that in turn produce the fantasies that guarantee Hal's desirability. Falstaff, of course, figures prominently here. Goldberg explains:

If we desire [Falstaff's] repeated comebacks it is because it is on his desire that ours floats. (Falstaff teaches us to see the prince as a sweet wag.) That desire is, importantly, the desire to take abuse. If we accept his banishment, it is then because we take it up as our position, because we have been accepting it all along, and because it is part of the way in which we need never give up our desiring Hal. (153–54)

By the end of the film, Scott rejects Bob and Mike; they join the other queer men previously discarded. While Mike may serve in the film to unsettle the hegemony of normative sexual identities, he nonetheless never relinquishes his desire for Scott. In his "banishment" of both Bob and Mike, Scott banishes his own queerness, too. This exchange reinforces what Goldberg, referring to the Shakespeare plays, identifies as "a masochism which, in the political register, signals an abjection coincident with the fantasy of empowerment" (154).

Gay cultural critic and activist Michelangelo Signorile, holding Van Sant and Hollywood accountable for the proliferation of such problematic gay representations, contextualizes this experience for gay men when he writes that "Private Idaho is, after all, a beautiful film with hot boys who have sex with men. What more do we want?"[48] For Signorile, much more is desired, including a more sophisticated, and politically invested, critique of Van Sant's popularity with mainstream critics and gay audiences. Signorile's "Hello, is anybody out there?"—directed toward gay people for their uncritical glorification of the film—at once suggests the immediate submission of gay male viewers seduced by sexy boy actors and, more importantly, the politics of outing and gay visibility he is famous for championing. Who is out there? As I have argued, this remains the central nagging question concerning the film's (boy) actors, director, and audience. It is ironic then that since My Own Private Idaho, it is Van Sant who seems to have adapted the Hal/Scott model, although with a defining difference. If Van Sant had earlier eschewed gay politics and the concerns around gay identity and representation articulated by gay and lesbian activists like Signorile, he now, in a very striking reversal, has publicly embraced gay and lesbian causes. Not only did he consider directing the controversial film version of Randy Shilts' biography of slain gay activist Harvey Milk, The Mayor of Castro Street, only to withdraw due to artistic differences with the producers, but he also came forth in the fall of 1992 as a driving force in Portland's gay and lesbian community to counter the perilous activities of the Oregon Citizens Alliance, an antigay group that put forth an initiative—which was defeated in the November elections—that would have amended the state constitution to define homosexuality as "abnormal behavior" and would have forbidden state and local governments from including gays and lesbians in antidiscrimination laws. Van Sant's new public identification as an "out" gay director involved in and supportive of the gay and lesbian community, like Hal and Scott's prodigality, has been championed by various gay activists in the Pacific Northwest, Hollywood, and throughout the United States.

In the film, the viewer is invited to pass through Portland's side streets with the knowledge secured by Scott's first soliloquy in the first reel, where he announces that his performance as a male hustler is only a performance of power, one that will culminate by the film's end with his embracement of the yuppie comforts of the Pacific Northwest. For those of us inclined to skip that route—the narcoleptics among us—there is perhaps some comfort in the following exchange that concludes the discussion with Keanu Reeves and River Phoenix in *Interview*. When asked what they plan to do next, the boy actors, never types to assume foreclosure, discuss some pending collaborative ideas. "To do more Shakespeare perhaps?" questions *Interview:*

KR: Um, who knows? I really would like to do more Shakespeare with River. I think we'd have a hoot. We could do *A Midsummer Night's Dream* or *Romeo and Juliet*.
RP: I'll be Juliet.[19]

Boy actors—in the 1590s and in the 1990s, in Shakespeare's plays and in Van Sant's film—incite the social forces of their cultures to inscribe them in the polemical debates around sexuality and gender circulating in these periods. Each of these cultures produces narratives that divorce performances from their historical contingencies and the specific social effects that give shape to them, and circulate these narratives in a continual but ultimately unresolvable search for epistemological certainty. Much of this quest for gender and sexual certainty involves the repression of the homoerotic and its transference into a cultural phenomenon I have called homoneuroticism. The homoneurotic reveals the instability of the categories, categories perhaps initiated by the regulatory regimes of the early

modern period that now—four hundred years later—have been misguid-
edly translated and naturalized as the more modern regimes of hetero-
and homosexualities. Mike's mantra—"I always know where I am by the
way the road looks"—finds an interesting translation in these comments
by Reeves and Phoenix, who recognize that the road before us continues
to take us on journeys that keep bringing us back, like Mike, to the very
place where we started: "Shakespeare," the controversies engendered by
boy actors, and the homoneurotic tendencies of cultures who seem to
have no idea where they've been or where they're going.[50]

NOTES

Earlier versions of this paper were presented at the Dangerous Liaisons?: Literature, Film, Video Conference at the University of Southern California in the
spring of 1992 and at the Looking Out/Looking Over: Lesbian and Gay Male
Film Conference at the University of California-Davis in the spring of 1993. I
would like to thank the participants at the USC conference—particularly Michael
Du Plessis, Richard Iosty, Joe Boone, Nancy Vickers, and Tania Modleski—for
their critical engagement and support. Thanks are also due to David Van Leer for
inviting me to speak on this topic at the UC-Davis conference; the participants at
the UC-Davis conference, especially Stephen Orgel, for insightful comments and
encouragement; the editors at *Genders* and the three outside readers, whose
suggestions for revision were very helpful; Will Fisher at the University of Pennsylvania; Douglas Swenson—my actor boyfriend and favorite movie date—for his
support; and finally, Susan Jeffords and Yvonne Yarbro-Bejarano—my exemplary
colleagues at the University of Washington—who read and commented on various drafts of this essay and who are unquestionably among the very best colleagues
any junior faculty person can find in this profession.

1. This is not to say, by any means, that the boy actor in the Renaissance was
   the only site of cultural contestation. Furthermore, River Phoenix and Keanu
   Reeves are not "boys" as one could, less problematically perhaps, identify an
   actor such as Macaulay Culkin. Maybe, as a friend wittily suggested to me in
   conversation, Phoenix and Reeves can be described more aptly as boy(ish)
   actors. Reeves and Phoenix are, of course, young men. In 1991, Keanu Reeves
   was twenty-seven years old and River Phoenix was twenty-one. I am inspired,
   however, by Marjorie Garber who, in her phenomenal book *Vested Interests:
   Cross-Dressing and Cultural Anxiety* (New York: Routledge, 1992), writes, "An
   actor is a changeling; a boy, in Shakespeare's culture as—somewhat differently, but still pertinently—in ours, is a medium, and a counter, of exchange"
   (92).

2. Gregory W. Bredbeck, *Sodomy and Interpretation: Marlowe to Milton* (Ithaca, N.Y.: Cornell University Press, 1991), 77.
3. See, for example, Greil Marcus, "The Elvis Strategy," *New York Times*, October 27, 1992, A16.
4. Marjorie Garber, "Shakespeare as Fetish," *Shakespeare Quarterly* 41 (1990): 242–50.
5. Ibid., 243. For other accounts of the Shakespeare myth-making industry see *The Shakespeare Myth*, ed. Graham Holderness (Manchester: Manchester University Press, 1988); and Michael D. Bristol, *Shakespeare's America, America's Shakespeare* (New York and London: Routledge, 1990).
6. See, for instance, Barry G. Edelstein's witty "Macbluff," *New Republic*, November 11, 1991, where he locates the various moments Shakespeare is mentioned during the hearings.
7. Stephen Orgel, *The Illusion of Power: Political Theater in the English Renaissance* (Berkeley: University of California Press, 1975).
8. This quote from *The Merry Wives of Windsor*, Shakespeare's only English comedy, is spoken by young Master Fenton who is associated with Hal's excesses and who similarly repents (*The Merry Wives of Windsor* [London and New York: Routledge, 1971], 90). The character of the prodigal son is a stock one in classical comedy; see Leo Salingar, *Shakespeare and the Traditions of Comedy* (Cambridge: Cambridge University Press, 1974), for a discussion of its origins. For the sociological implications of such conversions, see David Konstan, *Roman Comedy* (Ithaca, N. Y.: Cornell University Press, 1983).
9. Vincent Canby, review of *My Own Private Idaho*, *New York Times*, September 27, 1991, B4.
10. Owen Gleiberman, review of *My Own Private Idaho*, *Entertainment Weekly*, October 11, 1991, 44.
11. Peter Bowen, "His Own Private Idaho," *Off Hollywood Report* 6 (1991): 26–29.
12. Ibid., 28.
13. For useful bibliographies, see Lisa Jardine, *Still Harping on Daughters: Women and Drama in the Age of Shakespeare*. 2d ed. (New York: Columbia University Press, 1989); and Jean Howard, "Crossdressing, the Theater, and Gender Struggle in Early Modern England," *Shakespeare Quarterly* 39 (1988): 418–40.
14. Quoted in Jardine, 9. The epigraph to this section is from *Anatomy of Abuses*, quoted in Alan Bray, *Homosexuality in Renaissance England* (London: Gay Men's Press, 1982), 35.
15. Jardine, 9.
16. Jonathan Goldberg, *Sodometries: Renaissance Texts, Modern Sexualities* (Stanford, Calif.: Stanford University Press, 1992), 19.
17. Goldberg, *Sodometries*, 20.
18. See also Bruce R. Smith, *Homosexual Desire in Shakespeare's England* (Chicago: University of Chicago Press, 1991). Smith offers a fascinating recuperative argument for male-male sexual activity in the Renaissance—what he calls "homosexual behavior"—when he claims that the "structures of power in early modern England fostered the homosexual potentiality in male bonding"

(73). For Smith, sodomy is both an indeterminate and an unstable category;
the very indeterminacy of sodomy and, relationally, "homosexuality," allows
for the "apparent tolerance, even positive valuation, of homoerotic desire in
the visual arts and ... in the political arena" (13). Goldberg's axiom in
Sodometries, borrowed from Foucault's description of sodomy as "that utterly
confused category" in *The History of Sexuality*, Vol. I, materializes in Smith
with his occasional conflation of such terms as "sodomy," "homosexuality,"
and "homoerotic." Such lapses inadvertently prove Smith's very point, and
more so, Goldberg's, that the instability of the term "sodomy" is not exclusive
to the early modern period.

19. Jean Howard, "Renaissance Antitheatricality and the Politics of Gender and
Rank in *Much Ado about Nothing*," in *Shakespeare Reproduced: The Text in
History and Ideology*, ed. Jean Howard and Marion O'Conner (London and
New York: Routledge, 1987), 165.

20. Ibid., 168.

21. Stubbes writes that "there is such a confuse of mingle mangle of apparel in
Ailgna (England), and such preposterous excess thereof, as everyone is permitted to flaunt it out, in what apparel he lust himself, or can get by anie kind
of meanes. So that it is verie hard to knowe, who is noble, who is worshipfull,
who is a gentleman, who is not" (quoted in Howard, "Renaissance Antitheatricality," 166).

22. But see also Stephen Orgel, "Nobody's Perfect, or, Why Did the English
Stage Take Boys for Women?" in *Displacing Homophobia: Gay Male Perspectives
in Literature and Culture*, ed. Ronald Butters, John Clum, and Michael Moon
(Durham, N. C.: Duke University Press, 1989). Orgel suggests the potential
allure of boy actors for women spectators in early modern theater audiences.

23. Bray, *Homosexuality*, 54–59. Still, as Bray and Goldberg both make clear,
anyone could be a sodomite. Goldberg, for example, insists—rightfully so—
that to collapse sodomy into cross-dressing and "homosexuality," to undiffer-
entiate between boys and women, not only neglects to construct a history of
sexuality but often itself becomes a homophobic and/or misogynist practice.

24. J. W. Binns, "Women or Transvestites on the Elizabethan Stage?: An Oxford
Controversy," *Sixteenth Century Journal* 5 (1974): 95–120; but see also Laura
Levine, "Men in Women's Clothing: Antitheatricality and Effeminization
from 1579 to 1642," *Criticism* 39 (1988): 121–143.

25. Bray, *Homosexualities*, 55–56.

26. See, for example, Howard's "Crossdressing" for an overview of these diverse
positions, Garber's "Shakespeare as Fetish" for comments on this phenomenon, and Goldberg's chapter 4 of *Sodometries* for a critique of all these players.

27. See David Halperin, *One Hundred Years of Homosexuality and Other Essays on
Greek Love* (New York and London: Routledge, 1990), for a discussion of the
"emergence" of the modern homosexual.

28. Eve Kosofsky Sedgwick, *Between Men: English Literature and Male Homosocial
Desire* (New York: Columbia University Press, 1985), 89.

29. Goldberg discusses three of the most salient examples of what I would call

localities of homoneurotics: first, in his brilliant appraisal of how Saddam Hussein was constructed in the U.S. popular imagination and media during the Persian Gulf War; second, in his discussion of *Bowers v. Hardwick*; and third, in his (unfortunately) brief commentary on how AIDS and homosexuality are rendered synonymous. For Goldberg, these are understood as sodometries. David Norton, in an important dissertation on contemporary U.S. cultural politics and textual practices, includes a chapter that discusses two of these relationally, namely, Saddam Hussein and AIDS.

30. This is not to suggest that it worked the same way in both periods. Bruce Smith, in *Homosexual Desire in Shakespeare's England*, for example, argues that in certain contexts sex between men correlates with masculinity. He writes, "Behavior that we ["contemporary Europe and America"] would label homosexual, and hence a rejection of maleness, was for them ["early modern English society"] an aspect of manliness" (75; Smith's emphasis). I'm grateful to the *Genders'* reader who called this to my attention. For further readings in this area, see also Jonathan Dollimore's discussion of boy actors in the Renaissance in chapter 19 of his important project *Sexual Dissidence: Augustine to Wilde, Freud to Foucault* (Oxford: Oxford University Press, 1991), and Peter Stallybrass's related essay, "Transvestism and the Body Beneath: Speculating on the Boy Actor," in *Erotic Politics: Desire on the Renaissance Stage*, ed. Susan Zimmerman (New York and London: Routledge, 1992). In the contemporary scene, the media blitz of editorials positioned around such recent films as Alek Keshishian's Madonna "documentary" *Truth or Dare*, Ridley Walker's *Thelma and Louise*, Todd Hayne's *Poison*, and Jennie Livingston's *Paris Is Burning*, to cite only a few examples, provides ample proof that representations that blur sex and gender binarisms incite both neoconservative wrath and mass critical confusion. As far as issues of (homo)sexuality are concerned, current anxieties are informed by the ongoing activism of such groups as Queer Nation, ACT UP, and GLAAD, who monitor representations of lesbians and gays in the media, and by the growing self-proclaiming "Christian" radical right movement, who are equally equipped to rally a boycott against any positive gay or lesbian representation.

31. For the heterosexual indications of Scott's desire, see Donald Lyons's profile on Van Sant and the film in *Film Comment* 27 (1991): 6–12.

32. Moreover, the scene suggests the omnipresence of homoeroticism in popular culture. On this issue, see Alexander Doty's related study *Making Things Perfectly Queer: Interpreting Mass Culture* (Minneapolis: University of Minnesota Press, 1993).

33. River Phoenix explains, "In society there's this confusion between love and sex, people think they want love and that they'll get it through sex. Very rarely do the two merge cohesively. Mike is very clear on the difference between love and sex, because he has sex for a living" (quoted in Adam Block, "Interview with Gus Van Sant," *Advocate* 586 [1991]: 80–85, at 82).

34. Steve Warren, "Interview with Gus Van Sant," *San Francisco Sentinel*, October 10, 1991, 39.

35. Lance Loud, "Shakespeare in Black Leather," *American Film* 16, no. 9 (1991): 34.
36. Dario Scardapane, "Lost Boys on the Set," *US*, November 19, 1991, 75.
37. Gini Sikes and Paige Powell, *Interview* 11 (1991): 78–89.
38. Warren Sonbert, "Tale of Two Hustlers," *Bay Area Reporter*, October 17, 1991, 29.
39. Ibid., 34.
40. Judith Butler, *Gender Trouble: Feminism and the Subversion of Identity* (New York and London: Routledge, 1990).
41. Block, "Interview," 83.
42. See Goldberg's "Desiring Hal" in *Sodometries* for a different and more specifically antiheterosexist reading.
43. See, for instance, Stephen Greenblatt, *Marvelous Possessions: The Wonders of the New World* (Chicago: University of Chicago Press, 1991).
44. Steven Mullaney, *The Place of the Stage: License, Play, and Power in Renaissance England* (Chicago: University of Chicago Press, 1988), 71.
45. Ibid., 71.
46. Ibid., 84.
47. Ibid., 86.
48. Michelangelo Signorile, "Absolutely Queer," *Advocate* 590 (1991): 35.
49. Sikes and Powell, 88.
50. This paper was written and revised between the spring of 1992 and the fall of 1993. The week *Genders* notified me of its acceptance for publication was also the week of the stunning news of River Phoenix's death. My points about River Phoenix and his career are to be understood as a reading of a specific cultural moment—the fall of 1991—in contemporary U.S. culture. And yet I am compelled to convey a more direct appreciation for his work in light of the unfolding events of this month (November 1993). This week's media coverage of Phoenix's death, for example, focuses on his alleged substance abuse and "lifestyle," reporting that both infantilizes Phoenix and disciplines him posthumously. To continue to refer to him as a boy actor seems now dismissive and inaccurate. (River Phoenix was twenty-three years old at the time of his death.) More to the point, Phoenix's impressive body of work and his own inspired personal politics impress me as mature, responsible, and fully realized in ways generally unarticulated by other Hollywood actors regardless of their age or experience; his work on *My Own Private Idaho*—as offered by Gus Van Sant's comments—indicates as much. For these reasons alone, his death is surely a loss to the industry. Still, I am reluctant to mark River Phoenix's death in such a way as to make me complicit with the inevitable icon-shaping of popular figures who die young and/or mysteriously—Marilyn Monroe, Elvis, Shakespeare—and recirculate as a cultural fetish. The current speculations surrounding Phoenix's cause of death already signal the probability of this fetishization process. Like the search for Shakespeare, such speculations conflate the material bodies of actors and playwrights with the bodies of work they produced in their lifetimes. The quest

for authenticity—whether it concerns debates over the "authentic" Shakespeare or the "true" cause of Phoenix's death—suggests how cultures divorced from history enact narratives of truth as substitutions for the anxieties embedded within history. The material bodies of actors and playwrights enshrined as fetish relieve us of the responsibility to account for our losses on the one hand, and provide the location for our perpetual return to an imaginary site of "original cultural wholeness" on the other. Recast in the mise-en-scène of the fetish, these bodies are made vulnerable to the endless cannibalistic excavations that seem to characterize our times.

Contributors

D. A. BOXWELL is currently pursuing doctoral studies at Rutgers University. Previous articles on gender and the two world wars have appeared in *Tulsa Studies in Women's Literature* 12, no. 1 (Spring 1993) and *War, Literature, and the Arts* 3, no. 1 (Spring 1991).

LAUREN CHATTMAN is a lecturer in the department of English at Yale University. Her essay is part of a manuscript in progress, "Pictures of Progress: Femininity on Display in the Nineteenth-Century British Novel," on gender, realism, and visual culture.

WENDY GRAHAM is assistant professor of English at Vassar College. She is currently writing a book about Henry James, which situates his portrayals of hysterics, invalids, and homosexuals within the framework of late-nineteenth-century concepts of degeneracy and race suicide.

ANDREA L. HARRIS teaches English and women's studies at Mansfield University. She received her Ph.D. from the State University of New York at Buffalo. This essay is part of a manuscript in progress on alternatives to the gender binary in twentieth-century fiction and theory, entitled "The Third Sex: Women Rewriting Gender." Her other project examines female sexuality in the novels of Kathy Acker, Marianne Hauser, and Dorothy Allison.

MARCIA KLOTZ is a graduate student in the department of German Studies at Stanford University. Her dissertation is titled, "White Women and the Dark Continent: Sexuality and Gender in German Colonial Discourse, 1885–1945."

DEBORAH LUPTON lectures in medical sociology at the Faculty of Humanities and Social Sciences, University of Western Sydney, Nepean, Australia. She is the author of two books, *Moral Threats and Dangerous Desires: AIDS in the News Media* (Taylor and Francis, 1994) and *Medicine as Culture: Illness, Disease, and the Body in Western Societies* (Sage, 1994).

ROBERT McRUER is completing a Ph.D. at the University of Illinois at Urbana-Champaign. His dissertation, "Reading the Queer Renaissance," examines the work of Edmund White, Audre Lorde, Randall Kenan, Gloria Anzaldúa, John Weir, and Sarah Schulman.

SANGEETA RAY is an assistant professor in the department of English at the University of Maryland, College Park. She has published on post-colonial literature and theory in *Hypatia: A Journal of Feminist Philosophy* and in *Modern Fiction Studies*. She has an essay forthcoming in an anthology published by Westview Press. She is currently working on a book-length manuscript tentatively titled "Feminism, Nationalism, Imperialism: Representations of the East-Indian Woman in British and Indian Texts from 1857 to 1920."

DAVID ROMÁN is assistant professor of English at the University of Washington in Seattle and, for 1994–95, visiting assistant professor of women's studies at Yale University, where he teaches courses on lesbian and gay studies. His book, *Acts of Intervention: Gay Men, U.S. Theatre, AIDS* is forthcoming from Indiana University Press. He serves on the editorial board of *GLQ: A Journal of Lesbian and Gay Studies* and co-chairs the Gay and Lesbian Caucus of the Modern Language Association.

SANDHYA SHETTY is assistant professor of English at the University of New Hampshire, where she teaches postcolonial literary and cultural studies. Currently, she is preparing a book manuscript on constructions of colonial pathology in late nineteenth- and twentieth-century India and coediting an anthology on modern Indian subjectivities.

KAYANN SHORT is completing her Ph.D. at the University of Colorado. This essay is from her dissertation, "Publishing Feminism: Theory, Politics, and the Feminist Press Movement in the United States, 1969–1994," which examines the print apparatus of feminist production.

Guidelines for Prospective Contributors

Genders welcomes essays on art, literature, media, photography, film, and social theory. We are specifically interested in essays that address theoretical issues relating sexuality and gender to social, political, racial, economic, or stylistic concerns.

All essays that are considered for publication are sent to board members for review. Your name is not included on the manuscript in this process. A decision on the essay is usually reached in about four months. Essays are grouped for publication only after the manuscript has been accepted.

We require that we have first right to any manuscript that we consider and that we have first publication of any manuscript that we accept. We will not consider any manuscript that is already under consideration with another publication or that has already been published.

The recommended length for essays is twenty-five pages of double-spaced text. Essays must be printed in letter-quality type. Quotations in languages other than English must be accompanied by translations. Photocopies of illustrations are sufficient for initial review, but authors should be prepared to supply originals on request.

Place the title of the essay and your name, address, and telephone number on a separate sheet at the front of the essay. You are welcome to include relevant information about yourself or the essay in a letter to the editor, but please be advised that institutional affiliation does not affect editorial policy. Since the majority of manuscripts that we receive are photocopies, we do not routinely return submissions. However, if you would like your copies returned, please enclose a self-addressed, stamped envelope.

To submit an essay for consideration, send *three* legible copies to:

Thomas Foster
Genders
Department of English
Ballantine Hall 442
Indiana University
Bloomington, IN 47405-1201